CATHOLIC
BIOETHICS

AND THE GIFT OF

HUMAN LIFE

THIRD EDITION

THIRD EDITION

CATHOLIC BIOETHICS

AND THE GIFT OF

HUMAN LIFE

William E. May

Our Sunday Visitor Publishing Division
Our Sunday Visitor, Inc.
Huntington, Indiana 46750

Nihil Obstat
Msgr. Michael Heintz, Ph.D.
Censor Librorum

Imprimatur
✠ Kevin C. Rhoades
Bishop of Fort Wayne-South Bend
June 7, 2013

The *Nihil Obstat* and *Imprimatur* are official declarations that a book is free from doctrinal or moral error. It is not implied that those who have granted the *Nihil Obstat* and *Imprimatur* agree with the contents, opinions, or statements expressed.

Our Sunday Visitor Publishing Division
Our Sunday Visitor, Inc.
200 Noll Plaza
Huntington, IN 46750

ISBN: 978-1-61278-702-2 (Inventory No. T1407)
eISBN: 978-1-61278-308-6
LCCN: 00-130461

Cover design: Amanda Falk
Cover art: Thinkstock
Interior design: Sherri L. Hoffman

PRINTED IN THE UNITED STATES OF AMERICA

Dedicated to the memory of
my father, Robert W. May (1893-1985), and
my mother, Katherine Agnes May (1898-1987),
and to the memory of
Thomas J. Davin, Jr. (1930-2007),
who helped me greatly in preparing
the 2008 Second Edition of this book.

Contents

CHAPTER TWO
Making True Moral Judgments and Good Moral Choices   **59**

CHAPTER THREE
Generating Human Life: Marriage and the New Reproductive Technologies

CHAPTER FOUR
Contraception and Respect for Human Life   121

CHAPTER FIVE
Abortion and Human Life   159

CHAPTER SEVEN
Euthanasia, Assisted Suicide, and Care of the Dying   **251**

Acknowledgments

Introduction to the Third Edition

Our Sunday Visitor published the second edition of *Catholic Bioethics and the Gift of Human Life* at the beginning of September 2008. The text had been completed earlier in the year. On September 8, 2008, the Congregation for the Doctrine of the Faith (CDF) finished its instruction entitled *Dignitas personae: On Certain Bioethical Questions*, although the document was not officially released until December 8, 2008.

This document had been awaited for many years — I myself had been appointed by then Cardinal Ratzinger as a member of one of the four groups of Catholic bioethicists meeting under the leadership of Bishop Elio Sgreccia to study new questions that had arisen since the publication of the Vatican *Instruction on Respect for Human Life in Its Origin and on the Dignity of Procreation* (*Donum vitae* [DV]). I had been informed erroneously, however, that the new document would not be published for some time. I thus decided to finish a substantive revision of my book, which had originally been published in 2000.

In this revised third edition I have added a section to Chapter One, "Church Teaching and Major Issues in Bioethics," to provide an overview of this new document. I have also made appropriate changes in other chapters where specific passages and the teaching of *Dignitas personae* are particularly relevant. In addition I have substantively revised all of the chapters in order to integrate up-to-date scientific data and significant scholarly literature on the issues considered. Thus in Chapter Two I have added a section on the recent development of "virtue ethics" and reflected on the relationship between an ethics of principles (natural law as illumined and transformed by divine revelation) and "virtue ethics." In Chapter Three I have radically reduced in size Part 5, " 'Rescuing' Frozen Embryos," in light of a specific passage in DV (no. 19) whose interpretation is debated by theologians/bioethicists committed to support magisterial teaching. In Chapter Four I have taken into account some of the literature occasioned by the fiftieth anniversary of "the pill" in 2010 and strengthened arguments to show the moral evil of contraception.

In Chapter Five I have added new arguments against abortion and a new section devoted to "hard cases" for both defenders of the inviolability of unborn human life and champions of abortion as a woman's right. In Chapter Six I have thoroughly revised the parts on stem-cell research, genetic therapy, prenatal diagnosis and screening of the unborn, genetic counseling, and the human genome project. In Chapter Seven I have added material summarizing important new scholarly studies and legislative actions over euthanasia and assisted suicide. And in Chapter Eight I have cut some of the material providing in some depth the different views of D. Alan Shewmon and others over the validity of so-called brain death as one way of determining that a human person has died in order to devote attention to the contemporary debate and discussion among Catholic scholars loyal to the Magisterium who disagree profoundly among themselves. I have also updated the Bibliography and the list of helpful websites to include the most recent scientific and scholarly studies of the issues taken up.

In preparing this third edition of my book I have been helped greatly by my former student Mark Latkovic, now professor of moral theology at Sacred Heart Seminary in Detroit, and by E. Christian Brugger, my colleague as a senior research fellow of the Culture of Life Foundation, and William Cardinal Stafford Professor of Moral Theology at St. John Vianney Seminary in Denver.

CHAPTER ONE

Church Teaching and Major Issues in Bioethics

It is important and helpful to begin this book by summarizing the teaching of the Church on major issues in bioethics. I believe that the most important magisterial documents relevant to the topics to be considered in this book are: (1) Pope John Paul II's 1995 encyclical *Evangelium vitae* ("The Gospel of Life"); (2) the Congregation for the Doctrine of the Faith's 1987 *Instruction on Respect for Human Life in Its Origin and on the Dignity of Procreation* (entitled *Donum vitae* in Latin); (3) the same Congregation's 1974 *Declaration on Procured Abortion*; and (4) the same Congregation's 1980 *Declaration on Euthanasia*.

Other magisterial documents, in particular the *Catechism of the Catholic Church* and many addresses of Popes Pius XII and John Paul II, are also quite relevant to matters taken up in this book. In addition, the 1994 *Charter for Health Care Workers* prepared by the Pontifical Council for Pastoral Assistance to Health Care Workers, the 1994 *Ethical and Religious Directives for Catholic Health Care Services* promulgated by the bishops of the United States, and pastoral letters of individual bishops and episcopal conferences bear on topics to be considered. Thus, in chapters to follow, reference will be made to these sources of Church teaching when it is relevant to do so. But five documents are of paramount importance: 1. John Paul II's encyclical *Evangelium vitae;* 2. the Vatican *Instruction on Respect for Human Life in Its Origin and on the Dignity of Procreation* (*Donum vitae*); 3. the Declaration on Procured Abortion; 4. the Declaration on Euthanasia; and 5. *Dignitas personae: On Certain Bioethical Questions.* The teaching found in these documents will be referred to time and again in the following chapters; hence, presentation of their principal ideas here will eliminate the need for doing so in later chapters where specific topics taken up in these documents are examined. A simple reference to the matter found in this chapter will suffice.

1. John Paul II's Encyclical *Evangelium Vitae*

Pope John Paul II's encyclical is a wonderful manifesto eloquently presenting the reasons why human life is of incomparable dignity and, indeed, sanctity. It is also an incisive analysis and critique of the various factors and ideologies underlying the terrible threats menacing human life today, in particular, the life of the weakest members of the human family: the unborn, the severely impaired, the sick, and the dying. It is, above all, an impassioned plea to all people of goodwill to recognize the dignity and sanctity of human life, to defend it from the vicious and at times subtle attacks launched against it today, and to love it as a precious gift from the God whose only-begotten-Son-made-man poured forth his life on the Cross precisely so that everyone might have life in abundance and in union with him conquer death and rise to everlasting life in fellowship with the Triune God, the Giver of Life and Love.

A. Chapter One: "Present-Day Threats to Human Life"

This chapter begins with a meditation on the story of Cain and Abel in Genesis (nos. 7-9) and goes on to take up in detail the threats menacing human life today. John Paul II goes to the root causes of these threats, zeroing in on the emergence of a perverse idea of human freedom, understood as the autonomous freedom of individuals to be the arbiters of good and evil, right and wrong. This has blinded them to the value of human life, has eclipsed the sense of God and of man as a being of incomparable worth, and has led to the claim that *some* members of the human family, the strong and the able, have the *right* to dispose of the lives of the weak and vulnerable, in particular, the unborn, the "useless," the suffering, and the dying.

John Paul II, mincing no words, correctly claims that today we are confronted "by a culture which denies solidarity and in many cases takes the form of a veritable 'culture of death,'" one "actively fostered by powerful cultural, economic, and political currents which encourage an idea of society excessively concerned with efficiency." It is thus possible, he continues, "to speak in a certain sense of a *war of the powerful against the weak*" which unleashes a "*conspiracy against life*," a conspiracy involving "not only individuals in their personal, family or group relationships, but go[ing] far beyond, to the point of damaging and distorting, at the international level, relations between peoples and States" (no. 12).

This "culture of death" has its roots in "the mentality which *carries the concept of subjectivity to an extreme* and even distorts it, and recognizes as a subject of rights only the person who enjoys full or at least incipient autonomy and who emerges from a state of total dependence on others" (no. 19). It is likewise rooted in a *"notion of freedom* which exalts the isolated individual in an absolute way, and gives no place to solidarity, to openness to others and service of them" (no. 19), a misunderstanding of freedom which *"leads to a serious distortion of life in society"* (no. 20). This culture of death results ultimately in an *"eclipse of the sense of God and of man* typical of a social and cultural climate dominated by secularism" (no. 21). Citing Vatican Council II's Pastoral Constitution on the Church in the Modern World, *Gaudium et spes* (no. 36), which affirmed: "Without the Creator the creature would disappear. . . . But when God is forgotten the creature itself grows unintelligible," John Paul II continues:

> Man is no longer able to see himself as "mysteriously different" from other earthly creatures; he regards himself merely as one more living being, as an organism which, at most, has reached a high stage of perfection. Enclosed in the narrow horizon of his physical nature, he is somehow reduced to being "a thing," and no longer grasps the "transcendent" character of his "existence as man." He no longer considers life as a splendid gift from God, something "sacred," entrusted to his responsibility, and thus also to his loving care and "veneration." (no. 22)

After this incisive critique of the culture of death, its root causes and effects, John Paul II concludes the first chapter by reviewing "signs of hope," which invite all to commit themselves to welcoming, loving, and serving human life (nos. 26-28). Among these "signs of hope" are many married couples who generously accept children as the supreme gift of marriage; families which serve life and give themselves to the least of their brothers and sisters (abandoned children and elderly persons, handicapped people, teenagers in difficulty); people who generously volunteer to offer hospitality and a supportive environment to the weak; medical scientists, agencies, and organizations mobilizing efforts to bring the benefits of modern medicine to the poor and needy (no. 26); movements and initiatives to raise social awareness to defend human life, particularly the life of the unborn and the sick and dying; the daily struggle of countless people to care for others; a new sensitivity ever more opposed to war as an instrument for resolving conflicts and to the use of capital punishment; concern for the quality of life and the ecology (no. 27). In concluding this chapter, the Holy Father points out that "the unconditional choice for life reaches its full religious and moral meaning when it flows from, is formed by, and nourished by *faith in Christ*" (no. 28).

B. Chapter Two: "The Christian Message Concerning Life"

This chapter first focuses our gaze on Christ, "the Word of life" (1 Jn 1:1), in order to show us that the Gospel of Life is "something concrete and personal, for it consists in the proclamation of the *very person of Jesus*" (no. 29), the One who has come to reveal to us the complete truth about man and human life. Jesus, through word and deed, served life — in particular, the life of the poor and the weak. His words and deeds, John Paul II points out, "are not meant only for those who are sick or suffering or in some way neglected by society. On a deeper level they affect the *very meaning of every person's life in its moral and spiritual dimensions*" (no. 32). Jesus himself fully experienced life's contradictions and risks, living poverty throughout his life "until the culminating moment of the Cross: 'he humbled himself and became obedient unto death, even death on a cross. Therefore, God has highly exalted him and bestowed on him the name which is above every name' (Phil 2:8-9)." "It is precisely," the Pope continues, "*by his death* that *Jesus reveals all the splendor and value of life*, inasmuch as his self-oblation on the Cross becomes the source of a new life for all people (cf. Jn 12:32)" (no. 33).

Human life is surpassingly good because "the life which God gives man is quite different from the life of all other living creatures, inasmuch as man, although formed from the dust of the earth (cf. Gn 2:7, 3:19; Job 34:15; Ps 103:14; 104:29), *is a manifestation of God in the world, a sign of his presence, a trace of his glory* (cf. Gn 1:26-27; Ps 8:6)" (no. 34). Jesus brings human life, which is always a precious gift from God, to fulfillment. For Jesus shows us that God, in giving us life, shares something of himself with us precisely so that we can, in union with Jesus, fully participate in the life of the "Eternal One" by literally becoming his very own children (nos. 37-38). "Eternal life is ... the life of God himself and at the very same time the *life of the children of God* (cf. 1 Jn 3:1-2).... *Here the Christian truth about life becomes most sublime.* The dignity of this life is linked not only to its beginning, to the fact that it comes from God, but also to its final end, to its destiny of fellowship with God in knowledge and in love of him" (no. 38). Human life thus becomes the " 'place' where God manifests himself, where we meet him and enter into communion with him" (no. 39). The life of every human being is sacred and inviolable because God himself personally treasures and cares for it. His commandment that we are not to kill is rooted in the love and reverence due to the life he has given and confided to our trust (nos. 39-41).

Because he loves and trusts us, God allows us to share in his lordship by taking responsibility for human life. Husbands and wives, in particular, are privileged to "become partners in a divine undertaking: through the act of procreation, God's gift [of life] is accepted" lovingly and given the home where it is to take root and grow (no. 43). But "the task of accepting and serving life involves everyone; and this task must be fulfilled above all towards life when it is at its weakest," for Christ himself has told us that what we do to his littlest ones we do to him (cf. Mt 25:31-46) (no. 43).

Human life, God's precious gift, is most vulnerable when it comes into the world and when it leaves the realm of time to embark upon eternity (no. 44). When it comes into the world, it comes from the hand of God himself: "Before I formed you in the womb I knew you" (Jer 1:5; cf. Job 10:8-12; Ps 139: 13-14; 2 Mc 7:22-23). Thus the life of every individual, from its very beginning, is part of God's loving plan for human existence, a truth confirmed and deepened by the incarnation of God's only-begotten Son, who, while still in his mother's womb, was greeted with joy by his cousin John, an unborn child himself, who leapt for joy in Elizabeth's womb when Mary came to visit her cousin, who, despite her advanced age, was "with child" (cf. Lk 2:22-23) (nos. 40-45).

Human life, inescapably bodily in nature, is precious, in itself and to God, at every moment of its existence, even and especially when it is weak, when it suffers, when it draws near to death (nos. 47-48). God's command "You shall not kill" (Ex 20:13; Dt 5:17) is a specific command intended to protect the dignity and sanctity of human life; indeed, the whole of God's law, his wise and loving plan for human existence, fully protects human life. This law finds its fulfillment in Jesus, who shows us the authentic meaning of human life, namely, "that of being a *gift which is fully realized in the giving of self*," in the "*gift of self in love for one's brothers and sisters*" (no. 49).

The Gospel of Life is ultimately fulfilled on the tree of the Cross. From the pierced side of our Redeemer we have given to us "the very life of God." Jesus "proclaims that *life finds its center, its meaning, and its fulfillment when it is given up*" in love (no. 51).

C. Chapter Three: "God's Holy Law"

This chapter is devoted to the intimate bond between the Gospel of Life and the commandment, grounded in self-giving love, that we are not to kill. In this chapter, as he did in the first chapter of his encyclical *Veritatis splendor*, John Paul II begins with a meditation on the Gospel story of the rich young man who asked our Lord what he must do to enter into eternal life and was told that to do so he must keep the commandments (cf. Mt 19:6ff) (no. 52). The Gospel of Life is both a great gift of God and an exacting task for humanity: "In giving life to man God *demands* that he love, respect, and protect life. The *gift* has become a *commandment*, and the *commandment is itself a gift*" (no. 52).

Because it is God's precious gift and is thus sacred and inviolable, human life, particularly when weak and helpless, has God as its "*goel*," its defender (no. 53). The negative commandment "You shall not kill" simply indicates an extreme that can never be exceeded; but it implicitly encourages a positive attitude toward human life. This attitude, deepened and immeasurably enriched by the command that we are to love our neighbor as ourselves, helps to show us the enormity of the crime of murder, the intentional killing of innocent human beings (nos. 53-54).

The Pope, noting that "Christian reflection has sought a fuller and deeper understanding of what God's commandment prohibits and prescribes," reaffirms the Catholic tradition's teaching on the right to self-defense and on the right, and at times the duty, "for someone responsible for another's life, the common good of the family or of the State" to defend life even if one foresees that as a result of legitimately defending one's own or another's life from an unprovoked attack the life of the aggressor may be taken (no. 55). In such instances, one is not violating God's command, nor is one engaging in an act of killing. Rather, one's human act, as specified by the object chosen,[1] is rightly described as an act of legitimate defense and not as an act of killing.

It is in this context that the Pope takes up the question of capital punishment or the death penalty. Here it is important to note that he does not condemn capital punishment as intrinsically evil. Nonetheless, he teaches that, in order to defend the common good from criminal attacks and to punish evildoers for their unjust actions, society "ought not go to the extreme of executing the offender except in cases of absolute necessity; in other words, when it would not be possible otherwise to defend society." He concludes that today, "as a result of steady improvements in the organization of the penal system, such cases are very rare, if not practically non-existent" (no. 56). In other words, he is saying that under contemporary conditions one ought not to inflict the death penalty. Those wishing to do so have the burden of proving that doing so is absolutely necessary, and John Paul II seriously doubts that this can be so today.

The command "You shall not kill" is absolute, i.e., without exceptions, when it refers to innocent human life, "and all the more so in the case of weak and defenseless human beings, who find their ultimate defense against the arrogance and caprice of others only in the absolute binding force of God's commandment" (no. 57).

In developing this central truth, John Paul II makes it clear that the Church's teaching on the absolute inviolability of innocent human life and on the intrinsic evil of every freely chosen act of deliberately killing innocent human beings has been infallibly proposed by the ordinary Magisterium of the Church. He is *not* solemnly defining this truth by an *ex cathedra* pronouncement, but he definitely claims that this truth pertains to the patrimony of faith as proclaimed by the ordinary and universal Magisterium. He introduces the subject by writing as follows:

> Faced with the progressive weakening in individual consciences and in society of the sense of the absolute and grave moral illicitness of the direct taking of all innocent human life, especially in its beginning and its end, *the Church's Magisterium* has spoken out with increasing frequency in defense of the sacredness and inviolability of human life. The Papal Magisterium, particularly insistent in this regard, has always been seconded by that of the bishops, with numerous and comprehensive doctrinal and pastoral documents issued either by Episcopal Conferences or by individual bishops. The Second Vatican Council also addressed this matter forcefully, in a brief but incisive passage.[2] (no. 57)

He then goes on to say:

> Therefore, by the authority which Christ conferred upon Peter and his Successors, and in communion with the Bishops of the Catholic Church, *I confirm that the direct and voluntary killing of an innocent human being is always gravely immoral.* This doctrine, based upon that unwritten law which man, in the light of reason, finds in his own heart (cf. Rom 2:14-15) is reaffirmed by Sacred Scripture, transmitted by the Tradition of the Church, and taught by the ordinary and universal Magisterium. (no. 57)

Since John Paul II explicitly refers, at the conclusion of the passage just cited, to the teaching of Vatican Council II in *Lumen gentium*, no. 25, it is both useful and necessary, to properly understand the significance of this centrally important passage, to see what the Council Fathers said in the passage referred to. It reads:

> Although the bishops, taken individually, do not enjoy the privilege of infallibility, they do, however, *proclaim the doctrine of the Church infallibly*

on the following conditions: namely, when, even though dispersed throughout the entire world but preserving for all that amongst themselves and with Peter's successor the bond of communion, in their authoritative teaching concerning matters of faith or morals, they are in agreement that a particular teaching is to be held definitively and absolutely. (*Lumen gentium*, no. 25; emphasis added)

Note that John Paul II, before invoking the authority conferred upon Peter and his successors, made it a point to call attention to the universal teaching of the bishops and to the teaching of Vatican Council II on the intrinsic and grave malice of every direct and voluntary killing of innocent human beings. Surely this is a teaching on a matter of "morals," and the universal Magisterium agrees in judging that this teaching is to be held definitively and absolutely. Consequently, one can legitimately conclude that here John Paul II is asserting that this truth of Catholic moral teaching has been infallibly proposed by the ordinary and universal Magisterium of the Church, according to the criteria set forth in Vatican Council II's Dogmatic Constitution on the Church, *Lumen gentium*.[3]

Later in this chapter, in condemning the intrinsic evil of direct abortion, John Paul II first reviews the teaching of Scripture (no. 61), the two-thousand-year Tradition of the Church (no. 61), recent papal teaching (no. 62), and the Church's canonical discipline from the earliest times to the present on this question. He then writes:

Given such unanimity in the doctrinal and disciplinary tradition of the Church, Paul VI was able to declare that this tradition is unchanged and unchangeable (cf. encyclical letter *Humanae vitae*, no. 14). Therefore, by the authority which Christ conferred upon Peter and his Successors, in communion with the Bishops — who on various occasions have condemned abortion and who in the aforesaid consultation [which preceded publication of *Evangelium vitae*], albeit dispersed throughout the world, have shown unanimous agreement concerning this doctrine — *I declare that direct abortion, that is, abortion willed as an end or as a means, always constitutes a grave moral disorder,* since it is the deliberate killing of an innocent human being. This doctrine is based upon the natural law and upon the written Word of God, is transmitted by the Church's Tradition and taught by the ordinary and universal Magisterium [here again John Paul II explicitly refers to *Lumen gentium*, no. 25]. (no. 62; emphasis in original)

Clearly, here John Paul II affirms that the teaching on the grave immorality of direct abortion has been infallibly proposed by the ordinary and universal Magisterium.

Later, in unequivocally condemning euthanasia or mercy killing as always gravely immoral, John Paul II uses similar language:

> In harmony with the Magisterium of my Predecessors [here a note refers to the teaching of Popes Pius XII and Paul VI and to *Gaudium et spes*] and in communion with the Bishops of the Catholic Church, *I confirm that euthanasia is a grave violation of the law of God*, since it is the deliberate and morally unacceptable killing of a human person. This doctrine is based upon the natural law and upon the written Word of God, is transmitted by the Church's Tradition and taught by the ordinary and universal Magisterium [again a note refers to *Lumen gentium*, no. 25]. (no. 65; emphasis in original)

The Pope thus affirms here that this truth of Catholic moral teaching has been infallibly proposed by the ordinary and universal Magisterium.[4]

In this chapter, John Paul II also insists that we must have the courage "to look truth in the eye and to call things by their proper names" (no. 58). Truth requires us to say that procured abortion is "the deliberate and direct killing, by whatever means it is carried out, of a human being in the initial phase of his or her existence, extending from conception to birth" (no. 58). The legalization of abortion is "a most serious wound inflicted on society and its culture by the very people who ought to be society's promoters and defenders" (no. 59).

It is also an affront to the dignity of human life to perform experiments on human embryos that are not intended to benefit them. Human life, even in its earliest stages of development, can never be regarded as "biological material" for research or as a source of organs or tissues for transplants: "the killing of innocent human creatures, even if carried out to help others, constitutes an absolutely unacceptable act" (no. 63).

The temptation "to have recourse to euthanasia, that is, to take control of death and bring it about before its time, 'gently' ending one's own life or the life of others" must be totally rejected (no. 64). Although it is morally licit to forgo medical procedures that "no longer correspond to the real situation of the patient, either because they are by now disproportionate to any expected results or because they impose an excessive burden on the patient and his family," "euthanasia is a grave violation of the law of God, since it is the deliberate and morally unacceptable killing of a human person" (no. 65). The same is true of suicide and "assisted suicide." Euthanasia and assisted suicide must be recognized as a " '*false mercy*,' and indeed a disturbing 'perversion' of mercy. True 'compassion' leads to sharing another's pain; it does not kill the person whose suffering we cannot bear" (no. 66). The quite different "*way of love and true mercy*" leads us to recognize, in the pleas of the dying and the suffering, a "request for companionship, sympathy and support in the time of trial ... a plea for help to keep on hoping when all human hopes fail" (no. 67).

Today, some, at times many, claim that abortion and euthanasia must be regarded as human rights, or at least as legally permissible options if approved by the majority. Unfortunately, the civil law of far too many societies has given legal sanction to such claims (nos. 68-69). When ethical relativism, the root of these tendencies, prevails, it perverts democratic societies. Democracy "cannot be idolized to the point of making it a substitute for morality or a panacea for immorality." The moral value of a democracy depends on conformity to the moral law, whose truths do not depend on changeable "majority" opinions (no. 70).

If sound democracy is to develop, there is an urgent need to "rediscover those essential and innate human and moral values which flow from the very truth of the human being and express and safeguard the dignity of the person: values which no individual, no majority and no State can ever create, modify or destroy, but must only acknowledge, respect and promote" (no. 71). Public authority at times can tolerate moral evils in order to prevent more serious harms to human persons, but "it can never presume to legitimize as a right of individuals ... an offense against other persons caused by the disregard of so fundamental a right as the right to life." Nor can the legalization of abortion or euthanasia be justified by appeals to respect for the consciences of others, "precisely because society has the right and the duty to protect itself against the abuses which can occur in the name of conscience and under the pretext of freedom" (no. 71). Thus civil laws legalizing the direct killing of innocent human beings through abortion and euthanasia are totally opposed to "the inviolable right to life proper to every individual and thus deny the equality of everyone before the law" (no. 72). Since no human law can authorize such evils, there is a grave obligation in conscience to oppose them; it is never right to obey them or take part in propaganda campaigns in favor of them or to vote for them (no. 73).

John Paul II recognizes that "a particular problem of conscience can arise in cases where a legislative vote would be decisive for the passage of a more restrictive law, aimed at limiting the number of authorized abortions, in place of a more permissive law already passed or ready to be voted on." In such cases,

> when it is not possible to overturn or completely abrogate a pro-abortion law, an elected official, whose absolute personal opposition to procured abortion was well known, could licitly support proposals aimed at *limiting the harm* done by such a law and at lessening its negative consequences at the level of general opinion and public morality. This does not ... represent an illicit cooperation with an unjust law, but rather a legitimate and proper attempt to limit its evil aspects. (no. 73)

A grave obligation of conscience requires persons not to cooperate formally in practices that, even if permitted by civil law, are contrary to "God's law." Such cooperation, which can never be justified, occurs "when an action, either by its very nature or by the form it takes in a concrete situation, can be defined as a direct participation in an act against innocent human life or a sharing in the immoral intention of the person committing it" (no. 74).

The commandment "You shall not kill," by absolutely excluding intrinsically evil acts such as the deliberate killing of innocent human beings, is the point of departure for true freedom because "it leads us to promote life actively, and to develop particular ways of thinking and acting which serve life" (nos. 75-76). The new law of love immeasurably enriches and deepens this commandment: "for the Christian it involves an absolute imperative to respect, love, and promote the life of every brother and sister, in accordance with the requirements of God's bountiful love in Jesus Christ" (no. 77).

D. Chapter Four: "For a New Culture of Human Life"

This chapter is an appeal to proclaim the good news of the "Gospel of Life" and to carry out the work of evangelization, "an all-embracing, progressive activity through which the Church participates in the prophetic, priestly and royal mission of the Lord Jesus" (no. 78). Ransomed by the "author of life" (Acts 3:15) at the price of his blood (cf. 1 Cor 6:30), and made his members by baptism, we are now *"the people of life* and we are called to act accordingly,"* sent into the world as a people to celebrate and serve life (no. 79). To proclaim Jesus is to proclaim life because he is "the Word of life" (1 Jn 1:1). Because of our union with Jesus, we are adopted children of God, members of the divine family (no. 80). We are thus called to proclaim the "living God who is close to us, who calls us to profound communion with himself, who awakens in us the certain hope of eternal life"; we are sum-moned to affirm "the inseparable connection between the person, his life and his bodiliness" (no. 81).

Teachers, catechists, and theologians must show the anthropological reasons on which respect for every human life is based and help everyone discover how the Christian message "fully reveals what man is and the mean-ing of his being and existence." The task of proclaiming the Gospel of Life is primarily entrusted to bishops (no. 82).

To carry out our mission, we must foster in ourselves "a contemplative outlook," that "of those who see life in its deeper meaning, who grasp its utter gratuitousness, its beauty and its invitation to freedom and respon-sibility," accepting reality as a gift and with deep religious awe in order to "rediscover the ability to *revere and honor every person*" (no. 83).

Celebrating the Gospel of Life means celebrating the God of life, the God who gives life (no. 84). It requires us to "appreciate and make good use of the wealth of gestures and symbols present in the traditions and customs of different cultures and peoples" (no. 85). Above all, the Gospel of Life must be celebrated in our daily lives, filled with self-giving love for others. Only in this way can we provide the context within which "heroic actions ... are born," actions proclaiming the Gospel of Life "by the total gift of self." Such heroism is reflected quietly in the lives of brave mothers "who devote themselves to their own families without reserve, who suffer in giving birth to their children, and who are ready to make any effort, to face any sacrifice, in order to pass on to them the best of themselves" (no. 86).

The Gospel of Life must be proclaimed by works of charity, a pressing need today. In carrying out these works, our attitude must be to "care for the other as a person for whom God has made us responsible." Appropriate and effec-tive programs to support new life in particular must be implemented (no. 87).

A tremendous educational effort is needed to proclaim the Gospel of Life, including the development of centers for natural methods of regulating fertility, for marriage preparation and support, for helping unwed mothers welcome new life and care for it. Needed too are communities to help treat people suffering from drug addiction, from AIDS; and for all who are dis-abled. The elderly and terminally ill must be given the support necessary to sustain them in their final days. This requires a reconsideration of the role of hospitals, clinics, and convalescent homes, which must be "places where suffering, pain and death are acknowledged and understood in their human and specifically Christian meaning" (no. 88).

In proclaiming the Gospel of Life, a unique responsibility belongs to health-care personnel: doctors, pharmacists, nurses, chaplains, men and women religious, administrators, and volunteers (no. 89). Effective works of charity need certain forms of social activity and commitment in the political field. Civil leaders have a grave obligation to serve human life through legislative measures. Political leaders must not enact laws "which by disregarding the dignity of the person, undermine the very fabric of society." It is not enough to remove unjust laws; it is necessary to root out the underlying causes of attacks on life, "especially by ensuring proper support for families and motherhood. A *family policy must be the basis and driving force of all social policies*" (no. 90).

The issue of population growth must be addressed by respecting the primary and inalienable responsibility of married couples and families and "cannot employ methods which fail to respect the person and fundamental human rights, beginning with the right to life of every innocent human being" (no. 91).

The family has a decisive responsibility with respect to the Gospel of Life. "This responsibility flows from its very nature as a community of life and love, founded on marriage, and from its mission to 'guard, reveal and communicate love.'" The family is the true "sanctuary of life." It is indeed the "domestic church," summoned to proclaim, celebrate, and serve the Gospel of Life. Married couples are called upon to be givers of life; they must recognize that procreation is "a unique event which clearly reveals that human life is a gift received in order to be given as a gift." They must raise their children in the love and service of God and neighbor (no. 92). To carry out its mission, the family must pray daily, practice solidarity within the home, and extend hospitality and solidarity to others (no. 93).

The neglect or, worse yet, the rejection of the elderly, who have a valuable contribution to make to the Gospel of Life, is an intolerable offense (no. 94).

Because the future of humanity passes through the family, the sanctuary of life, "the *family urgently needs to be helped and supported.*" Tragically today, social, economic, and cultural conditions, far from serving the family, make its tasks more difficult. This must change (no. 94).

There is an urgent need for "general mobilization of consciences and a unified ethical effort to activate a great campaign in support of life. All together, we must build a new culture of life" (no. 95). To do this, the first and fundamental step is to form consciences rightly about the incomparable and inviolable worth of every human life and to reestablish the essential link between life and freedom, inseparably related goods of the human person. Of crucial importance in forming consciences is "the rediscovery of the necessary link between freedom and truth." Men must acknowledge that they are God's creatures: "Where God is denied and people live as though he does not exist, or his commandments are not taken into account, the dignity of the human person and the inviolability of human life also end up being rejected or compromised" (no. 96).

Education for life must emphasize its inherent value from its beginning. This demands that young people learn to value their sexuality and come to see the intimate bond between sexuality and authentic human love. Education in sexuality is education in chastity, a virtue enabling persons to respect the "spousal" meaning of the body, the responsibility of married couples to respect the beauty of human procreation and to be open to the gift of life by using natural methods of regulating fertility. Education for life also requires an education in the true meaning of suffering and death (no. 97).

In short, to develop a new culture of life we must have the courage "to *adopt a new life-style*" based on a correct scale of values: "*the primacy of being over having, of the person over things*"; it requires passing from indifference to concern for others, from rejection to acceptance. In developing this culture, everyone has a role. An indispensable one belongs to intellectuals, in particular Catholic intellectuals; likewise universities, especially Catholic universities, and centers, institutes, and committees of bioethics have an indispensable role. So too do those involved in the mass media, who should "present the positive values of sexuality and human love, and not insist on what defiles and cheapens human dignity" (no. 98). Women play a particularly important role in developing a new culture of life. They are to bear witness to the meaning of genuine love, especially of love for human life at its inception. Women who have had abortions should remember that the "Father of mercies is ready to give [them] forgiveness and peace," and enable them to re-commit themselves to the service of life (no. 99).

In developing a new culture of life, we must always remember that God, the Giver of Life, is our greatest friend and helper. We need to ask for his help in prayer and fasting "so that the power from on high will break down the walls of lies and deceit: the walls which conceal from the sight of so many of our brothers and sisters the evil of practices and laws which are hostile to life" (no. 100). The Gospel of Life, finally, is not for believers only, but for *everyone*. The value at stake, the value of human life, "is one which every human being can grasp by the light of reason." To be actively pro-life is "to contribute to the renewal of society through the promotion of the common good"; no genuine democracy can exist "without a recognition of every person's dignity and without respect for his or her rights." Nor can true peace exist unless "*life is defended and promoted*" (no. 101).

Conclusion

In the conclusion of his encyclical, Pope John Paul II turns to gaze on Mary, the Virgin Mother so intimately and personally associated with the Gospel of Life (nos. 102-104). She helps the Church to "*realize that life is always at the center of a great struggle* between good and evil, between light and darkness." She helps us realize that "it is precisely in the 'flesh' of every person that Christ continues to reveal himself and to enter into fellowship with us, so that *rejection of human life . . . is really a rejection of Christ*" (no. 104). She is the one who helps us face our mission to proclaim life. Like her, we are not "to be afraid," for "with God nothing is impossible" (Lk 1:30, 37) (no. 105).

2. The Vatican *Instruction on Respect for Human Life in Its Origin and on the Dignity of Procreation* (*Donum Vitae*)

On February 22, 1987, the Congregation for the Doctrine of the Faith issued this document, which is divided into an introduction and three principal parts. I will now summarize its contents.

A. Introduction

The Introduction contains five sections. Section 1 deals with biomedical research and Church teaching. The purpose of the document is to put "forward the moral teaching corresponding to the dignity of the person and to his integral vocation" with reference to issues posed by contemporary biomedical research. Section 2 takes up the contributions science and technology can make to the human person. But science and technology are not morally neutral. They require respect for the "fundamental criteria of the moral law," the service of the human person, of his inalienable rights and his integral good according to God's design. Section 3 relates truths about human anthropology to procedures in the biomedical field. Interventions upon the human body affect the human person, especially in the field of sexuality and procreation, where "the fundamental values of life and love are actualized." Biomedical interventions must be morally evaluated in light of the dignity of the human person and his divine vocation. Section 4 proposes two basic criteria for moral judgment in this area, namely,

(1) the inviolability of innocent human life "from the moment of conception until death" and (2) the special character of the transmission of human life, which has been "entrusted by nature to a personal act." Section 5 recalls the teaching of the Magisterium, which offers human reason the light of revelation on these two points, holding (1) that human life, from the moment of conception, must be absolutely respected because man is the only creature on earth that God "has wished for himself" and because the spiritual soul of man is "immediately created by God"; and (2) that human procreation requires the responsible collaboration of spouses with God's fruitful love. Human procreation must be realized in marriage through the acts proper and exclusive to spouses.

B. Part I: Respect for Human Embryos

This part has six major sections. Section 1, on respect due to the human embryo, reminds us that "the human being is to be respected as a person from the first moment of his existence." Modern science recognizes that the biological identity of a new human individual is already constituted in the zygote resulting from fertilization. This scientific conclusion gives a valuable indication for discerning by the use of reason a personal presence at the moment of the first appearance of human life: How could a human individual not be a human person?

The moral condemnation of procured abortion is reaffirmed. "Since the human embryo must be treated as a person, it must also be defended in its integrity, tended and cared for, to the extent possible, in the same way as any other human being." This is the principle determining the answers to the moral questions that will follow.

Section 2 deals with prenatal diagnosis. This is licit if the methods used with the informed consent of parents respect the life and integrity of the embryo and the mother without subjecting them to disproportionate risks. It is gravely immoral when the diagnosis is done with the thought of possibly inducing an abortion depending on its results. One must deny to the state or any other authority the right to link in any way prenatal diagnosis and procured abortion.

Section 3, concerned with *therapeutic* procedures on human embryos, affirms that they are licit if they respect the embryo's life and integrity and do not involve disproportionate risks. Procedures menacing the life or integrity of human embryos are illicit.

Section 4 takes up medical *research and experimentation* on human embryos. If the research is intended to benefit the embryo, it can be undertaken provided there is certainty that it will not harm the embryo's life or integrity and provided that proper consent has been given. Research and experimentation not directly therapeutic is absolutely illicit. Moreover, the corpses of human embryos and fetuses must be respected.

Section 5 affirms that it is absolutely immoral to produce human embryos *in vitro* as research material.

Section 6, which deals with procedures for manipulating human embryos engendered by new reproductive technologies, brands as absolutely immoral efforts to obtain a human being asexually through "twin fission," cloning, or parthenogenesis. It likewise brands as immoral efforts to make animal-human hybrids or to gestate human embryos in artificial or animal uteruses, as well as the freezing of embryos, attempts to engineer the "sex" of embryos, etc.

C. Part II: Interventions Upon Human Procreation

Here concern is with "artificial procreation and insemination," i.e., different technical procedures directed toward obtaining a human conception in a manner other than the sexual union of man and woman. This part begins by noting the ideological link between procured abortion and *in vitro* fertilization. This deathly dynamic, however, does not exempt us from a further and thorough ethical study of artificial fertilization, whether heterologous (when the gametic cells used come from persons not married to each other) or homologous (when these cells come from persons married to each other).

(1) Heterologous Artificial Insemination

Section 1 deals with the intimate link between marriage and human procreation. From the moral point of view, human procreation must be the fruit of marriage: this is the key principle. Every human being must be accepted as a gift and blessing. The procreation of a new human person must be "the fruit and sign of the mutual self-giving of the spouses." The child has a right to be conceived, carried in the womb, brought into the world and brought up within marriage. The good of society as well demands this. This is the only truly *responsible* way of generating human life.

Thus Section 2 repudiates heterologous artificial fertilization as immoral because it is contrary to the unity of marriage, to the dignity of the spouses, to the right of the child to be conceived and brought into the world in marriage and from marriage. Moreover, the fertilization of a woman who is unmarried or widowed, whoever the donor may be, is not morally justified.

Section 3 rejects "surrogate" motherhood as unacceptable for the reasons given already in repudiating heterologous artificial fertilization.

(2) Homologous Artificial Insemination

The key moral principle here is the intimate connection between procreation and the marital act. Three arguments are then given in Section 4, concerned with the connection between procreation and the marital or conjugal act.

(a) There is an inseparable connection, willed by God and unlawful for man to break on his own initiative, between the unitive and procreative meanings of the conjugal act. But artificial fertilization and procreation, even if the gametic cells used come from husband and wife, severs this bond. Fertilization is licitly sought when it is the result of a "conjugal act which is per se suitable for the generation of children to which marriage is ordered by its nature and by which the spouses become one flesh." From the moral point of view, procreation is deprived of its proper perfection when it is not desired as the fruit of a conjugal act, of the one-flesh unity of the spouses.

(b) The "language of the body" likewise shows that it is immoral for spouses to generate human life outside of their marital union, an act inseparably corporeal and spiritual. The origin of a new human person should be "linked to the union, not only biological but spiritual," of husband and wife.

(c) Respect for a human person in his origin requires that he not be treated as a product. When a child is begotten through the conjugal act, he comes to be as a gift from God, a gift crowning the spouses' mutual gift of themselves to each other. When a child is "produced," it comes to be, not as a gift from God, which in truth it is, but as a product of human control.

Section 5 specifically addresses the morality of homologous *in vitro* fertilization and embryo transfer. Even if we prescind from the ideological link between these procedures and procured abortion, the conclusion must be that these ways of generating human life are immoral. They dissociate the begetting of human life from the conjugal act and in fact establish the dominion of technology over the origin and destiny of the human person. Conception *in vitro* is not achieved or positively willed as the expression and fruit of a specific conjugal act; in homologous *in vitro* fertilization and embryo transfer, the generation of human persons is objectively deprived of its proper perfection, namely, that of being the result and fruit of a conjugal act expressing the love of husband and wife. The child so obtained has not been respected in his origin.

However a child comes into the world, whether as the fruit of a conjugal act or through these technologies, he must be respected as a person and as a gift from God.

Section 6 deals with homologous artificial insemination. This is rejected because it dissociates the two meanings of the conjugal act. The basic principle is this: if the procedure *replaces* or *substitutes* for the conjugal act, it is immoral; if, however, it *assists* or *helps* the conjugal act to achieve its purpose, it may be morally licit. Masturbation is repudiated as a morally illicit means of obtaining human sperm.

Section 7 treats of the moral criteria for medical intervention in human procreation. The physician is at the service of persons and of human procreation. He does not have the authority to dispose of them or to decide their fate. He is to aid the spouses and not, by his technique, substitute for them.

Section 8 concerns the suffering of spouses who cannot have a child or fear to bring a handicapped child into the world. The desire of spouses for children is natural and legitimate. But they do not have a "right" to a child because the child is not an object but a gift from God. Spouses suffering from sterility must bear their cross.

D. Part III: Moral Law and Civil Law

The inviolable right of every innocent human person and the institution of marriage are moral values and constitutive elements of the civil society and its order.

New technological possibilities require the intervention of political authorities and of legislators. Such intervention should be directed to ensuring the common good of the people through respect for their fundamental rights, the promotion of peace, and public morality. It furthermore ought to preserve the human community from temptations to selfishness and from discrimination and prejudice.

Among fundamental rights are these: (a) every human being's right to life and physical integrity and (b) the rights of the family and of the child.

Political authority may not approve making human beings through procedures exposing them to the grave risks noted in the document. The recognition by positive law of techniques of artificial transmission of human life would widen the breach already opened by the legalization of abortion. The law cannot tolerate, and in fact must forbid, that human beings, even at the embryonic stage of development, be treated as objects of experimentation, mutilated, or destroyed.

Civil law cannot approve techniques of artificial procreation that, for the benefit of third parties, take away what is a right inherent in the spousal relationship; therefore, civil law cannot legalize donation of gametes between persons who are not united in marriage. Legislation also ought to prohibit embryo banks, postmortem insemination, and surrogate motherhood.

Conclusion

In its conclusion, the document issues an invitation to all who can to exercise a positive influence and ensure that, in family and society, due respect is accorded to human life and love. In particular, it invites theologians, above all moralists, to study more deeply and make ever more accessible to the faithful the teaching of the Magisterium in the light of a valid anthropology of human sexuality and marriage.

All are invited to act responsibly in the area proper to each and, like the Good Samaritan, to recognize as a neighbor even the littlest among the children of men.

3. Declaration on Procured Abortion

This document was issued by the Congregation for the Doctrine of the Faith on November 18, 1974, during the pontificate of Pope Paul VI.

Consisting of 27 numbered sections, it is structured as follows: (A) an Introduction (nos. 1-4); (B) In the Light of Faith (nos. 5-7); (C) In the Additional Light of Reason (nos. 8-14); (D) Reply to Some Objections (nos. 15-18); (E) Morality and the Law (nos. 19-23); and (F) a Conclusion (nos. 24-27).

A. Introduction

This stresses that the Church cannot remain silent about the question of abortion because of her obligation to defend man against whatever destroys or degrades him and because the issue is so grave, concerned as it is with human life, the most basic of all man's goods (no. 1). The claim that abortion should be legalized since it does not violate anyone's conscience and reflects legitimate ethical pluralism is specious, because no one can claim freedom of thought as a pretext to attack the rights of others, especially the right to life (no. 2). Thus Christians, both clerical and lay, and notably bishops, have rightly resisted efforts to legalize abortion (no. 3). It is appropriate and necessary for the Congregation for the Doctrine of the Faith, charged with protecting and fostering faith and morals in the Church, to speak out on this matter; all the faithful must realize the need to assent to the truths of faith and morals proposed by the Magisterium. The *Declaration*'s teaching, therefore, lays a serious obligation on the consciences of the faithful (no. 4).

B. In the Light of Faith

Here the document stresses that God is the God of life, not death (no. 5), that the Church's Tradition from earliest times (e.g., the *Didache* of the second century) has always taught that human life must be protected at every stage in its course, including the beginnings (no. 6), despite different opinions regarding the precise time when a spiritual soul is infused. The teaching condemning abortion as gravely sinful, even by those who thought that the soul was not infused at conception, has been consistent throughout Church history and has been forcefully proclaimed by the Magisterium, especially in our day. As Pope Paul VI has said, the teaching of the Church on this matter is "unchanged and immutable" (no. 7).

C. In the Additional Light of Reason

Key points made here are: (1) human beings are persons because they have a rational nature and are radically capable of knowing the truth and making free choices; as a person, a human being is the subject of inviolable rights, among them the right to life (no. 8); (2) as a person, a human being is not subordinate to society but only to God, although a person must subordinate individual interests to the common good of society; his bodily life is a fundamental good (no. 9); (3) conscience must be enlightened to recognize that society is not the source of fundamental human rights but rather is obligated to respect and protect them (no. 10); the first right is the right to life, and society must respect this (no. 11); human life must be respected at all stages of development, from fertilization until natural death (no. 12).

Number 13 of this section is particularly interesting. It declares that modern genetic science confirms belief that all the characteristics of the person are fixed at conception. However, in footnote 19 of this number, the *Declaration* says that it deliberately leaves untouched the question, philosophical in nature, of when the spiritual soul is infused. It does so because "the tradition is not unanimous in its answer and authors hold different views: some think that animation occurs in the first moment of life, others that it occurs only after implantation." But it insists that the moral position it takes on abortion does not depend on the answer to that question, and this for two reasons: (1) Even if one supposes that animation occurs after conception, the life in question is incipiently human, preparing for and calling for a soul in which the nature received from the parents is completed. (2) It is enough that the presence of a soul is at least probable — and the contrary cannot be established with certainty — to show that taking the life of the fetus at least runs the risk of killing a person already in possession of a soul.

It is very important, I believe, to note that in *Evangelium vitae* Pope John Paul II addressed this question when he considered the view of those who "try to justify abortion by claiming that the result of conception, at least up to a certain number of days, cannot yet be considered a personal human life" (no. 60). After explicitly referring to no. 13 of the *Declaration on Procured Abortion*, he then said:

> What is at stake is so important that, from the standpoint of moral obligation, the mere probability that a human person is involved would suffice to justify an absolutely clear prohibition aimed at killing a human embryo. Precisely for this reason, over and above all scientific debates and those philosophical affirmations to which the Magisterium has not expressly committed itself, the Church has always taught and continues to teach that the result of human procreation, from the first moment of existence, must be guaranteed that unconditional respect which is morally due to the human being in his or her totality and unity as body and spirit.

He then concluded by making his own the teaching of *Donum vitae*, namely, that " '*The human being is to be respected and treated as a person from the moment of conception*; and therefore from that same moment his rights as a person must be recognized, among which in the first place is the inviolable right of every innocent human being to life' " (no. 60).

D. Reply to Some Objections

There can be serious reasons or motives for having an abortion (e.g., dangers to the mother's life and health, abnormal condition of the unborn child, extreme poverty, etc.). But life is too fundamental a good to be weighed against even very serious disadvantages. No reason can justify deliberately killing the unborn (no. 14). Women's liberation does not justify abortion (no. 15), nor does sexual freedom (no. 16), nor technological advance (which must be ruled by morality [no. 17]) — nor is birth control the answer (no. 18).

E. Morality and the Law

Cannot a legitimate pluralism legalize abortion, particularly to avoid harm to desperate women who seek abortion clandestinely (no. 19)? While civil law must tolerate some evils, it cannot accept the killing of the unborn (no. 20); civil law is subordinate to natural law, and the state has the obligation to protect the weak from the strong (no. 21). No one can rightly obey a law immoral in itself, nor can anyone take part in campaigns in favor of such laws, nor vote for them, nor collaborate in their application, etc. (no. 22). Law must reform society so that children will be welcomed and received worthily (no. 23).

F. Conclusion

At times heroism is needed to follow conscience and obey God's law, but fidelity to truth is necessary for true progress of human persons (no. 24). A Christian, whose outlook cannot be confined to this world, knows that he cannot measure happiness by the absence of sorrow and misery here below (no. 25). Every Christian must attempt to remedy such sorrows and miseries; while never approving abortion, Christians must work to combat its causes by effective means, including political action and development of suitable institutions to help pregnant women (no. 26). Action will never change unless hearts and minds are changed so that people will consider fertility a blessing, not a curse, and responsible cooperation with God in giving life a privilege and honor. Christians know that in facing these tasks Jesus will help them (no. 27).

4. Declaration on Euthanasia

This *Declaration*, promulgated by the Congregation for the Doctrine of the Faith on May 5, 1980, contains an Introduction, four parts (I. The Value of Human Life; II. Euthanasia; III. The Meaning of Suffering for Christians and the Use of Painkillers; IV. Due Proportion in the Use of Remedies), and a Conclusion.

A. Introduction

Here the document reminds readers of Vatican II's reaffirmation of the dignity of the human person and its unequivocal condemnation of crimes such as abortion, euthanasia, and willful suicide, and also of the Congregation's earlier *Declaration on Procured Abortion*. The Congregation now judges it opportune to set forth Church teaching on euthanasia, particularly in view of progress in medical science and issues this has raised.

B. Part I: The Value of Human Life

This part reaffirms that human life is the basis of all human goods. Most people regard it as sacred; no one may dispose of it at will; and believers regard it even more highly as a precious gift of God's love "which they are called upon to preserve and make fruitful." It then declares:

> 1. No one can make an attempt on the life of an innocent person without opposing God's love for that person, without violating a fundamental right, and therefore without committing a crime of the utmost gravity. 2. Everyone has the duty to lead his or her life in accordance with God's plan. That life … must bear fruit already here on earth, but … finds its full perfection only in eternal life. 3. Intentionally causing one's own death, or suicide, is therefore equally as wrong as murder.... However, one must clearly distinguish suicide from that sacrifice of one's life whereby for a higher cause … a person offers his or her own life or puts it in danger.

C. Part II: Euthanasia

The document defines euthanasia or mercy killing as "an action or an omission which of itself or by intention causes death, in order that all suffering may in this way be eliminated. Euthanasia's terms of reference, therefore, are to be found in the intention of the will and in the methods used." **NB:** One can kill a person mercifully or commit euthanasia by an act of *omission* as well as by one of commission.

It then articulates the *basic principle*, namely, "nothing and no one can in any way permit the killing of an innocent human being, whether a fetus or an embryo, an infant or an adult, an old person, or one suffering from an incurable disease, or a person who is dying." This is a "question of the violation of the divine law, an offense against the dignity of the human person, a crime against life, and an attack on humanity."

Some people, because of pain, suffering, etc., may ask to be killed mercifully; but many times when they ask for death they are really giving an anguished plea for help and love. What they need, besides medical care, is love.

D. Part III: The Meaning of Suffering for Christians and the Use of Painkillers

Physical suffering is an inevitable part of the human condition; it serves a useful purpose but so affects human psychology that it can become so severe that one wishes to remove it at any cost. Christians recognize that suffering has a special place in God's saving plan as a sharing in Christ's passion and union with his redemptive work. But there is nothing wrong in using painkillers as such so long as their use does not prevent one from carrying out religious and moral duties, even if one foresees that their use may shorten life. Painkillers that cause unconsciousness need special consideration because it is not right to deprive a person of consciousness without a serious reason for permitting this to happen.

E. Part IV: Due Proportion in the Use of Remedies

This is a very important part. The *Declaration* recalls the use in the past Catholic tradition of the distinction between "ordinary" and "extraordinary" means and notes that today — although the principle behind this distinction is good — it is sometimes difficult to understand because of the imprecision of these terms. Thus some today distinguish between "proportionate" and "disproportionate" means. The *Declaration* says that in any event one can make a "correct judgment as to means by studying the type of treatment to be used, its degree of complexity or risk, its cost and the possibilities of using it, and comparing these elements with the result that can be expected, taking into account the state of the sick person and his or her physical and moral resources."

This means that, although it is always gravely immoral to kill a person because of his or her alleged bad quality of life, the condition of a person's life can be used in judging whether a particular medical treatment is "proportionate" or "disproportionate."

In saying this, the *Declaration* in no way supports the proportionalist method of making moral judgments (as some proportionalists have claimed). First of all, the *Declaration* had previously affirmed unambiguously the existence of an absolute moral norm prohibiting an intrinsically evil act, namely, the norm absolutely proscribing the intentional killing of an innocent human being. No proportionalist affirms but rather denies this truth. Second, there are contexts in which judgments of proportionality can be made, *when there is some measure that can be used to compare measurable things.* Here the things to be measured are medical treatments of different types, each with its own risks, hazards, pains, costs, etc., and with its benefits. The judgment to be made in such cases is basically a technical one requiring some help from the medical profession. Moreover, although it is always wrong to kill a person because of the alleged bad quality of his life, a person's physical and moral resources will be such that some can accept treatments that other persons cannot because for some the treatment would be useful and not unduly burdensome whereas for others the treatments would not be useful and would be unduly burdensome. This topic will be considered at length in a later chapter.

The document then notes that it is not always wrong for patients to undergo perhaps hazardous and untried treatments if they so desire, and they can also forgo their use when they are seen not to do what they were supposed to do. Doctors can help greatly in judging whether the investment in instruments, personnel, etc., is just in proportion to the results achieved. No one can force a person to accept a risky or burdensome treatment, etc. If death is imminent, only normal care is required.

5. *Dignitas Personae*: On Certain Bioethical Questions

A. Overview

Dignitas personae is a sequel to the CDF's February 1987 doctrinal *Instruction on Respect for Human Life in Its Origin and on the Dignity of Procreation* (entitled *Donum vitae* in Latin).

Dignitas personae (henceforth DP) is of a doctrinal nature and falls within the category of documents that "participate in the ordinary Magisterium of the successor of Peter" (see *Donum veritatis*, no. 18) and is to be received by Catholics "with the religious assent of their spirit" (DP, no. 37). Its predecessor, *Donum vitae* (henceforth DV) was an exceptionally clearly written and unambiguous document. Some passages of DP, however, are not so clearly written and are somewhat ambiguous, so Catholic bioethicists faithful to magisterial teaching, acknowledging that the meaning of particular texts is not unambiguously clear, offer different and at times contradictory interpretations of those texts. The principal ones, which I will indicate in this overview and summary, are identified in a "Symposium on *Dignitas Personae*," edited by E. Christian Brugger and published in the Autumn 2009 issue of *The National Catholic Bioethics Quarterly*.[5]

The document did *not* consider several issues on which no firm magisterial teaching exists and over which bioethicists who accept magisterial teaching are sharply divided, among them the morality of gamete intrafallopian tube transfer (GIFT), how to cope with ectopic pregnancies (whether salpingostomy and the use of methotrexate are morally permissible in addition to salpingectomy), and the determination of death by accepting the irreversible cessation of the functioning of the entire brain, including the brain stem, as one criterion that the person has died.

DP contains thirty-six numbered sections divided as follows:

Introduction (nos. 1-3); First Part: Anthropological, Theological and Ethical Aspects of Human Life and Procreation (nos. 4-10); Second Part:

New Problems Concerning Procreation (nos. 11-23); Third Part: New Treatments Which Involve the Manipulation of the Embryo or the Human Genetic Patrimony (nos. 24-35); Conclusion (nos. 36-37).

The Second Part, after introductory no. 11, is subdivided into "Techniques for assisting infertility" (nos. 12-16); "Intracytoplasmic sperm injection (ICSI)" (no. 17); "Freezing embryos" (nos. 18-19); "The freezing of oocytes" (no. 20); "The reduction of embryos" (no. 21); "Preimplantation diagnosis" (no. 22); and "New forms of interception and contragestation" (no.23).

The Third Part, after introductory number 24, contains "Gene therapy" (nos. 25-27); "Human cloning" (nos. 28-30); "The therapeutic use of stem cells" (nos. 31-32); "Attempts at hybridization" (nos. 33); and "The use of human 'biological material' of illicit origin" (nos. 34-35).

B. Purpose and Teaching

A major purpose is to bring DV up to date by taking into account and evaluating new biomedical technologies that have raised new problems in the critical area of human life and the family and to examine "some issues that were treated earlier, but are in need of additional clarification" (no. 1). A subsidiary purpose is to show how Catholic teaching, based on both reason and faith, seeks to present an integral vision of man and his vocation, and to offer encouragement and support for a culture that considers science an invaluable service to the integral good of the life and dignity of every human being (no. 3).

(1) First Part

The First Part reaffirms (nos. 4-6) two fundamental principles given by DV governing the bioethical issues with which DP is concerned. The basic criterion is this: "The human being is to be respected and treated as a person from the moment of conception; and therefore from that same moment his rights as a person must be recognized, among which in the first place is the inviolable right of every innocent human being to life" (no. 4, a citation from DV, I, 1). The second fundamental principle declares: "*The origin of human life has its authentic context in marriage and in the family*, where it is generated through an act which expresses the reciprocal love between a man and a woman. Procreation which is truly responsible vis-à-vis the child to be born 'must be the fruit of marriage'" (no. 6; the internal citation is from DV, II, A, 1; emphasis in original).

Although DV did not define the embryo as a person, it nonetheless indicated, DP declares, "an intrinsic connection between the ontological dimension and the specific value of every human life." Thus it holds that "the reality of the human being for the entire span of life, both before and after birth, does not allow us to posit either a change in nature or a gradation in moral value, since it possesses *full anthropological and ethical status*" (no. 5; emphasis in original). One can thus argue that DP goes further than any magisterial document issued because it not only affirms that every human embryo *should be treated* as a person, but virtually declares that every human embryo *is* a person, although it does not actually say, "Every human embryo is a person." However, it does say that the nature of a being, its "ontological dimension," and the value of a being are intrinsically connected and then asserts that the human being has the same nature and therefore the same moral value throughout the stages of human development. "Indeed, the reality of the human being for the entire span of life, both before and after birth, does not allow us to posit either a change in nature or a gradation in moral value, since it possesses *full anthropological and ethical status*. The human embryo has, therefore, from the very beginning, the dignity proper to a person" (no. 5; emphasis in original).[6]

While the natural law known through human reason is "the source that inspires the relationship between the spouses in their responsibility for begetting new children" (no. 6), it is "only in the mystery of the incarnate Word that the mystery of man truly becomes clear" (no. 7). This enables us (no. 8) to understand that there can be no contradiction between affirming the dignity of human life and affirming its sacredness: "These two dimensions of life, the natural and the supernatural, allow us to understand better the sense in which *the acts that permit a new human being to come into existence*, in which a man and a woman give themselves to each other, *are a reflection of trinitarian love*" (no. 9; emphasis in original).

Finally, the First Part emphasizes that in expressing ethical judgments on new developments in medical research, "The Church ... does not intervene in the area proper to medical science itself, but rather calls everyone to ethical and social responsibility for their actions," reminding all that "the ethical value of biomedical science is gauged in reference to both the *unconditional respect owed to every human being* at every moment of his or her existence, and the *defense of the specific character of the personal act which transmits life*" (no. 10).

(2) Second Part

The Second Part, after a brief introduction (no. 11), first takes up "Techniques for assisting infertility." No. 12 identifies three fundamental goods that must be respected in treating infertility: "a) the right to life and to physical integrity of every human being from conception to natural death; b) the unity of marriage, which means reciprocal respect for the right within marriage to become a father or mother only together with the other spouse; c) the specifically human values of sexuality which require 'that the procreation of a human person be brought about as the fruit of the conjugal act specific to the love between spouses'" (internal citation from DV, II, B, 4).

No. 12 also recapitulates the teaching of DV by declaring that "all techniques of heterologous artificial fertilization, as well as those techniques of homologous artificial fertilization which substitute for the conjugal act, are to be excluded. On the other hand, techniques that act *as an aid to the conjugal act and its fertility* are permitted" (emphasis in original). No. 13 approves techniques aimed at removing obstacles to natural fertilization, such as hormonal treatments, surgery to unblock fallopian tubes, etc., and encourages adoption and research to prevent infertility. Nos. 14 and 15 focus on *in vitro* fertilization and the deliberate destruction of embryos. DV had taken these acts up and condemned them, and as DP points out, "[s]ubsequent experience has shown … that all techniques of *in vitro* fertilization proceed as if the human embryo were simply a mass of cells to be used, selected and discarded" (no. 14).

No. 16 sums up the Church's teaching: "The Church … holds that it is ethically unacceptable to *dissociate procreation from the integrally personal context of the conjugal act:* human procreation is a personal act of a husband and wife, which is not capable of substitution. The blithe acceptance of the enormous number of abortions involved in the process of *in vitro* fertilization vividly illustrates how the replacement of the conjugal act by a technical procedure — in addition to being in contradiction with the respect that is due to procreation as something that cannot be reduced to mere reproduction — leads to a weakening of the respect owed to every human being" (emphasis in original). While the desire for a child is legitimate, this desire "cannot justify the 'production' of offspring, just as the desire not to have a child cannot justify the abandonment or destruction of a child once he or she has been conceived. In reality, it seems that some researchers, lacking any ethical point of reference and aware of the possibilities inherent in technological progress, surrender to the logic of purely subjective desires." Confronted with this reality, " 'The Magisterium of the Church has constantly proclaimed the sacred and inviolable character of every human life from its conception until its natural end' "[7]

No. 17 is devoted to "Intracytoplasmic sperm injection (ICSI)," a more recently developed method of artificial fertilization. This procedure, as footnote 32 explains, "is similar in almost every respect to other forms of *in vitro* fertilization with the difference that in [it] fertilization in the test tube does not take place on its own, but rather by means of the injection into the oocyte of a single sperm, selected earlier, or by the injection of immature germ cells taken from the man." Like *in vitro* fertilization, it is intrinsically evil because it causes "*a complete separation between procreation and the conjugal act*" (no. 17; emphasis in original).

Nos. 18 and 19 deal with the issues involved in "Freezing embryos." No. 18 describes the procedure and the problems it raises. It is used to avoid repeatedly removing the woman's oocytes from her body by hyperfertilizing the woman and simultaneously extracting many oocytes, fertilizing them, cryopreserving the human embryos so produced, and storing them for "retrieval" later if someone wishes to use them (the late Jerome Lejeune rightly described the procedure as putting embryonic human persons into "concentration cans"). DP judges cryopreservation "*incompatible with the respect owed to human embryos*," exposing them to the serious risk of death or physical harm, depriving them at least temporarily of maternal reception and gestation, and placing them in a situation in which they are susceptible to further offense and manipulation (emphasis in original). Moreover, no. 18 continues, "The majority of embryos that are not used remain 'orphans.' Their parents do not ask for them and at times all trace of the parents is lost." This raises the question, "What to do with the large number of frozen and abandoned embryos?"

No. 19 takes up this issue, definitively repudiating as intrinsically immoral proposals to *use these embryos for research* or *for the treatment of disease*. Such proposals "are obviously unacceptable because they treat the embryos as mere 'biological material' and result in their destruction." Similarly the proposal that these embryos "could be put at the disposal of infertile couples as a *treatment for infertility* is not ethically acceptable for the same reasons which make artificial heterologous procreation illicit as well as any form of surrogate motherhood; this practice would also lead to other problems of a medical, psychological and legal nature."

No. 19 then devotes two brief sentences to an issue on which Catholic theologians loyal to the Magisterium have been divided. It describes the issue as follows: "It has also been proposed, solely in order to allow human beings to be born who are otherwise condemned to destruction, that there could be a form of '*prenatal adoption*' " (emphasis in original). The following sentence reads as follows: "This proposal, praiseworthy with regard to the intention of respecting and defending human life, presents however various problems not dissimilar to those mentioned above."

Does this passage definitively reject the proposal concerning the "prenatal adoption" of frozen and orphaned embryos? There is a dispute among those who have read the document on this issue. Some scholars think that DP has definitely concluded that adopting frozen embryos prenatally is not morally licit. But others, and I am among them, think that a close reading of this sentence and the context in which it appears makes it clear that *it was not the intention* of the CDF to make a definitive judgment on this disputed question but that it left the issue open to further debate by Catholic theologians. DP's statement that embryo adoption presents problems not dissimilar to those involved in the immoral practice treated in the preceding paragraph can be reasonably interpreted as warning those engaging in embryo adoption to attend to all relevant medical, psychological, and legal problems and to exercise prudence in dealing with them.[8]

That paragraph of no. 19 also rejects any form of surrogate motherhood, which it defines, referring to the definition found in DV II, A, 3 (see footnote 38), a definition that supporters of embryo prenatal adoption completely accept.[9] The final paragraph of no. 19 declares: "All things considered, it needs to be recognized that the thousands of abandoned embryos represent a *situation of injustice which in fact cannot be resolved*" (emphasis in original).

This is definitely true. Does this sentence imply that embryo adoption is morally wrong and for that reason its practice cannot resolve the injustice that has been done to abandoned embryos? It does not. Even if the practice of embryo adoption were so widely accepted by upright people that no abandoned embryo was left to die, all of those embryos would have suffered an injustice not rectified by the upright people who came to their rescue, the injustice of having been made in a laboratory and not begotten in and through the marital act.

No. 20 considers "The freezing of oocytes" and declares that "*cryopreservation of oocytes for the purpose of being used in artificial procreation is to be considered morally unacceptable*" (emphasis in original). No. 21 takes up "The reduction of embryos," a procedure in which embryos or fetuses in the womb are directly exterminated, and judges this "an intentional selective abortion" and always constituting "a grave moral disorder." Appealing to the good that could be achieved by doing so is of no avail insofar as "it is never permitted to do something which is intrinsically illicit, not even in view of a good result: *the end does not justify the means*" (emphasis in original). "Preimplantation diagnosis" is the subject of no. 22. It is done to make sure "*that only embryos free from defects or having the desired sex or other particular qualities are transferred*" (emphasis in original). It is directed to the destruction of human embryos judged defective or undesirable for other reasons, treats the human embryo as mere biological material, and is a terrible affront to human dignity. No. 23 (the final number of the Second Part) focuses on "New forms of interception and contragestation." "Interceptive methods" interfere with human embryos prior to implantation in order to prevent their birth, while "contragestative" methods eliminate — i.e., kill — them after implantation in order to achieve the same purpose. Both are forms of intentional abortion and always gravely immoral.[10]

The Second Part leaves untouched the question debated by Catholic moral theologians regarding the procedure known as "gamete intrafallopian tube transfer" (GIFT). Some judge it an immoral *substitute* for the conjugal act; others consider it a legitimate way of *aiding* the conjugal act to achieve its procreative meaning. The issue thus remains open to debate.

(3) Third Part

The Third Part, after its introductory paragraph (no. 24), takes up new treatments involving the manipulation of the human embryo or the human genome patrimony. Nos. 25-27 concern "Gene therapy" — i.e., techniques of genetic engineering applied to human beings for therapeutic purposes.

There are two broad types: *somatic-cell* gene therapy and *germ-line* cell therapy. The first aims at eliminating or reducing genetic defects by manipulating a person's somatic or body cells — i.e., cells other than the reproductive cells. It affects only one individual person. *Germ-line* cell therapy aims at correcting genetic defects present in germ-line cells with the purpose of transmitting the therapeutic effects to the offspring of the individual. Both methods of gene therapy can be undertaken on a fetus *before his or her birth* as gene therapy in the uterus or *after birth* on a child or adult (nos. 25-26). The CDF judges that "*[P]rocedures used on somatic cells for strictly therapeutic purposes are in principle morally licit*," but since gene therapy can involve significant risks for the patient, "the ethical principle must be observed according to which ... it is necessary to establish beforehand that the person being treated will not be exposed to risks to his health or physical integrity which are excessive or disproportionate to the gravity of the pathology for which a cure is sought. The informed consent of the patient or his legitimate representative is also required." The "moral evaluation of *germ line cell therapy* is different. Whatever genetic modifications are effected on the germ cells of a person will be transmitted to any potential offspring. Because the risks connected to any genetic manipulation are considerable and as yet not fully controllable, *in the present state of research, it is not morally permissible to act in a way that may cause possible harm to the resulting progeny....* [I]n its current state, germ line cell therapy in all its forms is morally illicit" (no. 26; emphasis in original).

No. 27 rejects use of genetic engineering for purposes other than therapeutic — e.g., to manipulate human genes for improving the genetic pool. DP claims, "Apart from technical difficulties and the real and potential risks involved, such manipulation would promote a eugenic mentality and would lead to indirect social stigma with regard to people who lack certain qualities, while privileging qualities that happen to be appreciated by a certain culture or society; such qualities do not constitute what is specifically human" (no. 27). Moreover, the attempt "to create *a new type of human being*" embodies "*an ideological element* in which man tries to take the place of his Creator" (no. 27; emphasis in original).

Nos. 28-30 deal with "Human cloning" — i.e., the asexual or agametic "reproduction" of the entire human organism in order to produce one or more "copies" which, from a genetic perspective, are substantially identical to the single original. It has two purposes: *reproduction,* to obtain the birth of a new human being, and *medical therapy* or research (no. 28).

Reproductive cloning is gravely immoral; it imposes on "the resulting individual a predetermined genetic identity, subjecting him ... to a form of *biological slavery....* The fact that someone would arrogate to himself the right to determine arbitrarily the genetic characteristics of another person represents *a grave offence to the dignity of that person as well as to the fundamental equality of all people*" (no. 29; emphasis in original). "[S]o-called therapeutic cloning is even more serious. To create embryos with the intention of destroying them, even with the intention of helping the sick, is completely incompatible with human dignity, because it makes the existence of a human being at the embryonic stage nothing more than a means to be used and destroyed. It is *gravely immoral to sacrifice a human life for therapeutic ends*" (no. 30; emphasis in original).

The final paragraph of no. 30 touches on the creation of stem cells without bringing into being any human individual who could be the victim of injustice — an issue more fully considered later in no. 32. No. 30 points out that ethical objections to therapeutic cloning and the use of human embryos formed *in vitro* have led to proposed new techniques presented as capable of producing embryonic-type stem cells without involving the destruction of true human embryos. Footnote 49 names some of these new techniques: "human parthenogenesis, altered nuclear transfer (ANT) and oocyte assisted reprogramming (OAR)." No. 30 then declares: "These proposals have been met with questions of both a scientific and an ethical nature regarding above all the ontological status of the 'product' obtained in this way. Until these doubts have been clarified, the statement of the Encyclical *Evangelium vitae* needs to be kept in mind: 'what is at stake is so important that, from the standpoint of moral obligation, the mere probability that a human person is involved would suffice to justify an absolutely clear prohibition of any intervention aimed at killing a human embryo.'" DP neither condemns ANT and OAR, which many faithful Catholic theologians have proposed as morally legitimate and others have opposed, as intrinsically evil nor affirms the opinion of those who think that the entity brought into being by those processes is a human being. Instead, it observes that questions have been raised about the status of the results of those processes and recalls previous teaching of the sound prudential norm that those dealing with what might be a human being cannot rightly treat that entity as other than a human being unless they are certain beyond reasonable doubt that it is not a human being. But here, too, there are some scholars who think that DP rejects ANT and OAR.

The discussion of cloning leads DP to reflect on "The therapeutic use of stem cells" in nos. 31-32. No. 31 identifies stem cells, their sources, and the proven therapeutic value of adult stem cells. "Stem cells are undifferentiated cells with ... a) the prolonged capability of multiplying themselves while maintaining the undifferentiated state; b) the capability of producing transitory progenitor cells from which fully differentiated cells descend, for example, nerve cells, muscle cells and blood cells.... Among the sources for human stem cells ... identified thus far are: the embryo in the first stages of its existence, the fetus, blood from the umbilical cord and various tissues from adult humans (bone marrow, umbilical cord, brain, mesenchyme from various organs, etc.) and amniotic fluid."

No. 32 offers an ethical evaluation of the use of stem cells, emphasizing that "it is necessary to consider the *methods of obtaining stem cells* as well as *the risks connected with their clinical and experimental use....* Methods which do not cause serious harm to the subject from whom the stem cells are taken are to be considered licit. This is generally the case when tissues are taken from: a) an adult organism; b) the blood of the umbilical cord at the time of birth; c) fetuses who have died of natural causes. The obtaining of stem cells from a living human embryo, on the other hand, invariably causes the death of the embryo and is consequently gravely illicit.... The use of embryonic stem cells or differentiated cells derived from them — even when these are provided by other researchers through the destruction of embryos or when such cells are commercially available — presents serious problems from the standpoint of cooperation in evil and scandal.

"There are no moral objections to the clinical use of stem cells that have been obtained licitly; however, the common criteria of medical ethics need to be respected.... Research initiatives involving the use of adult stem cells, since they do not present ethical problems, should be encouraged and supported" (no. 32; emphasis in original).

No. 33 considers "Attempts at hybridization" — i.e., using animal oocytes to reprogram the nuclei of human somatic cells in order to obtain embryonic stem cells from embryos produced without having to use human oocytes. Procedures of this kind are a grave offense against human dignity because of the mixing of human and animal genetic elements that can disrupt man's specific identity. Moreover, the possible use of stem cells taken from these embryos may also involve additional and as yet unknown health risks because of the presence of animal genetic material in their cytoplasm. "To consciously expose a human being to such risks is morally and ethically unacceptable."

In nos. 34-35, DP addresses "The use of human 'biological material' of illicit origin." No. 34 identifies the problem of cooperation in evil and giving scandal insofar as cell lines originally obtained by illicit interventions against human life and integrity are at times used for scientific research or the production of vaccines and other products. Some general principles must be given to help people form their consciences rightly. Citing John Paul II's *Evangelium vitae*, no. 34 reminds all that the use of human embryos/fetuses as objects of experimentation " 'constitutes a crime against their dignity as human beings who have a right to the same respect owed to a child once born, just as to every person' " (*Evangelium vitae*, no. 63); thus "[t]hese forms of experimentation always constitute a grave moral disorder" (cf. ibid., no. 62).

No. 35 notes that a different situation exists when researchers use "biological material" of illicit origin produced apart from their research center or commercially obtained. It likewise notes that DV articulated the principle to be followed: "The corpses of human embryos and fetuses, ... deliberately aborted or not, must be respected just as the remains of other human beings. In particular, they cannot be subjected to mutilation or to autopsies if their death has not yet been verified and without the consent of the parents or of the mother. Furthermore, the moral requirements must be safeguarded that there be no complicity in deliberate abortion and that the risk of scandal be avoided" (I, 4). DP then considers "the criterion of independence" proposed by some. According to it, the use of "biological material" of illicit origin would be ethically permissible provided there is a clear separation between those who produce, freeze, and cause the death of embryos and researchers involved in scientific experimentation. DP expresses caution here, arguing that of itself this criterion might not be sufficient "to avoid a contradiction in the attitude of the person who says that he does not approve of the injustice perpetrated by others, but at the same time accepts for his own work the 'biological material' which the others have obtained by means of that injustice. When the illicit action is endorsed by the laws which regulate healthcare and scientific research, it is necessary to distance oneself from the evil aspects of that system in order not to give the impression of a certain toleration or tacit acceptance of actions which are gravely unjust. Any appearance of acceptance would in fact contribute to the growing indifference to, if not the approval of, such actions in certain medical and political circles." In fact, "there is a duty to refuse to use such 'biological material' even when there is no close connection between the researcher and the actions of those who performed the artificial fertilization or the abortion, or when there was no prior agreement with the centers in which the artificial fertilization took place. This duty springs from the necessity to *remove oneself,* within the area of one's own research, *from a gravely unjust legal situation and to affirm with clarity the value of human life.* Therefore, the above-mentioned criterion of independence is necessary, but may be ethically insufficient" (emphasis in original).

But "within this general picture there exist *differing degrees of responsibility.* Grave reasons may be morally proportionate to justify the use of such 'biological material.' Thus, for example, danger to the health of children could permit parents to use a vaccine which was developed using cell lines of illicit origin, while keeping in mind that everyone has the duty to make known their disagreement and to ask that their health-care system make other types of vaccines available. Moreover, in organizations where cell lines of illicit origin are being utilized, the responsibility of those who make the decision to use them is not the same as that of those who have no voice in such a decision."[11]

(4) Conclusion

The Conclusion (nos. 36 and 37) is in essence a reasoned and reasonable apologia for the purpose and spirit of the Magisterium's analysis and evaluation of contemporary developments in biomedicine affecting human persons and the institution of marriage. The entire matter is summarized this way: "In virtue of the Church's doctrinal and pastoral mission, the Congregation for the Doctrine of the Faith has felt obliged to reiterate both the dignity and the fundamental and inalienable rights of every human being, including those in the initial stages of their existence, and to state explicitly the need for protection and respect which this dignity requires of everyone. The fulfillment of this duty implies courageous opposition to all those practices which result in grave and unjust discrimination against unborn human beings, who have the dignity of a person, created like others in the image of God. *Behind every 'no' in the difficult task of discerning between good and evil, there shines a great 'yes' to the recognition of the dignity and inalienable value of every single and unique human being called into existence*" (no. 37; emphasis in original).

DP ends by saying: "The Christian faithful will commit themselves to the energetic promotion of a new culture of life by receiving the contents of this Instruction with the religious assent of their spirit, knowing that God always gives the grace necessary to observe his commandments and that, in every human being, above all in the least among us, one meets Christ himself (cf. Mt 25:40). In addition, all persons of good will, in particular physicians and researchers open to dialogue and desirous of knowing what is true, will understand and agree with these principles and judgments, which seek to safeguard the vulnerable condition of human beings in the first stages of life and to promote a more human civilization."

Conclusion to Chapter One

This chapter has reviewed in depth the teaching found in four major documents of the Magisterium relevant to the issues to be taken up in this book. The teaching found in Pope John Paul II's encyclical *Evangelium vitae* is pertinent to almost every topic that will be considered, while the teaching set forth in *Donum vitae* is crucially important relative to questions concerning the generation of human life; that presented in the *Declaration on Procured Abortion* is central to the problem of abortion; and that given in the *Declaration on Euthanasia* is, naturally, quite pertinent to issues regarding the care of the dying. In our subsequent study of these specific issues, reference will be made to the documents examined here as well as to other relevant sources of magisterial teaching.

―――――――― Endnotes for Chapter One ――――――――

1. On this, see John Paul II, encyclical *Veritatis splendor*, no. 78; see also St. Thomas Aquinas, *Summa theologiae*, II-II, 64, 7.
2. Here the Pope refers to an incisive passage in *Gaudium et spes*, no. 27, where the Council Fathers had said that "all offenses against human life itself, such as murder, genocide, abortion, euthanasia, willful suicide … are criminal; they poison civilization, and they debase their perpetrators more than their victims and militate against the honor of the Creator."
3. The truth of this conclusion is confirmed by what John Paul II subsequently declared in his *motu proprio*, entitled *Ad tuendam fidem* ("To defend the faith"), in May 1998, and by the "explanatory note" on this document prepared by the Congregation for the Doctrine of the Faith. In this note, the Congregation *explicitly* includes the "doctrine on the grave immorality of the direct and voluntary killing of an innocent human being" as an example of a truth proposed as divinely revealed, not through a "defining act," i.e., a truth "solemnly defined by an *ex cathedra* pronouncement of the Roman Pontiff or by the action of an ecumenical council, but through a "non-defining act," i.e., "by the ordinary and universal magisterium of the bishops dispersed throughout the world who are in communion with the Successor of Peter." The Congregation then notes: "Such a doctrine can be confirmed or reaffirmed by the Roman Pontiff, even without recourse to a solemn definition, by declaring that it belongs explicitly to the teaching of the ordinary and universal magisterium." The text of John Paul II's *Ad tuendam fidem* and of the Congregation's explanatory note, entitled "Commentary on the Profession of Faith's Concluding Paragraphs," is found in *Origins: CNS Documentary Service* 28.8 (July 16, 1998). The text of *Ad tuendam fidem* is given on pp. 114-116; that of the commentary on pp. 116-120. See in particular nos. 9 and 11 of the commentary.
4. In its explanatory note on John Paul II's *Ad tuendam fidem*, the Congregation for the Doctrine of the Faith explicitly recalls the teaching of *Evangelium vitae* and cites euthanasia as an example of a truth which, while not revealed, is connected by logical necessity to revealed truth and as one infallibly proposed by the ordinary and universal Magisterium of the Church. See no. 11 of "Commentary on the Profession of Faith's Concluding Paragraphs," in *Origins* (cf. endnote 3).
5. E. Christian Brugger, ed., "Symposium on *Dignitas Personae*," *The National Catholic Bioethics Quarterly* 9.3 (Autumn 2009), 461-483. The "Symposium" includes an introduction by Brugger and the following essays: Christopher Kaczor's "Anthropological, Theological, and Ethical Aspects of Human Procreation" (nos. 1-10); Peter Ryan, S.J.'s "New Problems Concerning Human

Procreation" (nos. 11-17 and 20-23); Luke Gormally's "The 'Various Problems' Presented by Embryo Adoption" (no. 19), pp. 10-14; John M. Finnis's "Understanding *Dignitas Personae* on Embryo Adoption," pp. 14-17; William E. May's "New Treatments That Involve the Manipulation of the Embryo or the Human Genetic Patrimony, and Conclusion" (nos. 24-37); and E. Christian Brugger's "Strengths and Weaknesses of *Dignitas Personae*," pp. 20-21.

6. However, Edward J. Furton points out: "Still, *Dignitas personae* has not stated point-blank that 'the embryo is a person.' We will not find that exact expression anywhere in the text. Nonetheless, it is apparent that this is the only possible conclusion that one can draw, for if it is true that the embryo undergoes no change in nature throughout its development, and if it is true that the embryo, by its very nature, has the dignity of a person, then it must also be true that the embryo is a person from the moment of conception." See his essay "Is the Time of Personhood Settled? *Dignitas personae* Advances the Debate," *Ethics and Medics* 34.4 (April 2009), 3-4.

7. The internal citation is from Benedict XVI, Address to the General Assembly of the Pontifical Academy for Life and International Congress on "The Human Embryo in the Pre-implantation Phase," February 27, 2006.

8. *The National Catholic Bioethics Quarterly* "Symposium on *Dignitas Personae*," referred to in endnote 1, includes an essay ("The 'Various Problems' Presented by Embryo Adoption") by Luke Gormally in which he presents an argument that *DP*, properly understood, does regard embryo adoption as intrinsically evil, although he admits that the text "does not offer well-defined teaching." It also includes an essay ("Understanding *Dignitas Personae* on Embryo Adoption") by John Finnis offering an argument to the contrary. Above all, the United States Conference of Catholic Bishops says that *Dignitas personae* "raises cautions or problems about these new issues but does not formally make a judgment against them" (http://usccb.org/comm/archives/2008/08-196.shtml). Thus the issue is still open for debate and discussion by Catholic scholars.

9. For this, see the debate between Luke Gormally and John Finnis in "Symposium on *Dignitas Personae*," E. Christian Brugger, ed., *The National Catholic Bioethics Quarterly* 9.3 (Autumn 2009), 10-17.

10. For this see Congregation for the Doctrine of the Faith's "Doctrinal Commentary on the Concluding Formula of the *Professio Fidei*" (especially notes 9 and 11), accessible at http://www.vatican.va/roman_curia/congregations/cfaith/documents/rc_con_cfaith_doc_1998_professio-fidei_en.html.

11. See *Dignitas personae*, no. 35, par. 4.

CHAPTER TWO

Making True Moral Judgments
and Good Moral Choices

B efore considering, in the following chapters, major bioethical issues, it is fitting and useful to consider first of all the subject of making true moral judgments and good moral choices. It is so precisely because the principles in light of which true moral judgments and good moral choices can be made in our everyday lives as husbands and wives, students, businessmen and businesswomen, or what have you, are the very same principles in light of which true moral judgments and good moral choices can be made in matters pertaining to bioethics.

Upright, virtuous men and women make true moral judgments and good moral choices insofar as doing so has become, as it were, second nature to them. Moreover, faithful Catholics can be confident that they make such judgments and choices by conforming them to the teaching of the Church, which speaks in the name of Christ. But everyone, even the virtuous person, is at times perplexed about what to do, and frequently there is no firm teaching of the Church to which one can appeal in order to make a true moral judgment about some difficult moral problem, and at times it is very difficult to apply such teaching to some complex issues. It is thus worthwhile to reflect more systematically on this matter.

Moreover, it is good for virtuous persons and faithful Catholics to reflect in this way so that they can more intelligently explain both to themselves and to others why they regard some human actions as morally good and others as morally bad, and why the Church's teaching on moral matters is true.

I will proceed as follows: First, I will clarify the meaning of a "human act," its religious and existential significance, and the sources of its moral goodness or badness. I do so because moral judgments bear upon human acts, assessing them for their moral quality. Second, I will consider different kinds of human dignity to show how human freedom of choice is related to truth, to God's wise and loving plan for human existence. Third, I will consider the relationship between the "good" and human choice and action and the first principle of natural law. Fourth, I will consider the basic normative truths or principles of natural law, i.e., truths enabling us to distinguish between morally good and morally bad alternatives of choice and action. Fifth, I will outline briefly an intelligent way to go about making good moral judgments. Sixth, I will consider how the natural law is fulfilled and perfected by the new law of love and what this means for Christians in making moral judgments and choices. Seventh, I will consider the role of virtue ethics in making true moral judgments and good moral choices.[1]

1. The Meaning of a "Human Act"; Its Existential and Religious Significance; the Sources of Its Moral Character

A. The Meaning of a "Human Act"

Human acts are *not* physical events that come and go, like the falling of rain and the turning of leaves, nor do they "happen" to a person. They are, rather, the outward expression of a person's choices, for at the core of a human act is a free, self-determining choice, which as such is something spiritual that abides within the person, determining the very *being* of the person.

The Scriptures, particularly the New Testament, are very clear about this. Jesus taught that it is not what enters a person that defiles him or her; rather, it is what flows from the person, from his or her heart, from the core of his or her being, from his or her choice (cf. Mt 15:10-20; Mk 7:14-23).

Although many human acts have physical, observable components, what is central to them is the fact that they embody and carry out human choices; because they do, they abide within the person as dispositions to further choices and actions of the same kind, until a contradictory kind of choice is made. Thus I become an adulterer and remain an adulterer once I freely adopt by choice the proposal to have sex with someone other than my wife. I commit adultery in the heart even before I engage in the outward, observable act. And I remain an adulterer, disposed to commit adultery again, until I make a contradictory choice, i.e., until I sincerely repent of my adultery, do penance, and commit myself to amending my life and being faithful to my wife. Even then, in a sense, I remain an adulterer because I freely gave myself that identity, but now I am a *repentant* adulterer, resolved to be a faithful, loving husband, and I am a repentant adulterer because I have given myself this identity by my freely chosen act (made, of course, with the help of God's grace) of repentance.

B. The Existential, Religious Significance of Human Acts as Freely Chosen

This great truth, namely, that human acts as freely chosen have an existential, religious significance, has already, to some extent, been brought out in our consideration of the meaning of a human act as a reality shaped by a free, self-determining choice. But this matter is so critically important — it is precisely because human acts as freely chosen have existential and religious significance that eternal life depends on our making *good* moral choices in the light of *true* judgments — that it merits further reflection.

John Paul II eloquently emphasizes this truth at the very beginning of his 1993 encyclical *Veritatis splendor*, in meditating on the dialogue between Jesus and the rich young man who asked, "Teacher, what good must I do to gain eternal life?" (Mt 19:16). Reflecting on this question, the Holy Father says: "For the young man the question is not so much about rules to be followed, but *about the meaning of life*.... This question is ultimately an appeal to the absolute Good which attracts and beckons us: it is the echo of a call from God, who is the origin and goal of man's life" (VS, no. 7). It is, he continues, "*an essential and unavoidable question for every man* for it is about the moral good which must be done, and about eternal life. The young man senses that there is a connection between moral good and the fulfillment of his own destiny" (VS, no. 8).

The rich young man's question has existential and religious significance precisely because it is in and through the actions we freely choose to do that *we determine ourselves* and establish our identity as moral beings. "It is precisely through his acts," the Pope writes, "that man attains perfection as man, as one who is called to seek his Creator on his own accord and freely to arrive at full and blessed perfection by cleaving to him." Our freely chosen deeds, he continues, "do not produce a change merely in the state of affairs outside of man, but, to the extent that they are deliberate choices, they give moral definition to the very person who performs them, *determining his most profound spiritual traits*" (VS, no. 71). Each choice involves a "*decision about oneself* and a setting of one's own life for or against the Good, for or against the Truth, and ultimately for or against God" (VS, no. 65).

To recapitulate: we *determine ourselves, make ourselves to be the kind of persons we are in and through the actions we freely choose to do.* We are free to choose what we are to do and through our choices make ourselves to be the kind of persons we are. But we are *not* free to make what we choose to do to be good or bad, right or wrong. We know this from our own experience, for we know that at times we have freely chosen to do things that we knew, at the very moment we chose to do them, were *morally wrong*. We can, in short, choose badly or well; and if we are to be fully the beings we are meant to be we need to choose well, i.e., in accordance with the truth. We will take this matter up in detail later in this chapter.

C. The Sources of the Morality of a Human Act

The morality of a human act depends on three factors: the *object* of the act, its *end*, and the *circumstances* in which it is done (cf. CCC, nos. 1750-1754; ST, I-II, 18). Of these, the *primary* source of the morality of a human act is the *object*, and no wonder, because the object of the act is precisely what the acting person *chooses to do*. This object is not some physical event in the external world. Since it is precisely what the acting person is choosing to do here and now, he or she ratifies this object in his or her heart and makes himself or herself to be the kind of person willing to do *this*. Thus, if I choose to lie, lying is the object of my act specifying it as an act of lying, and, because I freely choose to lie, I make myself *to be* a *liar*, no matter how I may want to describe myself to others or even to myself.

Pope John Paul II, rejecting some contemporary moral theories utterly incompatible with Catholic faith, has emphasized this great truth. Thus he wrote: "*the morality of the human act depends primarily and fundamentally on the 'object' rationally chosen by the deliberate will*" (VS, no. 78; emphasis in original). In a very important passage that not only well summarizes the Catholic tradition but also bears witness to the truth that a human act is no mere physical happening but rather a reality flowing from the inner core of the person insofar as it is a freely chosen deed, John Paul II goes on to say:

> In order to be able to grasp the object of an act which specifies that act morally, it is therefore necessary to place oneself *in the perspective of the acting person*. The object of an act of willing is in fact a freely chosen kind of behavior. To the extent that it is in conformity with the order of reason, it is the cause of the goodness of the will; it perfects us morally.... By the object of a given moral act, then, one cannot mean a process or an event of the merely physical order, to be assessed on the basis of its ability to bring about a given state of affairs in the outside world. Rather that object is the proximate end of a deliberate decision which determines the act of willing on the part of the acting person. (VS, no. 78; cf. ST, I-II, 18)

Note that in this passage John Paul II affirms that the object freely chosen, if it is "in conformity with the order of reason," is the "cause of the goodness of the will" and "perfects us morally." Obviously, if this object is *not* in conformity with the order of reason and is known not to be, then it will be the cause of the badness of the will and will debase us morally. The "order of reason" to which John Paul II refers will occupy us below, in considering the "natural law" or set of truths intended to guide human choices and enable human persons to distinguish between morally good and morally bad alternatives of choice/action.

Note too that in this passage John Paul II says that the "object" is also the "proximate end of a deliberate decision which determines the act of willing on the part of the acting person." The "object" is the "proximate" or "immediate" end of an act of willing because it is what one chooses to do here and now. There is also a further or ulterior end of most human actions, the end for whose sake one chooses to do this here and now. This further or ulterior end is a distinct source of the morality of a human act different from the object or proximate end. But both the object or proximate end and the further or ulterior end must be good or in conformity with the order of reason if the human act in its totality is to be morally good. One can choose to do something morally good and in conformity with the order of reason for very bad ulterior ends. Thus one can choose to help carry an elderly widow's groceries into her house in order to gain entry to her house and steal her silverware or computer. The whole action is vitiated by the bad end toward which it is ordered and for whose sake one chose to carry in the groceries.

Frequently people seek to justify their actions in terms of the further or remote end for whose sake they are done, and at times they even try to redescribe the "object" of their act in terms of its hoped-for benefits. Thus some may seek to justify an abortion by saying that what they are doing — their moral object — is to prevent human suffering (e.g., the suffering that a child afflicted by cystic fibrosis and his family might experience if he is allowed to be born). But this alleged justification is patently false, for the true "object" specifying their act of choice is aborting the unborn child. This is the means chosen, the act done, in order to bring about the remote or further end motivating the act.

The morality of an act also depends on the *circumstances* in which it is done. These, too, can be either good or bad. For instance, it is good to offer charitable correction to a friend, but to do so in front of his children rather than in private is a circumstance affecting the act, turning one otherwise morally good into one morally bad.

Because the morality of a human act, considered in its totality, depends on object (= proximate end), end (further or ulterior end), and circumstances, the act is morally good *only* if *all* these factors are morally good, i.e., in conformity with the order of reason. This is what can be called the principle of plenitude or perfection, expressed in Latin by the dictum *bonum ex integra causa*, which means that the act is morally good if and only if all the factors contributing to its moral quality are good. If *any* of these morally relevant factors are contrary to the order of reason, then the act is morally bad: *malum ex quocumque defectu* — an act is bad if it has any moral defect whatsoever (cf. CCC, nos. 1755-1756; ST, I-II, 18, 1; 18, 4, ad 3; 19, 6, ad 1).

Of these three sources of the morality of a human act, the "object," understood precisely as John Paul II has described it, is primary. An act morally bad by reason of the object freely chosen can never be made good by reason of any end, no matter how noble, or any circumstances, whatever they may be.

2. Kinds of Human Dignity; Human Freedom and God's Wise and Loving Plan for Human Existence

A. Kinds of Human Dignity

According to Catholic tradition, there is a threefold dignity predicable of human persons: (1) the first is intrinsic, natural, inalienable, and an endowment or gift; (2) the second is also intrinsic, but it is an achievement, not an endowment, an achievement made possible, given the reality of original sin and its effects, only by God's unfailing grace; (3) the third, again an intrinsic dignity, is also a gift, not an achievement, but is a gift far surpassing man's nature and literally divinizing him.

The first dignity proper to human beings is the dignity that is theirs simply as living members of the human species, which God called into being when, in the beginning, he "created mankind in his image ... male and female he created them" (Gn 1:27). Every human being is a living image of the all-holy God and can therefore rightly be called a "created word" of God, the created word that his uncreated Word became and is, precisely to show us how much God loves us.

When we come into existence, we *are*, by reason of this intrinsic dignity, *persons*. As God's "created words," as persons, we are endowed with the capacity to know the truth and the capacity to determine our lives by freely choosing to conform our lives and actions to the truth.[2] Yet when we come into existence, we are *not yet* fully the beings we are meant to be. And this leads us to consider the second sort of dignity proper to human persons, a dignity that is intrinsic but an achievement (made possible only by God's never-failing grace), not an endowment.

This second kind of dignity is the dignity to which we are called as intelligent and free persons capable of determining our own lives by our own free choices. This is the dignity we are called upon to *give to ourselves* (with the help of God's unfailing grace) by freely choosing to shape our choices and actions in accord with the truth. In other words, we give ourselves this dignity and inwardly participate in it by making good moral choices, and such choices are possible only in the light of true moral judgments. We give this dignity to ourselves by being true to our natural dignity as persons created in God's image and likeness.

The third kind of dignity is ours as "children of God," brothers and sisters of Jesus, members of the divine family. This kind of dignity is a pure gratuitous gift from God himself. He made us to be the *kind* of beings we are, i.e., persons made in his image and likeness, because he willed that there be beings inwardly capable of receiving, should he choose to grant it, the gift of divine life. And God has chosen to give this utterly supernatural gift to us in and through his Son become man, Jesus Christ. Just as Jesus truly shares our human nature, so too do human persons who are regenerated in the waters of baptism share in Jesus' divine nature. As true children of God and brothers and sisters of Jesus, we are called to walk in a way worthy of our vocation *to be* co-workers with Christ, his collaborators in redeeming the world. I will take up the relevance of this dignity for making true moral judgments and good moral choices in section 6, below. My concern here and in the next two sections is with the second kind of dignity proper to human persons, the dignity that, as intelligent and free persons made in God's image and likeness, they are to give themselves by choosing in accordance with the truth.

B. Human Freedom of Choice and God's Wise and Loving Plan for Human Existence

The nature of this dignity and the relationship between human freedom and God's wise and loving plan for human existence was beautifully developed by Vatican Council II. According to the Council, "the highest norm of human life is the divine law — eternal, objective, and universal — whereby God orders, directs, and governs the entire universe and all the ways of the human community according to a plan conceived in wisdom and in love" (DH, no. 3). Immediately afterwards, the Council went on to say: "Man has been made by God to participate in this law, with the result that, under the gentle disposition of divine providence, he can come to perceive ever increasingly the unchanging truth" (DH, no. 3). Precisely because he can do this, man "has the duty, and therefore the right, to seek the truth" (DH, no. 3). The truth in question here is the truth that is to inwardly shape and guide human choices and actions — moral truth.

The passage concludes by saying that "on his part man perceives and acknowledges the imperatives of the divine law through the mediation of conscience" (DH, no. 3). Another Council document, the Pastoral Constitution on the Church in the Modern World, *Gaudium et spes* (GS), develops this thought in a very significant passage:

> Deep within his conscience man discovers a law which he has not laid upon himself but which he must obey. The voice of this law, ever calling him to love and do what is good and to avoid evil, tells him inwardly at the right moment, do this, shun that. For man has in his heart a law written by God. *His dignity lies in obeying this law*, and by it he will be judged. His conscience is man's most secret core, and his sanctuary. There he is alone with God, whose voice echoes in his depths. By conscience, in a wonderful way, that law is made known which is fulfilled in the love of God and of one's neighbor. (GS, no. 16; emphasis added)

These passages make it clear that human persons give to themselves the dignity to which they are called only by choosing in accord with the truth. They likewise make it clear that God's divine, eternal law, his "wise and loving plan for human existence," is the highest norm of human life. They also affirm that human persons have been so made by God that they can inwardly participate in his divine, eternal law. Although these passages do not explicitly use the expression "natural law" to refer to our intelligent participation in God's eternal law, this is precisely what the expression "natural law" does mean in the Catholic tradition, and the Council Fathers, through official footnotes appended to the text, show that this is precisely how they understand natural law.[3]

3. The Relationship Between the "Good" and Human Choices and Action; the First Principles of Natural Law

Human choices and actions, whether morally good or morally bad, are intelligible and purposeful. Sinful choices, although *unreasonable* and opposed to the "order of reason," are not *irrational, meaningless, or absurd*. All human choice and action is directed to some end or purpose, and the ends or purposes to which human choices and actions are ordered are considered as "goods" to be pursued. The "good" has the meaning of what is perfective of a being, constitutive of its flourishing or well-being. Consequently, the proposition *good is to be done and pursued and its opposite, evil, is to be avoided* is a proposition to which every human person, as intelligent, will assent (ST, I-II, 94, 2). It is a "principle" or "starting point" for intelligent, purposeful human choice and action. If human persons are to do anything, whether *morally* good or *morally* bad, there must be some "point" in doing it, something promising a benefit to the acting person. The principle that good is to be done and pursued and evil is to be avoided is the first principle or truth of the natural law, and everyone can understand it.

Moreover, this is not an empty principle. It can be specified by identifying the real goods perfective of human persons, aspects of their flourishing or full-being, and these goods are grasped by our practical reason as purposeful ends of human choice and action. St. Thomas identified a triple-tiered set of such human goods, which, when grasped by our reason as ordered to action ("practical reason"), serve as first principles or starting points for intelligent human activity, as starting points for practical deliberation — "What am I to do?" The first set includes being itself, a good that human persons share with other entities; and since the being of living things is life itself, the basic human good at this level is that of life itself, including bodily life, health, and bodily integrity. The second set includes the bodily union of man and woman in order to hand life on to new human persons, who need education and care if they are to flourish, and this is a set of goods that human persons share with other animals, but, of course, in a distinctively human way. The third set includes goods unique to human persons, such goods as knowledge of the truth, especially truth about God, fellowship with other persons in a human community (friendship and justice, peace), and the good of being reasonable in making choices (cf. ST, I-II, 94, 2).

To sum up: the first principles — the "starting points" — or first truths of natural law are the truths (a) that *good is to be done and pursued and evil is to be avoided* and (b) propositions identifying real goods of human existence as the goods that are to be pursued and done and whose opposites are evils to be avoided, propositions such as *life is a good to be pursued and protected, knowledge of the truth is a good to be pursued, friendship is a good to be pursued,* etc. These propositions articulate truths, practical in nature (i.e., relevant to human action), that do not need to be demonstrated as true — their truth is immediately evident for anyone who knows what they mean.

None of these goods is the highest or greatest good, the *Summum Bonum*. God alone is this good. But each of these goods is a real good of human persons, inwardly perfective of them; each is a created participation in the uncreated goodness of God himself. The propositions directing that good is to be done and identifying these as the goods which authentically perfect human persons and which are, consequently, the goods to be pursued in and through human action do not, however, enable us to distinguish, prior to choice, between alternatives of action that are morally good and those that are morally bad. Indeed, even sinners appeal to these goods and the principles directing that they be protected in order to "justify" or, rather, rationalize their immoral choices. Thus a research scientist who unethically experiments on human subjects, failing to secure their free and informed consent because he knows that they will not give it should they be aware of the risks his experiment entails, may try to rationalize his immoral behavior both to himself and others by appealing to the good of knowledge to be gained through his experiments and its benefits for the life and health of other persons.

But in addition to these *practical* principles of natural law, there are also practical principles that are *moral* in function, i.e., truths that enable human persons to distinguish, prior to making choices, which alternatives are morally good and which are morally bad. I shall now turn to a consideration of these moral or normative truths of the natural law.

4. Normative Truths of Natural Law

St. Thomas, in an article devoted to showing that all of the moral precepts of the Old Law can be reduced to the ten precepts of the Decalogue, taught that the twofold law of love of God and neighbor, while not among the precepts of the Decalogue, nonetheless pertained to it as the "first and common precepts of natural law." Consequently, all the precepts of the Decalogue must, he concluded, be referred to these two love commandments as to their "common principles" (ST, I-II, 100, 3 and ad 1). In other words, for St. Thomas the very first *moral* principle or normative truth of natural law can be properly expressed in terms of the twofold command of love of God and neighbor. St. Thomas held this view, obviously, on the authority of Jesus himself, who, when asked, "Teacher, which commandment in the law is the greatest?" replied, citing two Old Testament texts (Dt 6:5 and Lv 19:18),

"You shall love the Lord, your God, with all your heart, with all your soul, and with all your mind. This is the greatest and the first commandment. The second is like it: You shall love your neighbor as yourself. The whole law and the prophets depend on these two commandments" (Mt 22:36-40; cf. Mk 12:28-31; Lk 10:25-28; Rom 13:10; Gal 5:14).

In short, for St. Thomas — and the entire Catholic tradition — the very first moral principle of natural law is that we are to love God and our neighbor as ourselves. Moreover, and this is very important, there is an inseparable bond uniting this first *moral* principle of natural law to the first *practical* principle of natural law, which directs us to do and pursue the good and the principles specifying the real goods of human persons that are to be pursued and done. For the goods that are to be done and pursued in human action — the goods perfecting human persons — are in truth *gifts* from a loving God that we are to welcome and cherish, and it is obvious that we can love our neighbors *only* if we are willing to respect fully the goods perfective of them, only by willing that these goods flourish in them, and by being *unwilling* intentionally to damage, destroy, or impede these goods, to ignore them or slight them or put them aside, substituting pseudo-goods for them.

Pope John Paul II has well expressed the indissoluble bond between love for the goods of human existence and love for our neighbor. Commenting on the precepts of the second tablet of the Decalogue, i.e., those concerned with actions regarding our neighbor, he reminds us (as did Aquinas before him) that these precepts are rooted in the commandment that we are to love our neighbor as ourselves, a commandment expressing "*the singular dignity of the human person*, 'the only creature that God has wanted for its own sake'" (VS, no. 13, with an internal citation from GS, no. 22).

After saying this, the Holy Father continues, in a passage of singular importance for grasping the *truth* that is meant to guide our choices and actions, by emphasizing that we can love our neighbor and respect his dignity as a person only by cherishing the real goods perfective of him and by refusing intentionally to damage, destroy, impede, ignore, neglect or in any other way shut ourselves off from what is truly good. Appealing to the words of Jesus, he highlights the truth that "the different commandments of the Decalogue are really only so many reflections on the one commandment about the good of the person, at the level of the many different goods which characterize his identity as a spiritual and bodily being in relationship with God, with his neighbor, and with the material world.... The commandments, of which Jesus reminds the young man, *are meant to safeguard the good of the person, the image of God, by protecting his goods*" (VS, no. 13). The negative precepts of the Decalogue — "You shall not kill; You shall not commit adultery; You shall not steal; You shall not bear false witness" — all these precepts, he concludes, "express with particular force the ever urgent need to protect human life, the communion of persons in marriage," and so on (VS, no. 13).

Here the Holy Father is simply articulating once more the Catholic moral tradition. Centuries ago St. Thomas Aquinas observed that "God is offended by us only because we act contrary to our own good" (SCG 3.122).

In summary: the first *moral principle* of natural law, requiring us to love God and to love our neighbor as ourselves, directs us, in every one of our freely chosen deeds, to respect fully *every real good* perfective of human persons and to refrain from intentionally choosing to damage, destroy, impede, neglect, ignore, or in any other way fail to honor these goods and the persons in whom they are meant to flourish. This first moral principle of natural law, expressed fittingly in religious language by the twofold commandment of love of God and neighbor, can be expressed in more philosophical language, some contemporary Catholic authors convincingly argue, by saying that "in voluntarily acting for human goods and avoiding what is opposed to them, one ought to choose and otherwise will those and only those possibilities whose willing is compatible with integral human fulfillment."[4]

In other words, if we are to choose well, in accordance with the truth or order of reason, our basic attitude must be that of persons eager to embrace, revere, and honor the real goods perfective of human persons and the persons in whom these goods are meant to flourish because these goods are *gifts* from God himself, created participations in his own uncreated goodness, and constitutive aspects of the *full being* of the human persons made in his image.

This basic, first principle of morality logically entails various "modes of responsibility," i.e., moral principles specifying ways in which we can fail to love human persons and the goods meant to flourish in them. These are moral principles such as the Golden Rule — we are to do unto others as we would have others do unto us and not do unto others as we would not have them do unto us (cf. Mt 7:12; Lk 6:31; ST, I-II, 94, 4, ad 1) — and the principle that we are not to do evil so that good may come about (cf. Rom 3:8) (on this subject cf. May, p. 103).

In light of the first moral principle of natural law and its modes of responsibility, we can show the truth of more specific moral norms, such as the precepts of the Decalogue, and come to understand that some human acts, as specified by their moral objects, are intrinsically evil and hence absolutely forbidden. If we were willing to make these objects the end of our will's act of choice, we would be willing that *evil be* and thus freely make ourselves *evil*-doers.

This truth will be grasped readily if we recall here what was said before about the "object" of a human act, namely, the "freely chosen kind of behavior." Morally good objects are compatible with a love for *all* the goods of human persons and for the God whose gifts these goods are. Human acts specified by such objects are capable of being ordered to God; they specify morally good kinds of human acts, whereas objects opposed to these goods and to the persons in whom they are meant to flourish are not capable of being ordered to God, and such objects specify morally bad kinds of human acts. As Pope John Paul II puts the matter, "reason attests that there are objects of the human act which are by their nature 'incapable of being ordered to God,' *because they radically contradict the good of the person made in his image*" (VS, no. 80). Acts so specified are *intrinsically evil* acts and the specific moral norms proscribing them are *absolute*, i.e., without any possible exceptions.

The Catholic moral tradition — and sound philosophical ethics as well — has recognized that there are human acts of this kind, i.e., human acts specified by "objects" which cannot be chosen by one with a will toward integral human fulfillment, by one who loves all the goods of human persons and the persons in whom these goods are meant to flourish, who regards these goods as precious gifts from God himself. Among such intrinsically evil acts are the intentional (direct) killing of an innocent human being, having sexual relations outside of marriage (fornication, adultery), and the like; norms proscribing such intrinsically evil acts are moral absolutes.

Precisely because the truth of these moral absolutes is so widely denied today, even by some theologians, John Paul II found it necessary to devote his encyclical *Veritatis splendor* to the defense of this truth. He declared that "the central theme of this encyclical ... is the reaffirmation of the universality and immutability of the moral commandments, particularly those which prohibit always and without exception intrinsically evil acts" (VS, no. 115). He clearly affirms that the truth of these moral commandments is rooted in God's love and in his call to each one of us to be holy as he is holy (cf. Lv 19:2), his commandment that we are to be as perfect as he is perfect (cf. Mt 5:48). "The unwavering demands of that commandment are based upon God's infinitely merciful love (cf. Lk 6:36) and the purpose of that

commandment is to lead us, by the grace of Christ, on the path of that fullness of life proper to the children of God" (VS, no. 115).

5. Steps in Making True Moral Judgments

In light of the normative truths of natural law, we can make true judgments regarding the morality of human acts as specified by their "objects,"
i.e., by *what* is proposed as an object of free choice. We have already seen
that there are certain kinds of human acts, as specified by their moral objects,
that we ought never to freely choose to do: intentionally to kill an innocent
human being, to commit adultery or fornication, etc. Obviously, one cannot
intentionally choose to kill an innocent human being without freely willing
that a great evil *be*, namely, the death of that person whose life, a good of
incalculable value, one has chosen to destroy. Similarly, one cannot freely
choose to commit adultery without being willing to damage the incalculable
human good of marital fidelity and communion.

What this shows us is that, in considering the moral quality of any proposed alternative of action — any "object" of a human act — one must
consider how this proposed action impinges on the *goods* of human persons.
If the proposed action is specified by an object of choice that one *cannot*
will without being willing to damage, destroy, or impede some true good
of human persons, or without being willing to ignore, slight, or repudiate
some real good of human persons, then this proposed action is specified by
a morally bad object and hence not referable to God because it contradicts
the good of persons made in his image.

Moreover, since the morality of human acts, though primarily settled by
the object freely chosen, also depends on the ends for whose sake they are
chosen and done and on the circumstances in which they are done, these
ends and circumstances must also be in accord with the order of reason, i.e.,
in accord with a love and respect for the goods of human persons. Actions
good by reason of their object can become bad by reason of the end for which
they are chosen or the circumstances surrounding them. Thus, while it is
morally good in itself to sing a beautiful aria — by doing so one is participating in the good of beauty and perhaps enabling others to do so as well — it
is not morally good to choose to do so in a dormitory at 3 a.m. and thus
disturb the sleep of others. But one can never justify a human act morally
bad by reason of its object (an intrinsically evil act) by *any* end, however
noble (cf. CCC, no. 1756).

To put matters another way: Some proposals of choice (the "objects" of the act), while relevant to one or perhaps more human goods, are *compatible with a love and respect for all human goods*. Such moral objects are in accord with the order of reason, and thus acts specified by them can be rightly chosen. Other proposals of choice, while relevant to one or perhaps more human goods and compatible with a love and respect for *some* human goods, *are not compatible with love and respect for at least one human good*, that good, namely, whose destruction or injury is indeed the "object" of choice. Human acts specified by moral objects of this kind are not in accord with the order of reason and must be judged immoral.

6. The "Fulfillment" or "Perfection" of Natural Law Through the Redemptive Work of Christ

In his introduction to *Veritatis splendor*, John Paul II calls attention to a truth of supreme importance. This is the truth that "it is only in the mystery of the Word Incarnate that light is shed on the mystery of man.... It is Christ, the last Adam, who fully discloses man to himself and unfolds his noble calling by revealing the mystery of the Father and the Father's love" (VS, no. 2, citing GS, no. 22). Jesus, in his very person, "fulfills" the law and brings it to perfection and thereby reveals to man his noble calling. As a consequence, to live a moral life means ultimately to follow Christ.

We follow him not by any outward imitation but by "becoming conformed to him who became a servant even to giving himself on the Cross" (VS, no. 21; cf. Phil 2:5-8). Following Christ means "holding fast to the very person of Christ" (VS, no. 19).

But how can we "hold fast" to Christ? We do so by shaping our lives — by making moral judgments and choices — in accord with the sublime truths that Jesus makes known to us. Jesus not only reconfirms the truths of the old law given to Moses (which embodied truths of natural law); he also gives us a new command of love. The old law — as well as the natural law — commands us to love our neighbor as ourselves. The new commandment Jesus gives us still requires this, but it goes beyond it, for Christians, Jesus' brothers and sisters, true children of God, are commanded by him to love one another even as he has loved us, with a healing, redemptive kind of love (cf. Jn 15:12; VS, nos. 18, 20), the kind of self-giving love that finds expression on the Cross.

In his Sermon on the Mount (Mt 5), Jesus specifies for us the nature of this self-giving love. Pope John Paul II, following St. Augustine, St. Thomas, and the Catholic tradition, regards our Lord's Sermon on the Mount as the *"magna carta* of Gospel morality" (VS, no. 15). The Beatitudes of this Sermon "speak of basic attitudes and dispositions in life and therefore they do not," John Paul II says, "coincide with the commandments.... [They are], above all, *promises* from which there also flow *normative indications* for the moral life.... They are a sort of self-portrait of Christ ... invitations to discipleship and communion of life with Christ" (VS, no. 16).

The Beatitudes are not optional for the Christian, precisely because they describe the dispositions and attitudes that ought to characterize the followers of Christ. Here we must keep in mind the supreme truth about our existence as Christians and the sublime dignity (cf. the third kind of dignity described above) that is ours as children of God, brothers and sisters of Jesus, members of the divine family.

The Beatitudes of the Sermon on the Mount can be regarded — as Germain Grisez has so well presented matters — as "modes of Christian response." They specify ways of acting (including ways of making good moral judgments) that mark a person whose will, enlivened by the love of God poured into his or her heart, is inwardly disposed to act with the confidence, born of his or her Christian hope, that integral human fulfillment is *indeed* possible and realizable in union with Jesus.[5]

In bearing our cross daily and shaping our judgments, choices, and actions in accord with the truth — and ultimately the truth made known to us by Jesus — we can be confident that the burden he gives us is sweet and his yoke is light because *he is with us!* He is our Emmanuel. And he is, in truth, our Simon of Cyrene, who will help us bear our cross so that we can carry on his work of redemptive love.

7. Virtue Ethics and the Making of Good Moral Choices

A. Thomistic Background

An in-depth study of Aquinas's teaching on virtue is not possible here. He devoted questions 56-67 of the *Primae Secundae* of his *Summa theologiae* to virtues in general and organized the first 170 questions of the massive *Secunda Secundae* around a detailed presentation of the virtues, beginning with the supernatural virtues of faith, hope, and charity, continuing with the same kind of presentation of the four cardinal virtues of prudence, justice, fortitude, and temperance, their integral and associated virtues, acts commanded by them, the vices opposed to them, and the gifts and graces corresponding to them. In brief it can perhaps be summarized as follows:

According to Aquinas the virtues are stable dispositions perfecting the powers of the soul that are the active principles of action, enabling the person to do something well. Thus intellectual virtues perfect the intellect, and the principal *moral* virtue perfecting the intellect is prudence, supernaturally infused or acquired; justice perfects the will, fortitude perfects what he called the irascible appetite, and temperance perfects the concupiscible appetite. Aquinas "seated" the virtues in the powers they perfect. Thus a chaste person (chastity is part of the cardinal virtue of temperance) not only knows intellectually what he must do or not do but "feels" that way, finding repugnant what is opposed to chastity and attractive what is in accord with it.[6]

B. Contemporary Developments in Virtue Ethics

Prompted in large measure by the stimulating and provocative work of Alasdair MacIntyre,[7] there is today an emergence of a strong movement advocating a virtue-based ethic as preferable to a morality of principles. Among the authors advocating this approach are Romanus Cessario, O.P., Jean Porter, Martin Rhonheimer, Livio Melina, and William C. Mattison III.[8]

According to these authors knowledge of moral principles and of norms derived from them does not make a person morally good; moreover a person who knows these principles and how to apply them does not necessarily choose to act in accordance with them and may choose to violate them. For instance, a professor of moral theology may have an excellent grasp of these principles and the norms derived from them and still act immorally. A virtuous, or morally good, person, on the other hand, is inwardly disposed and habituated to make good moral choices and to do them. After all, did not Jesus say, "A good person brings forth good out of a store of goodness" (Mt 12:35; cf. Mk 7:21-23; Lk 6:45)? In addition, did not St. Thomas advise us that, in cases of doubt, when we are not clear as to what the morally good option is, we should ask a virtuous person to tell us? In fact, St. Thomas explicitly taught that the "remote conclusions" from the "first and common principles of natural law" are known only to the wise and that in God's providence other members of society are to come to know these precepts or norms "through the discipline of the wise" (ST, I-II, 100, 3). And by the "wise" St. Thomas did not mean those with Ph.D.s from Harvard or doctorates in sacred theology from some pontifical university in Rome, but rather "saints." Surely, if one were perplexed about homologous *in vitro* fertilization, I think he or she would get enlightenment from a person like Mother Teresa and not from Masters and Johnson.

C. "Virtue Ethics" vs. "An Ethics of Principles"

I fully appreciate and acknowledge the truths about human life and existence central to virtue ethics, but I believe that it is wrong to oppose virtue ethics to the morality of principles. Both are needed. But which takes precedence? I believe that the morality of principles set forth in the previous parts of this chapter does so. First, we can ask how one acquires a virtue. One acquires virtue by acting virtuously, that is, in accordance with reason, in accordance with true moral principles and norms derived therefrom and known to us through our intelligent participation in "the highest norm of human life," i.e., "the divine law — eternal, objective and universal — whereby God orders, directs and governs the entire universe and all the ways of the human community by a plan conceived in wisdom and love. Man has been made by God to participate in this law, with the result that, under the gentle disposition of divine Providence, he can come to perceive ever more fully the truth that is unchanging."[9]

In addition, it is possible for virtuous persons to disagree among themselves and for their disagreements to be contradictory so that one view must be true and the other false. For instance, I know some very virtuous persons who vigorously disagree on whether it is morally permissible for a married woman and her husband to "adopt" a frozen and abandoned unborn baby "left over" from *in vitro* fertilization. Some judge this to be inherently bad; others morally justifiable and not inherently bad. These judgments are contradictory; one must be true, the other must be false. If a married couple, perplexed about what they should do, were to ask these persons for advice on this matter, the couple would still be perplexed.[10] I think what one must do, then, is to examine the *arguments* rooted in moral principles and norms relevant to this situation to see which party has rightly grasped and applied these principles and norms after settling relevant factual matters. Or in other words, which side has done its homework?

─────────────── **Endnotes for Chapter Two** ───────────────

1. The following sources are used for this chapter:
   Documents of the Church's Magisterium:
   (1) *Catechism of the Catholic Church*, abbreviated as CCC.
   (2) Vatican Council II, Dogmatic Constitution on the Church, *Lumen gentium*, abbreviated as LG.
   (3) Vatican Council II, Pastoral Constitution on the Church in the Modern World, *Gaudium et spes*, abbreviated as GS.

(4) Vatican Council II, Declaration on Religious Liberty, *Dignitatis humanae*, abbreviated as DH.

(5) Pope John Paul II, encyclical *Veritatis splendor* ("The Splendor of Truth"), abbreviated as VS.

Other Sources:

(1) St. Thomas Aquinas, *Summa theologiae*, abbreviated as ST. The *Summa theologiae* is divided into parts, questions, and articles. There are three parts in the *Summa*, and the second part is in turn divided into two parts. The parts will be referred to by roman numerals, the questions and articles by arabic numerals. Thus ST, I-II, 94, 2 means: *Summa theologiae*, First Part of the Second Part, question 94, article 2. Frequently, important material is contained in St. Thomas's responses to the objections he poses at the beginning of each article. These responses are indicated by "ad 1," "ad 2," etc., meaning "response to objection 1," "response to objection 2," etc.

(2) St. Thomas Aquinas, *Summa contra gentiles*, abbreviated as SCG. This work is divided into four books, and the books are divided into chapters. Both will be indicated by arabic numerals, with a period between the arabic numeral designating the book and the arabic numeral indicating the chapter. Thus SCG 3.111 means *Summa contra gentiles*, Book 3, Chapter 111. This work of St. Thomas has been translated into English as *On the Truth of the Catholic Faith* (New York: Doubleday Image Books, 1955), five volumes. **NB:** Perhaps the finest presentation of St. Thomas's moral thought is to be found in John Finnis, *Aquinas: Moral, Political, and Legal Theory* (Oxford and New York: Oxford University Press, 1998), pp. 20-186. Revised ed.: *Collected Essays of John Finnis*, Vol. 3 (Oxford and New York: Oxford University Press, 2011).

(3) Germain Grisez, *The Way of the Lord Jesus*, Vol. 1, *Christian Moral Principles* (Chicago: Franciscan Herald Press, 1983). All published volumes in *The Way of the Lord Jesus*, along with other writings of Grisez are now available online at http://www.twotlj.org/.

(4) William E. May, *An Introduction to Moral Theology* (2nd ed.: Huntington, IN: Our Sunday Visitor, 2003). This will be referred to as May. See also Joseph H. Casey, S.J., *Guiding Your Own Life on the Way of the Lord Jesus: Liberated by the Profound Theologian Germain Grisez* (Bloomington, IN: AuthorHouse, 2012).

2. A baby, born or preborn, does not, of course, have the *developed* capacity for deliberating and choosing freely, but he has the *natural* or *radical* capacity to do so because he is human and personal in nature. This matter will be taken up in more depth in a later chapter concerned with the moral status of the embryo.

3. Thus, in *Dignitatis humanae*, no. 3, after affirming that God has made man capable of sharing in his law and thus coming to know ever more the unchanging truth, the Council Fathers added an official footnote, in which they refer to three key texts of St. Thomas, namely, ST, I-II, 91, 1; 93, 1; and 93, 2, in which St. Thomas affirms, among other things, that "the eternal law is unchanging

truth, and everyone somehow knows the truth, at least the *common principles of natural law* (even though in other matters some people share more and some less in the knowledge of the truth)" (ST, I-II, 93, 2). Unfortunately, the commonly used English translations of the Documents of Vatican Council II (the "Abbott" edition and the first "Flannery" edition) fail to include this official footnote, which is, however, in the Latin original. Fortunately, subsequent editions of the "Flannery" translation include the footnote.

4. Germain Grisez, *The Way of the Lord Jesus*, Vol. 1, *Christian Moral Principles* (Chicago: Franciscan Herald Press, 1983), p. 184. In suggesting this way of formulating in non-religious and more philosophical language the first moral principle of natural law, Grisez and his associates (John Finnis, Joseph Boyle, and myself) are in large measure simply following a suggestion made by the Fathers of Vatican II. As we have seen already, they clearly affirmed that the "highest norm of human life," i.e., the *ultimate norm of morality*, is God's divine, eternal law, in which we participate through the natural law (cf. DH, no. 3). But, in speaking of human action in this world, they also said that the "norm for human activity is this: that, in accord with the divine plan and will, *human activity should harmonize with the genuine good of the human race*, and total vocation and fulfill it" (GS, no. 35).

5. Cf. ibid., pp. 653-655.

6. One of the best and clearest — and relatively brief — presentations of St. Thomas's teaching on virtues in my judgment is that of Shane Defcinski, "A Very Short Primer of St. Thomas Aquinas' Account of the Various Virtues," accessible at http://www.uwplatt.edu/~drefcins/233AquinasVirtues.html. A modern interpreter of Aquinas's thought, Josef Pieper (1904-1997), is well known for his excellent studies of the virtues in the writings of St. Thomas. His presentation of the cardinal virtues of prudence, justice, fortitude, and temperance is given in the book *The Four Cardinal Virtues: Prudence, Justice, Fortitude, and Temperance* (Notre Dame, IN: University of Notre Dame Press, 1966) — a reprint of three books, one on prudence, one on justice, and one on fortitude and temperance, published originally in the 1950s by Pantheon Books of New York. Pieper also wrote books on the theological virtues entitled *Belief and Faith* (New York: Pantheon, 1963), *Hope* (San Francisco: Ignatius Press, 1986), and *About Love* (Chicago: Franciscan Herald Press, 1978). In 1997 Ignatius Press published these three works under the title *Faith, Hope, and Love*.

7. Alasdair MacIntyre, *After Virtue* (2nd ed., Notre Dame, IN: University of Notre Dame Press, 1984; originally published 1981); *Whose Justice? Which Rationality?* (Notre Dame, IN: University of Notre Dame Press, 1983); and other books.

8. For Romanus Cessario, O.P., see his *Moral Virtues and Theological Ethics* (Notre Dame, IN: University of Notre Dame Press, 1991) and *The Virtues or the Examined Life* (New York: Continuum Books, 2002). For Jean Porter, see her *Recovery of Virtue* (Philadelphia: Westminster Press, 1991). For Livio Melina, see his *Sharing in Christ's Virtues: For a Renewal of Moral Theology in the Light of Veritatis Splendor*, trans. William E. May (Washington, DC: The Catholic Uni-

versity of America Press, 2001). For Martin Rhonheimer, see *Natural Law and Practical Reason: A Thomist View of Moral Autonomy,* trans. Gerald Marlsbury (New York: Fordham University Press, 2000), esp. pp. 279 ff. For William C. Mattison, III, see his *New Wine, New Wineskins: A Next Generation's Reflections Regarding Key Issues in Catholic Moral Theology* (New York: Rowman, Littlefield and Co., 2005) and *Introducing Moral Theology: True Happiness and the Virtues* (Grand Rapids, MI: Brazos Press, 2008). Of these authors Mattison — and others associated with him — seem to regard as misplaced in some way the debates noted already between proportionalists and defenders of the Church's teaching that some acts, specified by their moral objects, are intrinsically evil and that norms prohibiting them are absolute and without any exceptions.

9. Vatican Council II, *Declaration on Religious Freedom (Dignitatis Humanae),* no. 3.
10. On this see the different views of Catholic authors, all noted for their fidelity to magisterial teaching, in *Human Embryo Adoption: Biotechnology, Marriage, and the Right to Life,* eds. Thomas V. Berg, L.C., and Edward J. Furton (Philadelphia and Thornton, NY: National Catholic Bioethics Center and The Westchester Institute for Ethics & the Human Person, 2006).

CHAPTER THREE

Generating Human Life: Marriage and the New Reproductive Technologies

Introduction

If the human race is to continue, new human beings must come into existence. It is now possible to "make" human babies in the laboratory through an array of modern reproductive technologies. But, as we all know, the usual way for bringing new human persons into existence is for a man and a woman to engage in genital intercourse, either within marriage and through the marital act or outside of marriage through acts of adultery and fornication or, as the latter is euphemistically called today, "premarital" sex.

No matter how a new human being comes into existence, he or she is something precious and good, a person, a being of incalculable value, worthy of respect, a bearer of inviolable rights, a being *who ought to be loved*.[1] This is true no matter how the child comes to be: whether through the intimate and chaste embrace of husband and wife, through an act of adultery or fornication, or through use of modern reproductive technologies.

This chapter is divided as follows. Part One briefly considers moral issues raised by generating human life through acts of fornication and adultery. Part Two considers at greater length and in depth the bonds intimately uniting marriage, the marital act, and the gift of human life in order to show why, in God's loving plan for human existence, new human life is properly respected when it comes to be in and through the marital embrace and how the generation of human life in and through the marital act is an act of *procreation*, not one of *reproduction*. Part Three takes up in depth the new reproductive technologies; after describing them in some detail, it sets forth ethical and theological arguments to show that it is intrinsically immoral to make use of technologies that generate new human life outside the marital act. Part Four presents criteria for distinguishing between technological interventions that "assist" the marital or conjugal act in being fruitful and those that substitute for it and replace it. Part Five considers the harm cause by IVF and other new reproductive technologies both to the children made by these procedures and to the women engaged in them. Part Six concerns the "rescuing" of frozen embryos produced by the new reproductive technologies. The discussion of this issue has been completely revised and shortened in light of the controversies over the correct interpretation of an ambiguous text in *Dignitas personae* by Catholic scholars known for their fidelity to magisterial teaching who defend contradictory and irreconcilable positions.

1. Part One: Fornication, Adultery, and the Generation of Human Life

Here we can state straightforwardly that it is *not* good to generate human life through acts of adultery and fornication. It is not good because fornicators and adulterers have not made themselves *fit* to receive the great gift of human life. They do not have the moral capacity to receive this surpassingly great gift because they have not, through their own free and self-determining choices, capacitated themselves to cooperate with God in raising up new life and giving it the home where it can take root and grow.[2] Indeed, practically all civilized societies have, until recently, regarded as irresponsible the generation of new human life through the coupling of unattached males and females. Even today, secular society judges fornicators and adulterers to be acting "responsibly" only if they take care to prevent unwanted pregnancies (and for the most part fornicators and adulterers do not want a pregnancy) by using contraceptives and, should contraceptives fail, abortion as a backup to prevent the birth of an unwanted child (the issues of contraception and abortion will be taken up in depth in later chapters).[3] It is, unfortunately, symbolic of a new barbarism — of the culture of death — that many today claim that unmarried individuals have the "right" to generate human life if they so choose, whether through freely chosen genital acts of fornication or adultery or through new laboratory methods of producing new human life.[4]

2. Part Two: Marriage and the Generation of Human Life

Two of the documents examined in Chapter One (*Evangelium vitae* and *Donum vitae*) testify to the Church's profound love and respect for marriage and the family. Married couples, as Pope John Paul II affirmed, are summoned to be givers of life and to recognize that procreating human life is "a unique event which clearly reveals that human life is a gift received in order to be given as a gift" (*Evangelium vitae*, no. 92). The *Instruction on Respect for Human Life in its Origin and on the Dignity of Human Procreation* (*Donum vitae*) insisted that the procreation of new human life must be the fruit of marriage and the marital act. As we saw in Chapter One, this document gave three reasons why it is wrong to generate human life outside the marital act: the first was based on the inseparable connection, willed by God and not lawful for man to sunder on his own initiative, between the unitive and procreative meanings of the marital act; the second, on the "language of the body"; the third, on the obligation to regard the child always as a person and never as a product. When children are engendered through the loving embrace of husbands and wives, the "inseparable connection" and the "language of the body" are fully respected, and the children are in no way treated as products. To show that this is true, I will consider (A) how men and women, by getting married, give themselves rights and capacities that unmarried persons simply do not have. Next (B), I will reflect on the meaning of the marital act as inherently unitive and procreative, and I will then (C) show that the life given in and through the marital act is truly "begotten, not made."

A. Marriage, Marital Rights, and Capacities

Fornicators and adulterers do not have the right either to "give" themselves to one another in genital sex or to "receive" the great gift of human life. They do not have the right to do these things precisely because they have failed to capacitate themselves to do them, to make themselves *fit* to do them.

But husbands and wives, precisely because they have given themselves irrevocably to each other in marriage, have established each other as irreplaceable, nonsubstitutable, nondisposable persons and by doing so have *capacitated* themselves to do things that unmarried individuals simply cannot do: among them, to "give" themselves to each other in the act proper and exclusive to spouses — the marital act — and to receive the gift of life.

In and through his act of marital consent — an act of free self-determination — the man, forswearing all others, has given himself irrevocably the identity of this particular woman's *husband*, while the woman, in and through her self-determining act of marital consent, has given herself irrevocably the identity of this particular man's *wife*, and together they have given themselves the identity of *spouses*. They have established each other as absolutely unique and irreplaceable.[5]

Moreover, in and through the choice that makes them to be husband and wife, a man and a woman give to themselves new capacities and new rights, and they freely take upon themselves new responsibilities. They are now able to do things that unmarried men and women simply cannot do, precisely because the latter have failed to capacitate themselves to do them by getting married. In short, men and women who give themselves irrevocably to each other in marriage have the right and the capacity to do what husbands and wives are supposed to do. And among the things that married persons are supposed to do are (1) to give each other a unique kind of love, conjugal or spousal or marital love, (2) to engage in the marital act, and (3) to "welcome life lovingly, nourish it humanely, and to educate it religiously," i.e., in love and service of God and neighbor.

B. The Meaning of the Marital Act

The marital act is not simply a genital act between men and women who happen to be married. Husbands and wives have the capacity to engage in *genital* acts because they have genitals. Unmarried men and women have the same capacity. But husbands and wives have the capacity (and the *right*) to engage in the *marital* act only because they are married, i.e., husbands and wives, spouses. The marital act, therefore, is more than a simple genital act between people who just happen to be married. As marital, it is an act that inwardly participates in their marital union, in their one-flesh unity, a unity open to the gift of children.[6] The marital act, in short, is an act inwardly participating in the "goods" or "blessings" of marriage, i.e., the good of steadfast fidelity and exclusive conjugal love, the good of children, and, for Christian spouses, the good of the "sacrament."

The marital act expresses, symbolizes, and manifests the exclusive nature of marital love, and it does so because it is both a communion in being (the unitive meaning of the act) and the sort or kind of an act in and through which the spouses open themselves to the good of human life in its transmission, to the blessing of fertility (its procreative meaning).[7]

The marital act is unitive, that is, a communion in being or in an intimate, exclusive sharing of personal life, because in and through it husband and wife come to "know" each other in a unique and unforgettable way, revealing themselves to each other as unique and irreplaceable persons of different but complementary sex.[8] In and through this act, they become personally "one flesh," renewing the covenant they made with each other when they gave themselves to each other in marriage.[9] In the marital act, husbands and wives "give" themselves to each other in a way that concretely expresses their sexual complementarity, for the husband gives himself to his wife in a receiving sort of way while she in turn receives him in a giving sort of way. His body, which expresses his person as a male, has a "nuptial significance," for it enables him to give himself personally to his wife by entering into her body-person and doing so in a receiving sort of way, while her body, which expresses her person as a female, likewise has a "nuptial significance," for it is so structured that she is uniquely equipped to receive his body-person into herself and in so receiving him to give herself to him.[10] The marital act thus indeed, as Pope John Paul II has said, speaks "the language of the body."

The marital act is also a procreative kind of an act. In giving themselves to each other in this act, in becoming "one flesh," husband and wife also become one complete organism capable of generating human life. Even if they happen to be sterile, their marital union is the sort or kind of act in and through which human life can be given should conditions be favorable: it is procreative in kind.[11] Moreover, precisely because husbands and wives are married, they have capacitated themselves, as nonmarried persons have not, to cooperate with God in bringing new human persons into existence in a way that responds to the dignity of persons. They have capacitated themselves to "welcome life lovingly, nourish it humanely, and educate it in the love and service of God and neighbor," to give this life the "home" it needs and merits in order to grow and develop.

The marital act, therefore, is not, as Pope Pius XII rightly said, "a mere organic function for the transmission of the germ of life." It is, rather, "a personal action, a simultaneous natural self-giving which, in the words of Holy Writ, effects the union in 'one flesh' ... [and] implies a personal cooperation [of the spouses with God in giving new human life]."[12] Indeed, as Pope Paul VI put matters, "because of its intimate nature the conjugal act, which unites husband and wife with the closest of bonds, also *makes them fit* [the Latin text reads: *eos idoneos facit*] to bring forth new human life according to laws inscribed in their very being as men and women."[13]

The marital act, therefore, precisely as marital, participates inwardly in the goods or blessings of marriage. It is inherently love-giving (unitive) and life-giving (procreative). And this is why the Church teaches that "there is an inseparable connection, willed by God and not lawful for man to break on his own initiative, between the unitive and procreative meaning of the marital act."[14] The bond inseparably uniting these two meanings of the marital act is the marriage itself, and "what God has joined together, let no man put asunder."

The marital act is thus an utterly unique kind of human act. It is a collaborative, personal act executing the choice of the spouses to actualize their marital union and participate in the goods proper to it. It is integrally unitive and procreative, and it speaks the "language of the body."

C. "Begetting" Human Life Through the Marital Act

When human life comes to be in and through the marital act, it comes as a "gift" crowning the act itself. The child is "begotten" through an act of intimate conjugal love; he or she is not "made," treated like a product. Husband and wife do not "make" a baby, just as they do not "make" love, for neither a human baby nor love are products one makes. In engaging in the marital act, husbands and wives are not *making* anything. They are, rather, *doing* something, i.e., *giving* themselves to each other as irreplaceable and nonsubstitutable persons complementary in their sexuality and *opening* themselves to the gift of human life. They are rightly regarded as "procreating" or "begetting" a child through an act of love; they are *not* producing one, making one. Their act is properly one of "procreation" and not one of "reproduction."

To grasp this truth properly, it is necessary to understand the difference between "transitive" and "immanent" human activity, between "making" and "doing." In the one mode of human activity, making, the action proceeds from the agent or agents to something produced in the external world by the use of various materials (e.g., cars, cookies, a poem). Such action is *transitive* insofar as it passes from the acting subject(s) to an object or objects fashioned by him or her or them. In this mode of human activity, which is governed by the rules of art, interest centers on the product made, and those that do not measure up to standards are frequently discarded. Thus autoworkers produce cars, cooks bake cakes, novelists write books, and college and university teachers produce lectures and texts. In this mode of human activity, the action perfects (or fails to perfect) the object made, not the agent producing the object — and I would rather have delicious cookies baked by a culinary artist who might, for all I know, be a morally bad person, than inedible ones produced by a saint.

In another mode of activity, doing, the action abides in the acting subject. The action is *immanent* (i.e., within the subject) and is governed by the requirements of the virtue of prudence, not by the rules of art. If the action is morally good, it perfects the agent, who in and through it "makes" himself or herself *to be* the kind of person he or she is, i.e., morally good.[15]

It is important to note that every making involves a doing, for one *chooses* to make something, and the act of choice, whereby we determine ourselves and give ourselves our identity as moral beings, is something we "do." And there are some things that we *can* make that we know we *ought not* to make because choosing to make them is a morally bad kind of choice, e.g., pornographic films.

The marital act is *not* an act of making or producing. It is not a transitive act issuing from spouses and terminating in some object distinct from them. It is something that they *do*. In it they do not "make" love or "make" babies. They *give* love to each other by giving themselves bodily to each other, and they open themselves to the gift of human life. The life begotten through their one-flesh union is not the product of their art, but "a gift supervening on and giving permanent embodiment to" the marital act itself.[16] Thus when human life comes to be in and through the marital act, we can rightly say that the spouses are procreating or begetting. Their child is "begotten, not made."

3. Part Three: Generating Human Life Through New Reproductive Technologies

Chapter One provided an extended account of the teaching on this matter found in the Vatican *Instruction on Respect for Human Life in its Origin and on the Dignity of Procreation* (*Donum vitae*). Hence there is no need here to repeat this teaching. But I will, prior to describing and offering a moral evaluation of the various methods of generating human life outside the marital act, summarize the teaching of Pope Pius XII on this matter and also the teaching found in the 1997 document issued by the Pontifical Academy for Life on cloning, an issue not treated in *Donum vitae*.

A. The Teaching of Pius XII and the Pontifical Academy for Life

Pius XII died in 1958, twenty years before the birth of Louise Brown, the first baby conceived *in vitro* to be born. Yet he was quite farsighted and in several of his addresses took up the artificial generation of human life.[17] In one address, concerned with artificial insemination either by a third party or by the husband, he articulated the "inseparability principle." His teaching is quite clear, as the following passage shows:

> The Church has … rejected the … attitude which pretended to separate in procreation the biological activity from the personal relations of husband and wife. The child is the fruit of the marriage union, when it finds full expression by the placing in action of the functional organs, of the sensible emotions thereto related, and of the spiritual and disinterested

love which animates such a union; it is in the unity of this human act that there must be considered the biological condition of procreation. Never is it permitted to separate these different aspects to the point of excluding positively either the intention of procreating or the conjugal relation.[18]

Referring specifically to artificial insemination by the husband, he put matters very eloquently:

> To reduce the common life of a husband and wife and the conjugal act to a mere organic function for the transmission of seed would be but to convert the domestic hearth, the family sanctuary, into a biological laboratory. Therefore, in our allocution of September 29, 1949, to the International Congress of Catholic Doctors, We expressly excluded artificial insemination in marriage. The conjugal act in its natural structure is a personal action, a simultaneous and immediate cooperation of husband and wife, which by the very nature of the agents and the propriety of the act, is an expression of the reciprocal gift, which, according to Holy Writ, effects the union "in one flesh." That is much more than the union of two germs, which can be effected even by artificial means, that is, without the natural action of husband and wife. The conjugal act, ordained and designed by nature, is a personal cooperation, to which husband and wife, when contracting marriage, exchange the right.[19]

In another address, he condemned *in vitro* fertilization, at that time only a possibility. In no uncertain terms he declared: "As regards experiments of human artificial fecundation 'in vitro,' let it be sufficient to observe that they must be rejected as immoral and absolutely unlawful."[20]

Although condemning artificial insemination/fecundation by a husband as intrinsically immoral, he declared that "this does not necessarily proscribe the use of certain artificial means destined solely to facilitate the marital act, or to assure the accomplishment of the end of the natural act normally performed."[21] As we have seen, the Vatican *Instruction on Respect for Human Life in Its Origin and the Dignity of Procreation* some thirty years later affirms the legitimacy of technological interventions that "assist" the marital act and do not "replace" it or "substitute" for it.

In June 1997, the Pontifical Academy for Life issued its *Reflections on Cloning*. The document was issued after the success of Scottish scientists in cloning the sheep "Dolly." After noting that cloning "represents a radical manipulation of the constitutive relationality and complementarity which is at the origin of human procreation in both its biological and strictly personal aspects," the Academy pronounces on the morality of cloning: "All the moral reasons which led to the condemnation of *in vitro* fertilization as such and to the radical censure of *in vitro* fertilization for merely experimental purposes must also be applied to human cloning."[22]

B. The New Reproductive Technologies

These include two broad categories: (1) artificial fertilization, which embraces (a) artificial insemination, (b) *in vitro* fertilization and embryo transfer, (c) alternative technologies using male and female gametic cells; and (2) cloning or agametic reproduction.

(1) Artificial Fertilization

Fertilization naturally occurs when male sperm (male gametic cells) are introduced into a woman's body through an act of sexual coition and one of the sperm succeeds in penetrating the woman's ovum (female gametic cell) and fertilizing it. Artificial fertilization is brought about when male sperm are not united with the female ovum through an act of sexual coition but by some other means. In artificial *insemination*, male sperm are introduced into the female reproductive tract by the use of a cannula or other instruments, with fertilization occurring when one of the sperm so introduced fuses with the woman's ovum. Fertilization occurs within the woman's body. In *in vitro* fertilization, male sperm and female ova are placed in a petri dish (hence the name *in vitro*, "in a glass"), and subsequent fusion of sperm and ovum and fertilization occur outside the woman's body.

Both these forms of artificial fertilization can be either homologous or heterologous. *Homologous* artificial fertilization uses gametic cells of a married couple, whereas *heterologous* artificial fertilization uses the gametic cells of individuals not married to each other (although one or both of the parties may be married to another person).[23]

(a) Artificial Insemination

Homologous artificial insemination or artificial insemination by husband (AIH) introduces the husband's sperm into the wife's body by use of a cannula or other instruments. Ordinarily the husband's sperm are obtained through masturbation, although an alternative is intercourse using a perforated condom or, in cases of obstruction of the vas deferens, which serves as a conduit for spermatozoa, the surgical removal of sperm from the epididymis, where the sperm are stored.[24]

Some married couples resort to AIH in order to achieve pregnancy when, for whatever reason, the husband is not able to ejaculate within the vagina. It is also used when the husband suffers from oligospermia (when his sperm production is very low and thus makes conception less likely through sexual union) or when some allergy exists that cannot be treated hormonally. Today AIH involves "washing" the sperm in a laboratory procedure to remove antibodies and prostaglandins and to capacitate the sperm for fertilizing the ovum.[25]

With the ability to freeze and store sperm (the cryopreservation of sperm), AIH can also be used to help a widow conceive a child by her own husband's sperm after his death.

Heterologous artificial insemination is usually referred to by the acronym AID, signifying "artificial insemination by a donor." But, as Walter Wadlington correctly observes, "the term 'sperm donor' is a misnomer because compensation of persons supplying semen has been a long-standing practice."[26] It is thus far more accurate to call this form of artificial insemination "artificial insemination by a vendor."[27]

Traditionally, this form of artificial insemination was used by married couples so that the wife could bear a child genetically her own if her husband were infertile or if there was "genetic incompatibility" between the couple; i.e., when the couple were bearers of a recessive genetic defect and there was the likelihood that any child they might conceive might be actually afflicted by this genetic impairment. Today the procedure is still commonly used for these purposes, but it is now also used by single women who want to bear a child and who, as Wadlington puts it, "do not have a marital or other stable heterosexual partner or by a woman in a life partnership with another woman."[28] It is also used in implementing surrogacy agreements under which a woman will conceive and bear a child who will then be turned over to the sperm provider or another person or other parties after birth.

Because of the danger that the sperm provided by the "vendor" may carry the human immuno-deficiency virus (HIV) and thus threaten the woman and child with AIDS (acquired immune deficiency syndrome), today most doctors engaging in this form of artificial insemination use only frozen sperm from commercial sperm banks which have quarantined the samples long enough to test for HIV.[29]

(b) In Vitro *Fertilization and Embryo Transfer*

Until the late 1970s, artificial insemination was the only alternative to sexual union for effecting conception. But in the late 1970s, Patrick Steptoe and Paul Edwards succeeded in bringing to birth a child conceived *in vitro* and transferred a few days after fertilization to her mother's womb. Thus, with the birth of Louise Brown on July 25, 1978, a new mode of human reproduction became a reality: *in vitro* fertilization. It is ironic to note that Louise was born precisely ten years after Pope Paul VI signed his encyclical *Humanae vitae*, which affirmed the "inseparable connection willed by God and unlawful for man to break on his own initiative, between the unitive and procreative meanings of the marital act." *In vitro* fertilization makes it possible for human life to be conceived outside the body of the (genetic) mother, but it is still a form of generating human life that is gametic, i.e., possible only by uniting a male gametic cell, the sperm, with a female gametic cell, the ovum. The new human life is conceived in a petri dish using sperm provided by a man and an ovum provided by a woman. Approximately two days after the fertilization process has been completed, the embryo, which by then has developed to the four-to-eight-cell stage, is ready for transfer into a woman's uterus, where it can implant and, if implantation is successful, continue intrauterine development until birth.

Initially, *in vitro* fertilization and embryo transfer (hereafter IVF-ET) was carried out by obtaining a single egg (ovum) from a woman through a laparoscopy, a procedure requiring general anesthesia. When a laparoscopy is performed, the physician aspirates the woman's egg through a hollow needle inserted into the abdomen and guided by a narrow optical instrument called a laparoscope. The first time IVF-ET succeeded, it was carried out in a normally ovulating woman, Louise Brown's mother, whose fallopian tubes had been surgically removed. After a single egg was obtained through laparoscopy, it was fertilized by her husband's sperm *in vitro*, and the resulting embryo was then transferred to her womb two days after the fertilization process was completed.

Today the standard procedure is to overstimulate the ovaries with ovulatory drugs such as Clomid, Pergonal, and Metrodin so that the woman will produce several oocytes for retrieval and subsequent fertilization. Oocytes (ova) produced are retrieved not by laparoscopy, with its requirement of general anesthesia, but by ultrasound-guided transvaginal aspiration, which does not require general anesthesia. This greatly simplifies the procedure. Standard practice today also includes fertilization of many ova, mixing them in the petri dish with sperm (usually collected by masturbation) that have been "washed" to make them more apt to fertilize. Thus several new human zygotes (human beings at the earliest stage of development) are produced and allowed to grow to the early embryo stage. It is now customary to transfer two to four of these early embryos to the womb to increase probability of implantation and subsequent gestation until birth and to freeze and store the others so that they can be used for implantation later if the first attempts are unsuccessful. These "spare" frozen embryos can also be "donated" for research purposes. Eventually, if not claimed by the persons responsible for their manufacture or used in research, the frozen embryos will be destroyed.[30]

IVF-ET can be either homologous or heterologous. Initially, homologous IVF-ET was used almost exclusively for wives whose fallopian tubes had been damaged, to enable them and their husbands to have children of their own. But now this procedure has been extended to include male-factor infertility (oligospermia, for instance) and other cases in which no precise cause for the couple's infertility has been determined.[31] It can also be used, it is now increasingly possible, to help a married couple avoid conceiving a child who could be affected by a genetically inherited pathology. For example, in the summer of 1998 scientists succeeded in identifying and separating male sperm responsible for the conception of female and male children. Male children alone are afflicted by hemophilia. Hence a married couple legitimately worried about conceiving a male child so afflicted can now choose to conceive the child *in vitro*, fertilizing the wife's ovum with sperm provided by her husband but with the assurance that the sperm provided are female-producing and not male-producing sperm. In the future, it is likely that more gametic cells, both male and female, carrying the genes responsible for genetically induced pathologies will be identified and separated, and then only those identified as not carrying the genes causing the maladies can be used for fertilization *in vitro*.

Heterologous IVF-ET can now be used instead of artificial insemination in instances when the husband is completely infertile or when the wife lacks ovaries or when there is genetic incompatibility between the spouses. Sperm "donation" is easier than ova "donation," inasmuch as the latter is complicated by the need to synchronize the menstrual cycles of the woman who "donates" the ova and the wife into whom the embryo is to be implanted. Embryos conceived *in vitro*, as well as sperm and ova, can also be "donated," and embryo donation, like sperm donation, does not require synchronizing the menstrual cycles of different women. Both homologous and heterologous IVF can include implanting the resulting embryo into the womb of a woman other than the one who supplied the ovum, a so-called surrogate mother.[32]

As this makes evident, many permutations and combinations of generating human life are now technically feasible as a result of *in vitro* fertilization, among them such procedures as ZIFT (zygote intrafallopian tube transfer), which occurs when the zygote resulting from IVF is inserted into the fallopian tube rather than having the embryo transferred into the womb; and PROST (pro-nuclear tubal transfer), which transfers the very early embryo by use of a laparascope into the fallopian tube.[33]

Intracytoplasmic sperm injection (ICSI) is a more recently developed method of artificial fertilization. This procedure, as footnote 32 explains, "is similar in almost every respect to other forms of *in vitro* fertilization with the difference that in [it] fertilization in the test tube does not take place on its own, but rather by means of the injection into the oocyte of a single sperm, selected earlier, or by the injection of immature germ cells taken from the man." Like *in vitro* fertilization, it is intrinsically evil because it causes "*a complete separation between procreation and the conjugal act.*"

(c) Alternative Technologies Using Male and Female Gametic Cells

Certain contemporary techniques are not, strictly speaking, variants of *in vitro* fertilization inasmuch as fertilization itself occurs, not outside the woman's body in a petri dish, but within a woman's body. Thus these techniques are more closely related to artificial insemination than to *in vitro* fertilization as methods of artificial fertilization. But their development was stimulated by research into *in vitro* fertilization and embryo transfer. In these procedures, sexual union is not required in order to unite male and female gametic cells.

One such technique is called SIFT, or sperm intrafallopian tube transfer. This is sometimes used as an option for infertile couples who have not conceived following AIH. In this procedure, the woman's ovaries are hyperstimulated; this is coupled with a laparoscopy under general anesthesia to inject a "washed" or prepared concentrate of the husband's sperm (or that of a "donor," if necessary) into the fallopian tubes so that conception can occur there.[34]

Another procedure of special interest is GIFT, or gamete intrafallopian tube transfer. This is similar to IVF in that the woman's ovaries are hyperstimulated to produce multiple eggs, which are retrieved either by laparoscopy or ultrasound-guided transvaginal procedures. An egg (or group of eggs) is placed into a catheter with sperm (provided either by masturbation or by the use of a perforated condom during intercourse) that have been treated and "capacitated," with an air bubble separating ova from sperm to prevent fertilization from occurring outside the woman's body. The catheter is then inserted into her fallopian tube, the ovum (ova) and sperm are released from the catheter, and fertilization can then occur within the body of the woman, who can, of course, be the wife of the man whose sperm are used and who could have provided the ovum (ova).[35]

There is currently a debate among theologians over GIFT and some similar procedures, such as LTOT (low tubal ovum transfer) and TOT (tubal ovum transfer). Some hold that GIFT and other procedures can, if used by married persons in a way that avoids procuring sperm through masturbation, be regarded as "assisting" the marital act and not replacing it and hence morally permissible. Others hold that GIFT is definitely a procedure that replaces or substitutes for the marital act and that, therefore, its use is immoral. I will take up this question in Part Four of this chapter.

(2) Cloning or Agametic Reproduction

The February 27, 1997, issue of the journal *Nature* carried the news of the birth of the sheep Dolly through the work of Scottish researchers Ian Wilmut and K. H. S. Campbell and their associates at Edinburgh's Roslin Institute. They succeeded in generating a new sheep by a process called "cloning," or more technically "somatic-cell nuclear transfer."[36] What they did was to produce Dolly by fusing the nucleus of a somatic (body) cell of an adult sheep with a denucleated oocyte, that is, an oocyte deprived of the maternal genome. The genetic identity of the new individual sheep, Dolly, was derived from only one source, namely, the adult sheep whose somatic cell nucleus was inserted into the denucleated oocyte to "trigger" development into a new individual of the species. This procedure can, in principle, be used to generate new human beings whose genetic endowment would be identical to that of the human beings whose somatic cells were inserted into a denucleated human ovum.

A somewhat different procedure, developed by Ryuzo Yanagimachi and his team at the John A. Burns School of Medicine at the University of Hawaii, was used to clone mice and reported in the July 24, 1998, issue of *Nature* magazine. But their work, too, produced a new member of a mammalian species by a procedure that is asexual, or agametic, in nature, inasmuch as it does not require fertilization of the female gametic cell, the ovum, by the male gametic cell, the sperm. Thus, even from a biological perspective, cloning is a far more radical mode of reproduction than artificial insemination or *in vitro* fertilization and their permutations and combinations. As the Pontifical Academy for Life noted in the document previously referred to, cloning "tends to make bisexuality a purely functional leftover, given that an ovum must be used without its nucleus in order to make room for the clone-embryo."[37]

C. An Ethical and Theological Evaluation of the New Reproductive Technologies

(1) Ethical Reasons Why Non-Marital Ways of Generating New Human Life Are Intrinsically Immoral

As we saw in Chapter One, the *Vatican Instruction on Respect for Human Life in Its Origin and on the Dignity of Procreation* (*Donum vitae*) briefly sets forth three lines of reasoning to support the conclusion that it is always immoral to generate human life outside the marital act. The first is based on the "inseparability principle," which claims that it is not lawful for man on his own initiative to separate the unitive and procreative meanings of the conjugal act. The second is rooted in the "language of the body," and the third is that non-marital ways of engendering human life change its generation from an act of procreation to one of reproduction, treating the child as if he or she were a product.

I believe that in the first part of this chapter, in reflecting on the meaning of marriage and the marital act, I provided evidence to show that the bond uniting marriage, the marital act, and the generating of new human life is intimate, that the marital act, precisely *as* marital, is inherently both unitive and procreative, and that it speaks the language of the body. Thus I think that in that part of the chapter I offered good reasons to support the first two lines of argument used by *Donum vitae*. There I also emphasized that when a child comes to be in and through the marital act, he or she is "begotten, not made," and that in engaging in the marital act husbands and wives are not "making" anything, either love or babies, but are rather *doing* something, i.e., *giving* themselves to each other in an act that actualizes their marital union and expresses their sexual complementarity and *opening* themselves to the gift of human life. I thus touched on the third line of reasoning used by *Donum vitae* to show that it is wrong to generate human life outside the marital act, because doing so treats the child as if he or she were a product.

Here I wish to develop this third line of reasoning because I think that it is the one that more clearly shows how seriously wrong it is to generate human life outside the marital act.

In what follows I will focus attention on *homologous* artificial insemination and IVF-ET, i.e., ways of bringing new human life into existence by uniting the gametic cells of husband and wife outside the marital act. I do so because although some people in our society — and perhaps their number is increasing — find the Church's teaching on heterologous fertilization too restrictive of human freedom, most people, Catholic and non-Catholic alike, can understand and appreciate this teaching even if, in some highly unique situations, they might justify heterologous insemination and fertilization. Nonetheless, most people recognize that when a man and a woman marry, they "give" themselves exclusively to each other and that the selves they give are sexual and procreative persons. Just as they violate their marital covenant after marriage by attempting to "give" themselves to another in sexual union, so too they dishonor their marital covenant and the uniqueness and exclusiveness of their love and marital union by choosing to exercise their procreative powers with someone other than their spouse, the one to whom they have given themselves, including their power to procreate, irrevocably, "forswearing all others."

But many of these people, including Catholics, find the Church's judgment that *homologous* artificial insemination and IVF-ET are *always* wrong, intrinsically evil, difficult to understand and accept. This is a "hard" teaching, and strikes many as harsh, insensitive, and cruel. They ask, and not without reason, why *must* human life be given *only* in and through the marital act? What evil is being done by a married couple, unable to have children by engaging in the marital act, if they make use of the new reproductive technologies to overcome the obstacles preventing their marriage from being blessed with the gift of children?

It seems obvious that, if homologous artificial fertilization (whether artificial insemination or IVF-ET) is intrinsically immoral, it follows *a fortiori* that this is true of heterologous fertilization and cloning.

To show that even homologous artificial fertilization is intrinsically immoral, I will, as noted earlier, focus on the argument that generating children outside of the marital act, even by procedures making use of gametic cells of husband and wife, changes the generation of human life from an act of "procreation" to one of "reproduction," treating the child as if he or she is a product. I will argue that this is indeed the case, and that it is always gravely immoral to treat a human being, even in his or her initial stages of existence, as a product and not as a person.

The argument to be advanced is intelligible in the light of the distinction, made previously, between "making" and "doing." We have seen already that in engaging in the marital act husbands and wives are not "making" anything, but are rather "doing" something, and that any human life brought into being in and through this act is begotten, not made.

In "making," as we have seen already, the action proceeds from an agent or agents to something in the external world, to a product. In making, interest centers on the product made, and ordinarily products that do not measure up to standards are discarded or, at any rate, are little appreciated and for this reason are frequently called "defective." In making, moreover, the logic of manufacturing is validly applied: one should use the most efficient procedures available, keeping costs as low as possible, etc.

When new human life comes to be as a result of homologous artificial insemination or homologous IVF-ET, it comes to be as the end product of a series of actions, transitive in nature, undertaken by different persons in order to make a particular product, a human baby. The spouses "produce" the gametic materials, which others then manipulate and use in order to make the final product. When these new reproductive technologies are employed, one cannot deny that the child "comes into existence ... in the manner of a product of making (and, typically, as the end product of a process managed and carried out by persons other than his parents)."[38] With use of these technologies, it is true to say that the child is "made," not "begotten."

Precisely because homologous artificial insemination/IVF-ET — like heterologous artificial insemination/IVF-ET — is an act of "making," it is standard procedure, as we have seen in surveying the literature describing the technologies, to overstimulate the woman's ovaries so that she can produce several ova for fertilization by sperm, usually obtained most economically through masturbation and then washed and "capacitated" so that they can better do their job; of the resulting new human embryos, some are frozen and kept on reserve for use should initial efforts to achieve implantation and gestation to birth fail; it is also common to implant several embryos (two to four) in the womb to enhance the likelihood that at least one will implant and, should too large a number of embryos successfully implant, to discard the "excess" number through a procedure some euphemistically call "pregnancy reduction." Finally, it is common practice to monitor development of the new human life both prior to being transferred to the womb and during gestation to determine whether it suffers from any defects and, should serious defects be discovered or thought likely, to abort the product that does not measure up to standard. As a form of "making" or "producing," artificial insemination/fertilization, homologous as well as heterologous, leads to the use of these methods, for they simply carry out the logic of manufacturing commodities: one should use the most efficient, time-saving, and cost-effective means available to deliver the desired product under good quality controls.

One readily sees how dehumanizing such "production" of human babies is. It obviously treats them as if they were products inferior to their producers and subject to quality controls, not persons equal in dignity to their parents.

But some people, including some Catholic theologians, note — correctly — that homologous insemination/fertilization does not *require* hyperovulating the woman, creating a number of new human beings in a petri dish, freezing some, implanting others, monitoring development with a view to abortion should "defects" be discovered, etc. They think that if these features commonly associated with homologous insemination/fertilization are rejected, then a limited resort by married couples to artificial insemination/IVF-ET does not really transform the generation of human life from an act of procreation to one of reproduction.

A leading representative of this school of thought, Richard A. McCormick, S.J., argues that spouses who resort to homologous *in vitro* fertilization do not perceive this as the " 'manufacture' of a 'product.' Fertilization *happens* when sperm and egg are brought together in a petri dish," but "the technician's intervention is a condition for its happening, not a cause."[39] Moreover, he continues, "the attitudes of the parents and the technicians can be every bit as reverential and respectful as they would be in the face of human life naturally conceived."[40] In fact, in McCormick's view and in that of some other writers as well — for instance, Thomas A. Shannon, Lisa Sowle Cahill, and Jean Porter[41] — homologous *in vitro* fertilization can be considered an "extension" of marital intercourse, so that the child generated can still be regarded as the "fruit" of the spouses' love. While it is preferable, if possible, to generate the baby through the marital act, it is, in the cases of concern to us, impossible to do this, and hence their marital act — so these writers claim — can be, as it were, "extended" to embrace *in vitro* fertilization.

Given the concrete situation, any disadvantages inherent in the generation of human lives apart from the marital act, so these authors reason, are clearly counterbalanced by the great good of new human lives and the fulfillment of the desire for children of couples who otherwise would not be able to have them. In such conditions, they contend, it is not unrealistic to say that homologous IVF-ET is simply a way of "extending" the marital act.

I believe that it is evident that this justification of homologous insemination/IVF-ET is rooted in the proportionalistic method of making moral judgments. It claims that one can rightly intend so-called pre-moral or nonmoral or ontic evils (the "disadvantages" referred to above) in order to attain a proportionately greater good, in this case, helping a married couple otherwise childless to have a child of their own. But this method of making moral judgments is very flawed and was explicitly repudiated by Pope John Paul II in *Veritatis splendor*.[42] It comes down to the claim that one can never judge an act to be morally bad only by taking into account the "object" freely chosen and that it is necessary, in order to render any moral judgment of an action, to consider it in its totality, taking into account not only its object but the end and circumstances as well. If the end for whose sake something is chosen and done is a "proportionately greater good" than the evil one does by choosing this object (e.g., making a baby in a petri dish), then the act as a whole can be morally good. In Chapter Two this flawed method of making moral judgments was briefly criticized.[43]

Moreover, the reasoning advanced by McCormick and others is rhetorical in character and not based on a realistic understanding of what is involved. Obviously, those who choose to produce a baby make that choice as a means to an ulterior end. They may well "intend" — in the sense of their further intention — that the baby be received into an authentic child-parent relationship, in which he or she will live in a communion of persons which befits those who share personal dignity. If realized, this intended end for whose sake the choice is made to produce the baby will be good for the baby as well as for the parents. But, even so, and despite McCormick's claim to the contrary, their "present intention," i.e., the choice they are making here and now, is precisely "to make a baby" — this is the "object" specifying their freely chosen act. The baby's initial status is the status of a product. In *in vitro* fertilization, the technician does not simply *assist* the marital act (that would be licit) but, as Benedict Ashley, O.P., rightly says, he "*substitutes* for that act of personal relationship and communication one which is like a chemist making a compound or a gardener planting a seed. The technician has thus become the principal cause of generation, acting through the instrumental forms of sperm and ovum."[44]

Moreover, the claim that *in vitro* fertilization is an "extension" of the marital act and not a substitution for it is simply contrary to fact. "What is extended," as Ashley also notes, "is not the act of intercourse, but the intention: from an intention to beget a child naturally to getting it by IVF, by artificial insemination, or by help of a surrogate mother."[45] Since the child's initial status is thus, in these procedures, that of a product, its status is subpersonal. Thus, the choice to produce a baby is, inevitably, the choice to enter into a relationship with the baby, not as its equal, but as a product inferior to its producers. But this initial relationship of those who choose to produce babies with the babies they produce is inconsistent with and so impedes the communion of persons endowed with equal dignity that is appropriate for any interpersonal relationship. It is the choice of a bad means to a good end. Moreover, in producing babies, if the product is defective, a new person comes to be as *unwanted*. Thus those who choose to produce babies not only choose life for some, but — and can this be realistically doubted? — at times quietly dispose of at least some of those who are not developing normally.[46]

I think that the reasons advanced here to show that it is not morally right to generate human life outside the marital act can be summarized in a syllogism, which I offer for consideration:

- *Major:* Any act of generating human life that is non-marital is irresponsible and violates the respect due to human life in its generation.
- *Minor:* But artificial insemination, *in vitro* fertilization, whether homologous or heterologous, and other forms of generating human life outside the marital act, including cloning, are non-marital.
- *Conclusion:* Therefore, these modes of generating human life are irresponsible and violate the respect due to human life in its generation.

I believe that the minor of this syllogism does not require extensive discussion. However, McCormick, commenting on an earlier essay of mine in which I advanced a syllogism of this kind, claims that my use of the term "non-marital" in the minor premise is "impenetrable," because the meaning of a "non-marital" action is not at all clear.[47] This objection simply fails to take into account all that I had said in my previous essay and in the earlier part of this chapter about the *marital* act.[48]

It is obvious that heterologous insemination/fertilization and cloning are "non-marital." But "non-marital" too are homologous artificial insemination and IVF. Even though married persons have collaborated in these procedures and even though these procedures make use of gametic cells supplied by husband and wife, the procedures are "non-marital" because the marital status of the man and the woman participating in them is accidental and not essential, whereas, as we saw in the first part of this chapter, the marital status of man and woman *is essential* for a *marital* act. Indeed, the marital status of the parties involved in homologous artificial insemination/IVF is utterly irrelevant to the procedures as such. What makes husband and wife capable of participating in these procedures is definitely *not* their marital union, whereas the *marital act* is possible only by reason of their marital union. Their marital status is irrelevant to artificial insemination/IVF because they are able to take part in these procedures simply because, like *unmarried* men and women, they are producers of gametic cells that other individuals can then use to fabricate human life. Just as spouses do not generate human life *maritally* when this life (which is *always* good and precious, no matter how engendered) is initiated as a result of an act of spousal abuse, so they do not generate new human life maritally when what they do is simply provide the materials to be used in making a baby.

The foregoing reflections should suffice to clarify the meaning of the minor premise of the syllogism and to show its truth.

The truth of the major premise is supported by everything said about the intimate bonds uniting marriage, the marital act, and the generation of human life. Those bonds are the indispensable and necessary means for properly respecting human life in its origin. To sunder them is to break the inseparable bond between the unitive and procreative meanings of the conjugal act, to refuse to speak the "language of the body," and above all to treat a child in its initial stage of existence as a product, as something "made," not "begotten." We have seen already that non-marital modes of generating human life change the act generating such life from one of "procreation" or "begetting" to one of "reproducing." Such reproductive modes of generating human life are indeed instances of "making."

(2) The Basic Theological Reason Why Human Life Ought to Be Generated Only In and Through the Marital Act

There is a very profound theological reason that offers ultimate support for the truth that new human life ought to be given *only* in and through the marital act — the act proper and unique to spouses, the act made possible only by marriage itself — and not through acts of fornication, adultery, spousal abuse, or new "reproductive" technologies.

The reason is this: human life ought to be "begotten, not made." Human life is the life of a human person, a being inescapably male or female, made in the image and likeness of the all-holy God. A human person, who comes to be when new human life comes into existence, is, as it were, an icon or "created word" of God. Human beings are, as it were, the "created words" that the Father's uncreated Word became and is,[49] precisely to show us how deeply God loves us and to enable us to be, like him, children of the Father and members of the divine family.

But the Uncreated Word, whose brothers and sisters human persons are called to be, was "begotten, not made." These words were chosen by the Fathers of the Council of Nicaea in A.D. 325 to express unambiguously their belief that the eternal and uncreated Word of God is indeed, like the Father, true God. This Word, who personally became true man in Jesus Christ while remaining true God, is not inferior to his Father; he is not a product of his Father's will, a being made by the Father and subordinate in dignity to him. Rather, the Word is one in being with the Father, equally a divine person. The Word, the Father's Son, was begotten by an immanent act of personal love.

Similarly, human persons, the "created words" of God, ought, like the uncreated Word, to be "begotten, not made." Like the uncreated Word, they are one in nature with their parents, persons like their mothers and fathers; they are not products inferior to their producers. Their personal dignity is equal to that of their mothers and fathers, just as the uncreated Word's personal dignity is equal to the personal dignity of the Father. That dignity is respected when their life is "begotten" in an act of self-giving spousal union, in an act of conjugal love. It is not respected when that life is "made" as the end product of a series of transitive acts of making. Nor is it respected when generated by acts of fornication, adultery, or spousal abuse.

4. Part Four: "Assisted" Insemination/Fertilization

The Church's Magisterium, as we have seen, distinguishes between technological procedures, such as artificial insemination and *in vitro* fertilization, whether homologous or heterologous, that *substitute for or replace the marital act* and procedures that *assist* the marital act in being crowned with the gift of human life. Although married couples ought never to use techniques that replace the marital act, they can legitimately use those that assist it in generating new human life. As Pope John Paul II has said, "infertile couples ... have a right to whatever legitimate therapies may be available to remedy their infertility."[50]

But there is serious controversy, even among Catholics who defend the truth of the Church's teaching on the generation of human life, regarding the kinds of procedures that assist rather than replace the marital act. After presenting basic criteria to help distinguish procedures that "assist" the conjugal act from those replacing it, I will then examine some specific techniques. We will find that there is a consensus among Catholic theologians regarding some of these procedures, whereas over others there is controversy.

A. Basic Criteria

The basic principle operative here is accurately formulated in the following text from *Donum vitae*:

> The human person must be accepted in his parents' act of union and love; the generation of a child must therefore be the fruit of that mutual giving which is realized in the conjugal act wherein the spouses cooperate as servants and not as masters in the work of the Creator who is love.[51]

If the child is to be the "fruit" of the marital act, the marital act must be directly related (= have a direct causal relationship) to the origin of new human life. The marital act, in other words, must be the "principal" cause of the conception of the child. It is so because the marital act not only unites husband and wife in an intimate "one-flesh" unity but also directly and personally introduces into the wife's body the sperm of her husband, which then actively seek an ovum in order to fertilize it and cause the conception of the child. Given that the marital or conjugal act is and must be the principal cause of the child's conception if the dignity of human life in its origin is to be respected, then what basic criteria will enable us to determine whether a technological intervention "assists" the marital act rather than "replaces" it or "substitutes" for it?

In an excellent study of this issue,[52] John Doerfler offers a thorough review of relevant literature, offering perceptive critiques of several essays and judging as one of the most helpful an insightful (but neglected) essay by Josef Seifert.[53] Doerfler proposes that the marital act is and remains the principal cause of conception only if the technical procedure either enables it to be performed by removing obstacles preventing the conjugal act from being effective or enables it to be performed by providing active condition(s) for it to exercise its own principal causality (technical procedures of this type will be illustrated below). But the conjugal act is not or does not remain the principal cause of conception if the natural causal process initiated by the marital act and leading to conception is interrupted by the technical means, and it is so interrupted if the technical means terminates or stops the natural causal process, if these means require the husband's sperm to be removed from the wife's body after the marital act has taken place, if conception occurs outside the wife's body, or if the technical means initiates the process anew once it has been stopped. Obviously, too, the conjugal act is not the principal cause of conception if it merely serves as a means for obtaining sperm. These are the major criteria developed by Doerfler[54] (I have in some measure modified and simplified them for presentation here), and in my opinion these are very helpful in enabling us to determine whether a given technical intervention assists or replaces the conjugal act.

From this it follows, I believe, that a procedure assists the marital act if and only if a marital act takes place and the procedure in question either circumvents obstacles preventing the specific marital act from being fruitful or supplies condition(s) needed for it to become effective in causing conception.

With these criteria in mind, I will now examine some specific procedures claimed by Catholic theologians to be licit examples of techniques that "assist" rather than "replace" the conjugal act. As will be seen, there is sharp disagreement among these theologians over some of the procedures to be examined. I will begin with techniques that all commentators, so far as I know, regard as instances of "assisted" insemination or fertilization, and then take up techniques over which controversy exists, offering my own assessment, guided by the criteria developed by Doerfler in his comprehensive study.

B. Acknowledged Instances of Assisted Insemination or Fertilization

(1) Use of Perforated Condom to Circumvent Hypospadias

Hypospadias is an anomaly of the male penis in which the urethra does not open at the distal end of the penis but on its underside, close to the man's body. This frequently prevents the husband from ejaculating sperm into his wife's vagina during the marital act. The use of a perforated condom would prevent the husband's sperm from being emitted outside his wife's body and facilitate their entrance into her vagina. This would thus be an instance of a technical means that would *remove an obstacle* to the fruitfulness of the conjugal act; all Catholic theologians who have discussed this procedure agree that it assists and does not replace the marital act and that, consequently, it is morally licit. It surely meets the criteria developed by Doerfler.[55]

(2) Low Tubal Ovum Transfer (LTOT)

This procedure, originally designed for women whose infertility was caused by blocked, damaged, or diseased fallopian tubes, relocates her ovum, bypassing and circumventing the area of tubal pathology in order to place the ovum into the fallopian tube below the point of damage, disease, or blockage so that her own husband's sperm, introduced into her body by the marital act, can then effect fertilization. It is called "*low* tubal ovum transfer" because ordinarily the ovum is relocated in the lower part of the fallopian tube (or at times in the uterus itself).

This procedure evidently "removes an obstacle" preventing conception from occurring after the marital act has taken place or provides the conditions necessary if the marital act is to be fruitful. All the procedure does is to relocate the wife's ovum within her body prior to the marital act. The sperm that fertilize the ovum are introduced into her body-person directly as a result of the marital act. This technique clearly meets the criteria set forth by Doerfler.

All Catholic theologians who have addressed this technique agree that LTOT is a morally legitimate way of assisting the marital act.[56]

(3) Moving Sperm Deposited in the Vagina Into the Uterus and Fallopian Tubes

Apparently, the fruitfulness of some marital acts is impeded because the husband's sperm do not migrate far enough or rapidly enough into the reproductive tract of his wife, but linger in the vagina or at most migrate only very slowly to those portions of the wife's reproductive tract where conception is most likely to occur, with the result that most of the sperm die before they are able to unite with an ovum and fertilize it.

This obstacle to the fruitfulness of the marital act is removed and the conditions favorable for it to bear fruit can be fulfilled if the physician, after husband and wife have completed the marital act, uses some instrument(s) to propel the sperm deposited in the vagina into the uterus and fallopian tubes. If this is the way the technical intervention occurs, then it seems evident that it merely removes an obstacle preventing the marital act from being fruitful, supplying conditions necessary for it to be effective. It thus meets the criteria we have noted and can rightly be said to assist and not replace the marital act.[57]

C. Controverted Technologies

(1) Temporary Removal of Sperm or of Ova to "Wash" and "Capacitate" Them

The procedure just discussed, namely, moving and relocating within the wife's body sperm deposited by her husband during the marital act, may be modified somewhat, requiring the sperm to be removed temporarily from the wife's body or perhaps having her ovum temporarily removed and treated for some pathological condition, and then relocating one or both elements to the fallopian tube where they can unite. Many Catholic theologians who have discussed this procedure believe that it, too, can be regarded as a legitimate assistance of the marital act.[58] This procedure, too, so it seems to them, assists the marital act by removing an obstacle to its fruitfulness or by supplying the conditions under which it can be effective.

Despite my respect for this opinion, I believe that the procedure in question does not truly assist the marital act but rather substitutes for it. One of the criteria developed by Doerfler in his well-reasoned study and supported by the analysis given by Seifert is that a technical means which stops or terminates the natural causal process initiated by the marital act and then initiates the process anew after its termination can hardly be designated as assisting the conjugal act or the causal process initiated by it.[59] It seems to me quite clear that distinct human acts, specified by their objects, are being chosen and done, and that one of them definitely *stops* or *terminates* a causal process initiated by the other. One of the acts is the marital act; the other is the technical intervention of removing and treating either the sperm introduced into the wife's body by the marital act or the ova present within her body when the marital act occurred, treating them in some fashion. This act is not marital, nor does it assist the causal process initiated by the marital act to be fruitful. It does not assist because it terminates the act in order to do something else, i.e., to treat sperm or ova. A third human act is then required to initiate the causal process that leads to conception, since a new human choice is needed for the reintroduction of sperm and/or ovum into the wife's body. It thus seems clear to me that this procedure substitutes for the marital act and does not assist it.

(2) Accumulating Sperm From a Series of Marital Acts and Introducing Them Into the Wife's Vagina in Conjunction With a Marital Act

In order to cope with infertility caused by oligospermia (a condition causing relatively low sperm production by the husband), some theologians propose that the physician collect amounts of sperm from the husband's ejaculate (by morally permissible means, such as use of a perforated condom), conserve and centrifuge such accumulated sperm, and then place this concentrate into the wife's generative tract in association with a marital act (usually prior to one) in order to mix with and fortify the husband's ejaculate during the marital act.

Although some Catholic theologians who accept the teaching of *Donum vitae* think that this procedure assists the marital act,[60] I believe that a proper assessment of what is going on shows that this technique replaces the marital act and does not assist it.

First of all, in this procedure one does not know whether the sperm that fertilize the ovum are sperm introduced into the wife's body by the husband during the marital act or sperm contained in the concentrate obtained by collecting sperm into a perforated condom during previous marital acts. But if the sperm that fertilize the ovum derive from that concentrate, then they simply *cannot* and *must not* be considered as part of the marital act. They cannot and must not be so considered precisely because they have been *intentionally withheld* from prior marital acts in order to procure sperm in a nonmasturbatory way. The marital act merely serves as an instrument for obtaining sperm. And since one cannot say whether fertilization is caused by sperm introduced into the wife's body by the specific marital act in question or by sperm contained in the concentrate resulting from *deliberately withholding sperm* from prior marital acts, one cannot truly say that the procedure "assists" the specific marital act in question. This procedure clearly violates one of the criteria developed by Doerfler.[61]

(3) Gamete Intrafallopian Tube Transfer (GIFT) and Tubal Ovum Transfer with Sperm (TOTS)

GIFT has already been described: the wife's eggs are removed by laparoscopy or ultrasound-guided transvaginal procedures. An egg (or group of eggs) is placed in a catheter with sperm (provided either by masturbation or by using a perforated condom during previous marital acts) that have been treated and "capacitated," with an air bubble separating ovum (ova) from sperm in the catheter while outside the wife's body. Thus fertilization does not take place outside the wife's body. The catheter is then inserted into the wife's body (and this can be done either prior to or immediately following a marital act), the ovum and sperm are released from the catheter, and fertilization and conception can then take place within the wife's body, caused by the concentrate of sperm placed in the catheter and released after its insertion into the wife's body or perhaps by sperm released into her body by the marital act in association with which the catheter is inserted.

Several Catholic theologians — among them, Donald McCarthy, Orville Griese, Peter Cataldo, and John W. Carlson — strongly defend GIFT as a procedure that assists the marital act in being fruitful.[62]

With many others, I disagree completely with this approval of GIFT. First of all, the procedure was originally developed as an offshoot of IVF, and the husband's sperm was collected by masturbation. Informed that the Catholic Church condemns masturbation, even as a way of obtaining a husband's sperm, the doctors who used the method suggested that sperm be obtained by using a perforated condom during the marital act. This shows definitely that with GIFT the marital act is merely incidental to the entire procedure, used only as a way of obtaining sperm in a nonmasturbatory way. These sperm, since they have been *deliberately, intentionally withheld from a marital act or series of marital acts*, can then not be said truly to be integral to the marital act when the catheter containing these sperm and the wife's ovum are inserted into her body. Although subsequent fertilization of her ovum *may* be caused by sperm introduced into her body during the accompanying marital act, such fertilization would be *per accidens* and not *per se*. Thus with many others, including Doerfler, Seifert, DeMarco, Tonti-Filippini, Grisez, and Ashley-O'Rourke, I believe that GIFT definitely substitutes for or replaces the marital act and does not assist it; and that, therefore, it is immoral to make use of it.[63]

TOTS is similar to GIFT. In this procedure, sperm are procured from the husband either by masturbation or by use of a perforated condom. Sperm are then placed in a catheter along with the wife's ovum (ova) and separated by an air bubble, and the catheter is then inserted into the fallopian tube (hence the name Tubal Ovum Transfer with Sperm), where ovum (ova) and sperm are released and fertilization can then occur. As can be seen, TOTS is quite similar to GIFT and not similar to LTOT, or low tubal ovum transfer. Like GIFT, it substitutes for the marital act and does not assist it since the marital act is only incidental to retrieval of sperm and sperm so retrieved are intentionally withheld from a marital act and hence cannot be regarded as part of a marital act.

Someone might say that with respect to procedures where reputable Catholic theologians disagree, and since there is no specific magisterial teaching on them, Catholics are at liberty to follow whatever view they prefer as a "probable opinion." This way of looking at the issue is quite legalistic in my opinion. What one ought to do is examine the arguments and reasons given by theologians to support their claims to see which is true and takes into account the realities involved.

D. Conclusion to Part Four; a Word About Fertility Drugs

Some may think that the preceding analysis of procedures to determine which assist and which replace the marital act may be a bit nit-picking.

Nonetheless, it deals with a real situation. The proper way to "assist" the conjugal act, I think, is to do more research to discover the root causes of female/male infertility and cure these underlying pathologies. At present, the usual recommendation to overcome problems posed by blocked fallopian tubes (not an uncommon cause of inability to conceive) is to have recourse to IVF-ET. Yet such recourse does not cure the underlying pathology but rather responds to a human desire. It would be more in line with true medical research to reconstruct the fallopian tubes surgically or perhaps to attempt a tubal transplant. Why can't fallopian tubes be transplanted from cadavers just as kidneys are? This would permanently cure the pathological condition.

Moreover, efforts to overcome infertility through use of hormones are gradually meeting with more and more success. Hormone treatment, to which I will return briefly below, is a type of infertility treatment by drugs, but it does not cause the problems associated with use of hyperovulatory drugs. Although use of hyperovulatory drugs is not intrinsically immoral, their use raises very serious problems. Ordinarily they cause the wife to produce a large number of ova (more than four), which could be fertilized by her husband as a result of the marital act. If all are fertilized and implanted, this can cause serious problems affecting the life and health both of the mother and of the unborn children during pregnancy, leading some doctors who use such drugs to recommend "pregnancy reduction" — a euphemism for injecting potassium chloride into the hearts of some unborn children to kill them — as a means of protecting the health and life of some of the unborn babies. Usually, too, children conceived in this way are born prematurely and must thus spend long periods in the neonatal intensive-care unit. This is obviously burdensome to them, and the costs involved are extremely high. The burdens that these children will likely suffer and the extreme expenses involved are likely consequences of using hyperovulatory drugs in an effort to overcome infertility. It seems to me that one ought to avoid these foreseen consequences by not resorting to use of such drugs.

As noted before, hormonal treatments of some causes of infertility have had success. Such treatments and other alternatives have been developed and are being further developed by Thomas W. Hilgers, M.D., at his Pope Paul VI Institute. Dr. Hilgers, a member of the Pontifical Academy for Life, resolutely refuses to use IVF-ET, AIH, GIFT, TOTS, and other technologies that substitute for the marital act but has been able to be of help to many married couples through the programs he has developed.[64] There is hope for couples who have difficulty in conceiving. But all married couples must remember that they do not have a "right" to a child and that God may give them the cross of childlessness to carry. If he does, they must remember that he will be their Simon of Cyrene, ready to help them bear the cross he gives them.

5. Part Five: IVF's Harm to Babies Conceived *In Vitro* or by Other New Reproductive Technologies and the Women Who Participate in Such Procedures

There is abundant evidence that IVF and other new reproductive technologies can cause harm to the babies "made" using these procedures and to the women who engage in them. I will cite three relevant sources.

The most recent was posted on *BioEdge: Bioethics News from Around the World,* a weekly bioethics news magazine from Australia, edited by Michael Cook. In the April 28, 2012, issue, in an article entitled "Dark Side of IVF Makes an Impact," Cook reported the following:

> The negative side of IVF birth defects may finally be getting some publicity. IVF clinics are aware that there is a higher incidence of birth defects among children conceived through IVF. However, consumer awareness is low. But last week's news [in the latest issue of *Fertility and Sterility*] that birth defects are 37% higher is dramatic. "That is a huge number," writes Art Caplan, of New York University [Caplan is at the University of Pennsylvania] ... probably the most quoted bioethicist in the US, and possibly the world.... He writes in a column for *msnbc.com*: "the large risk factor now on the table needs to be a key part of how everyone thinks about making babies in medical settings. The authors of the *Fertility and Sterility* study say they do not know why the risk is so large. And it has taken far too long for this question to get asked. We need to be sure that long-term monitoring of children born by means of infertility treatment is routine and that more research is done into the causes of health problems for kids who cannot make choices about facing risk.
>
> "Infertility treatments have brought a great deal of joy to many. But, the price is high — so high that we need to be sure it is a key element in thinking about using these treatments."

Since Caplan has long been a champion of IVF, this is stunning news.

The second source, by Dr. Carlo Bellieni, professor of neonatal therapy at the School of Pediatrics of the University of Siena, offered an overview of major scientific studies demonstrating the dangers of artificial procreation for the child conceived. He cited three studies on large numbers of children conceived *in vitro* that were published in 2002 in prestigious international scientific journals and the conclusions found by those studies. They verify that "children who are underweight at birth run the risk of incapacity and death. The use of IVF implies an increase of children who are underweight at birth in the U.S. because it is associated with a high rate of twin births. Until 1997, IVF was the cause of 40% of triple births. Likewise, studies show that there are more underweight children at birth by IVF than in normal pregnancies."[65] (Bellieni's remarks were reported in *Zenit*, June 2004.)

Another study clearly indicated that "children born by IVF have an increased risk of developing cerebral problems, in particular cerebral paralysis."[66] Another showed that "children conceived with the use of 'Intracytoplasmic Sperm Injection' (ICSI) or IVF run a double risk of presenting a greater defect at birth in relation to the general population."[67]

These studies were used in other pediatric journals. Thus one declared:

> In February of 2002, a team of Uppsala, Sweden, referred to a retrospective work on 5,680 children born by IVF: it showed that in general, children born by IVF have greater need for rehabilitation centers in relation to the normal population and the risk of cerebral paralysis is 3.7. The greatest difference is observed among children of single birth, while the risk of those born as twins is similar to that of the normal population. In an Australian study, 8.6% of children born by IVF had greater defects at birth, double that of the control group.[68]

The third and final — and in my judgment the most powerful — source is the testimony of Dr. Anthony Caruso of Chicago, who was for fifteen years a practitioner of IVF. His testimony was given in an interview with MercatorNet.[69] In its policy statement MercatorNet says that it seeks to frame "ethical and policy debates in terms of human dignity, not dollars and cents or political calculation," placing "the person at the centre of media debates about popular culture, the family, sexuality, bioethics, religion and law."

In his interview Dr. Caruso, who had been a member of several infertility practices since 1995, replied to a series of questions MercatorNet proposed to him. In answering these questions Caruso made several truths crystal clear. The first is that he resigned from doing IVFs because he came to the realization that *Dignitas personae*, "a beautifully written document, using all current statistics in its analysis," speaks the truth about the personal dignity of the babies manufactured in fertility clinics and treated not as persons of inviolable dignity but as products to be used or destroyed by others.

Another great truth — and its violation by this laboratory manufacturing of children is what most distressed him — is that such manufacturing blurs a basic purpose of marriage. "Children," Caruso said in his interview, "as gifts from God have become desires and pawns in the life process. ... The nature of the act is not good." He went on to say that most people going through IVF are totally ignorant of this. They have been misled by the slogan of IVF clinics: "Every child is a wanted child." "This statement is the problem," he said. "Every child is a gift from God. However, the process that brought them [IVF children] into existence has led to an attitude towards the embryo that is no different than any other commodity. If you add preimplantation diagnosis into the equation, then you really have a situation that is no different than an auto dealership or a department store. 'I will take two of these and then freeze these and toss these.' The very people who are showing off their beautiful children will not answer questions about how many frozen embryos are still present or how many they asked to be destroyed. Also, I doubt that anyone has ever thought how they might describe these things to their children — the fate of their siblings — because they are not seen as such. They are seen as simply a means to an end."

Caruso also brought out the harmful effects on the women who participate in IVF procedures. Although the data are slow in coming in, it is definitely

> well-known that there are dangers in over-stimulating a woman's ovaries. Ovarian hyper-stimulation syndrome can be severe, especially in the environment of a pregnancy. Though the other immediate risks are very small, there is a risk of bleeding, injury to the intestines and infection. There is also a risk of blood clots and their sequelae. The long-term effects are now slowly coming into focus. Remember, the first IVF pregnancy was in 1978, but the first IVF pregnancy from a stimulated ovary was in 1981. That was only 30 years ago and the women going through that procedure are largely just entering the age of chronic disease. One study from the Netherlands suggests that 15 years after an IVF pregnancy, there is an increased risk of ovarian cancer. While there are no controlled trials, many reproductive endocrinologists anecdotally describe women who present with breast tumors after IVF stimulation.

There are other riches in his interview. For instance, Caruso notes that a common practice in IVF clinics is to "reduce" the number of multiple pregnancies caused by overstimulating the ovaries by aborting all in excess of two.

He likewise accuses IVF fertility clinics of being businesses that definitely do not practice medicine. "IVF does not cure infertility. It bypasses the barriers to natural fertility. As such, it is really a business. Just think about the number of clinics that offer cash-back programs. They guarantee that if the couple does not conceive within a certain number of cycles, they will get some or all of their money back. Where is the 'medicine' in that?"

6. Part Six: "Rescuing" Frozen Embryos

In no. 19 *Dignitas personae* devotes two brief sentences to an issue on which Catholic theologians loyal to the Magisterium have been divided. It describes the issue as follows: "It has also been proposed, solely in order to allow human beings to be born who are otherwise condemned to destruction, that there could be a form of *'prenatal adoption'* " (emphasis in original).

The following sentence reads: "This proposal, praiseworthy with regard to the intention of respecting and defending human life, presents however various problems not dissimilar to those mentioned above."

Does this passage definitively reject the proposal concerning the "prenatal adoption" of frozen and orphaned embryos? There is a dispute among those who have read the document on this issue. Some scholars think that *Dignitas personae* has definitely concluded that adopting frozen embryos prenatally is not morally licit. But others, and I am among them, think that a close reading of this sentence and the context in which it appears makes it clear that *it was not the intention* of the CDF to make a definitive judgment on this disputed question but that it left the issue open to further debate by Catholic theologians. *Dignitas personae's* statement that embryo adoption presents problems not dissimilar to those involved in the immoral practice treated in the preceding paragraph can be reasonably interpreted as warning those engaging in embryo adoption to attend to all relevant medical, psychological, and legal problems and to exercise prudence in dealing with them.[70]

--------------------- **Endnotes for Chapter Three** ---------------------

1. This truth, a matter of Catholic faith, will be discussed in more detail later in the chapter on abortion. In his book *Love and Responsibility*, trans. H. T. Willetts (New York: Farrar, Straus, Giroux, 1981; reprinted, San Francisco: Ignatius Press, 1993), Karol Wojtyla (Pope John Paul II) expressed matters this way: "A person is the kind of good which does not admit of use and cannot be treated as an object of use and as such the means to an end.... A person is a good towards which the only proper and adequate attitude is love."

2. Centuries ago St. Augustine rightly and wisely noted that one of the principal *goods* of marriage is the good of children, who are "to be received lovingly, nourished humanely, and educated religiously," i.e., in the love and service of God and neighbor. See his *De genesi ad literam*, 9.7 (PL 34.397).

3. It is worth noting here that the principal reason St. Thomas gave to show that fornication is intrinsically evil is that acts of fornication may cause (and are known to cause) the conception of new human life, that the life thus generated would be deprived of the home to which it has a right, and that, therefore, by fornicating one was unjustly exposing children who could be generated by fornication to this deprivation. He observed that one might try to prevent their conception by contraceptive acts, but he judged contraception to be even more gravely immoral insofar as it constitutes an attack on the survival of the human species. See his *Summa contra gentiles*, 3.122.

4. I realize that many women valiantly struggle to care for children whom they have conceived out of wedlock. Their caring for these children is *good*, and I praise them for it. Despite this, it is *not* good for them to conceive children in this way nor for their children to be deprived of the home that only loving spouses can provide — as these valiant women themselves realize. Nor is it good for the males who impregnate women outside of marriage to place themselves in a position where they cannot properly carry out their obligations to the women they have made pregnant or to the children they have fathered.

5. As the German theologian Helmut Thielicke put the matter: "Not uniqueness establishes the marriage, but marriage establishes the uniqueness." *The Ethics of Sex* (New York: Harper, 1964), p. 95.

6. Here see John Paul II's perceptive observations in his commentary on Genesis 2: "The unity of which Genesis 2:24 speaks ('they become one flesh') is undoubtedly what is expressed and realized in the conjugal act. The biblical formulation, extremely concise and simple, indicates sex, femininity and masculinity, as that characteristic of man — male and female — which permits them, when they become one flesh, *to submit at the same time their whole humanity to the blessing of fertility*" (emphasis added). See John Paul II, "Marriage Is One and Indissoluble in the First Chapters of Genesis," General Audience of November 21, 1979, in *Original Unity of Man and Woman: Catechesis on the Book of Genesis* (Boston: St. Paul Editions, 1981), pp. 79-80. All of John Paul II's Wednesday audiences on the "theology of the body," originally published in English in four volumes (in addition to *Original Unity* these were: *Blessed Are the Pure of Heart*, *Theology of Marriage and Celibacy*, and *Reflections on Humanae Vitae*), have now been reprinted in a one-volume edition entitled *The Theology of the Body: Human Love in the Divine Plan* (Boston: Pauline Books & Media, 1997). This volume will henceforth be referred to as TB. The passage in question appears in TB, p. 49.

7. On this, see Pope Paul VI, encyclical *Humanae vitae*, no. 12; Pope John Paul II, Apostolic Exhortation on the Role of the Christian Family in the Modern World (*Familiaris consortio*), no. 32; *Catechism of the Catholic Church*, no. 2369.

8. On this, see John Paul II, "Analysis of Knowledge and Procreation," General Audience of March 5, 1980, Original Unity of Man and Woman, nos. 4-5, pp. 149-150 (TB, pp. 77-80). Here the Pope notes that in the marital act, whereby they come to "know" each other, husband and wife "reveal themselves to each other, with *that specific depth of their own human 'self,' which, precisely, is revealed also by means of their sex*, their masculinity and femininity.... [T]he reality of the conjugal union ... contains a new and, in a way, a definitive discovery of the meaning of the human body in its masculinity and femininity."

9. On this, see John F. Kippley, *Sex and the Marriage Covenant: A Basis for Morality* (Cincinnati: Couple to Couple League, 1991), pp. 7-12, 76-86.

10. The ideas briefly set forth here are developed by me at more length in *Marriage: The Rock on Which the Family Is Built* (second edition, San Francisco: Ignatius, 2009), chap. 2, "Marriage and the Complementarity of Male and Female." See also Robert Joyce, *Human Sexual Ecology: A Philosophy of Man and Woman* (Washington, DC: University Press of America, 1980), pp. 35-50.

11. On this, see Robert P. George and Gerard V. Bradley, "Marriage and the Liberal Imagination," *The Georgetown Law Review* 84 (1995), 301-320; Germain Grisez, "The Christian Family as Fulfillment of Sacramental Marriage," a paper delivered to the Society of Christian Ethics Annual Conference, September 9, 1995 (unpublished manuscript, on file with *The Georgetown Law Review*).

12. Pope Pius XII, Address to the Italian Union of Midwives, October 21, 1951, text in *The Catholic Mind* 50 (1951), 61.

13. Pope Paul VI, encyclical *Humanae vitae*, no. 12. My translation.

14. Ibid., no. 12.

15. Classic sources for the distinction between *transitive* and *immanent* action, between making and doing, and the significance of this distinction are: Aristotle, *Metaphysics*, Bk. 9, chap. 8, 1050a23-1051b1; St. Thomas Aquinas, *In IX Metaphysicorum*, Lect. 8, no. 1865.

16. Catholic Bishops' [of England] Committee on Bioethical Issues, *In Vitro Fertilization: Morality and Public Policy* (London: Catholic Information Services, 1983), no. 23.

17. Four of his addresses take up this issue: (1) Allocution to the Fourth International Conference of Catholic Doctors, September 29, 1949; text in *Papal Teachings on Matrimony*, ed. The Benedictine Monks of Solesmes, trans. Michael J. Byrnes (Boston: St. Paul Editions, 1963), pp. 381-385; (2) Allocution to Italian Catholic Midwives, October 29, 1951, in ibid., pp. 405-434; (3) Allocution to the Second World Congress on Fertility and Human Sterility, May 19, 1956, in ibid., pp. 482-492; and (4) Allocution to the Seventh Hematological Congress, September 12, 1958, in ibid., pp. 513-525. He discussed artificial insemination in all four of these addresses, and in no. 3 he explicitly took up *in vitro* fertilization.

18. Allocution to the Second World Congress on Fertility and Human Sterility, ibid., p. 485.

19. Allocution to Italian Catholic Midwives, ibid., pp. 427-428.

20. Allocution to the Second World Congress on Fertility and Human Sterility, ibid., p. 470.

21. Allocution to the Fourth International Congress of Catholic Doctors, ibid., p. 559.

22. Pontifical Academy for Life, Reflections on Cloning (Vatican City: Libreria Editrice Vaticana, 1997), pp. 10, 14.

23. It is instructive to note that in his article on artificial insemination in the widely used and influential *Encyclopedia of Bioethics*, Luigi Mastroianni included under "homologous" fertilization procedures "utilizing the semen of the husband or *designated partner*" (emphasis added) ("Reproductive Technologies, Introduction," in *Encyclopedia of Bioethics*, ed. Warren T. Reich [2nd rev. ed.: New York: McGraw Hill, 1995], 2207). Inasmuch as this edition of the *Encyclopedia* now includes an essay entitled "Marriage and *Other Domestic Partnerships*" (emphasis added) by Barbara Hilkert Anderson (pp. 1397-1402), Mastroianni's apparent equation of husbands with "designated partners" is not too surprising.

24. See Mastroianni, "Reproductive Technologies, Introduction," 2207.

25. On this, see David S. McLaughlin, M.D., "A Scientific Introduction to Reproductive Technologies," in *Reproductive Technologies, Marriage, and the Church*, ed. Donald G. McCarthy (Braintree, MA: The Pope John Center, 1988), pp. 55-56.

26. Walter Wadlington, "Reproductive Technologies, Artificial Insemination," *Encyclopedia of Bioethics*, 2220.

27. George J. Annas, "Artificial Insemination: Beyond the Best Interests of the Donor," *Hastings Center Report* 9.4 (August 1979), 14-15, 43.

28. Wadlington, "Reproductive Technologies, Artificial Insemination," 2217.

29. See McLaughlin, "A Scientific Introduction to Reproductive Technologies," p. 57.

30. On this, see Mastroianni, "Reproductive Technologies, Introduction," 2209-2210; Andrea L. Bonnicksen, "Reproductive Technologies, In Vitro Fertilization and Embryo Transfer," *Encyclopedia of Bioethics*, 2221-2224; and McLaughlin, "A Scientific Introduction to Reproductive Technologies," pp. 58-59.

31. Mastroianni, "Reproductive Technologies, Introduction," 2211.

32. See Bonnicksen, "Reproductive Technologies, In Vitro Fertilization and Embryo Transfer," 2222.

33. On these and other technologies, see McLaughlin, "A Scientific Introduction to Reproductive Technologies," pp. 60-62.

34. Ibid.

35. Ibid. See also Mastroianni, "Reproductive Technologies, Introduction," 2211-2212.

36. "Somatic-cell nuclear transfer" is the expression used by the National Bioethics Advisory Commission to describe mammalian cloning in its document, released in June 1997: "Cloning Human Beings: The Report and Recommendations of the National Bioethics Advisory Commission." A summary of this report is printed in *Hastings Center Report* (September-October, 1997), 7-9.

37. Pontifical Academy for Life, *Reflections on Cloning*, pp. 10-11.

38. Catholic Bishops' (of England) Committee on Bioethical Issues, *In Vitro Fertilization: Morality and Public Policy*, no. 24.

39. Richard McCormick, *The Critical Calling: Reflections on Moral Dilemmas Since Vatican II* (Washington, DC: Georgetown University Press, 1989), p. 337. The internal citation is from William Daniel, S.J., "In Vitro Fertilization: Two Problem Areas," *Australasian Catholic Record* 63 (1986), 27.

40. Ibid.

41. See Thomas A. Shannon and Lisa Sowle Cahill, *Religion and Artificial Reproduction: An Inquiry into the Vatican "Instruction on Respect for Human Life"* (New York: Crossroads, 1988), p. 138; Jean Porter, "Human Need and Natural Law," in *Infertility: A Crossroad of Faith, Medicine, and Technology*, ed. Kevin Wm. Wildes, S.J. (Dordrecht/Boston/London: Kluwer Academic Publishers, 1997), pp. 103-105. It should be noted that Shannon and Cahill, using an argument proportionalistic in nature — that is, that it can be morally permissible to intend a so-called nonmoral evil (e.g., heterologous generation of human life) should a sufficiently greater nonmoral good be possible (e.g., providing an otherwise childless couple with a child of their own) — insinuate that, if the spouses consent, recourse to third parties for gametes and even to surrogate mothers might not truly violate spousal dignity or unity. See *Artificial Reproduction*, p. 115.

42. See Pope John Paul II, encyclical *Veritatis splendor*, nos. 71-83. An excellent collection of essays on this encyclical is *Veritatis Splendor and the Renewal of Moral Theology*, eds. J. A. DiNoia, O.P., and Romanus Cessario, O.P. (Chicago: Midwest Theological Forum, 1999).

43. For critiques of proportionalism see my *Introduction to Moral Theology* (2nd ed.: Huntington, IN: Our Sunday Visitor, 2003); Germain Grisez, *The Way of the Lord Jesus*, Vol. 1, *Christian Moral Principles* (Chicago: Franciscan Herald Press, 1983), chap. 6; Martin Rhonheimer, "Intrinsically Evil Acts and the Moral Viewpoint: Clarifying a Central Teaching of *Veritatis splendor*," in *Veritatis Splendor and the Renewal of Moral Theology*, pp. 161-194.

44. Benedict Ashley, "The Chill Factor in Moral Theology," *Linacre Quarterly* 57.4 (1990), 71.

45. Ibid., 72.

46. The argument just advanced was set forth originally in an earlier essay I wrote on this issue: "*Donum Vitae*: Catholic Teaching on Homologous In Vitro Fertilization," in *Infertility: A Crossroad of Faith, Medicine, and Technology*, pp. 73-92, esp. pp. 81-87, making use of material developed by Germain Grisez, Joseph Boyle, John Finnis, and me in our essay " 'Every Marital Act Ought to Be Open to New Life': Toward a Clearer Understanding," *The Thomist* 52 (1988), 365-426.

47. McCormick, "Notes on Moral Theology," *Theological Studies* 45 (1984), 102.

48. Here I must note that in her essay "Human Need and Natural Law" (see endnote 41), Jean Porter claims that my argument supporting *Donum vitae* is based on a "Kantian" sexual ethics that "gives pride of place to autonomy" (pp. 100-

101). She even claims that I "dissent" from Catholic teaching in my analysis of the marital act because of my emphasis on the role of intention in determining the moral significance of human actions. Porter's criticisms are ludicrous and can be attributed only to a woeful ignorance of Thomistic moral theory and the teaching of John Paul II in *Veritatis splendor*. I may dissent from a "Suarezian" understanding of natural law, which Porter perhaps employs along with her own proportionalism, but I am by no means Kantian. As far as the role of intention in determining morality is concerned, has Porter read St. Thomas, *Summa theologiae*, II-II, 64, 7 (for instance), where he clearly says that "moral actions are specified according to what is intended and not by what lies outside the scope of one's intentionality" (the Latin text reads: "*morales autem actus recipiunt speciem secundum id quod intenditur, non autem ab eo quod est praeter intentionem*")?

49. It is important to stress here that Christian faith proclaims that the Word Incarnate, although not a human person, is still a *human being, a man*. Christian faith rejects docetism, the doctrine that the uncreated Word only seemed to become human and ceased so appearing after the resurrection.

50. Pope John Paul II, "To my brother bishops from North and Central America and the Caribbean assembled in Dallas, Texas," in *Reproductive Technologies, Marriage and the Church*, p. xv.

51. *Donum vitae*, II B 4, 7.

52. Rev. John Doerfler, *Assisting or Replacing the Conjugal Act: Criteria for a Moral Evaluation of Reproductive Techniques*, unpublished 1999 S.T.L. dissertation on file at the John Paul II Institute for Studies on Marriage and Family, Washington, DC. A substantive summary of Doerfler's study has appeared in *Anthropotes: Rivista di Studi sulla Persona e Famiglia*. He has briefly summarized his work in "Technology and Human Reproduction," *Ethics & Medics* 24.8 (August 1999), 3-4.

53. Josef Seifert, "Substitution of the Conjugal Act or Assistance to It? IVF, GIFT and Some Other Medical Interventions. Philosophical Reflections on the Vatican Declaration 'Donum Vitae,'" *Anthropotes: Rivista di Studi sulla Persona e Famiglia* 4 (1988), 273-286.

54. See Doerfler, *Assisting or Replacing the Conjugal Act*, pp. 89-90.

55. See, for example, Thomas J. O'Donnell, S.J., *Medicine and Christian Morality* (2nd rev. ed.: New York: Alba House, 1991), p. 238.

56. See, for instance, the following: Donald T. DeMarco, "Catholic Moral Teaching and TOT/GIFT," in *Reproductive Technologies, Marriage and the Church*, pp. 122-139; Nicholas Tonti-Filippini, " 'Donum Vitae' and Gamete Intra-Fallopian Tube Transfer," *Linacre Quarterly* 57.2 (May 1989), 68-79; Benedict Ashley, O.P., and Kevin O'Rourke, O.P., *Health Care Ethics: A Theological Analysis* (4th ed.: Washington, DC: Georgetown University Press, 1997), pp. 242-247; Germain Grisez, *Difficult Moral Questions*, Vol. 3 of *The Way of the Lord Jesus* (Quincy, IL: Franciscan Press, 1997), pp. 244-249; reprinted Alba House, now available online at http://www.twotlj.org/.

57. See Grisez, *Difficult Moral Questions*, p. 248; Orville N. Griese, *Catholic Identity in Health Care: Principles and Practice* (Braintree, MA: Pope John XXIII Medical-Moral Research and Education Center, 1987), pp. 443-444; John W. Carlson, "Interventions upon Gametes in Assisting the Conjugal Act toward Fertilization," in *Infertility: A Crossroad of Faith, Medicine, and Technology*, pp. 110-111; Tonti-Filippini, " 'Donum Vitae' and Gamete Intra-Fallopian Tube Transfer," 70.

58. This seems to me to be the position of Grisez, Griese, and Carlson (see preceding endnote for bibliographical details).

59. On this, see Doerfler, *Assisting or Replacing the Conjugal Act*, pp. 89ff.

60. Two Catholic theologians explicitly accepting this procedure are: O'Donnell, *Medicine and Christian Morality*, p. 238; and Griese, *Catholic Moral Identity in Health Care*, p. 46.

61. Good critiques of this procedure are provided by Grisez, *Difficult Moral Questions*, pp. 247-249; Tonti-Filippini, " 'Donum Vitae' and Gamete Intra-fallopian Tube Transfer."

62. The most extensive and initially plausible defense of GIFT is given by Peter J. Cataldo. His most detailed effort to justify it is found in his essay, "The Newest Reproductive Technologies: Applying Catholic Teaching," in *The Gospel of Life and the Vision of Health Care*, ed. Russell Smith (Braintree, MA: Pope John XXIII Medical-Moral Research and Education Center, 1996), pp. 61-94. A briefer presentation of his argument is given in "Reproductive Technologies," *Ethics & Medics* 21.1 (January 1996), 1-3. See also Donald McCarthy, "Infertility Bypass," *Ethics & Medics* 8.10 (October 1983), 1-2; McCarthy, "Catholic Moral Teaching and TOT/GIFT: A Response to Donald T. DeMarco, in *Reproductive Technologies, Marriage, and the Church*, pp. 140-145; Griese, *Catholic Identity in Health Care*, pp. 47-49.

63. For Doerfler, in addition to the study referred to in endnote 52, see his "Is GIFT Compatible with the Teaching of Donum Vitae?" *Linacre Quarterly* 64.1 (February 1997), 41-47. See also Grisez, *Difficult Moral Questions*, pp. 246-248; Tonti-Filippini, " 'Donum Vitae' and Gamete Intra-fallopian Tube Transfer," 68-89; DeMarco, "Catholic Moral Teaching and TOT/GIFT," in *Reproductive Technologies, Marriage, and the Church*, pp. 122-140; Ashley/O'Rourke, *Health Care Ethics*, pp. 246-247; Seifert, "Substitution of the Conjugal Act or Assistance to It?"

64. Personal letter from Thomas W. Hilgers, M.D., June 9, 1999. He has developed the *Creighton Model Fertility/Care System* for helping married couples experiencing difficulties in conceiving.

65. L. A. Schieve, et al., "Low and Very Low Birth Weight in Infants Conceived with Use of Assisted Reproductive Technology," *New England Journal of Medicine* 346 (2002), 731-737.

66. B. Stromberg, et al., "Neurological Sequelae in Children Born after In-Vitro Fertilization: A Population-Based Study," *The Lancet* 359 (2002), 461-465.

67. M. Hansen, et al., "The Risk of Major Birth Defects after Intracytoplasmic Sperm Injection and In Vitro Fertilization," *New England Journal of Medicine* 346.10 (2002), 725-730.

68. G. Koren, "Adverse Effects of Assisted Reproductive Technology and Pregnancy Outcome," *Pediatric Research* (2002).

69. http://www.mercatornet.com/articles/view/charge_of_heart.

70. *The National Catholic Bioethics Quarterly*, "Symposium on *Dignitas Personae*," edited by E. Christian Brugger, includes an essay ("The 'Various Problems' Presented by Embryo Adoption," no. 19) by Luke Gormally, in which he presents an argument that *Dignitas personae*, properly understood, does regard embryo adoption as intrinsically evil, although he admits that the text "does not offer well-defined teaching." It also includes an essay ("Understanding *Dignitas Personae* on Embryo Adoption") by John Finnis offering an argument to the contrary. But of greater significance than either of these worthwhile essays is the statement issued by the United States Conference of Catholic Bishops: "The document [*Dignitas personae*] raises cautions or problems about these new issues but does not formally make a definitive judgment against them" (United States Conference of Catholic Bishops, Questions and Answers on *Dignitas personae*, http://www.usccb.org/issues-and-action/marriage-and-family/natural-family -planning/upload/nfp-forum-newsletter-winter-spring-2009.pdf). This means that the issue is still open for debate and discussion by Catholic scholars loyal to the Magisterium.

CHAPTER FOUR

Contraception and Respect for Human Life

Introduction

In this revised edition I have entirely rewritten Part 6, "Condoms and the Prevention of HIV," in order to present and comment on the book *Light of the World: The Pope, the Church and the Signs of the Times*, by Benedict XVI and Peter Seewald, on the use of condoms by spouses to prevent AIDS. I have also sought to strengthen some arguments to show the moral evil of contraception and added a final section on Elaine Tyler May's 2010 book commemorating the fiftieth anniversary of the discovery of the pill. In her book, May, a champion of contraception, was compelled to acknowledge that today many women *and their gynecologists* reject oils, IUDs, diaphragms, condoms, etc. and instead use the "Fertility Awareness Method" (= NFP), and one major reason is that it requires women to talk to their husbands about this, fostering deeper communication between spouses and leading husbands to have a more mature love for their wives.

Contraception is usually considered an issue in sexual ethics rather than one proper to bioethics. But, as I hope to show here, contraception is very much relevant to respect for human life inasmuch as it is not, of itself, a *sexual* act but rather an *anti-life* kind of act. It is indeed the "gateway to abortion"; widespread social acceptance of contraception has led to the culture of death described by John Paul II in his encyclical *Evangelium vitae*.

The suggestion that contraception is "anti-life" and has led to the culture of death will offend many people, both Catholic and non-Catholic, who do not regard contraception as an anti-life kind of act and who can see no connection whatsoever between contraception and the culture of death. Most people in our society, Catholics and non-Catholics, regard contraception by married persons as "natural." It is the obvious thing to do if there are good reasons for avoiding a pregnancy; and the suggestion that there is a link between contraception and the culture of death is considered outrageous, in particular by married couples who are "pro-life" but nonetheless believe that there is nothing wrong with contraception.

This is illustrated by some of the contributors to the December 1998 symposium on contraception in the journal *First Things*. Gilbert Meilaender, a Lutheran theologian known widely for his opposition to abortion, and Philip Turner, an Anglican theologian also "on the side of life," in their joint contribution expressed the view that "contraceptive intercourse may sometimes be a fitting means by which husband and wife aim to nourish simultaneously the procreative and unitive purposes of their marriage."[1] Similarly, the editor of *First Things*, James Nuechterlein, reflecting on the symposium in a subsequent number of the journal, began by observing that he and his wife did not want children immediately because of their circumstances, although, had she become pregnant, "we would not for a moment have considered abortion. But," he continued,

> neither for a moment did we morally hesitate to practice contraception. We no more debated whether we would use contraception than we debated whether we would, in the fullness of time, have children. Of course we would someday, God willing, have children; in the meantime we would practice (non-abortifacient) contraception. This was not, for us, a matter of presuming on God's providence. It seemed rather a right use of reason in fulfilling the various goods of our marriage. We intended both the unitive and the procreative goods of marriage, but not necessarily both in every act of love.[2]

Concluding, Nuechterlein said: "The point of this self-revelation is to suggest how utterly typical that view was and is. There is nothing singular in our experience. I believe it is, mutatis mutandis, the experience of most Protestant couples of our generation and after."[3]

Note that Nuechterlein refers to the common experience of contemporary *Protestants* (and this, seemingly, was also in the mind of Meilaender and Turner). However, it is no doubt true that a great majority of Catholic couples agree with these writers. On reading their essays, in fact, I was reminded of the views set forth in the celebrated "Majority Papers" of the Papal Commission on Population, the Family, and Natality.[4] Two passages from these papers — to which I will return later for closer examination — seem in particular to express the view articulated by these contributors to *First Things*.

In one passage, the Majority justify contraception by married couples as an intelligent use of reason to control biological nature:

> The true opposition is not to be sought between some material conformity to the physiological processes of nature and some artificial intervention. For it is natural for man to use his skill in order to put under human control what is given by physical nature. The opposition is to be sought really between one way of acting which is contraceptive [in the sense of selfishly excluding children from marriage] and opposed to a prudent and generous fruitfulness, and another way which is in an ordered relationship to responsible fruitfulness and which has a concern for education and all the essential human and Christian values.[5]

In another passage, they justify the use of contraception by married couples by distinguishing between individual acts of sexual union within marriage and the totality of the marriage. According to them,

> When man interferes with the procreative purpose of individual acts by contracepting, he does this with the intention of regulating and not excluding fertility. Then he unites the material finality toward fecundity which exists in intercourse with the formal finality of the person and renders the entire process human. Conjugal acts which by intention are infertile or which are rendered infertile are ordered to the expression of the union of love; that love, however, reaches its culmination in fertility responsibly accepted. For that reason other acts of union are in a certain sense incomplete, and they receive their full moral quality with ordination toward the fertile act. Infertile conjugal acts constitute a totality with fertile acts and have a single moral specification.[6]

The "single moral specification" of such acts, as the Majority make clear, is "the fostering of love responsibly toward a generous fecundity."

In this view, what married couples who use contraception as a way of spacing children *in* their marriage and not of excluding them *from* their marriage are doing is simply using appropriate means for nourishing both the procreative and unitive purposes of marriage. This is their "intention" — as Meilaender/Turner and Nuechterlein indicate in the passages previously cited — and surely this intention is not immoral.

This way of viewing the use of contraception by married couples who have serious reasons to avoid having children, at least for a time, is quite common in our society. Many, Catholic and non-Catholic alike, who hold it regard abortion with horror, and they also unambiguously judge sex outside of marriage to be immoral. But they can see nothing wrong with the "responsible" use of contraception within marriage, nor do they believe that there is some inexorable link between contraception and the culture of death.

This widely held view, however, is mistaken. For centuries, Christian writers regarded contraception as an "anti-life" kind of act. In fact, one of the contributors to the *First Things* symposium, Alicia Mosier, an editorial assistant of the journal, forcefully expressed this view. She began by emphasizing that the issue does not center on the "artificiality" of the means used to prevent conception but with the nature of contraception itself. As she said, "what is wrong is contraception itself: the deliberate will, the choice, to subvert the life-giving order and meaning of the conjugal act."[7] Commenting on Pope Paul's description of contraception as "every action ... which proposes ... to render procreation impossible,"[8] she wrote:

> Proposing to render procreation impossible means, simply put, willing directly against the order of intercourse and consequently against life.... Couples who contracept introduce a countermeasure ... whose sole purpose is to make it impossible for a new life to come to be. Contraception is an act that can only express the will that *any* baby that might result from *this* sexual encounter not be conceived.... [I]t manifests a will aimed directly against new life.[9]

Mosier's way of expressing this view echoes the argument against contraception mounted by Germain Grisez, Joseph Boyle, John Finnis, and me in 1988.[10] But, as noted already, she articulates a position that was traditional in the Church, both East and West, both Catholic and Protestant, from the early days of Christianity to the mid-twentieth century. It is found in such Church Fathers as John Chrysostom, Ambrose, and Jerome; in medieval theologians such as Thomas Aquinas; in the canon law operative in the Roman Catholic Church from the mid-thirteenth century until 1917; in the thought of reformers such as John Calvin; and in the teaching of the *Roman Catechism*, popularly known as the *Catechism of the Council of Trent*. There is no need here to recapitulate this tradition. In the accompanying note, I cite representative witnesses.[11] There is thus a long and respected Christian tradition that judges contraception to be anti-life, expressing a will that is indeed at the heart of the culture of death.

Here I will show why contraception is intimately related to the culture of death and, indeed, is the gateway to this culture. I will begin by considering

Pope John Paul II's thought regarding the roots of the culture of death and his way of relating contraception to that culture. I will then take up his claim that the difference, anthropological and moral, between contraception and recourse to the rhythm of the cycle is enormous and involves ultimately "irreconcilable concepts of the human person and of human sexuality." This section will show that the acceptance of contraception is based on a dualistic anthropology of the human person and a consequentialist/proportionalist understanding of the morality of human acts: an anthropology and moral perspective central to the culture of death. This section will likewise show how confusing and misleading talk about "intentions" can be. I will follow this with an analysis of the human act of contraception to show that it is and cannot not be anti-life, and that this is *the* reason why contraception is indeed the gateway to the culture of death. In conclusion, I will consider contraception as an act both anti-love and anti-life, utterly incompatible with the culture of life and the "civilization of love." In an appendix, I will briefly consider the morality of seeking to prevent conception if a woman is in danger of being raped or has already suffered this violence to herself. I will integrate more recent scientific studies demonstrating that NFP is more effective than contraception in helping a married couple avoid causing a pregnancy if there is serious reason to do so and how NFP can help a married couple achieve a pregnancy when there are no grave reasons for not causing one. I shall also show how, in her 2010 book celebrating the fiftieth anniversary of the pill, *America and the Pill: History of Promise, Peril, and Liberation*, Elaine Tyler May (an ardent champion of contraception) was compelled to include a section in which many women and their gynecologists lauded the "Fertility Awareness Method" (= NFP) both because it was more effective than contraception *and* because it made the women discuss the issue with their husbands and in this way strengthened their marriage. An appendix treats contraception to avoid getting pregnant after rape.

1. Pope John Paul II on the Roots of the Culture of Death and Contraception's Relationship to It

In the first chapter of his encyclical *Evangelium vitae*, Pope John Paul II identifies two roots of the culture of death. This culture, he says, is rooted first of all in the "mentality which *carries the concept of subjectivity to an extreme* and even distorts it, and recognizes as a subject of rights only the person who enjoys full or at least incipient autonomy and who emerges from a state of total dependence on others" (no. 19). It is rooted, secondly, in a "*notion of freedom* which exalts the isolated individual in an absolute way" (no. 19).

Of these two roots, the first is most relevant for showing the relationship of contraception to the culture of death. At its heart is the idea that only those members of the human species who enjoy at least "incipient autonomy," i.e., individuals with exercisable capacities of reasoning and will, are *truly* persons with rights that ought to be recognized by society. This mentality, John Paul II points out, "tends to *equate personal dignity with the capacity for verbal and explicit*, or at least perceptible, *communication*" (no. 19). On this view a "person" is preeminently a subject aware of itself as a self and capable of relating to other selves; and not all members of the human species are persons in this understanding of "person." This idea, as will be seen later, fits in well with the anthropology underlying the acceptance of contraception.

In the first chapter of *Evangelium vitae*, John Paul II also discusses the relationship between contraception and abortion, whose justification and legalization is, of course, a hallmark of the culture of death. To the common claim that contraception, "if made safe and available to all, is the most effective remedy against abortion," John Paul II replied:

> When looked at carefully, this objection is clearly unfounded. It may be that many people use contraception with a view to excluding the subsequent temptation of abortion. But the negative values inherent in the "contraceptive mentality" — which is very different from responsible parenthood, lived in respect for the full truth of the conjugal act — are such that they in fact strengthen this temptation when an unwanted life is conceived.... Certainly, from the moral point of view contraception and abortion are *specifically different* evils: the former contradicts the full truth of the sexual act as the proper expression of conjugal love, whereas the latter destroys the life of a human being; the former is opposed to the virtue of chastity in marriage, the latter is opposed to the virtue of justice and directly violates the divine commandment "You shall not kill." (no. 13)

It is important to emphasize that here John Paul II does *not*, as did the long Christian tradition noted above, identify contraception as an "anti-life" kind of act, akin to murder. He rather characterizes it as an "anti-love" kind of act, one that, as he says elsewhere, "falsifies" the meaning of the conjugal act as one in which the spouses give themselves unreservedly to one another.[12] But he nonetheless insists that despite their differences "contraception and abortion are often closely connected, as fruits of the same tree," and he points out that the close link between the two "is being demonstrated in an alarming way by the development of chemical products, intrauterine devices and vaccines which, distributed with the same ease as contraceptives, really act as abortifacients in the very early stages of the development of the life of a new human being" (no. 13).

John Paul II obviously sees a real and substantive link between contraception and abortion and — through it — the culture of death. But he does not here *directly* relate contraception to the culture of death. For him, contraception directly violates marital chastity and not the good of human life.

2. Contraception vs. "Recourse to the Rhythm of the Cycle": Their Anthropological and Moral Differences, One Ultimately Entailing "Irreconcilable Concepts of the Human Person and of Human Sexuality"

In his apostolic exhortation on the *Role of the Christian Family in the Modern World* (*Familiaris consortio*), Pope John Paul II made the following bold claim:

> In the light of the experience of many couples and the data provided by the different human sciences, theological reflection is able to perceive and is called to study further *the difference, both anthropological and moral,* between contraception and recourse to the rhythm of the cycle: it is a difference which is much wider and deeper than is usually thought, one which involves in the final analysis *two irreconcilable concepts of the human person and of human sexuality.* (no. 32)[13]

Perhaps many people who *practice* contraception — and many who *practice* periodic abstinence — are not consciously aware of the difference between these two ways of exercising responsible parenthood, but the difference is profound. I will show this by examining the rationale used to defend the legitimacy of contraception in order to disclose its underlying anthropology and moral methodology. I will then contrast this by presenting the anthropology and moral methodology on which the practice of natural family planning or periodic abstinence or what John Paul II calls here "recourse to the rhythm of the cycle" is based.

A. Contraception: Its Underlying Anthropology and Moral Methodology

A dualistic understanding of the human person and of human sexuality is at the heart of the defense of contraception. This anthropology regards the body as an instrument of the person, a good for the person insofar as it is a necessary condition for goods and values intrinsic to the person; the latter, so-called personalistic goods and values, are those whose existence depends on their being consciously experienced. This anthropology underlies several key arguments given to support contraception, in particular, the argument defending contraception as the exercise of intelligent human dominion over nature and the argument justifying it on the basis that it is in harmony with the nature of *human* sexuality.

Several passages from the Majority documents of the Papal Commission illustrate the first line of reasoning, based on humankind's dominion over the world of nature. I cited one of these at the beginning of this chapter, in which the authors stressed that "it is natural for man to use his skill in order to put under human control what is given by physical nature."[14] In another passage they declare that, "in the matter at hand," namely, contraception,

> there is a certain change in the mind of contemporary man. He feels that he is more conformed to his rational nature, created by God with liberty and responsibility, when he uses his skill to intervene in the biological pro-cesses of nature so that he can achieve the institution of matrimony in the conditions of actual life, than if he would abandon himself to chance.[15]

In yet another passage, the Majority emphasized that "it is proper to man, created in the image of God, to use what is given in physical nature in a way that he may develop it to its full significance with a view to the good of the whole person."[16]

These passages make it clear that those defending contraception con-sider the biological fertility of human persons and the biological processes involved in the generation of new human life as physical or biological "giv-ens." Human fertility, in other words, is part of the world of subhuman or subpersonal nature over which persons have been given dominion. The majority theologians of the Papal Commission, in fact, assert that "biologi-cal fertility ... ought to be assumed into the human sphere and be regulated within it."[17] Obviously, if the biological fecundity of human persons is intrin-sically human, it does not need to be "assumed into the human sphere." Nothing assumes what it already is or has of itself. This passage is a clear assertion of dualism.

In other words, in this view human fertility is in and of itself a biological given belonging to the physical, not human, world over which the person has been given dominion. Biological givens, such as fertility, confront the person who is to control and regulate them by "assuming" them into the human and personal sphere, i.e., by making use of them when they serve "personalist" goods and by suppressing or impeding them when their continued flourishing inhibits participation in these goods, whose existence, as noted already, depends on their being consciously experienced.

The notion that human biological fertility is, of itself, subhuman and subpersonal is closely related to the understanding of human sexuality central to the defense of contraception. One of the major reasons for changing Church teaching on the matter, the majority theologians argued, is the "changed estimation of the value and meaning of human sexuality," one leading to a "better, deeper, and more correct understanding of conjugal life and the conjugal act."[18] According to this understanding, *human* sexuality, as distinct from *animal* sexuality, is above all relational or unitive in character. As one theologian put it, "the most profound meaning of human sexuality is that it is a relational reality, having a special significance for the person in his relationships."[19] Human sexuality, as some other theological defenders of contraception contend, "is preeminently ... the mode whereby an isolated subjectivity [= person] reaches out to communion with another subject. Embodied subjectivity reaches out to another body-subject in order to banish loneliness and to experience the fullness of being-with-another in the human project."[20]

Proponents of this understanding of human sexuality acknowledge that human sexual union can be procreative — or, to use the term that the more secularistic of them prefer, "reproductive." Yet in addition to these "biological" needs, sexual union serves other, more personal values, those, namely, whose existence depends on their being consciously experienced. The fact that such union, at times, results in the conception of a new human being has, in the past and even today, frequently inhibited the realization of these more personal purposes. But today — and this is *the* important consideration — it is possible through efficient methods of contraception to sever the connection between the procreative and unitive or relational dimensions of human sexuality.

The more radical, secularistic proponents of contraception sever this connection totally. As George Gilder so perceptively observed over a quarter of a century ago,

> The members of the sex coalition go well beyond a mere search for better contraceptives. They are not satisfied merely to control the biological tie between intercourse and childbirth. They also want to eliminate

the psychological and symbolic connections. . . . By far the most frequent and durably important long-term use of sex, they would say, is the fulfillment of the physical and psychological need for orgasmic pleasure and the communication of affection. For these purposes, sex is most adaptable if it is not connected with procreation, if it is regarded as a completely separate mode of activity.[21]

It cannot be denied that many people in the Western (and increasingly the non-Western) world regard the emergence of contraceptive technologies as a truly liberating event. They believe that the effective use of contraceptives enables human persons to liberate the *personal* and *human* purposes of sexuality and of genital intercourse from the tyranny of biology. Many today would agree with the claim of the well-known British writer Ashley Montagu that

> [t]he pill provides a dependable means of controlling conception. . . . [T]he pill makes it possible to render every individual of reproductive age completely responsible for both his sexual and his reproductive behavior. *It is necessary to be unequivocally clear concerning the distinction between sexual behavior and reproductive behavior.* Sexual behavior may have no purpose other than pleasure . . . without the slightest intent of reproducing, or it may be indulged in for both pleasure and reproduction.[22]

The majority theologians of the Papal Commission, and Protestant authors such as Meilaender, Turner, and Nuechterlein, would not go so far as Montagu and other secular supporters of contraception and sever completely the bond between the unitive and procreative meanings of human sexuality. Nonetheless, they deem the relational or unitive meaning its *personal,* as distinct from its procreative or *biological,* significance, the latter needing to be assumed into consciousness in order to become human and personal. Coupling this understanding of human sexuality with the dominion that human persons have over their biological fertility, they contend that if the continued flourishing of biological fecundity inhibits the expression of the relational or unitive meaning of sexuality, it is then licit to suppress this "biological given" so that the *personal,* relational good of sexuality can be realized. They do not want to sever the bond between the unitive (personal) and procreative (biological) meaning of our sexuality for the *whole* of the marriage, but they think it proper intentionally to separate them in *individual acts* if doing so is thought necessary for serving the procreative-unitive meaning of marriage as a whole. Biological fertility is, for them, a lesser good

— a good *for* the person (something like a coat), not a good *of* the person. For them, goods *of* the person are goods whose existence depends on being consciously experienced. Since fertility does not so depend, it is not this kind of a good. On the other hand, they consider the union made possible by sexual coition — the unitive or relational aspect of our sexuality — to be a good *of* the person because its existence and flourishing depends on being consciously experienced.

The foregoing has clearly shown the dualistic anthropology and understanding of the human person and of human sexuality crucial to major arguments used to justify contraception. This anthropology distinguishes the person, i.e., the conscious subject of experiences (or, as John Paul II noted in *Evangelium vitae*, no. 19, the subject having "the capacity for verbal and explicit, or at least perceptible, communication"), from the *body* that this person uses, now for this purpose, now for that. If the person is really not his or her own body, then the person's sexuality can be "liberated" from regulation by biological laws and used for "interpersonal communication" or the "fostering of conjugal love."

This anthropology or understanding of the human person is central to the culture of death. For, if the person is not his or her own body, then, as Germain Grisez has noted, "the destruction of the life of the body is not directly and in itself an attack on a value intrinsic to the human person." Continuing, he said:

> The lives of the unborn, the lives of those not fully in possession of themselves — the hopelessly insane and the "vegetating" senile — and the lives of those who no longer can engage in praxis or problem solving, become lives no longer meaningful, no longer valuable, no longer inviolable.[23]

The dualistic anthropology that has led to the justification of abortion on the grounds that the life thus taken, while "biologically" human, is not "meaningfully" human or the life of a "person," and to the justification of euthanasia on the grounds that it serves the needs of the "person" when biological life becomes a burden, is thus definitely operative in the ideology behind contraception, even if this is not acknowledged by many.

I turn now to consider the *moral methodology* employed in the justification of contraception, in particular, contraception by married couples. This methodology is clearly evident in the argument based on the distinction between individual or "isolated" marital acts and marriage as a whole or totality. This argument acknowledges (as Montagu and the most secular advocates of contraception do not) that procreation is indeed a good of marriage, and that marriage and children go together. But, this argument claims, the procreative good of marriage is properly respected and honored even when individual acts of marriage are deliberately made infertile, as long as those acts are ordered to the expression of love and to a generous fecundity within the marriage as a whole.

It will be useful here to review this very illuminating passage. It reads:

> When man interferes with the procreative purpose of individual acts by contracepting, he does this with the intention of regulating and not excluding fertility. Then he unites the material finality toward fecundity which exists in intercourse with the formal finality of the person and renders the entire process human. . . . Conjugal acts which by intention are infertile or which are rendered infertile are ordered to the expression of the union of love; that love, however, reaches its culmination in fertility responsibly accepted. For that reason other acts of union are in a certain sense incomplete, and they receive their full moral quality with ordination toward the fertile act. . . . Infertile conjugal acts constitute a totality with fertile acts and have a single moral specification.[24]

The "single moral specification" or moral object of this totality is the fostering of love responsibly toward a generous fecundity.

Note that this passage considers "recourse to the rhythm of the cycle" or periodic abstinence as simply another way of contracepting; it equates "acts which by intention are infertile," that is, marital acts chosen while the wife is not fertile, and acts "which are rendered infertile." The authors, in other words, see absolutely no *moral* difference between contraception and "recourse to the cycle." The latter is simply another way of contracepting.[25] They do so because they consider the moral "intentions" to be the same in both cases. Their "intention" is to avoid a pregnancy, perhaps for very serious and good reasons. I will return to this issue below.

The central claim of this passage is that the moral object specifying what couples who "responsibly" contracept individual acts of marital congress are doing is "fostering love responsibly toward a generous fecundity." Their aim, their "intention," as Meilaender and Turner later put it in their *First Things* essay, is to "nourish simultaneously the procreative and unitive purposes of their marriage."

This claim is rooted in the idea that we can identify the moral object specifying a human act *only* by considering the act in its "totality." According to this method of making moral decisions, it is not possible to determine the moral species of an action — its "moral object" — without taking into account the "intention" or end for whose sake the choice is made along with the foreseeable consequences for the persons concerned. If one does this, so the argument goes, one can conclude that, if the choice to contracept individual acts is directed to the end of nourishing conjugal love so that the good of procreation can also be served, then one can rightly say that *what* the spouses are doing — the *moral object* of their choice — is to foster conjugal love toward a generous fecundity, obviously something good, not bad.

But this reasoning is specious. It is so because it *redescribes* the contraceptive act, in fact, a whole series of contraceptive acts, in terms of hoped-for benefits. The *remote* or *further* end for whose sake the couple contracepts individual acts of sexual union may indeed be to nourish simultaneously the unitive and procreative goods of marriage. This end is indeed "intended," and this end, this "intention," is good. "Intended" also, however, is the *choice* to contracept — and the couple cannot *not choose*, cannot *not intend*, to contracept. But this specious moral reasoning conceals this "moral object." This reasoning, moreover, relies on a faulty understanding of the marital *act*. According to this reasoning, which redescribes the spouses' behavior in terms of hoped-for benefits, the marital act is intended to foster love between spouses, to unite them. But it is not, as such, intended to be open to the gift of life; rather the marriage *as a whole* in which particular acts occur is so intended. Its proponents would surely hold that spouses ought not, in choosing to unite genitally, freely intend to set aside its unitive dimension. Why, then, do they hold that they can freely intend, in uniting genitally, to set aside its procreative dimension? They can do so only because, as we have seen, they regard this dimension as merely "biological," a "lesser" good than the "personal" good of being sexually united.

The moral methodology used, in other words, is consequentialistic. It fails to recognize that the morality of human acts, as we saw in Chapter Two and as John Paul II has so correctly said, "depends primarily and fundamentally on the 'object' rationally chosen by the deliberate will."[26] With respect to contraception, that object is *not* "to foster love responsibly toward a generous fecundity" or to nourish simultaneously the unitive and procreative goods of marriage. Precisely what this object is will be taken up below. My point here is that the consequentialist moral reasoning used in this central argument to justify contraception is plausible only because it redescribes the object of choice — contraception — in terms of the hoped-for benefits of contracepting individual acts of sexual union.

We have now seen the anthropology and moral methodology underlying the defense of contraception. The anthropology, a dualistic one, regards the person primarily as a subject of enduring experiences who uses his or her body now for this purpose, now for that. It likewise locates the *human* and *personal* meaning of human sexuality in its *relational* significance, i.e., its ability to allow two subjects of enduring experiences to enter into deep interpersonal union, while regarding the *procreative* meaning of human sexuality as of itself subpersonal, part of the subhuman world of nature over which the person has been given dominion. This anthropology, as has been shown, is central to the culture of death.

The moral methodology employed is a form of consequentialism or proportionalism, one that redescribes chosen deeds in terms of their hoped-for benefits and by doing so conceals their true nature. This moral methodology is also central to the specious rationalizations used to justify the killings characteristic of the culture of death. Thus abortion is not recognized as the intentional killing of an unborn child but is rather redescribed as an act protecting the mother's health or the family's stability or something of this kind; rather than being called killing, euthanasia is redescribed as helping persons to die with dignity, etc.

B. Recourse to the Rhythm of the Cycle: Its Underlying Anthropology and Moral Methodology

The anthropology supporting the practice of periodic continence as the way to harmonize the requirements of conjugal love with respect for the good of procreation is holistic; i.e., it regards the human person as a unity of body and soul. The person is, in the unity of body and soul, the subject of moral actions.[27] According to this anthropology, the body and bodily life are integral to the person, are goods *of* the person, not merely *for* the person.

Human persons are, in other words, body persons. When God created man, he did not, as some dualistic-minded defenders of contraception claim, create "an isolated subjectivity … who experiences existence in [either] a female body-structure … [or] a male body-structure."[28] Quite to the contrary, God, in creating *human* persons, created bodily, sexual persons: "male and female he created them" (Gn 1:27). The human body expresses the human person; and since the human body is inescapably either male or female, it expresses a man-person or a woman-person. Precisely because of their sexual differences, manifest in their bodies, the man-person and the woman-person can give themselves to each other bodily. Moreover, since the body, male or female, is the expression of a human person, a man and a woman, in giving their bodies to each other, give their *persons* to each other. The bodily gift of a man and a woman to each other is the outward sign, the sacrament, of the *communion of persons* existing between them. The body is, therefore, the means and the sign of the gift of the male-person to the female-person. Pope John Paul II calls this capacity of the body to express the communion of persons the *nuptial meaning* of the body.[29]

In addition, human fertility or fecundity is *not* some subhuman, subpersonal aspect of human sexuality. As Vatican Council II clearly affirms, "Man's sexuality and the faculty of generating life wondrously surpass the lower forms of life" (*Gaudium et spes*, no. 51). Pope John Paul II pointedly observes that human fertility "is directed to the generation of a human being, and so by its nature it surpasses the purely biological order and involves a whole series of personal values" (*Familiaris consortio*, no. 11). The procreative meaning of human sexuality, in this non-dualistic anthropology, is *not* subhuman or subpersonal, in need of "being assumed" into the human. It is human and personal to begin with.

The rationale supporting recourse to the rhythm of the cycle does not judge the morality of human acts in terms of hoped-for results or of the anticipated overall proportion of good and evil that will come about. It holds, rather, that the morality of human actions depends on both the *end intended* and the *object chosen* and, because chosen, also *intended*. It distinguishes between the ulterior or remote end for whose sake one chooses to do *this*, and the proximate or immediate end, which is precisely the freely chosen object. Both end intended and object chosen must be morally good, i.e., in conformity with right reason; if either is not in accord with the truth, then the entire action is vitiated. But the primary source of the morality of the act is, as noted above, the "object" freely and rationally chosen by the acting subject. This is precisely *what one chooses to do*. The moral methodology underlying the practice of contraception ignores this object, the immediate end of one's choice to do *this* here and now, and focuses on the remote end or further intention of the act, i.e., the reason one chooses to do this here and now. As we have seen, this consequentialist methodology conceals and keeps hidden from view the precise object of one's freely chosen act and *redescribes* it in terms of its hoped-for benefits, the remote end intended by the acting person, the object of one's "further" intention.

The non-consequentialist way of making moral judgments on which recourse to the rhythm of the cycle is based recognizes, as Pope John Paul II emphasizes, "that there are objects of the human act which are by their nature 'incapable of being ordered' to God, because they radically contradict the good of the person made in his image." Continuing, the Pope says:

> These are the acts which, in the Church's moral tradition, have been termed "intrinsically evil" (*intrinsece malum*); they are such *always and per se,* in other words, on account of their very object, and apart from the ulterior intentions of the one acting and the circumstances. (*Veritatis splendor*, no. 80)

We need now to examine the moral object specifying the act of contraception in order to show that it is indeed an anti-life kind of act.

3. Contraception: An Anti-Life Act

In order to pass moral judgment on contraception, it is first necessary to know precisely of what we are speaking. It is essential to provide an accurate description of the kind of human act an act of contraception is and then to judge whether it is a human act in accordance with right reason, with the truth, and, if not, why not.

We have seen already that human acts are specified primarily by the "object" freely and rationally chosen by the deliberate will. But what is the "object" freely chosen in contraception? Pope Paul VI offers a good description when he says that the Church's teaching on the immorality of contraception excludes "every action, whether in anticipation of the conjugal act, or in its accomplishment, or in the development of its natural consequences, [that] proposes [the Latin text reads *intendat*], either as end or as means, to impede procreation [here the Latin text reads: *ut procreatio impediatur*]" (*Humanae vitae*, no. 14). Paul here refers to the conjugal act, since his encyclical was concerned with contraception by married couples. But, if "conjugal act" is changed to "genital act," Paul's description accurately identifies the "object" morally specifying an act as contraceptive, whether within marriage or not.

As this description shows, the object freely chosen and willed by someone who engages in an act of contraception is precisely to impede the beginning of a new human life or to impede procreation. It is reasonable to think that a certain kind of behavior — genital behavior — is one in and through which new human life can come to be. If one does not want that life to come to be, perhaps for very good reasons (e.g., the woman's health, inability to properly care for a new baby, etc.), one therefore chooses to do something to impede the beginning of the new human life that one believes that genital behavior might initiate. If one did not reasonably think that this kind of behavior — genital behavior — could result in the beginning of a new human life, one would have no reason to contracept. If one wanted that life to come to be, obviously one would not contracept in order to impede its beginning. Contraception makes sense, i.e., is an *intelligible* human act, only because one does not want new human life to come into existence as a result of another kind of human activity, namely, genital activity. As Mosier so well put it in the essay cited early in this work, "contraception is an act that can only express the will that *any* baby that might result from *this* sexual encounter not be conceived.... [I]t [thus] manifests a will aimed directly against new life."[30]

This analysis of the object specifying an act as one of contraception makes it clear that contraception, although related to genital/sexual acts, is not itself a sexual or genital act. Fornication, adultery, masturbation, and marital coition are sexual/genital acts. But if a fornicating couple, an adulterous couple, or a married couple contracept, they choose to do something distinct from the genital act they likewise choose to engage in. In other words, they choose (a) to engage in genital coition and (b) to do something prior to, during, or subsequent to their freely chosen genital coition precisely to impede procreation, i.e., to impede the beginning of the new human life that they reasonably believe could begin in and through the freely chosen genital coition. The act specified by the second choice, (b), is the act of contraception. It is not even necessary for the person who contracepts to engage in genital coition. For instance, suppose a father provides a home for his newly married daughter and her husband. His daughter and her husband abhor contraception, deeming it a grave moral evil. They would never contracept, although perhaps they plan to practice periodic continence until they can move into their own quarters. But the girl's father, in order to make sure that she does not conceive while living in his house, regularly puts contraceptive pills into his daughter's cereal in the morning. He is the one who is choosing to contracept, not his daughter.[31]

Since the contraceptive act is distinct from any sexual act to which it is related, it cannot be considered a part or element of a sexual act and justified on the alleged grounds that it is merely a part of a larger whole, for instance, the marital or conjugal act. This, in essence, is what the specious argument considered above seeks to do, namely, to justify contraception as simply an aspect of a totality of marital acts that nourish both the unitive and procreative goods of marriage. But, as has now been made clear, contraception is not a part or aspect of any marital act or series thereof; it is a distinct kind of human act, specified by the choice to impede the beginning of new human life, either as an end or as a means to some further end, one perhaps good in itself.

Since contraception is specified precisely by the choice to impede the beginning of new human life, it is an anti-life kind of act, one expressing a contra-life will. It is precisely because contraception is specified by a contra-life will that it was, as we saw earlier, regarded for centuries as analogous to homicide by Christian writers. This analogy, a contemporary author rightly says, "no longer surprises us if we look not exclusively at the material nature of the behaviour in the two cases [contraception and homicide], but rather at the intention or movement of the will that has recourse to contraception. Ultimately, in fact, the decision is rationalized and motivated by the judgment: 'It is not good that a new human person should exist.' "[32] Contraception is always seriously wrong because it is always gravely immoral to adopt by choice the proposal to damage, destroy, or impede the good of human life.

If the contraception fails and a child is conceived despite the steps taken deliberately to prevent its life from beginning, the child comes to be as an "unwanted" child. This does not mean that those who sought to prevent his or her conception will now resort to abortion — for they may resolutely have set their hearts and minds against abortion, as did Nuechterlein and his wife, as we have seen. But one can hardly say that a child conceived despite efforts to prevent its conception is a "wanted child." Its initial status is that of an unwanted child and is so because its parents have intentionally done something to "unwant" it, namely, to contracept, to impede the beginning of its life.

This is not true of couples who have "recourse to the rhythm of the cycle" or to periodic abstinence and who avoid irresponsibly causing a pregnancy by abstaining from the marital act at times when they believe that the wife is fertile and hence could conceive.[33] It is true that, like a contracepting couple, they do not "want" to have a child in the sense that they do not, for good reasons, want to cause a pregnancy. But not wanting to have a child in this sense is quite different from not wanting to have the child one could have as a result of *this freely chosen act of sexual union* and then freely choosing to do something to *impede that prospective child's coming into being*. Couples who contracept do not "want" a child in this second sense, and hence if it does come to be despite their contraceptive efforts to prevent it from coming to be, it comes to be as an "unwanted" child. But a child conceived by a couple having recourse to the rhythm of the cycle does not come to be as an "unwanted" child because they have done nothing to "unwant" this particular child. He or she may be a "surprise" baby, but not an "unwanted" baby.[34]

4. Contraception: Both Anti-Love and Anti-Life

As we have seen, the principal argument proposed by John Paul II as pope against contraception is that it violates marital love and falsifies the language of the body: the natural dynamism of the conjugal act, which is ordered to the procreation and education of children and the mutual love of the spouses, is overlaid with an objectively contradictory language: a refusal to give oneself fully to the other (see *Familiaris consortio*, no. 32).[35] For John Paul II, contraception directly violates marital love and marital chastity and only indirectly is opposed to the good of human life.

This argument, which has featured prominently in John Paul II's teaching on marriage and on the malice of contraception, was well expressed by Paul Quay, S.J., in the early 1960s and has been developed by Dietrich von Hildebrand, Mary Joyce, and others.[36] I believe it true that, by contracepting, a married couple fail to give themselves to each other fully and unreservedly. Yet the "not giving" entailed is *not* the object specifying the choice to contracept, and most married couples who do contracept would vehemently deny that they are refusing to give themselves to each other. Nuechterlein, in his *First Things* article, illustrates this. He says that "if someone had told us [his wife and him] ... that we were 'withholding our fertility from one another' [or not giving themselves to one another] he would have met with blank incomprehension."[37] The "not giving" is *praeter intentionem* or outside the scope of the intentions of the married couples who are contracepting. It is, I believe, an *effect* or *consequence* of their contracepting their sexual union, but for the most part they do not consciously recognize this. It is surely *not* "the proximate end of a deliberate decision which determines the act of willing on the part of the acting person," as John Paul II himself describes the object morally specifying a human act in *Veritatis splendor*, no. 78. Indeed, contracepting married couples commonly attempt to justify their choice to contracept by claiming that contraception *is necessary* in order for them to express their love for each other. I will return to this issue later.

Although the argument summarized here is the principal one used by John Paul II to show that it is wrong for married couples to contracept, in some of his writings he has focused attention on the anti-life character of contraception. Thus, in a homily during a Mass for youth in Nairobi, Kenya, he pointed out that the fullest sign of spousal self-giving occurs when couples willingly accept children. Citing *Gaudium et spes*, no. 50, he said: "That is why *anti-life* actions such as contraception and abortion are wrong and are unworthy of good husbands and wives."[38] Moreover, writing as the philosopher Karol Wojtyla, Pope John Paul II had earlier stated that the ultimate end served by the sexual urge in human persons, men and women, "is the very existence of the [human] species. It follows therefore that that urge, on account of its very own nature, aims at the transmission of life, because on that depends the good of the human species."[39]

In addition, the human sexual urge aims at transmitting *personal* life, and the love of husband and wife, the philosopher Wojtyla argued, is shaped by this good. Indeed, as he says:

> Looked at more closely and concretely, these two persons, the man and the woman, facilitate the existence of another concrete person, their own child, blood of their blood, and flesh of their flesh. This person is at once an affirmation and a continuation of their own lives. The natural order of human existence is not in conflict with love between persons but in strict harmony with it.[40]

Thus John Paul II clearly recognizes the anti-life nature of contraception. It is both *anti-love* and *anti-life*. In his papal writings on marriage and the family, John Paul has obviously concluded that he can best persuade married couples to reject contraception by stressing its character as an act incompatible with conjugal love. And, if we think clearly about things, this is true, even if the precise "object" of contraception is to impede the beginning of new human life and *not* the "not giving of spouses to one another."

Spouses cannot contracept merely by taking thought. They do so by choosing to do something to their body-persons, and different contraceptives work in different ways to "impede procreation." I here omit discussion of devices allegedly "contraceptive" that are either definitively abortifacient (e.g., morning-after pills, Norplant, Ensure) or may "work" by preventing implantation in the event that conception occurs (e.g., the pills in use today and, for the most part, IUDs). I hence limit consideration to the so-called barrier (condoms, diaphragms, etc.) and "chemical" (spermicidal jellies and the like) methods.

Now consider this. A person does not put on gloves to touch a beloved one tenderly, unless he or she thinks that some disease may be communicated. But is pregnancy a disease? And is not the use of condoms, diaphragms, spermicidal jellies, and the like similar to putting on gloves? Do husband and wife really become "one flesh" if they must arm themselves with protective gear before "giving" themselves to each other genitally? The answers to these questions are obvious, and they help us see why the argument that contraception is anti-love and a falsification of the "language of the body" is true. Spouses who must "protect" themselves from each other in such ways are "not giving" themselves unreservedly to each other as bodily, sexual beings, even if this "not giving" is "outside the scope of their intention."

Contraception is thus anti-love as well as anti-life. It is utterly incompatible with the culture of life and the civilization of love. It is rather the gateway to the culture of death. This is implicit in the slogan frequently on the lips of those who defend our contraceptive culture by saying that "No unwanted child ought ever to be born." This banal slogan typifies the culture of death, which seeks to avert the tragedy of an "unwanted child" by preventing its coming into being through contraception or, should this fail, by abortion. It is utterly opposed to the truth that "no person, i.e., no human being, whether born or unborn, male or female, young or old, genius or demented, ought ever to be unwanted, i.e., unloved." And the only way to build a civilization in which every human person is indeed wanted is to respect both the love-giving (unitive) and life-giving meanings of human sexuality and marriage.

5. Sterilization

Partly because of the dangers of the pill and IUDs, more and more people are resorting to sterilization as a means of preventing conception. Naturally, those who justify contraception use the same reasoning to justify sterilization, although dissenting Catholic theologians usually require a "greater proportionate reason" to justify sterilization since it is very difficult to reverse.[41] Many advocate sterilization as the most appropriate way to cope with the problems faced by a couple who have serious reasons to avoid a pregnancy, for instance, if a pregnancy would endanger the mother's life or if there were a serious risk of generating a child crippled by a severe recessive genetic defect such as Tay-Sachs disease.

A. Why Contraceptive Sterilization Is Morally Wrong

The Church's Magisterium has constantly taught that contraceptive or direct sterilization is always gravely immoral.[42] The Church, along with theologians faithful to her teachings, distinguishes between direct or contraceptive sterilization and "indirect" sterilization. The former is an act specified by the choice to impede procreation from freely chosen genital acts; it is thus contraceptive in nature, no matter what further good ends are appealed to in order to "rationalize" this contraceptive choice. Contraceptive sterilization is just as much anti-life and anti-love as are other methods of contraception. So-called indirect sterilization is an unintended side effect of medical procedures morally specified by the choice to remove pathological reproductive organs (ovaries, wombs, testes, etc.) or to inhibit their natural functioning when such functioning (e.g., abnormal hormonal production) aggravates a pathological condition within a person.

Contraceptive sterilization is not only, as is contraception by other means, an anti-life kind of act; it is also an act of mutilation and is therefore more seriously wrong than other methods of contraception.

From the time of *Humanae vitae* through the 1990s, revisionist theologians time and again sought to justify contraceptive sterilization by interpreting the principle of totality as a form of proportionalistic moral reasoning. They argued that contraceptive sterilization is morally good if necessary to prevent a future pregnancy that may be hazardous to the life of the mother or may result in the conception of a severely handicapped child, and in this way contribute to the "total" well-being of individuals and families.[43] In essence, this is an argument that some hoped-for good to come can justify the willingness to do evil here and now.

B. Medical Dangers of Tubal Ligation

Several Catholic moralists, among them Bernard Häring, C.Ss.R., and Richard A. McCormick, S.J., recommended tubal ligation, one form of contraceptive sterilization, as the best way, morally and medically, of helping families cope with serious problems that arise when a wife is told that her life might be endangered should she get pregnant.[44] They redescribed the act of sterilization in terms of its hoped-for benefits by calling it a "marriage-saving" act. Ironically, tubal ligation is *not always effective*. As Hanna Klaus, M.D., has noted, women who choose tubal ligation run the risk of subsequently conceiving and of having a tubal pregnancy that can seriously threaten their lives and that are frequently not considered by medical personnel precisely because of their history of sterilization. As Klaus has written:

> Female sterilization by tubal ligation has been shown to be less effective than previously thought. Most publications say 2% failure now.... Depending on the type of sterilization performed and the age of the

woman, the risk of ectopic pregnancy, if there is post-surgical conception, is quite high and persists into menopause. For women who have been sterilized before the age of 30 the likelihood of ectopic pregnancy ranges from 1.2 per 1000 for postpartum open surgery to 31.9 per 1000 for bipolar coagulation.... If a woman has symptoms of an ectopic pregnancy she should be investigated immediately and aggressively irrespective of the history of sterilization.[45]

Because we live in a technological age, the temptation to resort to sterilization either of husband or wife to cope with difficult problems is understandable because it is touted by many in our culture as the most "effective" way of handling serious problems. One can, in light of Dr. Klaus's studies, call this assumption into doubt, and one can also ask serious questions about the "love" a husband has for his wife if he allows her or requires her to undergo a tubal ligation in order to avoid a pregnancy and to run the risk of having an ectopic pregnancy later, particularly when effective use of modern methods of natural family planning have been shown to be 99 percent effective in helping a couple avoid a pregnancy by periodic abstinence.[46]

C. Moral Dangers of Contraception and Sterilization

The most serious danger of contraception and of sterilization is to the good of the person who chooses any form of contraception. A grave sin, such as contraception or sterilization, is something freely chosen. And, as we saw in Chapter Two, our choices *last* insofar as they are self-determining. Contraceptive sterilization is not only *physically* mutilating but *spiritually* so. This self-mutilation lasts until the person repents and freely chooses to do penance and to reform his or her life.

Moreover, studies now show that contraception — and today in the United States contraceptive sterilization is the most popular method — contributes greatly to divorce and the breakup of families precisely because women in particular feel "used" by their husbands.[47]

D. What to Do if One Has Been Sterilized

Ought couples of whom one or both have been sterilized abstain entirely from the conjugal act or try to have the sterilization reversed? There is no Church teaching explicitly devoted to this issue. Grisez believes that general principles indicate a negative answer to both questions at least for most cases.[48] He maintains, however, that those who repent of being sterilized must consider their responsibilities consciously and that some couples will judge correctly that they still should seek to have children if they can and that they can and should accept the burdens that attempts to reverse the sterilization might involve. He likewise notes that repentant couples could sin by deliberately rejoicing over their self-inflicted sterility and so "in order to maintain and confirm their repentance and verify its sincerity to themselves and each other, they should abstain during periods which would be fertile except for the sterilization."[49]

I agree with Grisez, although I think that *if* surgery to correct the sterilization does *not* impose the kind of serious burdens Grisez speaks of, then the sterilized party should seek to have it reversed. I also think that a single person should do so prior to getting married, *if*, again, doing so imposes no grave burdens. Such a sterilized person is free to marry because sterilization, whether caused by some pathology or deliberately done as a contraceptive measure, is not a diriment impediment to marriage.

John Kippley, the founder and first president of the Couple to Couple League, differs from Grisez and me. He believes that sterilized couples are morally obliged to abstain from intercourse during times that would otherwise be fertile.[50]

An interesting discussion of this matter is provided by Janet Smith and Christopher Kaczor in their 2007 book *Life Issues, Medical Choices: Questions and Answers for Catholics.*[51]

6. Use of Condoms and the Prevention of HIV

In the late fall of 2010 Pope Benedict XVI wrote *Light of the World.* In answering one question that his interviewer, Peter Seewald, posed, the Pope said, "The secular realm has developed the so-called ABC Theory: Abstinence-Be Faithful-Condom, where the condom is understood only as a last resort, when the other two points fail to work. This means that *the sheer fixation on the condom implies a banalization of sexuality,* which ... is precisely *the dangerous source of the attitude of no longer seeing sexuality as the expression of love, but only a sort of drug*" (emphasis added). Benedict went on to say, "There may be a basis in the case of some individuals, as perhaps when a male prostitute uses a condom, where this can be a first step in the direction of a moralization, a first assumption of responsibility, on the way toward recovering an awareness that not everything is allowed, and that one cannot do whatever one wants. *But it is not really to deal with the evil of HIV infection. That can really only lie in a humanization of sexuality*" (emphasis added).[52] Seewald then asked: "Are you saying, then, that the Church is actually not opposed in principle to the use of condoms?" To this Benedict replied: "She *of course does not* regard it as a real or moral solution, but, in this or that case, there can be nonetheless the intention of reducing the risk of infection, a *first step* in a movement toward . . . a more human way of living sexuality" (emphasis added).[53]

I believe it is obvious, in light of the passages emphasized above, that Pope Benedict in no way said that the use of condoms to prevent HIV/AIDS is morally good and acceptable. Quite to the contrary. But several dissenting Catholic theologians, among them Jon D. Fuller, S.J., and James F. Keenan, S.J., in a September 23 essay, "The Vatican's New Insights on HIV Prevention," insisted that Benedict's remarks and those of other Vatican officials clearly showed that the Church was now approving condom use to prevent HIV/AIDS not only for male prostitutes but also for married couples.

What does the Magisterium teach about this use of condoms? So far as I know or can discover, the most authoritative teaching of the Congregation for the Doctrine of the Faith on this matter was probably set forth by Joseph Cardinal Ratzinger, then prefect of the CDF, in a letter, authorized by Pope John Paul II, to Archbishop Pio Laghi, at that time the papal pronuncio to the United States, on May 29, 1988, after the "lively discussion, widened and sometimes distorted by the press worldwide, which followed the publication of the NCCB Administrative Board's well-known document, *The Many Faces of AIDS*," a document in which this issue was considered but in a way that was not very clear. Confronting this precise issue head-on, Cardinal Ratzinger wrote as follows:

> I want to draw attention to the clarification which appeared in the March 10 edition of *L'Osservatore Romano*, in an unsigned article entitled "Prevention of AIDS: Christian Ethical Aspect," and I quote, "To seek a solution to the problem of infection by promoting the use of prophylactics would be to embark on a way not only insufficiently reliable from the technical point of view, but also and above all, *unacceptable from the moral aspect* [emphasis added]. . . ." In the case here under discussion, it hardly seems pertinent to appeal to the classical principle of tolerance of the lesser evil on the part of those who exercise responsibility for the temporal good of society. In fact, even when the issue has to do with educational programs promoted by the civil government, one would not be dealing simply with a form of passive toleration but rather with *a kind of behavior which would result in at least the facilitation of evil* [emphasis added].

Ratzinger then wrote: "The problem of educational programs in specifically Catholic schools and institutions requires particular attention. These facilities are called to provide their own contribution for the prevention of AIDS, *in full fidelity to the moral doctrine of the church* [emphasis added]. . . . [T]he church's responsibility is to give that kind of witness which is proper to her, namely, an unequivocal witness of effective and unreserved solidarity with those who are suffering and, at the same time, *a witness of defense of the dignity of human sexuality which can only be realized within the context of moral law* [emphasis added]." In closing his letter Ratzinger emphasized that Pope John Paul II fully supported this teaching.

Do any later magisterial documents disagree with the teaching set forth in this 1988 letter of the CDF? The answer, in my judgment, is that none do. I have already argued that Pope Benedict XVI's comments on this matter in *Light of the World* in no way indicate that the Church's teaching has changed on this matter. Moreover, John Paul II himself, in numerous homilies and addresses throughout the world, particularly in Africa, reaffirmed this teaching again and again. Moreover, Father John Flynn, L.C., in an article published in *Zenit*, February 11, 2008, cited several texts from Pope Benedict XVI affirming the same doctrine. For example:

> Benedict XVI addressed the HIV/AIDS issue in a couple of recent speeches made when receiving the credentials of new ambassadors. On Dec. 13, in his address to Peter Hitjitevi Katjavivi from Namibia, the Pope recognized the urgent need to halt the spread of infections. "I assure the people of your country that the Church will continue to assist those who suffer from AIDS and to support their families," the Pope stated. The Church's contribution to the goal of eradicating AIDS, the Pontiff continued, "cannot but draw its inspiration from the Christian conception of human love and sexuality." This vision sees marriage as a total, reciprocal and exclusive communion of love between a man and a woman, Benedict XVI explained.

I am convinced that when spouses use condoms as a means of preventing HIV/AIDS, they change the act they perform from one of true marital union (the marriage act) into a *different kind of act*. Why? To show why we must be clear about the "object" morally specifying human acts. As we have seen already in *Veritatis splendor*, no. 78, Pope John Paul II had clearly identified what this "object" is: "In order to be able to grasp the object of an act which specifies that act morally, it is therefore necessary to place oneself in the perspective of the acting person. The object of the act of willing is in fact a freely chosen kind of behavior.... [T]hat object is the proximate end of a deliberate decision which determines the act of willing on the part of the acting person." For example, the "object" of an act of adultery is having intercourse with someone who is not one's spouse or with the spouse of another. This is *what* adultery is.

In using condoms to prevent HIV/AIDS the "object" freely chosen and primarily specifying the spouses' act is precisely to put on a condom while engaging in intercourse; this is also the "immediate" or "proximate" end. The "further" or "more remote" end for whose sake the couple chooses to use condoms while engaging in intercourse is the hoped-for benefit of not harming a spouse by transmitting HIV/AIDS. This further end is good; but the act freely chosen as the means to this end has as its morally specifying object the use of condoms while having intercourse. This "object" is different from the "object" morally specifying a *marital or spousal act*. In that act the spouses are choosing here and now "to give and receive each other in a bodily act, that is the *only* bodily act 'apt' for generating new human life, even if one or the other is not fertile."

7. Elaine Tyler May's *America and the Pill*

Although she is a champion of contraception, May is honest enough to report in the final chapter of her book *America and the Pill: A History of Promise, Peril, and Liberation* that among young women who responded to an Internet inquiry (details are given in note 8 of Chapter 7, p. 196), many reported that the pill decreased their libido. But more significantly, the same Internet inquiry showed that today some gynecologists refuse to prescribe artificial contraceptives and instead advise couples to use a natural method, FAM (Fertility Awareness Method), to regulate conception. One woman, Sue G., voices the view of many young married women today who reject artificial methods and think that "cutting off one of my body's natural, normal functions just does not set well with me" (p. 160). Another participant in the survey, Jacqueline G., is a FAM enthusiast who had originally taken the pill when she was twenty-six. She said that as a result of doing so, "for the next two and a half years my body felt numb, my sexuality dimmed, and my brain felt cloudy and dull." When she heard of FAM she said: "I was stunned to hear about scientific birth control that was completely natural and engaged both partners in the method.... I told my husband about the method as soon as I got home, and he was as excited about it as I was. We both loved how natural the new method is." They took an eight-hour course that "pretty much blew our minds." They learned how to chart temperatures and analyze cervical secretions to determine scientifically the exact times she was fertile. "Suddenly," Jacqueline says, "my fertility wasn't something wild or uncontrollable. . . . I find it deeply satisfying to be so attuned to my own body's rhythms and fertility signals. . . . It's like we both [her husband and her] learned a new language — the language of my body's rhythms" (pp. 161-162).

It seems obvious that the method Jacqueline and others identify as the Fertility Awareness Method (FAM) is precisely the method that millions of women and men know as Natural Family Planning. It is just as reliable — indeed more reliable — than any "artificial" method of birth control in enabling wives and husbands to avoid causing a pregnancy if, for good reasons, it would not be prudent for the wife to become pregnant. All one has to do is to abstain from engaging in the conjugal act when it is reasonable to think that engaging in it will cause a pregnancy because the wife is fertile at the time — in short, to practice periodic continence. During this time the married couple can find other ways of expressing their deep love for one another. And unlike *any* contraceptive, FAM or NFP also enables a couple to *achieve* a pregnancy when there is no good reason not to cause one. No woman ever took the pill or used condoms or diaphragms or spermicidal jellies or IUDs in order to become pregnant, but millions of women (and their husbands) use FAM precisely in order to become pregnant. Moreover, this natural method allows spouses to "speak the language of the body" and to respect their fertility as a blessing and not a curse. Use of this method requires the active knowledge and cooperation of the wife's husband as well, and this cooperation helps them to grow in their love for one another and to strengthen their marriage. In particular, it helps the husband to deepen his respect for his wife as a person whose sexuality differs from and complements his own. In addition FAM does not cost a cent; rather than using some artificial device, those who practice FAM use their *brains*. As more women (and men) come to realize that "artificial" means of regulating conception actually serve to distance couples from each other and even contribute to divorce, we will come to realize that there is no need to celebrate the pill's fifty-first or sixtieth birthday. We can celebrate its demise.

Appendix: Preventing Conception When in Danger of Rape or After Rape

As we have seen, contraception is an intrinsically evil act and can never be morally justified. Contraception, as a human, moral act is specified by the object freely chosen, and this object is precisely *to impede the beginning of new human life that one reasonably foresees may come into existence through freely chosen genital acts.* Moreover, the *object specifying* a human act, as we have seen and as St. Thomas and Pope John Paul II make clear, is *not* merely some physical performance or outward behavior but is rather shaped by the present *intention* of the acting person: it is precisely what the acting person is freely choosing to do;[54] in contracepting, one is choosing to impede the beginning of a new human life that one believes might begin through a freely chosen genital act.

If a woman is in serious danger of being raped (for instance, if she is in an area where invading soldiers have already raped the women they have encountered), she has a right to protect herself from the rapist's sperm and the further violation to her bodily and personal integrity that his sperm could cause. Were she to use some device that would prevent the rapist's sperm from penetrating her ovum (e.g., a diaphragm or spermicidal jellies), the *object* specifying her act would *not* be *to impede the beginning of a new life that could begin through her freely chosen genital act,* but rather *to protect herself from further bodily and personal violation by a rapist,* and a human act, specified by this object, is *not* an act of contraception, nor does it violate any moral norm. The woman has absolutely no obligation to permit the rapist's sperm to penetrate and fertilize her ovum, because she has not consented to a genital act but has rather refused such consent and has been sexually violated by the rapist. In a fine passage, Germain Grisez has put the matter this way:

> Rape is the imposition of intimate, bodily union upon someone without her or his consent, and anyone who is raped rightly resists so far as possible. Moreover, the victim (or potential victim) is right to resist not only insofar as he or she is subjected to unjust force, but insofar as that force imposes the special wrong of uniquely intimate bodily contact. It can scarcely be doubted that someone who cannot prevent the initiation of this intimacy is morally justified in resisting its continuation; for example, a woman who awakes and finds herself being penetrated by a rapist need not permit her attacker to ejaculate in her vagina if she can make him withdraw. On the same basis, if they cannot prevent the wrongful intimacy itself, women who are victims (or potential victims) of rape and those trying to help them are morally justified in trying to prevent conception insofar as it is the fullness of sexual union.
>
> The measures taken in this case are a defense of the woman's ovum (insofar as it is a part of her person) against the rapist's sperms (insofar as they are parts of his person). By contrast, if the intimate, bodily union of intercourse is not imposed on the woman but sought willingly or willingly

permitted, neither she nor anyone who permits the union can intend at the same time that it not occur. Hence, rape apart, contraceptive measures are chosen to prevent conception not insofar as it is the ultimate completion of intimate bodily union but insofar as it is the beginning of a new and unwanted person.[55]

In other words, the moral object specifying the rape victim's (or potential rape victim's) human act is *not* to prevent the conception of a new human person but rather to prevent ultimate completion of an unjust act of sexual violence.

Similarly, a woman who has suffered the horrible violence of being raped, but who has not, prior to being raped, sought to protect herself from further violence from the rapist's sperm, can legitimately protect herself from the further violation that would be done to her were the rapist's sperm to penetrate her ovum. Thus Directive 36 of the *Ethical and Religious Directives for Catholic Health Care Services*, promulgated by the National Conference of Catholic Bishops of the United States in 2009, reads as follows:

A female who has been raped should be able to defend herself against a potential conception from the sexual assault. If, after appropriate testing, there is no evidence that conception has occurred already, she may be treated with medications that would prevent ovulation, sperm capacitation, or fertilization. It is not permissible, however, to initiate or to recommend treatments that have as their purpose or direct effect the removal, destruction, or interference with the implantation of a fertilized ovum. In other words, human acts can legitimately be taken to protect the woman who has been raped from being made pregnant by the rapist's sperm. Such acts are *not acts of contraception,* which is intrinsically evil and can *never* be morally justified. Such acts are not acts of contraception because the *object* freely chosen and morally specifying them is *not* the impeding of a new human life that could begin through a freely chosen genital act [= definition of contraception] but is rather the *protecting of the raped woman from further violence by the rapist.*[56]

──────────────── Endnotes for Chapter Four ────────────────

1. Gilbert Meilaender and Philip Turner, "Contraception: A Symposium," *First Things* 88 (December 1998), 24.
2. James Nuechterlein, "Catholics, Protestants, and Contraception," *First Things* 92 (April 1999), 10.

3. Ibid.

4. Pope John XXIII established this commission, whose function was exclusively to offer advice to the Pope, in 1963. After Pope John's death, Pope Paul VI ordered that it continue its work. The commission's original charge was to determine whether the newly discovered "anovulant" pill was indeed a contraceptive (as Pope Pius XII had judged in an address given to a Congress of Hematologists on September 12, 1958, less than a month before he died), but it soon began to open up the entire issue of contraception. The commission soon divided into a "minority," which held that the Church's teaching on the immorality of contraception is true and cannot change, and a "majority," which held that contraception by married couples can be justified. The commission completed its work in 1966. Although its findings were supposed to have been given *only* to the Holy Father, the commission's papers were leaked to the press in July 1967 and published in the United States in the *National Catholic Reporter*. The commission issued four documents; all can be found in *The Birth-Control Debate: Interim History from the Pages of the National Catholic Reporter*, ed. Robert Hoyt (Kansas City: National Catholic Reporter, 1969). One, expressing the minority view, was entitled in Latin "*Status Quaestionis: Doctrina Ecclesiae Eiusque Auctoritatis*" and was given the title "The State of the Question: A Conservative View" in the Hoyt volume. Three documents set forth the majority position: (1) a rebuttal of the minority view: "*Documentum Syntheticum de Moralitate Nativitatum*" ("The Question Is not Closed: The Liberals Reply" in Hoyt); (2) the final theological report of the majority: "*Schema Documenti de Responsabili Paternitate*" ("On Responsible Parenthood: The Final Report" in Hoyt); and (3) a pastoral paper, written in French under the title "*Indications Pastorales*" ("Pastoral Approaches" in Hoyt).

An interesting account of the commission and its work, written by one fully in agreement with the "majority" position, is given by Robert McClory in *Turning Point: The Inside Story of the Papal Birth Control Commission, and How Humanae Vitae Changed the Life of Patty Crowley and the Future of the Church* (New York: Crossroad, 1995).

5. "On Responsible Parenthood," in Hoyt, p. 88.

6. "The Question Is not Closed," in ibid., p. 72.

7. Alicia Mosier, "Contraception: A Symposium," *First Things* 88 (December 1998), p. 26.

8. A better translation of the Latin text of *Humanae vitae* to which Mosier refers is "to impede procreation" insofar as the Latin reads "*ut procreatio impediatur.*"

9. Mosier, "Contraception: A Symposium," pp. 26-27.

10. See Germain Grisez, Joseph Boyle, John Finnis, and William E. May, " 'Every Marital Act Ought to Be Open to New Life': Toward a Clearer Understanding," *The Thomist* 52 (1988), 365-426; reprinted in *The Teaching of Humanae Vitae: A Defense* (San Francisco: Ignatius Press, 1988), pp. 33-116.

11. See, for instance, the following:

(1) St. John Chrysostom, *Homily 24 on the Epistle to the Romans*, PG 60.626-627: "Why do you sow where the field is eager to destroy the fruit? Where

there are medicines of sterility? Where there is murder before birth? You do not even let a harlot remain only a harlot, but you make her a murderess as well. Do you see that from drunkenness comes fornication, from fornication adultery, from adultery murder? Indeed, it is something worse than murder and I do not know what to call it; for she does not kill what is formed but prevents its formation. What then? Do you contemn the gift of God, and fight with his law? What is a curse, do you seek as though it were a blessing? Do you make the anteroom of birth the anteroom of slaughter? Do you teach the woman who is given to you for the procreation of offspring to perpetuate killing?" Cited by John T. Noonan, Jr., in his *Contraception: A History of Its Treatment by Catholic Theologians and Canonists* (Cambridge, MA: The Belknap Press of Harvard University, 1965), p. 98. On pp. 91-94 of this work, Noonan shows that contraception, along with abortion, was considered equivalent to murder in such early Christian writings as the *Didache* and the *Epistle to Barnabas*. As Noonan shows in later sections of his work, e.g., pp. 146, 232-237, this tradition perdured in the Church for centuries.

(2) St. Thomas Aquinas, *Summa contra gentiles*, Bk. 3, chap. 122: "Nor, in fact, should it be deemed a slight sin for a man to arrange for the emission of semen apart from the proper purpose of generating and bringing up children.... [T]he inordinate emission of semen is incompatible with the natural good of preserving the species. Hence, after the sin of homicide whereby a human nature already in existence is destroyed, this type of sin appears to take next place, for by it the generation of human nature is impeded."

(3) The *"Si aliquis"* canon, which was integrated into the canon law of the Church in the *Decretum Greg. IX,* lib. V, tit., 12, cap. V, and was part of the Church's canon law from the mid-thirteenth century until 1917, clearly likened contraception to murder. It declared: "If anyone for the sake of fulfilling sexual desire or with premeditated hatred does something to a man or a woman, or gives something to drink, so that he cannot generate or she cannot conceive or offspring be born, let him be held as a murderer." Text in *Corpus iuris canonici*, ed. A. L. Richter and A. Friedberg (Leipzig: Tauchnitz, 1881), 2.794.

(4) In its treatment of marriage, the *Roman Catechism* declared: "Whoever in marriage artificially prevents conception, or procures an abortion, commits a most serious sin: the sin of premeditated murder" (Part II, chap. 7, no. 13). It should be noted that Pope Paul VI explicitly refers to this text in a footnote to no. 14 of *Humanae vitae* (footnote no. 16), precisely where Paul defines contraception as every act prior to intercourse, during it, or in the course of its natural effect that proposes (the Latin text reads *intendat*), either as end or as means, to impede procreation (*ut procreatio impediatur*).

(5) John Calvin, in his commentary on the sin of Onan in Genesis 38, had this to say: "Onan not only defrauded his brother of the right due him, but also preferred his semen to putrefy on the ground.... The voluntary

spilling of semen outside of intercourse between man and woman is a monstrous thing. Deliberately to withdraw from coitus in order that semen may fall on the ground is doubly monstrous. For this is to extinguish the hope of the race and to kill before is born the hoped-for offspring.... If any woman ejects a foetus from her womb by drugs, it is reckoned a crime incapable of expiation, and deservedly Onan incurred upon himself the same kind of punishment, infecting the earth by his semen in order that Tamar might not conceive a future human being as an inhabitant of the earth." *Commentaries on the First Book of Moses Called Genesis*, 38:9, 10; quoted in Charles D. Provan, *The Bible and Birth Control* (Monongahela, PA: Zimmer Printing, 1989), p. 15. Provan points out that the editor of the *unabridged* series of Calvin's Commentaries, published by Baker Book House, has omitted the commentary on these two verses of Genesis.

12. See, for instance, his apostolic exhortation *Familiaris consortio* (*The Role of the Christian Family in the Modern World*), no. 32.

13. On this, see Paul F. deLadurantaye, " 'Irreconcilable Concepts of the Human Person' and the Moral Issue of Contraception: An Examination of the Personalism of Louis Janssens and of Pope John Paul II," *Anthropotes: Rivista di Studi sulla Persona e la Famiglia* 13.2 (1997), 433-456. This essay is a summary of deLadurantaye's 1997 S.T.D. dissertation under the same title at the John Paul II Institute for Studies on Marriage and Family, Washington, DC.

14. See endnote 5, above.

15. "The Question Is not Closed," in Hoyt, p. 69.

16. "On Responsible Parenthood," in Hoyt, p. 87.

17. "The Question Is not Closed," in Hoyt, p. 71.

18. "On Responsible Parenthood," in Hoyt, p. 89.

19. Louis Janssens, "Considerations on *Humanae Vitae*," *Louvain Studies* 2 (1969), 249.

20. Anthony Kosnik, et al., *Human Sexuality: New Directions in American Catholic Thought* (New York: Paulist, 1977), p. 83.

21. George Gilder, *Sexual Suicide* (New York: Quadrangle Books, 1973), p. 34.

22. Ashley Montagu, *Sex, Man, and Society* (New York: G. P. Putnam's, 1969), pp. 13-14; emphasis in original.

23. Germain Grisez, "Dualism and the New Morality," *Atti del congresso internazionale Tommaso d'Aquino nel suo settimo centenario*, vol. 5, *L'agire morale* (Naples: Edizioni Domenicane Italiane, 1977), p. 325.

24. "The Question Is not Closed," in Hoyt, p. 72.

25. In fact, some Catholic advocates of contraception, for instance, Rosemary Ruether and Louis Janssens, claim that with barrier methods of contraception one puts a "spatial" barrier between ovum and sperm, whereas with the use of periodic abstinence one puts a "temporal" barrier between ovum and sperm. Thus Ruether writes: "sexual acts which are calculated to function only during the times of sterility are sterilizing the act just as much as any other means of rendering the act infertile. *It is difficult to see why there should be such an absolute*

moral difference between creating a spatial barrier to procreation and creating a temporal barrier to procreation" ("Birth Control and Sexuality," in *Contraception and Holiness: The Catholic Predicament*, Introduction by Thomas D. Roberts, S.J. [New York: Herder and Herder, 1964], p. 74; emphasis added).

26. Pope John Paul II, encyclical *Veritatis splendor* (*The Splendor of Truth*), no. 78.

27. See ibid., no. 48. In this section of his encyclical, Pope John Paul II explicitly refers to defined Catholic teaching on the unity of the human person as a unity of body and soul, namely, the Council of Vienne, Constitution *Fides Catholica, DS*, 902; Fifth Lateran Council, Bull *Apostolici Regiminis, DS*, 1440; and Vatican Council II, Pastoral Constitution on the Church in the Modern World (*Gaudium et spes*), no. 14. See footnotes 66 and 67 to no. 48 of *Gaudium et spes*.

28. Kosnik et al., *Human Sexuality: New Directions in American Catholic Thought*, pp. 83-84.

29. The "nuptial meaning" of the body is developed in many of the addresses of Pope John Paul II on the "theology of the body." See in particular "The Nuptial Meaning of the Body" (General Audience of January 9, 1980) in John Paul II, *The Theology of the Body: Human Love in the Divine Plan* (Boston: Pauline Books and Media, 1997), pp. 60-63; "The Man-Person Becomes a Gift in the Freedom of Love" (General Audience of January 16, 1980), in ibid., pp. 63-66; "Mystery of Man's Original Innocence" (General Audience of January 30, 1980), in ibid., pp. 66-69. On this issue, see my essay, "Marriage and the Complementarity of Male and Female," chap. 2, of my *Marriage: The Rock on Which the Family Is Built* (second edition, San Francisco: Ignatius, 2009), pp. 29-56.

30. Mosier, "Contraception: A Symposium," p. 27.

31. In criticizing an earlier version of the argument given here (see endnote 10 above for bibliographical details of the Grisez et al. argument), Janet Smith accused the authors of "subjectivism" and of failing to recognize that "what one intends to do is defined as good or bad *independently of any act of the will*" (Janet Smith, *Humanae Vitae: A Generation Later* [Washington, DC: The Catholic University of America Press, 1991], p. 355). This criticism overlooks the fact that Paul VI, in order to reject every sort of contraception, had to define it in terms of the intention to impede procreation. Smith's critique in fact completely misunderstands the Grisez et al. argument; nowhere in her critique does she even report on the *arguments* given by Grisez et al. to show why it is always wrong to have an anti-life will. For a response to her criticisms, see William E. May, "A Review of Janet Smith's *Humanae Vitae: A Generation Later*," *The Thomist* 57 (1993), 155-161.

32. Carlo Caffarra, "*Humanae Vitae* Venti Anni Dopo," in *"Humanae Vitae: 20 Anni Dopo: Atti del II Congresso Internazionale di Teologia Morale* (Milan: Edizioni Ares, 1989), p. 192; English translation in *Why Humanae Vitae Was Right: A Reader*, ed. Janet Smith (San Francisco: Ignatius, 1993), p. 267.

33. I acknowledge that some individuals *can* abuse "recourse to the rhythm of the cycle," regarding it merely as another way of impeding new human life. Such individuals have, in fact, a "contraceptive mentality" and may decide to impede

new life by this means rather than by barrier or chemical means for aesthetic or hygienic reasons. St. Augustine, who used a primitive form of "fertility awareness" (refraining from having sex with his mistress during certain periods), testifies to this, for in his *Confessions* he acknowledges that his son Adeotatus "was conceived against our wills," but that, once born, he forced Augustine and his mistress to love him (see Bk. 4, chap. 2). Such individuals are, in effect, putting a "temporal barrier between sperm and ovum" (as Rosemary Ruether claims) precisely in order to impede procreation. But those who have recourse to the rhythm of the cycle, choosing to abstain, not as a means of impeding procreation but of not causing a pregnancy when it would not be prudent to do so, do not have this anti-life will. If told that they "are putting a temporal barrier between sperm and ovum," they would rightly find the charge incomprehensible. Augustine would not find it so because he apparently thought that this was precisely what he was doing, for he was contracepting.

34. The argument briefly set forth in this section is developed at much greater length by Grisez et al. in the essay " 'Every Marital Act Ought to Be Open to New Life': Toward a Clearer Understanding." It is masterfully presented by Grisez in Vol. 2, *Living a Christian Life*, of his *The Way of the Lord Jesus* (Quincy, IL: Franciscan Press, 1993), pp. 506-519.

35. Pope John Paul II develops this argument in many of his papal writings. Janet Smith provides an excellent synthesis of his thought on this matter in her *Humanae Vitae: A Generation Later*, pp. 98-129. See also Paul deLadurantaye, " 'Irreconcilable Concepts of the Human Person' and the Moral Issue of Contraception: An Examination of the Personalism of Louis Janssens and of Pope John Paul II."

36. See Paul Quay, S.J., "Contraception and Conjugal Love," *Theological Studies* 22 (1961), 18-40. See also Mary Joyce, *The Meaning of Contraception* (Collegeville, MN: The Liturgical Press, 1969); Dietrich von Hildebrand, *The Encyclical Humanae Vitae: A Sign of Contradiction* (Chicago: Franciscan Herald Press, 1969); and John Kippley, *Sex and the Marriage Covenant: A Basis for Morality* (Cincinnati: Couple to Couple League, 1991), pp. 50-76. In *Contraception and the Natural Law* (Milwaukee: Bruce, 1964), pp. 33-35, Germain Grisez offers an appreciative critique of this argument as expressed by Paul Quay.

37. Nuechterlein, "Catholics, Protestants, and Contraception," p. 10.

38. Pope John Paul II, "Homily at Mass for Youth, Nairobi, Kenya," *L'Osservatore Romano*, English ed., August 26, 1985, no. 8, p. 5; emphasis added. In saying this, John Paul II was in some ways also reaffirming the thought of Pope Paul VI, who referred to *Humanae vitae* as a defense of life "at the very source of human existence," and, citing the teaching of *Gaudium et spes*, no. 51, on abortion and infanticide, added: "We did no more than accept this charge when, ten years ago, we published the Encyclical *Humanae vitae*. This document drew its inspiration from the inviolable teachings of the Bible and the Gospel, which confirms the norms of the natural law and the unsuppressible dictates of conscience on respect for human life, the transmission of which is entrusted to responsible

fatherhood and motherhood" (Paul VI, "Homily on the Feast of Sts. Peter and Paul," *L'Osservatore Romano*, English ed., July 6, 1978, no. 2, p. 3).

39. Karol Wojtyla, "Instynkt, milosc, malzenstwo," *Tygodnik Powszechny* 8 (1952), p. 39. Quoted in John M. Grondelski, *Fruitfulness as an Essential Dimension in Acts of Conjugal Love: An Interpretative Study of the Pre-Pontifical Thought of John Paul II* (New York: Fordham University Press, 1986), p. 49. I am indebted to Paul deLadurantaye for calling this text to my attention. This entire section of this chapter owes much to the final portion of deLadurantaye's unpublished S.T.D. dissertation, " 'Irreconcilable Concepts of the Human Person' and the Moral Issue of Contraception: An Examination of the Personalism of Louis Janssens and Pope John Paul II," esp. pp. 259-280. As noted in endnote 13 above, a summary of this excellent study is provided in the journal *Anthropotes*.

40. Karol Wojtyla, *Love and Responsibility*, trans. H. Willetts (New York: Farrar, Strauss, Giroux, 1981), pp. 53-54. See *Evangelium vitae*, no. 81: "The meaning of life is found in giving and receiving love, and in this light human sexuality and procreation reach their true and full significance."

41. See, for example, Charles E. Curran, "Sterilization: Exposition, Critique, and Refutation of Past Teaching," in *New Perspectives in Moral Theology* (Notre Dame, IN: Notre Dame University Press, 1976), pp. 207-211.

42. See, for example, Pope Paul VI, *Humanae vitae*, no. 14; National Conference of Catholic Bishops, *Ethical and Religious Directives for Catholic Health Care Services* (Washington, DC: United States Catholic Conference, 1995), no. 53.

43. A remarkable presentation of this view is given by Martin Nolan, "The Principle of Totality," in *Absolutes in Moral Theology*, ed. Charles E. Curran (Washington, DC: Corpus Books, 1968). Paul Ramsey provided a brilliant critique of Nolan in his *Patient as Person* (New Haven: Yale University Press, 1970), pp. 178-181.

44. On this, see Bernard Häring, *Medical Ethics* (Notre Dame, IN: Fides, 1973), p. 90. Richard McCormick, *How Brave a New World: Dilemmas in Bioethics* (New York: Doubleday, 1981), p. 272.

45. One of Klaus's (religious name Sister Miriam) excellent articles showing why contraception and contraceptive sterilization (e.g. tubal ligation of women who refuse to be open to new human life) are evil was called "The Reality of Con-traception," formerly available at www.catholic.net/RCC/Periodicals/Dossier/sept97/reality.html. This website is no longer available. Sister Doctor Miriam Paul (Hannah) Klaus was born in Vienna, Austria, and is a Medical Mission Sister who celebrated her Golden Jubilee as a sister in 2010. She was raised in the United States, became an M.D. in gynecology/obstetrics and served in the Mission Sisters' hospitals in Pakistan and Bangladesh, taught medicine at various hospitals in the United States, and is internationally recognized as a leading authority on Natural Family Planning. For the past 35 years, she has been Executive Director of the Natural Family Planning Center in Washington, DC, and of the international Teen-Star education program she developed to help teenage girls learn how to be chaste and understand why NFP is good and contraception evil.

46. On this, see Richard Fehring, D.N.Sc., R.N., Stella Kitchen, and Mary Shiva-nandan, "A Word about Effectiveness," in *An Introduction to Natural Family Planning*, ed. Therese Notare (Washington, DC: USCCB, 1999).

47. See W. Bradford Wilcox, "Social Science and the Vindication of Catholic Moral Teaching," in *The Church, Marriage, & the Family: Proceedings from the 27th Annual Convention of the Fellowship of Catholic Scholars, September 24-26, 2004, Pittsburgh, PA*, ed. Kenneth Whitehead (South Bend, IN: St. Augustine's Press, 2007), pp. 330-340.

48. Grisez, *Living a Christian Life*, p. 545: "On the one hand, having repented sterilization, married couples have the same right to intercourse and reasons for it which other couples have after the wife's menopause. On the other hand, there usually are good reasons not to try to have the operation reversed: doing so involves costs and other burdens, the attempt often fails to restore fertility, and even if it were to succeed many such couples would have no moral obligation to try to have a child."

49. Ibid.

50. On this, see his *Sex and the Marital Covenant: A Basis for Morality* (Cincinnati: Couple to Couple League, 1991), pp. 209-212.

51. See their book *Life Issues, Medical Choices: Questions and Answers for Catholics* (Cincinnati: Servant Books, published by St. Anthony Messenger, 2007), Question 34, pp. 95-97.

52. William E. May, in *Fellowship of Catholic Scholars Newsletter* 11.23 (June 1988), pp. 1-2.

53. Pope Benedict XVI, *Light of the World: The Pope, The Church, and the Signs of the Times: An Interview with Peter Seewald* (San Francisco: Ignatius Press, 2010), pp. 118-119.

54. Fuller and Keenan, in *America: The National Catholic Weekly*, September 23, 2010.

55. Germain Grisez, *Living a Christian Life*, p. 512.

56. National Conference of Catholic Bishops, *Ethical and Religious Directives for Catholic Health Care Services* (Washington, DC: NCCB, 2009), no. 36.

CHAPTER FIVE

Abortion and Human Life

Introduction: The Structure of This Chapter

Although Chapter One set forth in some detail the Church's teaching on abortion, I begin this chapter with a résumé of that teaching, particularly in order to clarify that teaching on the "definition" of abortion, the question of "ensoulment," and the distinction between "direct" and "indirect" abortion. After a presentation of relevant scientific data, I then defend the proposition that it is reasonable to believe that most people begin at fertilization* and unreasonable to deny this (in defending this proposition, I criticize opposing views).

I do so because the great majority of the arguments advanced to justify abortion, either throughout the entire pregnancy or at least during its early stages, contend that the being killed by abortion is not a human person. Next I consider the special gravity of abortion and the fallacies characterizing the major arguments used to justify it as a woman's right even if one grants that it kills a human person. I then focus on the distinction made by some thinkers today between abortion as "killing" and abortion as "removal" and the argument that the latter can, under certain conditions, be morally justified. Debates among Catholic theologians on the proper moral management of ectopic pregnancies are then considered.

The chapter, therefore, is divided as follows: (1) Résumé and Clarification of Church Teaching; (2) Relevant Scientific Data; (3) It Is Reasonable to Believe That Most People Begin at Fertilization and Unreasonable to Deny This; (4) The Special Moral Gravity of Abortion, a Woman's "Right" to Abortion, the Difference Between a "Right" and a "Liberty"; (5) Abortion as "Removal" vs. Abortion as "Killing"; (6) The Management of Ectopic

---

* As we will see in this chapter, the only persons who do not begin at fertilization are some monozygotic twins or triplets, etc., of whom *one* may come into existence after fertilization, whereas another, so it will be argued, was in being from fertilization onward.

Pregnancies; (7) "Hard Cases" for Opponents and Supporters of Abortion. The issue of experimenting on unborn human life is taken up in Chapter Six.

1. Résumé and Clarification of Church Teaching

The *Catechism of the Catholic Church* succinctly summarizes the teaching of the Church — reviewed extensively in Chapter One — on the inviolability of human life from its beginning and on the grave moral evil of abortion. Here it will be useful to cite two passages from the *Catechism*, along with their internal citations from Scripture, from the second-century document called the *Didache* (also known as *The Teaching of the Twelve Apostles*), and from Vatican Council II.

> Human life must be respected and protected absolutely from the moment of conception. From the first moment of his existence, a human being must be recognized as having the rights of a person — among which is the inviolable right of every innocent being to life (cf. CDF, *Donum vitae* I, 1). "Before I formed you in the womb I knew you, and before you were born I consecrated you" (Jer 1:5; cf. Job 10:8-12; Ps 22:10-11). "My frame was not hidden from you, when I was being made in secret, intricately wrought in the depths of the earth" (Ps 139:15). (CCC, no. 2270)
>
> Since the first century the Church has affirmed the moral evil of every procured abortion. This teaching has not changed and remains unchangeable. Direct abortion, that is to say, abortion willed either as an end or a means, is gravely contrary to the moral law. "You shall not kill the embryo by abortion and shall not cause the newborn to perish" (*Didache* 2, 2: SCh 248, 148; cf. *Ep. Barnabae* 19, 5: PG 2, 777; *Ad Diognetum* 5, 6: PG 2, 1173; Tertullian, *Apol.* 9: PL 1, 319-320). "God, the Lord of life, has entrusted to men the noble mission of safeguarding life, and men must carry it out in a manner worthy of themselves. Life must be protected with the utmost care from the moment of conception: abortion and infanticide are abominable crimes" (*Gaudium et spes*, no. 51 § 3). (CCC no. 2271)

Moreover, as we saw in Chapter One, Pope John Paul II clearly affirmed that the teaching of the Church on the grave immorality of procured or direct abortion has been infallibly proposed by the ordinary and universal Magisterium of the Church. Mincing no words, he spoke as follows:

> ... by the authority which Christ conferred upon Peter and his Successors, in communion with the Bishops — who on various occasions have condemned abortion and who ... albeit dispersed throughout the world,

have shown unanimous agreement concerning this doctrine — *I declare that direct abortion, that is, abortion willed as an end or as a means, always constitutes a grave moral disorder,* since it is the deliberate killing of an innocent human being. This doctrine is based upon the natural law and upon the written Word of God, is transmitted by the Church's Tradition and taught by the ordinary and universal Magisterium. (*Evangelium vitae,* no. 62; emphasis in original)

A. The Definition of Abortion

Shortly before making this powerful declaration, John Paul II had defined direct or procured abortion as "the deliberate and direct killing, by whatever means it is carried out, of a human being in the initial phase of his or her existence, extending from conception to birth" (*Evangelium vitae,* no. 58; emphasis in original). Note that here the Pope defines abortion as an act of "killing" and not as the "expelling" from the mother's womb of a living but not yet viable fetus. Some older manuals of Catholic moral theology had defined abortion in this way and used other terms, e.g., "craniotomy," "embryotomy," "feticide," to describe interventions that deliberately caused the death of the unborn child but did not do so by "expelling" it from the womb.[1] I bring this matter up here because of its relevance to the distinction made today by some scholars loyal to the Magisterium between abortion as "killing" and abortion as "removal," a matter to be consider later.

B. "Ensoulment" or Infusion of the Immortal Soul

We saw also in Chapter One that the Magisterium of the Church had not expressly committed itself to the position that individual human personal life begins at conception until, as was noted in the final Part of Chapter One, where the teaching of *Dignitas personae* was summarized, an argument was advanced by Edward Furton of the *National Catholic Bioethics Center* that one passage in DP clearly teaches that human personal life does begin at conception. Although DP does *not* explicitly say that human personal life begins with conception/fertilization, it affirms "an intrinsic connection between the ontological dimension and the specific value of every human life." Thus it holds that "the reality of the human being for the entire span of life, both before and after birth, does not allow us to posit either a change in nature or a gradation in moral value, since it possesses *full anthropological and ethical status*" (no. 5; emphasis in original). It also says that the nature of a being, its "ontological dimension," and the value of a being are intrinsically connected and then asserts that the human being has the same nature and therefore the same moral value throughout the stages of human development. "Indeed, the reality of the human being for the entire span of life, both before and after birth, does not allow us to posit either a change in nature or a gradation in moral value, since it possesses *full anthropological and ethical status*. The human embryo has, therefore, from the very beginning, the dignity proper to a person" (no. 5; emphasis in original).

Furton pointed out that from DP, no. 5, personal human life must begin at the very beginning, because that is the "only possible conclusion that one can draw, for if it is true that the embryo undergoes no change in nature throughout its development, and if it is true that the embryo, by its very nature, has the dignity of a person, then it must also be true that the embryo is a person from the moment of conception."[2]

Before that, as John Paul II declared in *Evangelium vitae*, when commenting on the view of those who seek to justify abortion by claiming that the result of conception, at least for a time, cannot be considered personal human life, "what is at stake is so important that, from the standpoint of moral obligation, the mere probability that a human person is involved would suffice to justify an absolutely clear prohibition of any intervention aimed at killing a human embryo." He concluded by saying:

> Precisely for this reason, over and above all scientific debates and those philosophical affirmations [concerning the precise moment when a spiritual soul is infused] to which the Magisterium has not yet expressly committed itself, the Church has always taught and continues to teach that the result of human procreation, from the first moment of its existence, must be guaranteed that unconditional respect which is morally due to the human being in his or her totality and unity as body and spirit. (no. 60)[3]

In speaking in this way, Pope John Paul II voices the age-old tradition of the Church. No matter what their own personal views regarding the moment when the spiritual soul was infused into the body, the Apostolic Fathers, the early Christian apologists, the Fathers and Doctors of the Church, both East and West — indeed, the entire tradition — unanimously condemned procured or direct abortion of any kind as utterly immoral.[4] Thus, for example, the Greek Church Father St. Basil the Great declared that whoever purposely destroys a fetus is a murderer, and it makes no difference whatsoever whether it is formed (animated by a spiritual soul) or unformed (not yet so animated).[5]

I believe that the individual personal human life of most people begins at conception/fertilization and that empirical evidence supports this belief. Later in this chapter, this issue will be explored in depth. But it is very important to emphasize here that the Church's teaching on the grave immorality of procured or direct abortion deliberately left the question open for discussion — at least until 2008 and the publication of *Dignitas personae*, some of whose passages logically lead to the conclusion that such life begins at conception. As we saw in Chapter Four, a long tradition in the Church regarded contraception as a gravely immoral *anti-life* kind of act, analogous to murder. It is thus obvious that during the centuries when all Christians judged contraception and abortion as gravely immoral, theoretical differences regarding the precise moment of "ensoulment" or infusion of an immortal soul to "form" the fetus made little or no difference in the practical judgment that every attempt to terminate pregnancy was absolutely immoral, no matter when this attempt was made.[6]

C. "Direct" vs. "Indirect" Abortion

In *Evangelium vitae*, Pope John Paul II, like his predecessors in the chair of St. Peter and along with the *Catechism of the Catholic Church*, condemned as intrinsically evil and gravely immoral every act of "procured" or "direct" abortion. Moreover, he clearly defined the meaning of "direct" or "procured" abortion. Explicitly referring to and citing from the teaching of Pope Pius XII,[7] John Paul II said that "direct" abortion includes every act tending to destroy human life in the womb, "whether such destruction is intended as an *end* or only as a *means* to an end" (no. 62). By direct or procured abortion, then, one means a human act specified morally as an act of *killing the unborn*. It is so specified because its "object" as a human act is precisely the destruction of unborn human life. This "object" is either the *end* for whose sake the act is done or, more frequently, the *means chosen* in order to bring about some *further* end. In any event, this "object" is the *proximate end* willed by the agent; it is the *proximate end* specifying a freely chosen human act, which may also be willed as a *means* to some further or ulterior end that may have motivated the act (e.g., to avoid the embarrassment of out-of-wedlock pregnancy, to prevent the birth of a child probably suffering from some genetically induced malady, etc.). And this "object" is precisely the aborting or killing of unborn human life. The abortion (killing) of that life cannot *not* be willed by the acting person.[8]

In so-called indirect abortion, the killing of the unborn child, or its abortion, is *not* the object of the act, neither as an end nor as a means. It is rather, as the passage already cited from Pope Pius XII (see endnote 7) makes clear, the foreseen but "unintended" consequence or result of a medical procedure that itself is specified as an act of healing a sick woman or protecting her life. Neither the end intended nor the means chosen to attain the end in question is the abortion or killing of the unborn. This is foreseen as an inevitable and unavoidable result of the deed chosen to protect or heal or safeguard the mother's life, but it is *not willed by the acting person*. It is "outside the scope of his or her intentions" and can be justified if there is urgent need to protect a great good, such as the life of the mother, and no other alternatives can be used to do so. Thus, for instance, it is morally permissible for a woman suffering from cancer of the uterus to have a hysterectomy or undergo radiation therapy to cure the cancer or protect her from dying of it even if she is pregnant and realizes that the unborn child will die as a result of the hysterectomy or radiation therapy, provided that no alternative therapies exist and those that do exist cannot be postponed until after the baby's safe delivery. The "abortion" in such conditions is no more "directly" willed than is one's baldness, which one foresees will occur as a result of undergoing chemotherapy for a life-threatening cancerous condition. The baldness is surely "outside the scope of the agent's intention" and is definitely *not* willed in any way. Similarly, in cases of so-called indirect abortion, the abortion or death of the unborn child is also outside the scope of the agent's intention and is definitely *not* willed in any way, even indirectly, either as an end or as a means. It is precisely an *unintended* side effect of an action good in itself because the "object" specifying it is precisely the saving or protecting of the mother's life. The unborn child's death is thus not "intended" in any way.

2. Relevant Scientific Data

I will first consider an important essay by Nicanor Pier Austriaco, O.P., and I will then show the relevance of an article by Patrick Lee and Robert George.

In a most important essay, Austriaco summarizes "a systems biology view of the beginning of human life." Addressing the issue of fertilization and embryogenesis, Austriaco reviews the biology by describing the molecular and cellular events at the beginning of life. Fertilization, traditionally the point that marks the origin of the human organism,

> is initiated by fusion of the sperm and egg.... Between eleven and eighteen hours after insemination, the two pro-nuclei, one from each of the gametes, become visible and eventually unite, forming the embryonic

nucleus with its complete set of forty-six chromosomes. About thirty hours after sperm-egg fusion, the first cell division occurs, and two- to four-cell stage embryos can usually be observed by day two. By day three, the embryo reaches the eight cell stage. Sometimes between days two and three, the embryonic genome is activated representing the transition of control from maternally-derived to embryonically-derived molecules. By day five, the embryo appears as a ball of cells, called the blastocyst, which is ready for implantation in his mother's womb. This sequence of orchestrated changes makes up the early stages of human development called embryogenesis.[9]

He then gives an analysis of the human egg or oocyte before it is in a state called meiotic arrest. "In a sense, the egg is a structured collection of *inert molecules awaiting activation*.... In this state the egg only has a lifespan of about twenty-four hours after it has been expelled by the ovary. It cannot maintain itself and soon depletes its energy resources. If it is not fertilized, the system will deteriorate, collapse, and the egg will die" (emphasis added).[10]

The fusion of egg and sperm (fertilization) has two effects. First, by introducing paternally derived molecules into the network of maternally derived molecules, it initiates a new structure, an entirely new system or organism. Second, fertilization

> triggers a change in the dynamics of the egg by reorganizing and reactivating the interconnected network of inert maternal molecules in its contents ... trigger[ing] the chain of reactions and molecular interactions that drive cell division and differentiation. If left alone, this self-driven, self-perpetuating process of molecular interactions will continue for nine months and beyond, transforming the living system called an embryo into the living system called a gurgling eight pound baby. Whereas the living system before fertilization only had a lifespan of twenty-four hours, the new living system after fertilization now has a span of seventy or eighty [years] for those who are strong. Furthermore, since this new system is capable of independent and self-sustaining existence, it is an organism. Fertilization is the paradigmatic example of cell-to-organism transition.[11]

Summarizing, Austriaco says that from the systems perspective,

> the beginning of life should be understood, first and foremost, as the transformation of one dynamic system, the egg, into another, the embryo. The *egg is a cell*, an embodied process in stasis that has only a

life expectancy on the order of hours because it *is not self-sustaining....* In contrast, the *embryo is an organism*, an embodied process that has a life expectancy on the order of decades precisely because *it has the ability to sustain itself as an independent entity.* It is a dynamic system which arises from the necessary interactions among the mix of molecules that is created by the fusion of the egg and the sperm, and it manifests itself as the visible and morphological changes which we call human development.[12]

It is easy to see, after this summary of Austriaco's essay, why standard embryology texts locate the beginning of the human individual at fertilization, not at implantation.[13] But some people claim that at implantation maternal signaling factors transform a bundle of cells into a human organism. However, as Patrick Lee and Robert George point out,

> there is much dispute about whether any such maternal signaling actually occurs. As Hans-Werner Denker observes, it was once assumed that in mammals, in contrast to amphibians and birds, polarity in the early embryo depends upon some external signal, since no clear indications of bilateral symmetry had been found in oocytes, zygotes, or early blastocysts. But this view has been revised in light of emerging evidence: "[I]ndications have been found that in mammals the axis of bilateral symmetry is indeed determined (although at first in a labile way) by sperm penetration, as in amphibians. Bilateral symmetry can already be detected in the early blastocyst and is not dependent on implantation."

Continuing, Lee and George write:

> Denker refers specifically to the work of Magdalena Zernicka-Goetz and her colleagues at Cambridge and that of R. L. Gardner at Oxford, which shows that polarity exists even at the two-cell stage.
>
> The test of whether a group of cells constitutes a single organism is whether they form a stable body and function as parts of a whole, self-developing, adaptive unit. Compaction, cavitation, the changes occurring earlier to facilitate these activities, and implantation — all of these activities are clear cases of the cells acting in a coordinated manner for the sake of a self-developing and adaptive whole. In other words, such activities are ordered to the survival and maturation of the whole, existing embryo. This fact shows that the unity of the blastomeres (the cells of the early embryo) is *substantial* rather than incidental; the blastomeres are integrated parts of a functional whole, not separate parts that lead to the

creation of a whole. This is compelling evidence that what exists from day 1 to day 6 is not a mere aggregate of cells but a multi-cellular organism.... The actions of the embryo from day 1 to day 6 are clearly part of a unitary development toward human maturation. None of the events occurring in the embryo could reasonably be interpreted as creating a new and distinct direction. Implantation does not change the *nature* (kind of being) of the embryo; it is an event in the unfolding life of a whole human organism, not the initiation of an entirely new organism.[14]

In his 2011 masterful study, *The Ethics of Abortion: Women's Rights, Human Life, and the Ethics of Abortion,* Christopher Kaczor takes up this crucial issue. In Chapter 5, "Does Human Life Begin at Conception?", Kaczor, who had in Chapters 2 through 4 demolished claims that human personal life begins after birth, at birth, or during pregnancy, points out that to determine when an individual human begins to be is a biological or scientific, not a moral, question. Making his own the scientific studies of Arey, Larsen, and Moore, to which reference has already been given, Kaczor shows that "this evidence leaves no doubt about the beginning of human beings; they come to be at conception, when the sperm from the man fuses with the oocyte of the woman and a new organism, distinct from mother and father, begins to be with the active potency to develop into an embryo, fetus, newborn ... senile old person." He then offers another argument, which he calls the "constitutive property" argument, to support this conclusion (pp.105-120). The "constitutive property" is that all human beings from conception on are *rational animals,* i.e., bodily beings with the *active potency* or *radical capacity,* rooted in their being the *kind* of beings they are, i.e., rational animals endowed with reason and freedom of choice, to develop and exercise the rational acts of forming concepts, judgments, and arguments. (On this see "Personhood Requires Exercisable Cognitive Abilities" below.)

3. It Is Reasonable to Believe That Most People Begin at Fertilization and Unreasonable to Deny This

Here I will defend the position that the individual personal human life of most people begins at conception/fertilization. This position, of course, is denied by many. It is denied first of all by those who claim that the being killed by abortion is not even a *human being,* let alone a person. It is denied also by many who grant that the being killed by abortion is a *human being* or *member of the human species,* but who contend that it simply cannot be regarded as a *person* with rights. Still others adopt one or another variant of the "gradualist" view, which holds that at some point during gestation the entity that was conceived *becomes* human and personal in nature. There are many variants of this view, with some holding that a human person is in existence early on in the process — for instance, at implantation — while others claim that the being does not become a person until some later stage — say, at the formation of the neocortex of the brain, the presence of all organ systems, viability, etc. This view, which has wide rhetorical appeal, regards early abortions (those done prior to the event that marks the beginning of personal as opposed to merely biological life, whatever that event might be) as morally permissible, while abortions done later are questionable; and the later an abortion is done, the closer it is to being wrong or more seriously wrong. Among the finest presentations and critiques of these different views are the studies by Patrick Lee in *Abortion and Unborn Human Life* and by Robert George and Christopher Tollefsen in *Embryo: A Defense of Human Life*, and I urge readers to consult these rigorously argued works.[15] Many others have also examined this matter in depth, and my obvious debt to them will be noted throughout.

I will first briefly consider some opinions, unfortunately common in our society, that are utterly incompatible with what we *know* about human procreation. I will then take up positions that at least seem more plausible. The falsification of the even more plausible views will help corroborate the claim that it is reasonable to hold that the human personal life of most people begins at conception/fertilization and that it is unreasonable to deny this.

There is no need to waste time with the utterly rhetorical and/or euphemistic assertions identifying the being brought into existence at fertilization as "protoplasmic rubbish" or a "gobbet of meat"[16] or a "blueprint"[17] or "gametic materials" or the "product of conception,"[18] or only a "part of the mother's body."[19] Such views, which rely on rhetoric and the abuse of language, are patently either false or totally inadequate in light of what we actually *know* about the process of human generation. They simply cannot be and ought not to be taken seriously.

Another common set of claims, slightly more credible, that deny the humanity and *a fortiori* the personhood of the human zygote and early embryo appeal to the fact that these organisms do not *appear* to be human or persons. Pictures and drawings of human beings at these stages of development *seem* to support claims of this kind. "How," they ask, "can you say that an organism with no face or hands or feet or organs can possibly be a human being, much less a person?" Or, "How can an organism no larger than the period at the end of a sentence possibly be regarded as a human being, a person?" Germain Grisez points out that arguments of this kind are plausible "because they use imagery and directly affect feelings. Usually, in judging whether or not to apply a predicate [such as *human being* or *person*] to an experienced entity, one does not examine it to see whether it meets a set of intelligible criteria; instead, one judges by appearances, using as guide past experience of individuals of that kind." However, he continues, such claims can be falsified by pointing out "that, while the particular difference [between a human zygote or early embryo and an embryo or fetus at a later stage of development] is striking because of the normal limits of human experience, nevertheless entities that are different in that way certainly are living human beings."[20] Stephen Schwarz, whom Grisez commends, has identified the element common to these denials of humanity and/or personhood to the zygote and early embryo and has responded to it decisively. He points out that all these objections are "based on the expectation that what is a person must be like us. It must be the right size (a size like ours); it must have a level of development comparable to ours; it must look like us; it must, like us, be conscious."[21]

But, he continues, "these are not true criteria for being a person [or for being a human being]." They are rather "simply expressions of our expectations, of what we are used to, of what appears familiar to us. It is not that the zygote fails to be a person [or a human being] because it fails these tests; rather, it is we who fail by using these criteria to measure what a person [or a human being] is."[22]

It is unreasonable to expect that a human being in the first stages of his or her development will look like a familiar human being, or like a newborn baby or a four-year-old or a teenager, or like a mature adult or a wheelchair-bound elderly man or woman. The way these persons *appear* during the early stages of their development says nothing of the status of their *nature* or *being*. Each of us develops and unfolds his or her personality every day of our lives, and we were developing and unfolding them before we were born, just as we have done since, because we were alive then. This ought not to cause anyone surprise. Horton, one of Dr. Seuss's lovable characters, hits the nail on the head in *Horton Hears a Who* when he says, "A person's a person, no matter how small."

Another claim denying personhood to the unborn, or at least to many unborn human beings, is widely held today, but it too is readily falsifiable. It is the claim that personhood is a status conferred on entities by others, and it is, surprisingly, held by many in our society. Proponents of this view contend that personhood is a *social status* conferred on an entity by others, and that an entity is a *person* only when recognized by others as a person. They believe that this view is supported by the truth that persons exist only with other persons — personhood is *relational* in character.

One advocate of this view, Marjorie Reiley Maguire, proposes that the personhood of the unborn "begins when the bearer of life, the mother, makes a covenant of love with the developing life within her to birth.... The moment which begins personhood ... is the moment when the mother accepts the pregnancy." And, if she does not accept it and decides to abort the "developing life within her," that life must be regarded as not a person, for personhood has not been bestowed on it.[23]

This position, of course, leads to the absurdity that the same being can be simultaneously both a person and not a person; it is a person, for instance, if at least one other person, say its father, recognizes and esteems it as a person; but it is not a person if another, say its mother, refuses to consider it a person. This claim presupposes that human meaning-giving *constitutes* persons; the truth is that human meaning-giving and human societies *presuppose* human persons.[24]

I will now consider and rebut more plausible views that deny personhood to the unborn. These have been well identified by Grisez, who offers excellent critiques of them.[25] In what follows, I will use categories somewhat different from the ones he uses, but mine are essentially the same. The principal positions of this kind are the following: (A) personhood requires exercisable cognitive abilities; (B) personhood is dependent on sense organs and a brain (= the "delayed hominization" position); (C) individual persons, as phenomena such as twinning and the "wastage" of embryos prior to implantation indicate, are formed only two weeks after fertilization.

A. Personhood Requires Exercisable Cognitive Abilities

This view, widely held today, contends that for a human being to be regarded as a person, he or she must have developed at least incipiently exercisable capacities or abilities for understanding, choice, and rational communication. Many who hold it — and among its more influential proponents are Michael Tooley, Daniel Callahan, and Peter Singer[26] — are willing to grant that a human being, in the sense of a living biological member of the human species, is in existence from conception/fertilization or at any rate very early afterward. But they contend that membership in the human species is not a sufficient criterion for personhood because only some members of the human species acquire the property or set of properties necessary if an entity is to be regarded as a person. In fact, some who hold this position assert that those who believe that membership in the human species is of great moral significance are guilty of a form of discrimination, *speciesism*, a prejudice similar to such immoral prejudices as racism. Prominent among those who make this claim is Peter Singer, the champion of "animal rights," who contends that it is far more immoral to torture a kitten than it is to kill an unborn child or a young infant with a debilitating condition such as Down syndrome.[27] In this view, not only are unborn children nonpersons but so too are newborns and, apparently, adult humans who no longer possess exercisable faculties of knowledge, recognition, consciousness, etc.

The reasoning behind this claim is fallacious. It fails to distinguish between a *radical* capacity or ability and a *developed* capacity or ability. A radical capacity can also be called an *active*, as distinct from a merely *passive*, potentiality. An unborn baby or a newborn child, precisely by reason of its membership in the human species, has the *radical capacity* or *active potentiality* to discriminate between true and false propositions, to make choices, and to communicate rationally. But in order for the child, unborn or newborn, to *exercise* this capacity or set of capacities, his radical capacity or active potentiality for engaging in these activities — predictable kinds of behavior for members of the human species — must be allowed to develop. But it could never be developed if it were not there to begin with. Similarly, adult members of the human species may, because of accidents, no longer be capable of actually exercising their capacity or ability to engage in these activities. But this does not mean that they do not have the natural or radical capacity, rooted in their being the kind of beings they are, for such activities. They are simply inhibited from exercising this capacity by disease or accidents. Similarly, members of the species "bald eagle" have the *radical* capacity or *active* potentiality, rooted in their being the kind of beings they are, to soar loftily in the air; eaglets who have not as yet *developed* this capacity and adult eagles whose wings have been broken are not able to *exercise* this capacity, but the fact that this capacity is not presently exercisable does not mean that it is not a radical capacity or active potentiality rooted in the nature of all members of the species "bald eagle" and not merely potential in a passive sense.

A human embryo has the *active* potentiality or *radical* capacity to develop *from within its own resources* all that it needs to exercise the property or set of properties characteristic of adult members of the species. One can say that the human embryo is a human person *with potential*; he or she is *not* merely a *potential person*. Those, like Tooley and Singer, who require that an entity have *exercisable* cognitive abilities, recognize that the unborn have the *potentiality* to engage in cognitive activities. But they regard this as a merely *passive* potentiality and fail to recognize the crucially significant difference between an *active* potentiality and a merely *passive* one. In his excellent development of the significance of this difference, Patrick Lee makes two very important points. The first concerns the *moral* significance of the difference between an *active* and a merely *passive* potentiality. An active potentiality means "that the same entity which possesses it is the same entity as will later exercise that active potentiality. With a passive potentiality, that is not so; that is, the actualization of a passive potentiality often produces a completely different thing or substance [e.g., oxygen has the passive potentiality to become water when appropriately combined with hydrogen]." Lee's second key point answers the question "Why should higher mental functions or the capacity or active potentiality for such functions be a trait conferring value on those who have it?" The proper answer is that such functions and the capacity for them are "of ethical significance not because [these functions] are the only intrinsically valuable entities but because entities which have such potentialities are intrinsically valuable. And, *if the entity itself is intrinsically valuable, then it must be intrinsically valuable from the moment that it exists.*"[28]

The claim that not all human beings are persons but that only those who possess exercisable cognitive abilities are to be so regarded, moreover, is marked by debates among its advocates over precisely *which* ability or abilities must be exercisable if an entity is to be classified as a person. This claim thus inevitably leads to arbitrary and unjust criteria for "personhood." A group of Catholic thinkers in England gives a devastating critique of this arbitrariness, and it is worthwhile to cite it at some length because it so ably pinpoints the arbitrariness involved:

> The rational abilities necessary to these [cognitive] abilities are various, and come in varying degrees in human beings. If actual possession of such abilities is a necessary condition of the claim to be treated justly, questions will have to be faced precisely *which* abilities must be possessed, and how developed they must be before one enjoys this claim to be treated justly. And these questions can be answered only by *choosing* which to count as the relevant abilities and precisely how developed they must be to count. But any such line-drawing exercise is necessarily arbitrary.... Arbi-

trary choices may be reasonable and unavoidable in determining some entitlements.... But if one's understanding of human worth and dignity commits one to being arbitrary about who are to be treated justly (i.e., about who are the very *subjects* of justice), it is clear that one lacks what is recognisable as a framework of justice. For it is incompatible with our fundamental intuitions about justice that we should determine who are the subjects of justice by arbitrary choice. The need for a non-arbitrary understanding of who are the subjects of justice requires us to assume that *just treatment is owing to all human beings in virtue of their humanity.* This indispensable assumption is also intrinsically reasonable. It is true that the distinctive dignity and value of human life are *manifested* in those specific exercises of developed rational abilities in which we achieve some share in such human goods as truth, beauty, justice, friendship, and integrity. But the necessary rational abilities are acquired in virtue of an underlying or radical capacity, *given with our nature as human beings*, for developing precisely those abilities.[29]

The claim that "only those with exercisable cognitive abilities are persons" is also dualistic because it sharply distinguishes between the "person," the subject with exercisable cognitive abilities, and the living human body, which the person, as it were, possesses. It is, of course, true that human persons can do things — think, make free choices, etc. — which show that they are *more* than their bodies and that they are also (or can be) consciously experiencing subjects with cognitive abilities. But, as Grisez notes, "persons can be more than their bodies without being realities other than their bodies, since a whole can be more than one of its parts without being a reality other than that part."[30] There is not one being who breathes, eats, sleeps, feels bodily pain, etc., and another being who thinks, chooses, and is aware of his rights, etc. The same subject, the same *human being, is* the living human body and the subject of cognitive activities. The dualistic view of man underlying the claim denying personhood to human beings who lack *exercisable cognitive abilities* is, therefore, a false understanding of man, male and female.[31]

A final comment on this position is that, as Grisez has said, it simply misses "what *person* means in ordinary language," where the word refers to a living, human individual.[32] The legitimate application of this term to non-adult human beings is rooted in its use in referring to adult human beings, who regularly think of their personhood not as a trait that they have acquired at some time in their lives but as an aspect of their very being. If one asks a person when he or she was born, he or she will spontaneously say that he or she was born on his or her day of birth, clearly implying that the person so responding considers himself or herself to be identical in being with the one born on that day. And were one to ask a person, "When were you *conceived?*" the person addressed would spontaneously reply, "Approximately nine months before I was born," thereby implying that he or she regards himself or herself as the very same being, i.e., person, conceived and born.[33]

B. Personhood Depends on Sense Organs and a Brain: The "Delayed Hominization" Theory

Unlike the claim just considered, this position repudiates a dualistic understanding of the human person; nonetheless, its advocates contend that the early human embryo cannot be considered a person because it lacks sense organs and a brain, material organs necessary for exercising human cognitive and volitional powers.

Among its proponents are several Roman Catholic philosophers and theologians, the more influential of whom are Joseph Donceel, S.J., Thomas A. Shannon, and Allan Wolter, O.F.M.[34] These writers seek to rehabilitate the "delayed hominization" theory of St. Thomas Aquinas. According to this view, the human embryo undergoes a substantial change from a subhuman entity to a human, personal entity, and does so when its body becomes sufficiently organized to be fit matter for the infusion of a spiritual soul. Donceel proposes that the body formed at conception is capable only of biological, not rational actions. It is capable of the latter only when the neural integration of the entire organism has been established, and this occurs only around the twentieth week of gestation, when the cerebral cortex is present. Shannon and Wolter hold a similar view. Their central claim is that what specifically distinguishes human and personal nature as superior to that of other animals is reason, and that the necessary condition for reasoning is the operation of the cerebral cortex. Thus it is only after formation of the cerebral cortex that a *personal* as distinct from a merely *animal* body, fit for reception of a spiritual soul, is in being. It is at this point that the entity in question undergoes a substantial change; i.e., it changes from being a nonpersonal entity to a person. Donceel, Shannon, and Wolter realize that it is absurd to suggest that babies undergo a substantial change after birth, even though they cannot actually engage in thought until some time later in their development. They thus hold that the developed brain itself is not the bodily basis for intellectual activities but only its precursor, but they hold that this is all that the hylomorphic theory of St. Thomas requires.

The attempt by Donceel, Shannon/Wolter, and others to rehabilitate the "delayed hominization" theory in order to justify early abortions fails on several counts. First of all, these modern authors, in contrast to St. Thomas, assume that abortion of a pre-personal entity might be justified. But, as we saw earlier, various opinions during patristic and medieval times on the infusion of the spiritual soul in no way changed their judgment that procured abortion was always gravely immoral. All Christian writers, including St. Thomas, absolutely condemned all deliberate abortion, no matter whether the embryo/fetus was "formed" or not.

Secondly, the attempted rehabilitation of the "delayed hominization" theory is philosophically untenable, and untenable on *Thomistic* grounds in light of what we *know* about the process of human generation. Many writers, among them Grisez, Lee, Benedict Ashley, Albert Moraczewski, Jean Siebenthal, and Mark Johnson, have shown this very clearly.[35] Here I will summarize the critiques given by Grisez and Siebenthal.

Grisez first points out that even after birth, babies cannot think and make choices, the rational actions characteristic of human persons and the capacity for which distinguishes human, personal nature from subhuman, subpersonal nature. Thus, as the advocates of the "delayed hominization" theory admit, the beginning of the brain's development during the gestation period cannot be the bodily basis required for specifically personal acts but only its precursor. Since this precursor satisfies the requirements of St. Thomas's theory, why cannot precursors at earlier stages of development satisfy them? Moreover, modern biology demonstrates that every human embryo has from the very beginning a specific developmental tendency, including the epigenetic primordial, or sources for the development of *all* its organs, including the brain. The fact that a spiritual soul can exist only in matter able to receive it does not entail the conclusion that a human zygote cannot receive it, since it has within itself the active potency to develop all its organs. Grisez then concludes that the assumption on which this theory rests, namely, that the human embryo is at first a pre-personal entity and only later becomes personal, "posits two entities where only one is necessary to account for the observed facts. But entities," he continues, "are not to be multiplied without necessity. Consequently, the view that the embryo becomes a person when the brain begins to develop should be rejected, and the personal soul should be considered to be present from conception."[36]

Siebenthal's refutation of this view is most interesting because he roots it in a careful analysis of the thought of St. Thomas himself — to whom

Donceel, Shannon, and others appeal for support. Siebenthal first stresses that for St. Thomas the origin of the *human body* coincides with the infusion of a spiritual or intellectual soul. For St. Thomas, *human* flesh gets its being — its *esse* — from the human intellectual soul.[37] Since St. Thomas himself mistakenly thought, because he relied on the inadequate biological knowledge of his day, that in human generation the male seed was alone the active element, he concluded that the body first formed from the maternal blood by this seed was only vegetative in nature; later, a substantial change occurred and a new body, this time animated by an animal soul, was formed; finally, another substantial change occurred, and a new body, human in nature and animated by an intellectual soul, came into being. But note that for St. Thomas the *bodies* first generated were *not human* in nature. He thus concluded that there was a radical discontinuity between the bodies formed during gestation. Siebenthal's point is that St. Thomas, were he alive today and cognizant of the biological evidence known today, would not hesitate in concluding that the *body* that comes to be when fertilization is completed is indubitably a *human* body and hence that its organizing and vivifying principle can only be a *human soul,* an intellectual or spiritual soul.[38]

Today, in addition to those advocating the "delayed hominization" theory, several thinkers believe that authentically human and personal life begins only once the brain has developed in the unborn. They do so because they think that a functioning brain is an essential property of a human being. Scholars taking this position draw an analogy between the end and the beginning of human life. They note that today a widely accepted criterion to show that death has occurred and that a living human person no longer exists is the irreversible cessation of the functioning of *the entire brain, including the brain stem.* Since we can say that a person is dead, i.e., no longer alive and among us, when his or her brain in its entirety has irreversibly ceased to function, then why can we not say that human, personal life begins when the fetus acquires a functioning brain?[39]

Even if it is granted that irreversible cessation of all the functions of the entire brain, including the brain stem, is an acceptable criterion that death has occurred, the analogy invoked is not accurate, as Lee, in particular, clearly shows. While it is true that what we say about the end of human life should be consistent with what we say about its beginning, advocates of this view locate the analogy in the wrong place, i.e., in a *functioning brain,* and not in the *unity of the organism.* Irreversible cessation of all functions of the entire brain may indeed show that death has occurred, because in a mature human being the brain is the organ that integrates the functioning of all the systems of that mature human being. Hence, when the brain ceases to function (totally and irreparably) in a mature human being, all other tissues and organs cease to form a unified organism. A human being is essentially an organism, albeit a specific type, and so if the tissues and organs cease to constitute an organism, then the human being has ceased to be. But, since being an organism expresses in a very general way what a human being is, it is impossible for an organism to come to be at one time and, remaining the *same* organism, become human at a later time. Hence, "if an organism at one time is the same organism as a human organism at a later time, then the organism at the earlier time is a human organism also, the same human organism as the one which exists at a later time."[40] Proponents of this view must acknowledge that, before the formation of the brain in the developing biological organism, there is something in that organism during its zygotic and early embryonic stages that definitely integrates all its living activities — the essential function carried out by the brain in that same organism at later states of its existence. It is impossible to declare the organism dead or to deny that it is identifiably biologically as a member of the human species as distinct from other animal species. The organism is alive, is human in nature, and has within itself the active potential to develop its own brain. One cannot say this of the nonliving corpse of a person declared dead because there is certainty that there is irreversible cessation of all the functions of the entire brain, which serves, in the mature human, as the integrating, organizing factor.[41]

C. Individual Personhood Cannot Be Established Before Implantation

Another challenge to the thesis defended here, namely, that most persons begin at fertilization, is raised by those who contend, on the basis of certain facts (or alleged facts), that the thesis in question is unreasonable and that it is simply not possible for *individual human persons to come to be prior to implantation.*

The two major facts appealed to in support of this claim are the following: (1) the enormous "wastage" of life prior to implantation and (2) the phenomenon of monozygotic twins (triplets, etc.) and the possibility of "fusion" or recombination of two or more zygotic individuals into a different individual prior to implantation. As I will now show, the first of these alleged "facts" is highly questionable. The second raises some difficulties but definitely does *not*, as those who appeal to it claim, "rebut" the idea that human personal life begins at conception.

(1) The Question of "Wastage"

Some people, mainly Catholic theologians, contend that the loss or wastage of "fertilized eggs," "zygotes," "blastocysts," and other clusters of human genetic cells prior to implantation is so vast that it is highly unreasonable to call these entities "persons."[42] In fact, Shannon and Wolter say that "to ascribe such bungling of the [reproductive] process [as this "wastage" implies] to an all-wise creator would seem almost sacrilegious."[43]

The argument, in brief, is this: *Major:* An all-wise and providential God would not create new human persons made in his own image and likeness and then let them die even before they could be implanted in the wombs of their mothers. *Minor:* But enormous numbers of the beings resulting from human fertilization die before they can be implanted in the womb. *Conclusion:* Therefore, it is unreasonable and even sacrilegious to call these entities persons made in the image and likeness of God.

What can be said in response? First of all, the minor can be seriously challenged. Those who pose this problem cite studies claiming that from 40 to 60 percent of all "fertilized eggs" and their progeny are "wasted" prior to implantation. But if one carefully examines the studies in question — as several scholars have done, in particular, W. Jerome Bracken, C.P.[44] — one soon discovers that most such losses are the result of such severe chromosomal defects that the individuals in all likelihood lack the proper complement of genetic material for formation of a *human* body animated by a *spiritual* soul. In other words, the "fertilized eggs" that are "wasted" were not, in a great number of cases, individual human beings to begin with because of severe abnormalities in the process of fertilization.

How about the major? We are not God and do not know his mind. We need to remember that, for most of human history, infant mortality was very high. Would those who invoke the "fact" of "fetal wastage" to support their claim that it is unreasonable and even sacrilegious to say that individual personal life begins at conception want to deny that the millions of babies who have died in infancy were not persons and that an all-wise God would allow such "bungling" of the infancy period?

(2) The Question of Monozygotic "Twinning" and Possible "Fusion" or "Recombination" of Zygotes

It is a fact that two or more twins (triplets, etc.) known as "monozygotic" twins, etc., can be derived from the zygote (the human baby in its unicellular stage) formed after conception/fertilization but before implantation in the womb of the mother. It is also a possibility that a human individual might form from the "fusion" or "recombination" of two original zygotes (whether this possibility has ever in fact occurred in humans is not known). This fact and this possibility have led some to conclude that it is not possible for an *individual human person* to be in existence from fertilization, and that it is impossible for individual human persons to exist prior to implantation (a process that takes place approximately two weeks *after* fertilization and after which twinning is not possible).

Many today champion this position. It has been perhaps most extensively presented by an Australian Catholic priest, Norman Ford, S.D.B., in his highly influential book *When Did I Begin? Conception of the Human Individual in History, Philosophy, and Science,*[45] and by many others, for instance, Michael Coughlan.[46]

According to Ford, Coughlan, and others who hold this position, the zygote and the very early or "preimplantation" embryo (or, as they prefer to call it, the "pre-embryo," a term that ought not be employed, as Angelo Serra and Roberto Columbo emphasize in an important study[47]) is *genetically and biologically human* and distinct from its parents; but it is not as yet an *ontologically distinct human individual* until after "gastration," the formation of the "primitive streak," and implantation, events after which twinning and recombination cannot take place. What exists during this time of gestation, they insist, is not an ontologically distinct human individual but rather a colony of cells held together in an artificial way, each with the active potentiality and "totipotential" to become more than one human individual.

This is the basic claim made by proponents of this view. Shannon and Wolter, who adopt this view, attempt to strengthen it by appealing to the work of the biologists C. A. Bedate and R. C. Cefalo,[48] who contend that the early embryo or "pre-embryo" must receive information from the mother before a distinct human individual can begin to exist.

Before offering a definitive rebuttal to the claims made by Ford and others on the basis of the phenomenon of twinning and the possibility of recombination, I will first comment on Shannon and Wolter's assertion that the preimplantation embryo lacks the genetic information necessary for being a distinct human individual and must receive it from its mother. This contention has been devastatingly rebutted by the embryologist Antoine Suarez, who shows that contemporary research into early embryonic development definitively proves that "during pregnancy the embryo does *not* receive any messages or information from the mother able to control the mechanisms of development or to produce the type of cellular differentiation necessary for building the tissues of the new human adult." To the contrary, recent empirical research supports the conclusion that "*the pre-implantation embryo is the same individual of the human species (the same animal) as the adult into whom the pre-implantation embryo can in principle develop.*"[49]

The claims made by Ford and others based on the phenomenon of twinning have been subjected to devastating criticism by many, including philosophers, theologians, and embryologists. Among the more incisive critiques are those given by Grisez, Lee, Ashley/Moraczewski, Nicholas Tonti-Filippini, Anthony Fisher, and Angelo Serra/Roberto Columbo.[50] Here I will summarize the principal reasons given by these authors to show that the Ford-et-al. hypothesis is untenable.

The Ford-et-al. view claims that in the early embryo (or "pre-embryo") prior to implantation, formation of the "primitive streak," etc., the various cells within the *zona pellucida* (the membrane surrounding the zygote and early embryo) are all "totipotential," i.e., each *can* become distinct individual human persons (monozygotic twins, triplets, etc.), all with the same genetic endowment. Their thesis, as we have seen, is that while this entity is *biologically and genetically human* and distinct from its parents, it is not yet an *ontologically distinct* human individual person. It is rather a *colony* of individual cells, each capable of developing into a distinct human person.

However, as embryologists such as R. Yanagimachi and Antoine Suarez note in summarizing what is scientifically known about mammalian fertilization, "fertilization in mammals normally represents the beginning of life for an individual."[51] In light of all the evidence, the claim that cell division in the early embryo actually gives rise to a colony of really distinct individuals "until a small army of them form the true human individual" is not at all plausible.[52] Ford and those who agree with him think that the individual cells within the early embryo have the *active* potentiality to become individual human beings — and if so, then they would so develop unless some accident prevented such development. But they do not have such "active" potentiality; their "totipotentiality" is not "active" but hypothetical. It is hypothetical because, for it to be actualized, some extrinsic cause must separate the individual cells within the preimplantation embryo. We can grant that during the early stages of its development (i.e., prior to implantation) the individual cells of the embryo are as yet relatively unspecialized and therefore *can* become whole human organisms *if* they are divided and have an appropriate environment after division. But, as Patrick Lee points out, "this does not in the least indicate that prior to such an extrinsic division the embryo is an aggregate rather than a single, multicellular organism," and one identifiably of the human species, distinct from other members of the species.[53]

The crucial question raised by such phenomena as monozygotic twinning and possible recombination is this: Do they, *of themselves*, demonstrate that the "ontological" human individual comes into being only after implantation? The attempts to demonstrate this by Ford and others are very implausible and rest on the presupposition, not credible, that the individual cells within the *zona pellucida* surrounding the early embryo have the *active* potentiality to become individual human persons. But if they did have an *active* potency of this kind, then they would *all* become individual persons, and this is absurd. Thus, as Grisez says, "contrary to what Ford asserts (without argument), in those zygotes which develop continuously as individuals the facts do not evidence an *active* potentiality to develop otherwise. Rather, at most the facts show that all early embryos could *passively* undergo division or recombination."[54]

In short, the argument that individual human persons *cannot* begin at fertilization because of such phenomena as identical twinning is based on appearances and alleged common sense, but it fails to prove what it claims to prove. It is far more likely, as Ashley/Moraczewski and others argue, that identical twinning is a developmental accident and that the coming into being of identical twins can be explained reasonably as a mode of asexual reproduction (cloning).[55]

Twinning and similar facts in no way compel us to conclude that individual human persons do not begin to be at conception/fertilization. It is possible that *some* human individuals begin to be between fertilization and implantation, but *most* human individuals do come to be at fertilization/conception; it is reasonable to hold that they do and unreasonable to claim that they do not. I believe that this section of this chapter has provided evidence and arguments to support the truth of this proposition.

4. The Special Moral Gravity of Abortion, a Woman's "Right" to an Abortion, the Difference Between a "Right" and a "Liberty"

Here I will first reflect on the unique moral gravity of abortion. I will then comment on some of the principal arguments, passionately advanced, by those who claim that a woman has a "right" to abortion, and conclude by considering the crucial difference between a "right" and a "liberty" and the relevance of this distinction to the issue of abortion.

A. The Unique Moral Gravity of Abortion

Abortion, as we have seen, is the intentional killing of an innocent human person. As we saw in Chapter Two, the intentional killing of *any* innocent human person is an intrinsically evil act insofar as it is utterly opposed to *love* of the person made in the image and likeness of God. But the intentional killing of unborn human children and of infants has a unique kind of gravity. Human life, the life of human persons, is a magnificent gift from God, a truth that John Paul II develops eloquently in Chapter Two of his encyclical *Evangelium vitae*. Although we saw this in detail in Chapter Two, it is useful here to summarize what he had to say there and elsewhere.

Human life, the Pope reminds us, is surpassingly good because "the life which God gives man is quite different from the life of all other living creatures, inasmuch as man, although formed from the dust of the earth (cf. Gn 2:7; 3:19; Jb 34:15; Ps 103:14; Ps 104:29), *is a manifestation of God in the world, a sign of his presence, a trace of his glory* (cf. Gn 1:26-27; Ps 8:6)" (*Evangelium vitae,* no. 34). Human life indeed is the " 'place' where God manifests himself, where we meet him and enter into communion with him" (no. 38). This great truth is immeasurably deepened and enriched by the incarnation of God's only-begotten Son, his uncreated Word, who for love of us became, like us, God's "created word." And his Son, Jesus, has made known to us not only who we are — God's created "words," his living images — but also who we are meant to be! As John Paul II reminds us, "Eternal life ... is the life of God himself" and at the same time "is *the life of the children of God* (cf. 1 Jn 3:1-2).... *Here the Christian truth about [human] life becomes most sublime.* The dignity of this life is linked not only to its beginning, to the fact that it comes from God, but also to its final end, to its destiny of fellowship with God in knowledge and love of him" (no. 38).

God so loves us and wills that we share in his creative work that he entrusts to us in a special way the gift of new human life. This life, as the Pope reminds us, is entrusted "to each and every other human being." "But," he continues, it "is entrusted in a special way ... to woman, precisely because the woman, in virtue of her special experience of motherhood, is seen to have a *specific sensitivity* towards the human person and all that constitutes the individual's true welfare, beginning with the fundamental value of life."[56] New human life comes to be in and through the intimate union of man and woman (a union honored, as we saw in Chapter Three, only when *marital*). In its beginnings, this life is particularly vulnerable and dependent on others for its well-being. It is a gift to be welcomed and received with love, as each one of us knows. How grateful we must be if the man and the woman who gave us life welcomed our coming! And how sad it must be should one come to know that they did not, even if they did not kill one in the womb. Yes, the intentional killing of children, and in particular unborn children — and each one of us was, when we came into existence, an unborn child — has a particular gravity, a betrayal, as it were, of a sacred trust committed to our care. We must remember that God's eternal Word, his only-begotten Son, became man — became truly one of us — as a helpless and utterly dependent unborn child in the womb of his mother. He is one with unborn children in the wombs of their mothers.[57]

Unfortunately, many today, because of the contraceptive/abortifacient culture in which we live, fail to realize this truth or to take it into account. But it *is* a truth, one we must have the courage to face, even as we seek to care compassionately for women who experience pregnancies "unwanted" for one reason or another.

B. A Woman's "Right" to an Abortion

In our society, many claim today that a woman has a "right" to an abortion. It will be, I think, worthwhile to consider some of the major arguments given to support this claim and to show why they are not good arguments. In the final section of this part, I will show that the alleged right to an abortion is not a right at all but rather a supposed "liberty," one that cannot be genuine insofar as it is nonexistent in view of the unborn child's authentic right to life.

As Sidney Callahan remarks in an interesting essay,[58] the most highly developed feminist arguments for the morality and legality of abortion can be found in Beverly Wildung Harrison's *Our Right to Choose* (Boston: Beacon Press, 1983) and Rosalind Pollack Petchesky's *Abortion and Woman's Choice* (New York: Longmans, 1984). Callahan identifies four major strands of argumentation. Of these, the one dependent on the claim that the unborn child cannot be regarded as a person has already been sufficiently rebutted. Another, claiming that abortion is necessary if women are to be considered socially equal to men, simply avoids facing the basic questions. The other two lines of argument, however, are very popular, are somewhat more plausible, and appeal to many people today. They should therefore be confronted, the truth they inadequately express acknowledged, and their specious character identified.

The two arguments in question are: (1) the woman's moral right to control her own body, and (2) the moral necessity of autonomy and choice in personal integrity. The first claims that in choosing an abortion a woman is simply exercising a basic right of bodily integrity. If she does not choose to be pregnant, she should not be compelled to be so against her will. It is *her* body that is involved, and intimately so. If no one can be compelled to donate an organ to another or to submit to other invasive procedures on his or her own body for however noble a cause, why should women be so compelled just because they happen to become pregnant? This would seem especially the case, as another feminist author, Judith Jarvis Thomson, claimed in a celebrated essay originally published in 1970,[59] if the woman has taken precautions not to become pregnant by using an effective contraceptive. The alternatives, according to this argument, are these: either *compulsory pregnancy* or the right to terminate a pregnancy, i.e., have an abortion. Of these two alternatives, this argument contends, the second is obviously the right moral one, for it alone recognizes the woman's right to bodily integrity.

The second argument holds that in order for a woman to be a full adult in the moral sense, not only does she have a right to *bodily* integrity but also to make and keep commitments and determine her own lifestyle. In order to do this, she must have control over reproduction, because if she does not, she is not capable of keeping prior and present commitments, and/or of making future ones, particularly in the areas of family, work, and education. A right to abortion is integral to a woman's adult, mature responsibility and autonomy.[60]

With respect to the first argument, it simply refuses to take into consideration the truth that abortion affects the body and bodily integrity of the unborn child, whose life is destroyed by it, far more than it does the body and bodily integrity of his or her mother. As Callahan so well says in her critique of this argument, during pregnancy "one's own body no longer exists as a single unit but is engendering another organism's life. This dynamic passage from conception to birth is genetically ordered and universally found in the human species. Pregnancy is not like the growth of a cancer or infestation by a biological parasite; it is the way every human being comes into the world. Strained philosophical analogies fail to apply: having a baby is not like rescuing a drowning person, being hooked up to a famous violinist's artificial life-support system,[61] donating organs for transplant — or anything else."[62]

Proponents of this argument are correct in saying that civil law protects, and rightly so, one's own bodily integrity and considers as a crime against the person any invasions of that person's body without free and personal consent. This is the kernel of truth in the argument that gives it some plausibility. But the same civil law clearly and rightly holds that it is wrong and criminal to intentionally harm the bodies, bodily integrity, and lives of *other persons*, of other *bodies*. Although the protection that civil law thus affords has been unjustly removed from the unborn, it clearly recognizes the difference between invasive procedures affecting one's own body and attacks on the body of another. Thus the argument is specious.

The second major argument advanced by feminists is rooted in the individualistic understanding of human autonomy so prevalent in our culture, an understanding that refuses to recognize that human persons can exist only within a community of persons and that our freedom to choose is not independent of the truth and is not the same as the autonomy to determine what is right and what is wrong (cf. Chapters One and Two). The truth it contains, making it somewhat plausible, is that we must make commitments in our lives and be faithful to them. But these commitments, which are particular choices affecting broad areas of our lives, must themselves be morally good and in accord with the truth, and we may have to set some aside, once made, in the light of moral responsibilities that we have either freely taken upon ourselves or that have been placed on us (e.g., caring for an injured person when we are the only one able to do so, even if this means sacrificing something worthwhile in itself).

C. The Difference Between a "Right" and a "Liberty"

There is a great deal of talk in our society today about "rights." As we have seen, many claim that a woman has a "right" to an abortion; pro-lifers, on the other hand, claim that the unborn child has a "right" to life. How is it possible to distinguish between authentic rights and alleged rights? I believe that the distinction between a right in the strict sense or a "claim right" and a "liberty" or a "liberty right" is most helpful here. In what follows, I will paraphrase and to some extent simplify the brilliant discussion of this matter presented by John Finnis in Chapter 8 of his *Natural Law and Natural Rights*.[63]

Very frequently, particularly in popular discussions (as on TV talk shows, etc.), people talk about rights as two-term relations between persons and one subject-matter or *thing* (e.g., a woman's right to an abortion, an innocent person's right to life, a worker's right to a just wage, a smoker's right to smoke, etc.). In order to distinguish a right in the strict sense, or what can be called a "claim right," from a liberty or a "liberty right," it is necessary to speak of a three-term relationship between two persons (or groups of persons) and an act of a specific type. If we do so, we can speak of a "claim right" as follows:

> *A* (= a person or group of persons, or all persons if we are speaking of basic human and inalienable rights of human persons) has a *right* (a "claim right") that *B* (= another person or group of persons or all persons) should *x* (= some specifiable act), if and only if *B* has a *duty* to *A* to *x*.

To illustrate: Innocent human persons (= A) have a *right*, in the sense of a claim right, to life if and only if innocent human persons (= A) have a right that all other persons (= B) have a duty to innocent human persons (= A) to forbear from intentionally killing them (= x). In other words, the right of innocent human persons to life, if genuine, means that all other persons have an obligation or duty *not to kill them* intentionally. Applying this to unborn children, we can say: Unborn children have a strict right or claim right to life if, and only if, unborn children (= A) have a right that their mothers and other persons (= B) have a duty to unborn children *to forbear from aborting them, i.e., intentionally killing them* (= x). And, as we have seen, this right is genuine because all persons, including mothers, have a strict obligation or duty to forbear from intentionally killing innocent human persons, and abortion is the intentional killing of an innocent human person.

Note that with respect to a right in the strict sense, a claim right, the action in question is required, not of the right-holder, but of other persons. With reference to the right to life, the action required is first and foremost an act of forbearance (of refusal to kill intentionally) required of all who must respect this right. With respect to abortion, the action in question is not an action of the unborn, but an action of others (mothers, etc.) and is again an act of forbearance, of refusing intentionally to kill the unborn by aborting them.

What about the alleged "right" of a woman to an abortion? If we express this, not as a two-term relationship between a person (a woman) and a thing (an abortion), but in a three-term relationship between two persons and a specifiable action, we see that the alleged right is really a "liberty" claimed by women. It can be put generally as follows:

> *B* (= a person, group of persons, etc.) has a *liberty* relative to *A* (= a person, a group of persons, etc.) to *x* (= some specifiable act), if and only if *A* has no claim right that *B* should not *x*.

Translating this talk about the woman's alleged right to an abortion into this language, we have the following: A woman (= B) has a liberty relative to the unborn baby (= A) intentionally to abort it (= x) if and only if the unborn baby (= A) has no claim right that the woman (= B) should not abort it (= x). But, as we have seen, the unborn has the claim right that his or her mother (and others) forbear from aborting it. Consequently, the liberty (and not right) claimed by women to abort is spurious.

There are, of course, many genuine liberties or "liberty rights," e.g., the right to worship God, the right of persons of the opposite sex to marry and have children, etc.

5. Abortion as "Removal" vs. Abortion as "Killing"

Patrick Lee puts the title of the fourth chapter of his excellent book on abortion in the form of a question, "Is abortion justified as nonintentional killing?" In it he examines the view that abortions, or at least many of them, can be justified because they are not intentional killings of innocent human persons but are rather to be regarded as "indirect" abortions, or abortions that are not intended. As we have seen, the Magisterium condemns procured or "direct" abortion, i.e., acts in which the abortion is intended either as end or as means, but recognizes that under certain conditions one can rightly engage in an act which has abortion as a foreseen, even inevitable, yet unintended effect. In such instances, the abortion is unintended or nonintended.

If abortion is *defined* as the "removal" or "expulsion" of a living but not yet viable unborn child from the womb of his or her mother, then the question posed by Lee as the title of his chapter is intelligible, for it is at least conceivable that some "removals" or "expulsions" of a living but not yet viable unborn child from its mother's womb might not have as its moral object, either as end or as means, the killing or death of the unborn child. Assume, for the sake of argument, that the unborn child in the womb of a woman diagnosed with cancer of the uterus could be removed from her womb and placed in an artificial womb for the three months necessary for it to become viable. The woman is in danger of dying from the cancer, and traditionally Roman Catholic moralists (and the Magisterium) would justify the woman's having a hysterectomy or undergoing chemotherapy to protect her from dying of cancer, even though it was foreseen that the unborn child would die as a result of the hysterectomy or chemotherapy. The reasoning was that the "removal" of the child from the mother's womb — the abortion itself — and its consequent death were not "directly intended" but only foreseen as unavoidable but not intended effects of the hysterectomy or chemotherapy. It seems obvious that it would be far better, if it were possible, to save the life of the unborn child in such instances by "removing" it from the mother's womb to an artificial womb than to "allow" the child to die as a foreseen but nonintended result of the chemotherapy or hysterectomy. But one would, in this instance, definitely *intend* the "removal" of the unborn child from the mother's womb; one could not *not* intend this. Thus, if abortion is defined as "removal," then it seems that in at least some instances (like the hypothetical one I just gave) a "direct abortion" would be morally justifiable. This is the kind of issue with which Lee is concerned, and I will reflect on his treatment of this issue below.

But before doing so, it seems only obvious to note that if we *define* abortion as the *intentional killing of an innocent unborn child*, then it is not possible to distinguish between abortion as "removal" and abortion as "killing." If abortion is *defined* as the *intentional **killing** of an unborn child*, then directly intended *removals* of the unborn from their mothers' wombs cannot be considered *abortions*, **if** the *killing or death of the unborn* is intended neither as end nor as means, i.e., is not intended at all. But, as we have seen and as I emphasized in the first section of this chapter, Pope John Paul II in *Evangelium vitae* defines abortion as the *intentional killing of the unborn*. I will return to the relevance of this. I will begin, however, by summarizing and reflecting on Patrick Lee's analysis.

A. Lee's Analysis and Position

The question Lee poses is whether direct abortions, or at least many abortions (understood as removing or expelling nonviable unborn children from their mothers' wombs), can be justified because they are nonintentional killings of innocent human persons.

He notes that this line of justifying abortions (or most abortions) was developed by Judith Jarvis Thomson in her celebrated "In Defense of Abortion" article,[64] and Lee's first concern is to reject her claim that the great majority of abortions can be justified as nonintentional killings. She argued that even if we grant that the unborn baby is a human person with a right to life, this does not mean that it has a right to everything it needs to support its life, particularly the use of a woman's body. According to Thomson, no woman has the right to *kill* the fetus, but no woman has the obligation to let it use her body for life support *unless* she has voluntarily assumed this duty; and, particularly if she has tried to avoid conception by using contraceptives, very frequently she has not assumed that duty. Therefore, Thomson concludes, she can expel the unborn child from her body even if she knows that it will die as a result.

In short, she argues that there is a real difference between intentional killing or securing someone's death and causing death as a side effect. Many abortions are not intentional killings because the objective of the women having them is not the securing of the death of the children they are carrying; they are rather cases of causing death as a side effect of "removing" an unborn child from the womb, justifiable when one has no obligation to allow the unborn child the use of one's womb and one simply wants its removal. Consequently, many abortions are morally right even if we grant that the unborn child or fetus is a person.[65]

Lee grants that the distinction between intentional killing and causing death as a side effect is valid (and I agree, as can be seen from what was said above). But he argues, and rightly so, that the great majority of abortions are intentional killings because those who procure them want to get rid of the unborn. However, he continues, even if some abortions (= "direct" abortions understood as intentional "removals" of living but not yet viable unborn children from their mothers' wombs) are not intentional killings, they are not, for the most part, morally justified. He then distinguishes two types of abortion cases that are not (or at least need not be) intentional killings and in which the mother's life is not significantly in danger. In one type of case, the man and the woman freely choose to have sex, realizing that by doing so the woman can conceive (even if they use contraceptives). In such a case, even if one grants that the "object" of the abortion is not the securing of the child's death but its "removal" so that the woman could, for instance, maintain her figure, "removing" it and thereby "causing its death" as a foreseen side effect is gravely immoral because, Lee writes, "(a) they have a specific duty to the child because they placed him or her in that dependent relationship, and (b) the harm caused to the child is immensely worse than the harm that the woman (and others involved) is avoiding by having the abortion." In a second type of case, abortion is performed because of rape or incest. Here (a) does not apply, but because of (b) and other factors, such as the unborn child's innocence and the moral significance of the mother's biological relationship to it, abortion is not morally justified here either, even if it is not an instance of intentional killing but rather of intentional removal. It is not morally justified because it is grossly unjust and unfair and thus violates the moral principle of fairness or the Golden Rule in a serious way.[66]

Lee thus concludes that in the great majority of cases, one cannot justify direct abortion as "removal" rather than as "killing" because the death of the unborn child can and ought to be prevented; there are grave moral reasons why "allowing" its death would be seriously immoral.[67] But Lee goes on to argue that in cases in which the mother's life is significantly in danger, then permitting the death of the unborn child as a foreseen but not intended side effect of its removal could be morally justifiable. It is so, he says, "if the choice to save the mother rather than the child is fair" — for example, if both cannot be saved — because in such cases "it seems that it would be causing the child's death as a side effect and with a grave reason to do so." Lee says that he has no *philosophical* objections against (direct) abortion, understood as "removal" and not as "killing," in such cases, but in a footnote he advises his readers to follow the teaching of the Church if the act is against Catholic teaching.[68]

B. Critique

It is thus evident that Lee thinks that some abortions, clearly *intended* and hence "direct," can be justified in very special cases when necessary to save the mother's life as "removals" causing the death of the unborn child as a foreseen but *not intended* effect of its removal and an effect that one can rightly "permit." His position was set forth originally by Grisez (whom Lee follows on this matter) in his 1970 massive and superb defense of the unborn, *Abortion: The Myths, the Realities, and the Arguments*. Grisez applied St. Thomas Aquinas's analysis of killing in self-defense,[69] the classic source for the principle of double effect, to some sorts of procedures, for instance craniotomies and salpingostomies, that Catholic moral theologians — who, as we have seen at the beginning of this chapter, *defined* abortion as the "expulsion" of a living but not yet viable unborn child from the womb — considered "direct" abortions and therefore intrinsically immoral. Grisez argued (as does Lee in his book) that under certain conditions when such procedures are used, the death of the unborn child need be neither the end intended nor the means chosen and that, therefore, it is possible to regard the evil done by these procedures, namely, the death of the unborn child, as not intended and therefore justifiable.[70] As did Lee later, Grisez maintained that this was a position he had reached as a philosopher, but that, should Catholic teaching judge otherwise, Catholics like himself were not at liberty to set that teaching aside and act on the basis of his analysis.[71]

As indicated at the very beginning of this section, when I considered the possibility of "removing" an unborn child from the womb of a mother about to undergo a hysterectomy or chemotherapy (to save her life from cancer) to an artificial womb, I think that the distinction between abortion as "killing" and abortion as "removal" is a valid distinction, and is relevant to the issue of abortion when it is *defined* as the removal or expulsion of a nonviable fetus from the mother's body, and that if abortion is defined in this way, then some "direct" abortions are, at least in principle, justifiable. It is obvious, however, that if "direct" abortion, i.e., abortion intended either as end or as chosen means, is *defined* — as it is by Pope John Paul II — as the "killing" of an innocent unborn person, then all "direct" abortions are gravely immoral and in no way justifiable.

In the first edition, I rejected the defense offered by Grisez, Boyle, and Lee of craniotomy as an example of abortion as "removal" but not of "killing." I thought their analysis faulty; in particular, I thought their claim that the "object" morally specifying the act was to alter or change the dimensions of the baby's skull was simply a specious way of "redescribing" the act. I thus accepted the critique of their argument by Kevin Flannery, S.J.

I have since changed my mind. Before describing why I did, it is important, I think, to describe what a craniotomy is. The following description of it was sent to me by e-mail on October 20, 2007, by a great pro-life Catholic obstetrician-gynecologist, John Bruchalski, M.D.:

> The technical definition of a craniotomy is the surgical procedure where the physician creates a hole in the cranium (crani-otomy). The most common practical situation would be when a pre-born child has water on the brain, hydrocephalus. In that case the craniotomy is accomplished by an 18g needle[,] where the skull is punctured and fluid drained to decompress the child's skull enough to affect vaginal delivery. *The intent in that case is to affect delivery[,] not to kill the child* [my emphasis]. In a D&X abortion [= partial-birth abortion], the craniotomy is to kill the child and enable the delivery of the head. Today, a cesarean section would be done in most cases to safely deliver the child and "save" the mother's life in most medical situations. The intention of doing a craniotomy with anything other than a needle is the death of a child to save the mother's life. Craniotomy is the direct, intended destruction of the child in most medical cases where it is recommended as a therapy for delivery to protect the life of the mother. Cesarean sections are able to be done safely and quickly.[72]

It now seems to me that Boyle in essence put the matter correctly in a passage cited and criticized in the first edition. Boyle pointed out that in the case under consideration, "the death of the fetus in no way contributes to the continuation of labor and thus to saving the mother's life, and thus the bringing about of this effect just as such is not a means to these ends.... [I]t is not the *killing* which removes the threat; the means here appears to be the craniotomy itself insofar as it alters the dimensions of the skull *in order to* allow labor to proceed. It is the dimensions of the baby's skull being altered and not its being dead which saves the mother's life." I have also been led to change my mind by studying the article jointly published in *The Thomist*, in January 2001, by John Finnis, Germain Grisez, and Joseph Boyle, entitled " 'Direct' and 'Indirect': A Reply to Critics of Our Action Theory."

There they show that both Thomas Aquinas (cf. *In II Sent.* d. 40, a. 2, c and ad 2-3, *De Malo*, q. 2, a. 2, ad 8, ST II-II, q. 64, a. 7, *In V Metaphysics*, lect. 2, no. 9) and John Paul II (*Veritatis splendor*, no. 78) make it clear that the object morally specifying a human act *cannot be identified with a process or an event in the physical order* (what Thomas called the *natural species* of an act as distinct from its *moral* species) but is rather precisely what the acting person is *choosing to do* here and now, and that this object can be grasped only from the perspective of that acting person. It is thus possible that the very same physical performance, e.g., a craniotomy in its *natural species*, can be, if viewed *from the perspective of the acting person*, either the choice to engage in a partial-birth abortion (a morally bad object of choice) or the choice to reduce the size of the baby's head so that it or its corpse can be removed from the birth canal (an object of choice not in itself immoral), foreseeing as a nonintended side effect the death of the child, a death that could be accepted under the principle of double effect.

Finnis, Grisez, and Boyle respond to the charge that the Magisterium has condemned their view by acknowledging that toward the end of the nineteenth century the Holy Office (now the Congregation for the Doctrine of the Faith) issued three documents concerning craniotomies. But, they emphasize, "*none of these documents taught that craniotomies are intentional killings or morally wrong.*" But those documents did declare that one might not *teach* that craniotomies could be done and that craniotomies cannot safely be done. Our authors then write: "However, since the Holy Office did not assert that craniotomy is immoral, its responses cannot ground an argument against a position such as ours," inserting a footnote in which they write: "Our position is shared by some theologians completely faithful to the Church's magisterium, e.g., Marcellino Zalba, S.J." Zalba, I want to note, was a member of the minority commission of the "papal birth control commission" that defended the Church's teaching against contraception prior to *Humanae vitae* and subsequently heroically defended *Humanae vitae* and as a result suffered terribly.

Finnis, Grisez, and Boyle affirm that they regard as a truth of faith the Church's teaching that the intentional killing of the unborn is *always gravely immoral.* Their position, however, is that "a doctor could do a craniotomy, even one emptying a baby's skull, without intending to kill the baby — that is, without the craniotomy being a direct killing." Here they insert another footnote in which they acknowledge that *even if such killing is not directly intended or direct killing it could often be gravely wrong and that there might be reasons for condemning the practice of craniotomy other than that it is direct killing and that Catholics who reject their opinion certainly ought to form their consciences in the light of Church teaching in the light of faith.*[73]

I have come to accept their argument that a craniotomy could indeed *not* be a direct, intentional killing of the unborn and that the child's death could be accepted as a nonintended but foreseen consequence of an act not morally bad in itself. So far as I know, however, the Magisterium, although not declaring craniotomy in the case envisioned to be morally wrong, nonetheless still teaches that it is *not safe to teach* that craniotomies can be performed and also that *craniotomies are not safe.* Since neither our authors nor I have the right to instruct the faithful, whereas the Magisterium has both the right and the duty, I conclude this part of this chapter by citing an important passage from Grisez's *Abortion: The Myths, the Realities, and the Arguments* (pp. 345-346):

> Roman Catholic readers may notice that my conclusions about abortion diverge from common theological teachings, and also diverge from the official teaching of the Church as it was laid down by the Holy Office in the nineteenth century. I am aware of the divergence, but would point out that my theory is consonant with the more important and more formally definite teaching that direct killing of the unborn is wrong. I reach conclusions that are not traditional by broadening the meaning of "unintended" in a revision of the principle of double effect, not by accepting the rightness of direct killing or the violability of unborn life because of any ulterior purpose or indication.

He then continues:

> Most important, I cannot as a philosopher limit my conclusions by theological principles. However, I can as a Catholic propose my philosophic conclusions as suggestions for consideration in the light of faith, while not proposing anything contrary to the Church's teaching as a practical norm of conduct for my fellow believers. *Those who really believe that there exists on this earth a community whose leaders are appointed and*

continuously assisted by God to guide those who accept their authority safely through time to eternity, would be foolish to direct their lives by some frail fabrication of mere reason instead of by conforming to a guidance system designed and maintained by divine wisdom. (emphasis added)

6. The Management of Ectopic Pregnancies

Currently, there is a debate among non-dissenting Catholic theologians regarding the legitimacy of different methods of managing ectopic pregnancies, specifically tubal pregnancies. Before taking up this debate, I will briefly describe ectopic pregnancies, their frequency, and current medical procedures available for their management. I will also summarize relevant material from the *Ethical and Religious Directives for Catholic Health Care Services* promulgated by the bishops of the United States in November 1994.

A. Ectopic Pregnancies and Their Frequency

An ectopic ("out of place," from the Greek *ek*, "out of," and *topos*, "place") pregnancy occurs when a developing new human person does not implant in the uterus, where it belongs, but elsewhere in the mother's body, usually in the fallopian tube or, more rarely, in the ovary, the cornua, the abdomen, or the cervix. Such pregnancies pose serious risks to the mother's life because of the danger of hemorrhage. During the last thirty years, there has been an alarming increase in the number of ectopic, and particularly tubal, pregnancies. The principal factors responsible for this increase include the alarmingly growing number of sexually transmitted diseases, especially pelvic inflammatory disease, tubal sterilization, the use of intrauterine devices or progesterone contraceptive pills, and *in vitro* fertilization.[74]

B. Medically Available Procedures for Coping With Ectopic Pregnancies

Medical authorities recognize four major treatment procedures for managing ectopic pregnancies: (1) "expectant" therapy; (2) drug therapy; (3) conservative surgical treatment; and (4) radical surgical treatment.[75] (1) "Expectant" therapy simply means that nothing is done and one simply waits for the tubal pregnancy to resolve itself by spontaneous abortion or miscarriage. This may occur in as many as 64 percent of the cases. (2) Drug therapy involves the uses of methotrexate (MTX). MTX interferes with the synthesis of DNA and resolves tubal pregnancies by attacking the trophoblast, i.e., the outer layer of cells produced by the developing baby, connecting it to its mother. According to the scientific literature, actively proliferating trophoblastic tissue "is exquisitely sensitive to this effect [interference with the synthesis of DNA], which forms the rationale for its use in the treatment of ectopic pregnancies."[76] Under (3), "conservative surgical treatment," are included (a) partial salpingectomy or removal of the portion of the fallopian tube *affected* by the tubal pregnancy, i.e., that portion of the tube containing the tubal pregnancy, with subsequent resectioning of the fallopian tube and (b) salpingostomy, procedures in which an incision is made in the affected part of the fallopian tube and the developing embryo is extracted, along with portions of the fallopian tube itself, by the use of forceps or other instruments.[77] (4) "Radical surgical treatment" is necessary if the fallopian tube has ruptured and consists in a total salpingectomy or the removal of the entire affected fallopian tube and, with it, the unborn child.[78]

C. The Ethical and Religious Directives

In the 1971 set of *Ethical and Religious Directives for Catholic Health Care Facilities*, the bishops of the United States included the following directive, no. 16:

> In extrauterine pregnancy the affected part of the mother (e.g., cervix, ovary, or fallopian tube) may be removed, even though fetal death is foreseen, provided that (a) the affected part is presumed already to be so damaged and dangerously affected as to warrant its removal, and that (b) the operation is not just a separation of the embryo or fetus from its site within the part (which would be a direct abortion from a uterine appendage) and that (c) the operation cannot be postponed without notably increasing the danger to the mother.[79]

This directive clearly authorizes as morally licit the use of partial salpingectomy or total salpingectomy in order to safeguard the mother's life when there is grave danger of hemorrhaging from the fallopian-tube pregnancy. But it also clearly excludes use of a salpingostomy. At the time this directive was written, the management of tubal pregnancies by methotrexate was not known.

Yet the relevant directive in the 1994 *Ethical and Religious Directives for Catholic Health Care Services* is markedly different. It says simply: "In case of extrauterine pregnancy, no intervention is morally licit which constitutes a direct abortion" (no. 48).[80] But, theologians now ask, what constitutes a "direct abortion" in the management of tubal pregnancies?

D. Current Debates Over Management of Ectopic Pregnancies

In the first edition, I maintained that the salpingectomy was the only morally permissible, non-abortifacient way of coping with a tubal pregnancy. I rejected as abortifacient and hence immoral both salpingostomy and the use of methotrexate, repudiating the position defended by Albert Moraczewski, Patrick Clark, and others.[81]

I have since changed my mind and now accept the view held by Moraczewski and others. I have also now come to regard salpingostomy as a morally licit way of coping with tubal pregnancies, since it is, I judge, "abortion as removal" and not "abortion as killing," because the object specifying the act is not to kill the unborn child but to remove it from its place within the mother. Christopher Kaczor offers a good analysis of this matter, writing that

> removing the embryo from the fallopian tube in itself *is not* simply the same thing as intentionally killing. Although there is not yet an established procedure for facilitating this transfer, one can hope that advances in microsurgery and early detection of ectopic pregnancy would render possible both a preservation of embryonic human life as well as the reproductive capability of the fallopian tube. I believe that the removal of the embryo from its pathological site of implantation ... is *implicitly* recognized as a morally good or indifferent action, considered by itself and independently of its effects (condition 1 of double effect), even by those who condemn these procedures. A number of respected ethicists who vigorously oppose removing the embryo alone, including William E. May, Eugene F. Diamond, Thomas Hilgers, and Kelly Bowring, nevertheless endorse efforts at embryo transplantation from the fallopian tube to the uterus. But such transplantation necessarily involves detaching the embryo from its location in the fallopian tube — which, if truly evil in itself and not merely from its effects, would be an act that is intrinsically evil and therefore never to be performed regardless of the consequences. So at least implicitly, these authors do not hold that detaching the embryo from its pathological location in itself is intrinsically evil (or they should — to be consistent — condemn as intrinsically evil any effort to transplant an ectopic pregnancy into the uterus).[82]

I do not accept methotraxate as a morally licit way of coping with ectopic pregnancies because it is used before it has been clearly established whether the embryo has a real chance of survival or dies spontaneously and thus not cause a threat to the mother's life because of a ruptured fallopian tube.

7. "Hard Cases" for Opponents and Supporters of Abortion

We are all familiar with the so-called hard cases raised by defenders of abortion in response to the assertion that the free choice intentionally to kill an unborn human baby, a human person with the strict claim right not to be deliberately killed by anyone, either as means or as end, is wrong. These are (1) abortion because of rape or incest, (2) fetal anomalies such as Down syndrome, cystic fibrosis, Tay-Sachs disease, etc., and (3) the *health*, including mental health, and *life* of the mother (as legally permitted by *Roe v. Wade*).

We also know how to answer objections based on these cases. The first (1), abortion because of rape or incest, leaves unpunished the male who violated the woman's bodily integrity and instead punishes another innocent person, the baby conceived as a result of his vicious act. But the child so conceived, as Chicken George, the hero of Alex Haley's *Roots*, eloquently illustrates, can grow up to love and protect his mother, and she can come to love and cherish him throughout her life if she is given proper community support — and this is surely a mission Catholic dioceses and parishes can and ought to give by establishing centers for counseling and supporting women who have been sexually violated by males.

Regarding (2) "fetal deformity," an unborn baby — and every innocent living human person — has the inviolable claim right not to be intentionally killed by others, either by acts of omission or acts of omitting what is morally required. Their value as persons remains despite any handicaps they may suffer. Our duty is to seek to remove or alleviate their handicaps and not to kill them.

Regarding (3) abortion to protect the health, including the psychological health, of the mother, or her life, we know, first of all, that the woman's psychological health can and ought to be treated by appropriate psychological and/or psychiatric care; it is surely not removed by killing the child in her womb. We know also that if the mother's life is threatened—extremely rare today in most of the world—the principle or rule of double effect justifies therapeutic measures such as radiation therapy for cancer of the uterus and morally licit ways of coping with ectopic pregnancies (see above). Even if we realize that the death of the unborn child is a foreseen but unintended effect of the therapeutic act, its death is in no way the means chosen to protect her life.

What of "hard cases" for defenders of abortion? Kaczor considers several such hard cases in *The Ethics of Abortion* (pp. 193-214). I will here consider three that he takes up.

The first is the murder of pregnant women. "Most people," Kaczor writes, "find the raping of women morally abhorrent and particularly odious if the woman is pregnant and even more so if it causes her to have a miscarriage. So true is this that even proponents of capital punishment balk at executing a pregnant woman. At times the males who have caused a woman to become pregnant assault her in order to cause a miscarriage if she refuses to abort the child." He then cites the notorious example that occurred when Scott Peterson killed his wife, who was eight months pregnant. Missing since Christmas Eve 2002, their bodies washed ashore separately on April 14, 2003, and the baby's umbilical cord was still attached. The husband was legally charged by the California Court with two counts of murder, with "special circumstances" calling for tougher penalties (pp. 193-194).

The second is sex-selection abortion. If an abortion is done because a child of unwanted sex is known to be in the womb, another hard case is facing defenders of abortion. This almost always means the elimination of females and in some countries or cultures extends to their infanticide, should they survive until birth. In the United States 85 percent of women and 95 percent of men want a male child for their first baby, and the first may well be the last wanted. This kind of abortion troubles female defenders of abortion. How can they criticize such abortions without implying that abortion itself is problematic? In fact, as Kaczor says, "the American College of Gynecologists and Obstetricians (ACOG) opposes sex-selection abortion." He concludes: "It is not a simple matter to condemn sex selection abortion while upholding abortion for other reasons" (pp. 194-200).

The third hard case is abortion for frivolous reasons. "Abortions are frequently done for very frivolous reasons—parents want a child conceived during a certain astrological sign, a Leo, say, rather than an Aries—or a child of a certain hair color." Kaczor cites Naomi Wolf, who identified some trifling reasons used by classmates in her high school during the '70s (to find out if a girl could get pregnant and, if she did, to abort the pregnancy). This is enough to illustrate the problem (p. 200).[83]

Conclusion to Chapter Five

This lengthy chapter has examined in detail the issue of abortion and respect for human life and its dignity. Human life is truly a gift, and a surpassing one at that, from God himself. It is indeed the "place" where we encounter God in our everyday lives. It is a *good of the person*, not a mere good *for* the person. If we are to love God, we must love our neighbor; and if we are to love our neighbor, we must respect the good of his or her life; and our neighbor includes the unborn child hidden in his or her mother's body (or, perhaps, in petri dishes), no matter how small he or she may be. We ought never to adopt by choice the proposal to take an unborn child's life, to kill him or her. To kill an innocent person intentionally is always gravely immoral; to kill the innocent unborn intentionally is particularly heinous because of their utter dependence on others for the continuance of their existence. Their inviolable right to life makes no sense if adult members of the human species do not have the absolute obligation to forbear from intentionally killing them. But, as I have argued, all adult members of the human species have this obligation. In a certain way, the innocent unborn symbolize their adult brothers and sisters, for the latter must admit that, at one time, they, too, were innocent unborn human persons.

——————————————— Endnotes for Chapter Five ———————————————

1. On this, see the helpful essay by Angel Rodriguez Luño, "La valutazione teologico-morale dell'aborto," in *Commento Interdisciplinare alla "Evangelium Vitae,"* under the direction and coordination of Ramon Lucas Lucas, Italian edition by Elio Sgreccia and Ramon Lucas Lucas (Vatican City: Libreria Editrice Vaticana, 1997), p. 419. As examples of older moral manuals defining abortion as the expelling of a living but not yet viable fetus from the mother's womb, Luño refers to those by D. M. Pruemmer and H. Noldin.

   In his *Manuale Theologiae Morale* (Friburgi Brisg./Rome: Herder, 1961), vol. 2, no. 137, Pruemmer defined abortion as *"eiectio immaturi foetus viventis ex utero matris"* (expelling of an immature living fetus from the mother's womb). In his *Summa Theologiae Moralis* (Oeniponte-Lipsiae: P. Rauch, 1941), vol. 2, no. 342, Noldin offered a similar definition, *"foetus abortus est eiectio immaturi ex utero matris"* (abortion is the expelling of an immature fetus from its mother's womb).

2. See Furton's essay "Is the Time of Personhood Settled? *Dignitas personae* Advances the Debate," *Ethics and Medics* 34.4 (April 2009), 3-4.

3. See Chapter One, pp. 24-26.

4. On this, see, for example, Germain Grisez, *Abortion: The Myths, the Realities, and the Arguments* (New York/Cleveland: Corpus Instrumentorum, 1970), pp. 137-156.

5. St. Basil the Great, *Epistles* 188, 2. *PG* 32.671. Indeed, he condemned as quibbling unworthy of Christians debates over the precise moment when the soul is infused, and in saying this he simply voiced the view of *all* the early Fathers.

6. On the Magisterium's teaching on this matter, see the excellent essay by Ignacio Carrasco de Paula, "The Respect Due to the Human Embryo: A Historical and Doctrinal Perspective," in *Identity and Statute* [sic] *of the Human Embryo: Proceedings of the Third Assembly of the Pontifical Academy for Life* (Vatican City, February 14-16, 1997), ed. Juan de Dios Vial Correa and Elio Sgreccia

(Vatican City: Libreria Editrice Vaticana, 1998), pp. 48-74, esp. pp. 66-73. The title of the book should have "Status" where "Statute" is printed. An obvious error was made in the English version.

7. Pope Pius XII, "Address to the Biomedical Association of St. Luke," November 12, 1944, in *Discorsi e Radiomessagi di Sua Santità Pio XII* (Vatican City: Libreria Editrice Vaticana, 1945), 6 (1944-1945), p. 191; "Address to the Italian Catholic Union of Midwives," October 29, 1951, no. 2, in *Acta Apostolicae Sedis* 43 (1951), 838. In his "Address to the Biomedical Association of St. Luke," Pius had said: "We have on purpose always used the expression '*direct* attack on the life of the innocent,' '*direct* killing.' For if, for instance, the safety of the life of the mother-to-be, independently of her pregnant condition, should urgently require a surgical operation or other therapeutic treatment, which would have as a side effect, in no way willed or intended yet inevitable, the death of the fetus, then such an act could not any longer be called a *direct* attack on innocent life. With these conditions, the operation, like other similar medical interventions, can be allowed, always assuming that a good of great worth, such as life, is at stake, and that it is not possible to delay until after the baby is born or to make use of some other effective remedy."

8. On this, see Chapter Two, pp. 47-48. See also Pope John Paul II, encyclical *Veritatis splendor*, no. 78: "*The morality of the human act depends primarily and fundamentally on the 'object' rationally chosen by the deliberate will....* The object of the act of willing is in fact a freely chosen kind of behavior.... By the object of a given moral act ... one cannot mean a process or an event of the merely physical order, to be assessed on the basis of its ability to bring about a given state of affairs in the outside world. Rather, that object is the proximate end of a deliberate decision which determines the act of willing on the part of the acting person."

9. Nicanor Pier Austriaco, O.P., "On Static Eggs and Dynamic Embryos: A Systems Perspective," *The National Catholic Bioethics Quarterly* 2.4 (Winter 2002), 665.

10. Ibid., 665-666.

11. Ibid., 666.

12. Ibid., 666-667.

13. Cf., for example, William J. Larsen, *Human Embryology*, 3rd ed. (Churchill Livingstone, 2001); Keith Moore and T. V. N. Persaud, *The Developing Human, Clinically Oriented Embryology*, 7th ed., (Philadelphia: Saunders, 2003); and Ronan O'Rahilly and Fabiola Mueller, *Human Embryology and Teratology*, 3rd ed. (Wiley-Liss, 2001).

14. Patrick Lee and Robert George, "The First Fourteen Days of Life," *The New Atlantis* 13 (Summer 2006), 61-67.

15. Patrick Lee, *Abortion and Unborn Human Life* (Washington, DC: The Catholic University of America Press, 1997), and Robert George and Christopher Tollefsen, *Embryo: A Defense of Human Life* (New York: Doubleday, 2008). I am much indebted to Lee, George, and Tollefsen for material in the chapter.

16. Philip Wylie, *The Magic Animal* (Garden City, NY: Doubleday, 1968), p. 272. These characterizations are found in a particularly vitriolic passage, filled with invective against the notion of the sanctity of human life.

17. A claim made by the biologist Garrett Hardin, "Abortion — or Compulsory Pregnancy?" *Journal of Marriage and Family* (May 1968), 250. An obvious and insuperable difficulty with this way of describing the being in question is that it is alive and developing, whereas a blueprint is not.

18. A typical representative of this view is the late and widely influential ethicist Joseph Fletcher. See his essay "New Beginnings of Life," in *The New Genetics and the Future of Man*, ed. Michael Hamilton (Grand Rapids: Eerdmans, 1972), p. 76. Such descriptions conceal rather than reveal the nature of the being in question.

19. This claim, made early in the twentieth century by the sexologist Havelock Ellis in his *Studies in the Psychology of Sex* (New York: 1924), 6.607, is quite common today and seems in fact to be a tenet of some leading feminists. It is obviously false in view of the fact that every cell of the being that comes into existence at fertilization is identifiably quite different in nature from every cell of the mother.

20. Germain Grisez, *The Way of the Lord Jesus*, Vol. 2, *Living a Christian Life* (Quincy, IL: Franciscan Press, 1993), pp. 494-495.

21. Stephen Schwarz, *The Moral Question of Abortion* (Chicago: Loyola University Press, 1990), p. 73.

22. Ibid.

23. Marjorie Reiley Maguire, "Personhood, Covenant, and Abortion," in *Abortion and Catholicism: The American Debate*, ed. Patricia Beattie Jung and Thomas A. Shannon (New York: Crossroad, 1988), p. 109. Maguire's essay was originally published, it should be noted, in the 1983 volume of *The Annual of the Society of Christian Ethics* (Knoxville, TN: Society of Christian Ethics, 1983). Her essay, delivered at the annual convention of the society, was among those judged worthy of publication in the society's *Annual*. Others who hold this position include Pierre de Locht, former professor of moral theology at the Catholic University of Louvain, "Discussion," in *L'Avortement: Actes du Xieme colloque international de sexologie* (Louvain: Centre International Cardinal Suenens, 1968), 2.155; Louis Beinaert, S.J., "L'avortement est-il un infanticide?" *Etudes* 333 (1970), 520-523; Mary Warnock, "Do Human Cells Have Rights?" *Bioethics* 1 (1987), 2.

24. On this, see Grisez, "When Do People Begin?" *Proceedings of the American Catholic Philosophical Association* 63 (1989), 29; *Living a Christian Life*, p. 489.

25. See, in particular, Grisez, "When Do People Begin?" 27-47.

26. See Michael Tooley, *Abortion and Infanticide* (New York: Oxford University Press, 1983); Daniel Callahan, *Abortion: Law, Choice, and Morality* (New York: Macmillan, 1970), pp. 383-389, 497-498; Peter Singer, *Rethinking Life and Death: The Collapse of Our Traditional Ethics* (New York: St. Martin's Press, 1994).

27. See Singer, *Rethinking Life and Death*. Singer notes that the expression "speciesism," which "was coined by the Oxford psychologist Richard Ryder in 1970, has now entered the *Oxford English Dictionary*, where it is defined as 'discrimination against or exploitation of certain animal species by human beings, based on an assumption of mankind's superiority.' As the term suggests, there is a parallel between our attitudes to nonhuman animals, and the attitudes of racists

to those they regard as belonging to an inferior race. In both cases, there is an inner group that justifies its exploitation of an outer group by reference to a distinction that *lacks real moral significance*" (p. 173; emphasis added). See also pp. 202-206, where Singer elaborates on his "fifth new commandment: '*Do not discriminate on the basis of species.*'"

28. Lee, *Abortion and Unborn Human Life,* pp. 26-27; emphasis added.

29. This passage is found in a book dealing with the question of euthanasia, where debates over "personhood" similar to those over this issue in considering abortion are common. The book, authored by the members of a "Working Party" of the Linacre Centre of London, is entitled *Euthanasia, Clinical Practice and the Law,* ed. Luke Gormally (London: The Linacre Centre for Health Care Ethics, 1994), pp. 123-124. Among the members of the "Working Party," in addition to Gormally, were John Finnis and Elizabeth Anscombe.

30. Grisez, *Living a Christian Life,* p. 491; see "When Do People Begin?" 31-32. For another excellent defense of the proposition that membership in the human species is a sufficient criterion for personhood, see Lee, *Abortion and Unborn Human Life,* pp. 58-62.

31. For an excellent critique of the dualism underlying this position see Lee, *Abortion and Unborn Human Life,* pp. 32-37. See also Lee's essay, "Human Beings Are Animals," in *Natural Law and Moral Inquiry: Ethics, Metaphysics, and Politics in the Work of Germain Grisez,* ed. Robert P. George (Washington, DC: Georgetown University Press, 1998), pp. 135-151.

32. Grisez, *Living a Christian Life,* p. 490. In a footnote (no. 54), Grisez observes that both *Webster's New International Dictionary* and the *Oxford English Dictionary* say that a standard use of the term "person" is to refer to a living, human individual.

33. Grisez, *Living a Christian Life,* pp. 490-491; "When Do People Begin?" 30-31. See also *Euthanasia, Clinical Practice and the Law,* p. 41.

34. See the following: Joseph Donceel, S.J. "Immediate Animation and Delayed Hominization," *Theological Studies* 31 (1970), 76-105; Donceel, "A Liberal Catholic's View," in *Abortion and Catholicism: The American Debate,* pp. 48-53; Thomas A. Shannon and Allan B. Wolter, O.F.M., "Reflections on the Moral Status of the Pre-Embryo," *Theological Studies* 51 (1990), 603-636. Shannon and Wolter, in their efforts to rehabilitate the "delayed hominization" view, appeal to additional supposed facts made known by contemporary science.

35. For Grisez, see "When Do People Begin?" 33-34; *Living a Christian Life,* pp. 492-493. For Lee, see *Abortion and Unborn Human Life,* pp. 79-90. See also the following: Benedict Ashley, O.P., "A Critique of the Theory of Delayed Hominization," in *An Ethical Evaluation of Fetal Experimentation: An Interdisciplinary Study,* ed. Donald McCarthy (St. Louis: Pope John XXIII Medical-Moral Research and Education Center, 1976), pp. 113-133; Benedict Ashley, O.P. and Albert Moraczewski, O.P., "Is the Biological Subject of Human Rights Present from Conception?" in *The Fetal Tissue Issue,* ed. Peter Cataldo and Albert Moraczewski, O.P. (Braintree, MA: Pope John XXIII Medical-Moral Research and Education Center, 1994), pp. 33-60; Jean Siebenthal, "L'animation selon

Thomas d'Aquin," in *L'Embryon: Un Homme. Actes du Congrès de Lausanne 1986* (Premier Congrès de la Societé Suisse de Bioetique 8 et 9 novembre 1986) (Lausanne: Centre de documentation civique, 1987), pp. 91-98; Mark Jordan, "Delayed Hominization: Reflections on Some Recent Catholic Claims for Delayed Hominization," *Theological Studies* 56 (1995), 743-763; Stephen J. Heaney, "Aquinas and the Presence of the Human Rational Soul in the Early Embryo," in *Abortion: A New Generation of Catholic Responses*, ed. Stephen J. Heaney (Braintree, MA: Pope John XXIII Medical-Moral Research and Education Center, 1992), pp. 43-72; Augustine Reagan, C.Ss.R., "The Human Conceptus and Personhood," *Studia Moralia* 30 (1992), 97-127.

36. Grisez, *Living a Christian Life*, pp. 492-493.

37. Siebenthal refers to the following Thomistic texts to show this: ST, I, 118, 3; 76, 4 and 6, ad 1; III, 6, 4, ad 1; 2, 5.

38. Siebenthal, "L'animation selon Thomas d'Aquin," 96-97.

39. Among scholars who accept this view are the following: Baruch Brody, *Abortion and the Sanctity of Human Life: A Philosophical View* (Boston: Massachusetts Institute of Technology Press, 1975); Robert M. Veatch, "Definitions of Life and Death: Should There Be a Consistency?" in *Defining Human Life: Medical, Legal, and Ethical Implications*, ed. Margery W. Shaw and A. Edward Dondera (Ann Arbor, MI: AUPHA Press, 1983), pp. 99-113.

40. Lee, *Abortion and Unborn Human Life*, pp. 76-77.

41. See Grisez, "When Do People Begin?" 34; *Living a Christian Life*, pp. 493-494.

42. For this claim, see the following: Karl Rahner, S.J., "The Problem of Genetic Manipulation," in *Theological Investigations*, Vol. 9, *Writings of 1965-67: I*, tr. Graham Harrison (New York: Herder & Herder, 1972), p. 226; Lisa S. Cahill, "The Embryo and the Fetus: New Moral Contexts," *Theological Studies* 54 (1993), 124; Richard A. McCormick, S.J., "Who or What Is the Pre-embryo?" *Kennedy Institute of Bioethics Journal* 1 (1991), 3; Shannon and Wolter, "Reflections on the Moral Status of the Pre-Embryo," 618-619.

43. Shannon and Wolter, "Reflections on the Moral Status of the Pre-Embryo," 618, no. 60.

44. W. Jerome Bracken, C.P. "Is the Early Embryo a Person?" in *Life and Learning VIII: Proceedings of the Eighth University Faculty for Life Conference*, June 1998, ed. Joseph W. Koterski, S.J. (Washington, DC: University Faculty for Life, 1999), 443-467, where he cites a recent scientific study by D. Wilcox et al., "Incidence of Loss in Early Pregnancy," *New England Journal of Medicine* 319/4 (July 28, 1988), 189-194, and others to challenge the claims frequently made.

45. Norman Ford, S.D.B., *When Did I Begin?: Conception of the Human Individual in History, Philosophy, and Science* (Cambridge/New York: Cambridge University Press, 1988).

46. Michael Coughlan, *The Vatican, the Embryo, and the Law* (Iowa City: University of Iowa Press, 1990).

47. In their superlative study, "Identity and Status of the Human Embryo: The Contributions of Biology," in *Identity and Statute* [sic] *of the Human Embryo*,

in which they show the fatal flaws in the theory of Ford and others, Angelo Serra and Roberto Columbo note that the term "pre-embryo" was introduced into the literature in 1986 by A. McLaren. She and others (such as Shannon and Wolter) who use this term claim that until approximately the fourteenth day after fertilization, all that occurs is the preparation of the protective and nutritional systems required for the future needs of the embryo, and that only at the fifteenth day after fertilization, when the "primitive streak" appears, does the embryo in the strict sense appear (see A. McLaren, "Prelude to Embryogenesis," in *Human Embryo Research: Yes or No?* The Ciba Foundation [New York: The Ciba Foundation/Tavistok, 1986], p. 12). Serra and Columbo, along with others, point out that the embryonic disk, which appears on the fifteenth day and to which McClaren gives such significance, is a structure "which derives from a further differentiation *of the embryoblast,* which is *already present* when the embryo as a *whole* provides, under genetic control, for a faster differentiation of the trophoblastic derivatives, which are extremely necessary for a correct and smooth progress of the body-building process. As a matter of fact," they continue, "the trophoblast and the embryoblast, both deriving from the zygote, simultaneously make their own way as a whole, according to a finely orchestrated program" (p. 167). Serra and Columbo thus conclude (with the majority of human embryologists), that it is not correct to distinguish between the so-called "pre-embryo" and the "embryo" proper. It is more scientifically accurate to speak of the "preimplantation" embryo than of the "pre-embryo" when referring to the living human organism at the preimplantation stage of development. It is here important to note that Ronan O'Rahilly, internationally regarded as one of the most outstanding human embryologists of our day, regards the term "pre-embryo" as scientifically inaccurate and erroneous and refuses to use the term. See Ronan O'Rahilly and Fabiola Muller, *Human Embryology and Teratology* (New York: John Wiley & Sons, 1994), p. 55.

48. Shannon and Wolter, "Reflections on the Moral Status of the Pre-Embryo," refer to the work of C. A. Bedate and R. C. Cefalo, "The Zygote: To Be or Not to Be a Person," *Journal of Medicine and Philosophy* 14 (1989), 641-645.

49. Antoine Suarez, "Hydatidiform Moles and Teratomas Confirm the Human Identity of the Preimplantation Embryo," *Journal of Medicine and Philosophy* 15 (1990), 627. The same number of this journal carried an essay by Thomas J. Bole, III, "Zygotes, Souls, Substances, and Persons," ibid., 637-652. Bole criticized Suarez's essay on the grounds that normal zygotes have developed into partial hydatidiform moles (whereas Suarez argues that they cannot). Bole's claim, however, is contradicted by competent embryologists, for instance, Stanley J. Robboy, Marie A. Duggan, and Robert J. Kurnam, "The Female Reproductive System," *Pathology,* ed. Emmanuel Rubin and John L. Farber (2nd ed., Philadelphia: J. B. Lippincott, 1994), 967. On this, see Bracken, "Is the Early Embryo a Person?" p. 448.

50. See the following: Grisez, "When Do People Begin?" 35-40; *Living a Christian Life,* pp. 495-497; Lee, *Abortion and Unborn Human Life,* pp. 90-102; Ashley

and Moraczewski, "Is the Biological Subject of Human Rights Present at Conception?" 33-60; Nicholas Tonti-Filippini, "A Critical Note," *Linacre Quarterly* 56.3 (August 1989), 36-50; Anthony Fisher, O.P., "Individuogenesis and a Recent Book by Fr. Norman Ford," *Anthropotes: Rivista di studi sulla persona e la famiglia* 7 (1991), 199-244; Serra and Colombo, "Identity and Status of the Human Embryo: The Contribution of Biology," esp. pp. 166-176.

51. R. Yanagimachi, "Mammalian Fertilization," in *The Physiology of Reproduction*, ed. E. Knobil, J. Neill, et al. (New York: Raven Press, 1988), p. 135; cited by Grisez, "When Do People Begin?" 45, no. 49; *Living a Christian Life*, p. 495, no. 66. For Suarez, see his "Hydatidiform Moles and Teratomas Confirm the Human Identity of the Preimplantation Embryo," (note 42).

52. Grisez, "When Do People Begin?" 37.

53. On this, see Lee, *Abortion and Unborn Human Life*, pp. 92-93.

54. Grisez, "When Do People Begin?" 38.

55. Ashley and Moraczewski, "Is the Biological Subject of Human Rights Present from Conception?" pp. 50-53.

56. Pope John Paul II, apostolic exhortation *Christifideles laici*, no. 51. See also his apostolic letter *Mulieris dignitatem*, no. 30: "The moral and spiritual strength of a woman is joined to her awareness that *God entrusts the human being to her in a special way*. Of course, God entrusts every human being to each and every other human being. But this entrusting concerns women in a special way — precisely because of their femininity — and this in a particular way determines their vocation."

57. On this, see John Saward, *Redeemer in the Womb: Jesus Living in Mary* (San Francisco: Ignatius Press, 1993), in particular, pp. 165-168.

58. Sidney Callahan, "Abortion and the Sexual Agenda: A Case for Prolife Feminism," in *Abortion and Catholicism: The American Debate*, pp. 128-145, at 128-129.

59. Judith Jarvis Thomson, "In Defense of Abortion," *Philosophy and Public Affairs* (1970).

60. Here I have paraphrased Callahan's summary of these two arguments in "Abortion and the Sexual Agenda," pp. 128-129.

61. This was the analogy used by Thomson in her celebrated "defense" of abortion (cf. endnote 54).

62. Callahan, "Abortion and the Sexual Agenda," p. 131.

63. John Finnis, *Natural Law and Natural Rights* (Oxford/New York: Oxford University Press, at the Clarendon Press, 1980). Finnis's book is a volume in the Oxford Law Series. See pp. 199-205, "An Analysis of Rights Talk."

64. See endnote 59.

65. Here I follow Lee's summary, pp. 107-108, of Thomson's argument.

66. Ibid., pp. 113-116.

67. According to the principle of double effect, it is permissible to "allow" or permit an evil to result from an act that is not intrinsically evil provided that this effect is not intended either as end or as means *and* that there is a "proportionate reason" for "permitting" or "allowing" the evil effect. Lee's argument is that, even if

the abortions in question can legitimately be regarded as "removals" rather than "killings" — that is, the evil effect, the unborn child's death, is not intended either as end or as means — there is no "proportionate reason" for "permitting" or "allowing" the evil effect. On the contrary, there are serious moral reasons, based on justice, that require one *not* to "permit" this evil.

68. Lee, *Abortion and Unborn Human Life*, p. 116.

69. St. Thomas Aquinas, ST, II-II, 64, 7.

70. Grisez, *Abortion: The Myths, the Realities, and the Arguments*, pp. 340-346.

71. Ibid., pp. 345-346.

72. John Bruchalski, M.D., in an e-mail to William May, October 20, 2007.

73. John Finnis, Germain Grisez, and Joseph Boyle, Jr., " 'Direct' and 'Indirect': A Reply to Critics of Our Action Theory," *The Thomist* 61.1 (January 2001), 1-45.

74. John A. Rock, M.D., "Ectopic Pregnancy," in *TeLinde's Operative Gynecology* (Philadelphia: J. B. Lippincott, 1992), pp. 412-414. In 1970, approximately 17,800 ectopic pregnancies were reported in women aged 15 to 44; by 1980, the figure had risen to 52,000 women in this age group; today it is estimated that 1 pregnancy in every 60 is ectopic, with the rate increasing. It is ironic that among the causes of tubal pregnancies are *in vitro* fertilization (frequently resorted to as a way of providing children to women with blocked fallopian tubes) and the use of contraceptives.

75. Ibid., pp. 421-427.

76. J. Cannon and H. Jesionowska, "Methotrexate Treatment of Tubal Pregnancy," *Fertility and Sterility* 55 (June 1991), 1034.

77. Rock, "Ectopic Pregnancy," p. 427. See also Charles E. Cavagnaro III, "Treating Ectopic Pregnancy: A Moral Analysis," *The NaProEthics Forum* 3.6 (November 1998), 4.

78. Rock, "Ectopic Pregnancy," p. 427; Cavagnaro, "Treating Ectopic Pregnancy," 4.

79. National Conference of Catholic Bishops, *Ethical and Religious Directives for Catholic Health Care Facilities* (Washington, DC: NCCB, 1971), no. 16.

80. National Conference of Catholic Bishops, *Ethical and Religious Directives for Catholic Health Care Services* (Washington, DC: NCCB, 1995), no. 48.

81. See William E. May, "The Management of Ectopic Pregnancies: A Moral Analysis," in *The Fetal Tissue Issue: Medical and Ethical Aspects*, ed. Peter J. Cataldo and Albert S. Moraczewski, O.P. (Braintree, MA: Pope John XXIII Medical-Moral Research and Education Center, 1994), pp. 121-148, esp. pp. 133-145. I believe that I was the first moral theologian to consider the use of methotrexate in the management of ectopic pregnancies.

82. Christopher Kazcor, "Ectopic Pregnancy and the Catholic Hospital." Professor Kazcor kindly sent me a copy of this article, as yet unpublished.

83. See my extensive review of Kaczor's book in *Linacre Quarterly* 29.1 (February 2012), 104-117.

CHAPTER SIX

Experimentation on
Human Subjects

This chapter will take up the morality of experimentation on human subjects. I will (1) introduce the topic and articulate and explain the cardinal principle governing human experimentation, namely, the principle of free and informed consent. I will then (2) examine the meaning and limits of proxy consent, in particular, proxy consent for non-therapeutic experiments to be carried out on incompetent human persons or those whom the late Paul Ramsey called "voiceless patients," and follow the analysis of this issue with a consideration of (3) research on the unborn, in particular embryo stem-cell research, including updated scientific evidence regarding effectiveness of therapeutic use of adult stem cells, continued failure of the use of embryonic stem cells to effect cures, and evidence of harms they can and have caused, developments of induced pluripotent stem cells (IPPS); (4) gene therapy, (5) prenatal and preimplantation genetic screening, (6) genetic counseling, and (7) the human genome project.

1. Introduction: The Cardinal Principle of
Free and Informed Consent[1]

One of the most unforgettable television newscasts I ever witnessed was a May 1973 CBS Special Report, "The Ultimate Experimental Animal: Man." It included a scene that struck me as especially illuminating, which well serves to introduce the question of experimenting on human beings. A black woman, who had been a prisoner in a Detroit jail, had participated in a program testing a new type of birth-control pill. This particular pill was known to the researchers to carry a high risk of causing cancer, but this fact was deliberately withheld from the women who had "volunteered" to participate in the program testing its effectiveness. When the woman learned, after her release from prison, that the pill she and other women had been taking posed a serious risk of causing cancer, she was outraged at having been "used," declaring to the CBS correspondent that she had been "treated like an animal."

Her reaction is very instructive. In saying that she had been treated like an animal and in being outraged at having been so treated, she voiced the conviction that human beings ought not to be treated like animals. She was not necessarily denying that she — with other human beings as well — is an animal (for, after all, we are); rather, she was affirming that a human being is an *animal with a difference*, an entity of moral worth, a subject of rights that demand respect and protection from the society in which one lives. She was saying, in a simple and unsophisticated way, what the philosopher Roger Wertheimer has called a "standard belief" among human beings. This is the belief that "being human has moral cachet; a human being has human status in virtue of being a human being";[2] that being a member of the human species has *moral* significance and has so because every member of the human species is a *person*, not a thing or mere animal.[3]

She was also affirming that any experiment performed on the "human animal" must, if it is to be rightly carried out, respect the truth that human beings are persons, beings of moral worth, subjects of rights rooted in their being and not conferred on them by others. She was affirming, at least implicitly, that no human being can be regarded simply as a part subordinated to a larger whole, the society at large, but must be considered as a whole that cannot rightly be subordinated to the interests of others. Expressed in more philosophical terms, this woman was articulating what Karol Wojtyla called the "personalistic norm," which, "in its negative aspect, states that the person is the kind of good which does not admit of use and cannot be treated as an object of use and as such the means to an end," and which, "in its positive form ... confirms this: the person is a good towards which the only adequate attitude is love."[4]

This is the cardinal point to be kept in mind as we consider the ethics of experimenting on human subjects. The moral worth of every human being from conception/fertilization until death is *the* crucial truth in considering this important topic in all its ramifications. That every human being *is* indeed a being of moral worth, a person of irreplaceable and priceless value, is a truth central to the Gospel and is eloquently proclaimed by the Church, as we have seen in our review of relevant magisterial documents in Chapter One. It is this truth alone that renders intelligible the cardinal principle in human experimentation, namely, the principle of free and informed consent, that "canon of loyalty," as Paul Ramsey terms it,[5] which is operative in all situations wherein one human person is the experimenter and another is his "co-adventurer" in the experiment.

A. Basic Types of Experimentation

Before we look into this principle and its meaning, however, it will be useful to distinguish different types of experimental situations. There are many types of such situations, but from the perspective of moral analysis the two most basic kinds are *therapeutic* and *non-therapeutic* or purely *research* experiments. Among the first can be included experiments whose purpose is to (1) diagnose an illness or condition afflicting a person, (2) alleviate or cure a malady from which the subject is suffering, and (3) prevent a person from becoming afflicted with a specifiable malady. Therapeutic experiments, in short, can be diagnostic, curative or alleviating, or preventive. Despite the differences in these kinds of experiments, all are therapeutic in that they are aimed at being of medical benefit to the subject experimented on. Some therapeutic experiments are *research* experiments in the sense that they study the effects of using diagnostic, prophylactic/therapeutic, or preventive methods that depart from ordinary medical practice but nonetheless offer reasonable hope of success. Such research experiments are thus truly therapeutic insofar as they are designed not only to acquire knowledge but also *to be of benefit* to the subject.[6]

Non-therapeutic or purely research experiments are not, of themselves, designed to be of medical benefit to the subject. They are rather intended to further biomedical and behavioral research, to advance the frontiers of knowledge, and thus enable us eventually to develop new techniques for coping with the diverse maladies that plague humankind and thereby to enhance the common good. It is true that at times the subjects of such non-therapeutic experiments may be benefited in spiritual and psychological ways, but such benefits to the subject are incidental to the experiment (and experimenter!) as such, inasmuch as the experiment (and the experimenter) *intends* or *aims at* acquiring knowledge that *may* be beneficial to human beings in the future, whereas the therapeutic experiment is aimed at benefiting the subject of the experiment.

B. The Key Principle or "Canon of Loyalty": The Principle of Free and Informed Consent

The canon of loyalty that must be observed in experimental situations, whether therapeutic or non-therapeutic, is the principle of free and informed consent. This principle is at the heart of medical ethics and bioethics. It was eloquently expressed in the articles of the Nuremberg Code (1946-1949), and it is salutary today, a half century later, to recall that this code was formulated when the memories of the atrocities carried out on human subjects by the Third Reich in the name of scientific research was fresh in the minds of men. According to the first article of the Nuremberg Code,

> The voluntary consent of the human subject is absolutely essential. This means that the person involved should have legal capacity to give consent; should be so situated as to be able to exercise free power of choice, without the intervention of any element of force, fraud, deceit, duress, overreaching, or other ulterior form of constraint or coercion; and should have sufficient knowledge and comprehension of the elements of the subject matter involved as to enable him to make an understanding and enlightened decision. This latter element requires that before the acceptance of an affirmative decision by the experimental subject there should be made known to him the nature, duration, and purpose of the experiment; the method and means by which it is to be conducted; all the inconveniences and hazards reasonably to be expected; and the effects upon his health or person which may probably come from his participation in the experiment.[7]

The moral demand that a human person who is to be the subject of an experiment give free and informed consent is also embodied in the code of ethics adopted by the World Health Organization in the *Declaration of Helsinki* in 1964 and by the American Medical Association.[8] This principle is at the heart of traditional Jewish and Christian medical ethics and has been reaffirmed time and time again by the Magisterium of the Church.

(1) The Principle of Free and Informed Consent and Relevant Teaching of the Magisterium

As Gonzalo Herranz has emphasized, this principle was clearly recognized and affirmed by Catholic authors in the nineteenth century long before it was articulated in the very first article of the Nuremberg Code in 1949. Herranz calls attention to the work of the French Catholic medical doctor George Surbled, who clearly expressed this principle in the first edition (1891) of his *La morale dans ses rapports avec la médicine et l'hygiene,* and to the vigorous affirmation by his predecessor Max Simon of the principle of the supremacy of the human person over scientific research in his 1845 volume, *Déontologie Médicale ou des Devoirs des Médicins dans l'Etat Actuel de la Civilisation.*[9]

The 1994 *Charter for Health Care Workers*, promulgated by the Pontifical Council for Pastoral Assistance to Health Care Workers, provides a valuable summary of magisterial teaching on the need to secure the patient's informed consent in no. 72, citing liberally from and referring to relevant magisterial documents. Thus it will be useful here to present the text of this number and in the endnotes refer to the magisterial documents either cited in the text of this number or referred to in the footnotes contained in it:

> To intervene medically, the health care worker should have the express or tacit consent of the patient. In fact [as Pope Pius XII affirmed], "he does not have a separate and independent right in relation to the patient. In general, he can act only if the patient explicitly or implicitly (directly or indirectly) authorizes him."[10] Without such authorization he gives himself an arbitrary power.[11] Besides the medical relationship there is a human one: dialogic, non-objective. The patient [as Pope John Paul II insists] "is not an anonymous individual" on whom medical expertise is practiced, but "a responsible person, who should be given the opportunity of personally choosing, and not be made to submit to the decisions and choices of others."[12] So that the choice may be made with full awareness and freedom, the patient should be given a precise idea of his illness and the therapeutic possibilities, with the risks, the problems and the consequences that they entail.[13] This means that the patient should be asked for an *informed consent.*[14]

(2) Interpreting This Principle

It is frequently difficult, if not impossible, as many authorities have pointed out,[15] to secure *fully* informed consent. They have noted that frequently it is not possible to explain to the person about to undergo an experiment all of the complications involved. At times, some hazards may not be known; at other times the persons to be subjected to the experiment may not be capable of understanding all the pertinent and known factors; at other times, full details of all possible hazards and complications might so terrify a person that he or she may become paralyzed in thought and unwilling to consent to a procedure that is really not hazardous and that offers solid hope of being beneficial.

This means that this cardinal principle or canon of loyalty, demanding the subject's free and informed consent, is to be understood as requiring "reasonably" free and "adequately" informed consent, and the reasonableness and adequacy are to be determined in accord with the Golden Rule of doing unto others as you would have them do unto you and not doing unto them what you would not have them do to you. Ramsey puts matters this way: "A choice may be free and responsible despite the fact that it began in an emotional bias one way or another, and consent can be informed without being encyclopedic."[16] In their *Ethical and Religious Directives for Catholic Health Care Services* (1994), the bishops of the United States expressed the requirement of free and informed consent as follows: "Free and informed consent requires that the person or the person's surrogate [the issue of "proxy consent" will be explored below] receive all reasonable information about the essential nature of the proposed treatment and its benefits; its risks, side-effects, consequences, and cost; and any reasonable and morally legitimate alternatives, including no treatment at all."[17]

Basically, what is at stake here is *trust* between the subject and the doctor/researcher: trust that the doctor/researcher will *not* propose any experiment without communicating to the subject sufficient information for him or her to make an informed decision, for after all, it affects that person's life and health. Unfortunately today, this trust between patients and doctors/researchers has been to a great extent eroded for a wide variety of reasons, and it is imperative that such trust be restored. It can be restored only if doctors and researchers are willing, in informing subjects of proposed experiments, to shape their choices and actions in accord with the Golden Rule or basic principle of justice and fairness.[18]

This requirement, the canon of loyalty demanding reasonably free and informed consent, is imperative in *all* types of experimentation on human persons (who come to be at conception/fertilization and remain in being so long as they are living human bodies). The reason is rooted in the inviolability of the human person as a being of moral worth, as an entity surpassing in value the entire material-created world, the bearer of inalienable rights that must be recognized and respected by society and by all persons. As we have seen before, human beings are ends, not means, and all human beings are equal in their dignity as persons.[19] Ramsey has put the matter beautifully by saying, "No man is good enough to experiment upon another without his consent."[20] To experiment on a human subject without securing his consent is to treat him as a being who is no longer a person, no longer a being of moral worth, to make of him a means, not an end, to subordinate him to others, to deny his humanity.

With respect to medical treatments, there is one clear exception from the requirement of expressed consent, an exception that in no way weakens the normative demand governing medical practice by consent alone. This is the kind of case in which consent is reasonably presumed or implied when a person is in extreme danger and cannot explicitly give consent. As the *Charter for Health Care Workers* says, in extreme situations of this kind, "if there is a temporary loss of knowing and willing, the health care worker can act in virtue of *the principle of therapeutic trust*.... Should there be a permanent loss of knowing and willing, the health care worker can act in virtue of *the principle of responsibility for health care*, which obliges the health care worker to assume responsibility for the patient's health."[21] As Ramsey has said, "Indeed, we might say that if a doctor stops on the road to Jericho, instead of passing by on his way to read a research paper before a scientific gathering or to visit his regular, paying customers, he is self-selected as good enough to practice medicine without the needy man's expressed consent."[22]

(3) Other Ethical Principles/Norms Governing Biomedical Research on Human Subjects

Free and informed consent is not the only relevant moral principle to justify biomedical research on human subjects. Another key principle/norm is known as the "principle of descending order." The philosopher Hans Jonas suggested this principle in selecting subjects of research. It requires researchers to select the least vulnerable people as subjects.[23] The primary obligation is to protect *vulnerable persons* and to prevent taking advantage of them in selecting subjects of experimentation. Such subjects, of course, must give free and informed consent to the research project for which they are selected and for which they then volunteer. There are two major categories of "vulnerable persons." The first includes persons unable to give consent to experimentation: babies, born or unborn, and older persons who are mentally incompetent; the second group includes people vulnerable to manipulation or coercion (perhaps of a very subtle type) by others: for example, prisoners, residents of institutions, the poor, students attending institutes conducting research, etc. The criterion of descending order does not mean that vulnerable persons can never be rightly chosen or volunteer as subjects of biomedical research; it simply requires that research subjects be selected on the basis of justice. Benedict Ashley, O.P., and Kevin O'Rourke, O.P., offer the following general criterion relevant to this principle: "subjects should be selected so that risks and benefits will not fall unequally on one group in society."[24]

Two other good, sound subsidiary principles are formulated in Articles 9 and 10 of the Nuremberg Code. Article 9 states that "during the course of the experiment the human subject should be at liberty to bring the experiment to an end if he has reached the physical or mental state where continuation of the experiment seems to him to be impossible." Article 10 declares: "During the course of the experiment the scientist in charge must be prepared to terminate the experiment at any stage if he has probable cause to believe, in the exercise of good faith, superior skill and careful judgment required of him that a continuation of the experiment is likely to result in injury, disability or death to the experimental subject."[25]

2. Proxy Consent: Its Meaning, Justification, and Limits

There are many instances when it is impossible to secure adequately informed and free consent from the person who is to be the subject of the experimentation. It is obviously impossible to obtain such consent from incompetent human persons, the unborn, infants and children, the demented, etc., those whom Ramsey has called "voiceless patients."

A. Proxy Consent in the Therapeutic Situation

There is no serious debate among authorities — legal, medical, or moral — that proxy consent, i.e., consent given by another acting as a surrogate for the person on whom the experiment is to be performed, is justifiable when the experiment in question is therapeutic, that is, when it is designed to secure some benefit for the subject.

Frequently, the responsibilities of those who give proxy consent for therapeutic procedures on behalf of voiceless patients are described as making choices in accord with the incompetent individual's own preferences, if these are known, or else making these choices in accord with the "best interests" of the individual concerned, if he or she had never expressed personal preferences, for instance, if one is acting as a proxy for an infant or for an adult who has never been able to exercise moral responsibility because of some anomaly. Thus the bishops of the United States declare that decisions made on behalf of an individual by a designated surrogate (or responsible family member) should "be faithful to Catholic moral principles and to the person's intentions and values [so long as these are compatible with Catholic moral principles], or if the person's intentions are unknown, to the person's best interests."[26]

I believe that the basic moral principle justifying "proxy" consent in the therapeutic situation is in fact the Golden Rule. We are to do unto others as we would have them do unto us and not do unto them what we would not have them do unto us. If the health or life of a fellow human person for whom we have responsibility (as parents do for their children) is in danger and there are means that can be taken to protect and/or enhance that person's health and life and/or ameliorate his or her condition *without imposing grave burdens upon that person*, then we are morally obligated to authorize use of those means for protecting/preserving/enhancing/ameliorating the life and health of the person for whom we have responsibility. The *Charter for Health Care Workers*, I believe, expressed this requirement, rooted in the principle of the Golden Rule, in what it termed the "*principle of responsibility for health care*."[27]

In other words, I think that "proxy consent," when made on behalf of those who have never been able to articulate their own preferences with respect to the kind of therapeutic care they are willing to accept, is not so much "proxy consent," i.e., consent made in the name of another person (as godparents act as proxies for infants in consenting to baptism), as it is the *personal consent* of the one morally responsible for the care of the incompetent individual. In giving consent to *therapeutic* experiments, that is, those reasonably expected to *benefit* the subject, to protect his *goods*, on such incompetent persons, those giving it are not so much speaking in the name of those voiceless patients but are rather exercising their own proper moral responsibility.

If consent is given on behalf of a now incompetent person who, while competent, had expressed his or her preferences for the kind of therapeutic treatment he or she is willing to accept, then we are indeed speaking of "proxy consent," and the U.S. bishops are quite correct in saying that the choice made (the free consent given) ought to be faithful to the person's intentions and values, *as long as such a choice is faithful to Catholic moral principles*. This issue will be taken up in greater depth in Chapter Seven, where we set forth the criteria to be observed in making moral choices regarding the kind of therapeutic medical treatment proposed to persons.

B. Voluntary Consent in the Non-Therapeutic Situation: Can This Ever Be Morally Required?

Before considering "proxy" consent to both therapeutic and non-therapeutic experimentation, it is necessary to consider the question of whether there can be an *obligation* or *moral responsibility* for *competent persons* to volunteer as subjects in such experiments. For years I thought that there could be no such moral obligation and that volunteering to participate in such experimentation was an act of mercy, in the nature of a gift. But in preparing this paper and after discussing the matter with others, in particular Germain Grisez, I now believe that the principle of fairness can at times require a competent adult to choose freely to participate in biomedical non-therapeutic experiments under certain conditions. For instance, if one's personal physician asked one in the course of a routine medical examination to give a urine sample for a program designed to compare the urine of healthy adults with the urine of those suffering from a particular disease in order to test some hypothesis regarding treatment of the disease or of its symptoms, it seems that in fairness one could have a *moral* obligation to help out. In an instance of this kind, one can easily do something of benefit to fellow human persons with no cost or minimal cost to oneself. The situation is analogous, it seems, to that of a vigorous adult who sees a frail elderly person struggling to carry a suitcase across the street; fairness, rooted in the Golden Rule as understood in the Christian tradition, would normally require the vigorous adult to come to the older person's aid. Although such a responsibility could not be legally mandated, it is reasonable to think that a moral obligation can exist for a competent adult to participate in non-therapeutic biomedical experimentation in situations of this kind. If, however, the non-therapeutic experiment imposes significant burdens or inconveniences, then fairness would not require one to volunteer as a research subject; one's free and informed choice to be a participant would indeed be an act of mercy, a "gift" of oneself.

C. Proxy Consent in the Non-Therapeutic Situation

Can proxy consent be justified in the non-therapeutic situation, i.e., when the proposed research/experiment/treatment is *not intended* to benefit the human subject of such procedures but rather to gain knowledge that may in the future be of great benefit to others? Here I will first review arguments advanced to justify and to oppose proxy consent in the non-therapeutic situation. I will then examine relevant magisterial teaching.

(1) Arguments For and Against

A major argument advanced to justify proxy consent in the non-therapeutic situation was proposed in the 1970s by the late Richard McCormick, S.J. His basic argument was that proxy consent in the *therapeutic* situation is justified precisely because parents and other surrogates can presume that the subjects themselves *would*, if they could, consent because they *ought* to consent by virtue of their moral obligation to protect their own life and health. Similarly, he argued, in *non-therapeutic* situations posing no significant risk or minimal risk and in which great good is promised, proxy consent for children and other non-competents is justified inasmuch as one can reasonably assume that the non-competents themselves *would* consent if they could because they would realize that they *ought* to consent to such experiments because of their social nature and their obligation to promote the common good of society when they can do so with little effort and no danger or minimal risk to themselves.[28]

Paul Ramsey and I rejected McCormick's argument justifying proxy consent in both therapeutic and non-therapeutic situations precisely because there are no grounds for presuming that children and other non-competents *would*, if they *could*, consent in both situations because they would realize that they *ought* to do so. There is no need to infer, as did McCormick, that children and other non-competents have *any* moral obligations.[29] Precisely because they are non-competent, they are *not moral agents*, but they *are* persons who ought never to be used as mere means to ends extrinsic to themselves.[30] To treat them *as if* they were moral agents who had moral obligations to carry out, among them, to participate in non-therapeutic experiments promising great good at minimal or no significant risk, is to fail to recognize them for what, in truth, they *are*, namely, vulnerable, helpless human persons totally dependent on others.

I think that these considerations clearly show that McCormick's argument for justifying proxy consent to non-therapeutic experimentation is not at all valid. Although, as I noted earlier, competent adults could, under certain conditions, have a moral obligation to participate in certain kinds of non-therapeutic investigation, non-competent, "voiceless" persons can have no such obligation precisely because they have *no* moral obligations by reason of their condition.

With Ramsey I found McCormick's apologia for proxy consent in the non-therapeutic situation repugnant. In fact, from the 1970s until September 2002, when I presented a paper on which this material is based at a meeting sponsored by the Pontifical Academy for Life in preparation for the plenary session of February 2003 and found my position sharply challenged, I firmly held the view that it is *never* morally right for others to give so-called proxy consent for non-competent, voiceless human persons to non-therapeutic research/experimentation. Basically, the argument supporting this conclusion — advanced in the 1970s and subsequently by Ramsey and me — holds that incompetent or "voiceless" human persons, by reason of their *dignity precisely as persons*, ought *never* be used as subjects in procedures that are non-therapeutic and are undertaken not for their benefit but for the benefit of others. According to this argument, even if the procedures may not "harm" them and may pose no significant risk, they are immoral because they violate their dignity as persons. Ramsey well expressed this position when he said:

> To experiment on children [or other non-competent subjects] in ways that are not related to them as patients is already a sanitized form of barbarism; it already removes them from view and pays no attention to the faithfulness-claims which a child, simply by being a normal or sick or dying child, places upon us and upon medical care.... To attempt to consent for a child to be made an experimental subject is to treat the child as not a child.... Nontherapeutic, nondiagnostic, experimentation involving human subjects must be based on true consent if it is to proceed as a human enterprise. No child or incompetent adult can choose to become a participating member of medical undertakings, and no one else on earth should decide to subject those people to investigations having no relation to their own treatment. That is a canon of loyalty to them. This they claim simply by being a human child or incompetent.[31]

I was led to change my position unalterably opposing *all proxy consent to non-therapeutic procedures* because of the objections raised against it at a September 27-28, 2002, meeting of persons who had been invited to give papers at the plenary session of the Pontifical Academy for Life. I had prepared a paper reaffirming my long-standing complete rejection of proxy consent in the non-therapeutic situation. Criticism given at that meeting, along with discussions I subsequently carried out with Germain Grisez, led me to conclude that although McCormick's *argument* to justify proxy consent on behalf of "voiceless" subjects in the non-therapeutic situation may be severely criticized for the reasons given, the position he took can be defended on other grounds. Some participants in the September 2002 meeting suggested one line of reasoning used to justify such proxy consent. The basic claim is that it would not be unreasonable — and therefore not contrary to objective moral standards — if parents, for instance, were to allow experimentation involving their children for the benefit of others if the experiment involves no significant risk. After all, parents frequently take their children, including babies, on automobile trips not undertaken for their benefit (e.g., to purchase some clothes for the mother), and such journeys surely involve some risks, but, after all, risks of this kind are acceptable both for oneself and for those for whom one cares. And other examples could be given. Hence, if it is not wrong for parents to act in this way in exercising responsible stewardship of their children, why would it be always immoral for them to consent to have their children participate in non-therapeutic research/experimentation?

I believe that Germain Grisez has clearly formulated this line of reasoning:

> People making decisions for someone who is not competent — for instance, parents for a child — *may not accept any significant risk (that is, any risk beyond the level of life's common risks) to a dependent's health for the sake of an experiment's possible benefit to others. For parents and others in charge of the noncompetent have a special responsibility to act in their personal interests, not to subordinate them to others. Nor can such subordination of a dependent's interests be an act of mercy, since mercy is self-sacrifice, not imposing sacrifice on someone for whom one is responsible.*[32]

I wish to note some important features of Grisez's presentation. First of all, he offers a clear definition/description of "significant" risk. He identifies as "significant" a risk that is "beyond the level of life's common risks" — e.g., such risks as riding in an automobile, crossing a street, etc. — "risks" that parents commonly take for their children when they have their children accompany them in a host of activities that are not intended to be of any direct benefit to the children themselves. Grisez thus provides us with a clearly defined criterion to help us determine whether a risk is "significant." Obviously, however, application of this criterion would vary depending on social/cultural conditions. Thus what constitutes "significant" risk in Manhattan would seem to be different from what constitutes "significant" risk in, say, Wagga Wagga, Australia.

Second, Grisez clearly believes that such parental consent in no way "subordinates" their children to the interests of others since he rejects such subordination. When conditions warrant parental consent (or consent by other guardians) to participation by those entrusted to their care in non-therapeutic experimentation, in other words, such consent is given in fidelity to the trust given them to protect the inviolable *dignity precisely as persons* of the non-competent persons for whose well-being they are responsible. Moreover, he explicitly rejects the claim that such subordination can be "an act of mercy, since mercy is self-sacrifice, not imposing sacrifice on someone for whom one is responsible."

After reflecting on the reasons advanced by those who considered my view too restrictive and not necessary to protect the inviolable dignity of "voiceless" persons, I have concluded that it would not be unreasonable for parents to allow their children to be subjects of non-therapeutic studies posing no "significant" risk (as defined above) and causing no significant inconvenience or burden to their children. They would not be treating them as mere objects of use or failing in their serious responsibility to protect their lives and health by all reasonable means.

I now believe that the view I defended for many years was in fact an overreaction to unethical experiments on non-competent persons and a fear, reasonable in itself, that the intrinsic dignity of such vulnerable persons was endangered by a desire to subordinate them to the interests of others.

"Proxy" consent in such situations is, of course, not true proxy consent, i.e., consent given in the name of the non-competent persons themselves. It is the personal consent of the parents or guardians of voiceless persons to permit those for whom they have a grave responsibility to participate in non-therapeutic experimentations if, and only if, such experimentations pose no "significant" risk, promise great benefit, and cannot be carried out on other subjects. As noted previously, I believe that children who have reached the "use of reason" can make free and informed decisions, and that, if so, parents ought to give their children sufficient information for them to make a free and informed choice in the matter and to answer any of their concerns and to retain veto power over their children's choices in this matter when they judge this necessary.

(2) Relevant Magisterial Teaching

With respect to *magisterial* teaching relevant to this matter, it is very important to consider (a) proxy consent to non-therapeutic experimentation on *unborn* human persons and (b) such experimentation on human persons *already born*.

The universal Magisterium of the Church rejects as absolutely immoral proxy consent to non-therapeutic experiments on *unborn human persons*. A key passage in *Donum vitae* of central importance regarding this matter is the following:

> As regards experimentation, and presupposing the general distinction between experimentation for purposes which are not directly therapeutic and experimentation which is clearly therapeutic for the subject himself, in the case in point [experimentation on human embryos and fetuses] one

must also distinguish between experimentation carried out on embryos which are still alive and experimentation carried out on embryos which are dead. *If the embryos are living, whether viable or not, they must be respected just like any other human person; experimentation on embryos which is not directly therapeutic is illicit.* No objective, even though noble in itself, such as a foreseeable advantage to science, to other human beings, or to society, can in any way justify experimentation on living human embryos or fetuses, whether viable or not, either inside or outside the mother's womb. The informed consent ordinarily required for clinical experimentation on adults cannot be granted by the parents, who may not freely dispose of the physical integrity or life of the unborn child. Moreover, experimentation on embryos and fetuses always involves risk, and indeed in most cases it involves the certain expectation of harm to their physical integrity or even their death. To use human embryos or fetuses as the object or instrument of experimentation constitutes a crime against their dignity as human beings having a right to the same respect that is due to the child already born and to every human person.[33]

When I first read this passage in 1987, and in the years that followed, I read it in the perspective of my position that regarded as immoral *all proxy consent* on behalf of "voiceless" persons to non-therapeutic experimentation precisely *because it violated their dignity as persons.* I thus *assumed* that the fundamental reason *Donum vitae* absolutely repudiated proxy consent to non-therapeutic experimentation on the unborn was the same as my reason for repudiating it. Moreover, the text in question seemed capable of being interpreted in this way insofar as it prefaced its rejection of such consent by emphasizing the respect due to human embryos as persons equal in dignity to all other human persons. Moreover, I assumed that both *Donum vitae* and Pope John Paul II in the passage cited by *Donum vitae* considered non-therapeutic experimentation on human embryos — and indeed all human persons incapable of giving personal informed consent — to be immoral because such experimentation treated human embryos and other non-competent human persons as mere "objects" or "instruments" of use.

Thus, when I subsequently discovered that the U.S. bishops, who, with *Donum vitae* and Pope John Paul II, absolutely excluded as illicit proxy consent to non-therapeutic experiments on *unborn human persons*,[34] nonetheless *authorized* parents to give such consent to non-therapeutic experiments on children already born if the experiments posed no "significant risk to the person's well being,"[35] I accused them of unreasonably holding a "double standard," one for unborn children and another for children already born.[36] A position similar to that of the U.S. bishops was taken by the Australian hierarchy.[37] However, now, after changing my position regarding proxy consent to non-therapeutic experiments posing no "significant" risks to non-competent or "voiceless" persons, I realize that I was reading my views *into Donum vitae* and the passage from Pope John Paul II cited therein. I was guilty of *eisegesis* and failed to consider the possibility of interpreting the relevant texts differently. I now think that the fundamental reason *Donum vitae* repudiates proxy consent to non-therapeutic experiments on *unborn human persons* is that "experimentation on embryos and fetuses *always* involves risk, and indeed in most cases it involves the certain expectation of harm to their physical integrity or even their death" (*Donum vitae*, no. 1.4; emphasis added). It is for this reason that *Donum vitae* also judges that such experimentation treats a living human embryo as a mere "object" or "instrument."

One might reasonably question why all non-therapeutic experiments on the unborn are illicit because of the serious risks they pose and why such experiments are justifiable on human persons already born. An unborn child cannot be a legitimate subject of a non-therapeutic experiment, but apparently the same child, minutes after birth, can be. This seems unreasonable. In answer to this reasonable question, I think it important to emphasize that parents and others who have responsibility to care for "voiceless" or non-competent persons *cannot licitly* consent to their being subjects of non-therapeutic procedures *if these procedures pose "significant" risks*. I further maintain that newborn babies are very vulnerable subjects and that one can reasonably hold that non-therapeutic experiments performed on them would pose more significant risks in comparison to any benefits to be expected.

(3) Conclusion to "Proxy" Consent for Non-Competent or "Voiceless" Subjects to Participate in Non-Therapeutic Experimentation

I maintain that "proxy" consent here is a misnomer, since the potential subjects are, precisely because they are non-competent or "voiceless," incapable of giving consent, and no one should presume to give consent for them. The consent in question is the *personal* consent of parents and other guardians. The dignity proper to human beings precisely as persons and the dignity proper to them precisely as moral agents are both at stake. For parents and other guardians who might give consent for those under their care to participate in non-therapeutic experiments, the dignity primarily at stake is their dignity precisely as moral agents, who must respect fully the dignity precisely as persons of the voiceless, non-competent persons committed to their trust. If in their judgment, the proposed experimentation would not violate their charges' dignity precisely as persons, it would then not be unreasonable or a violation of the trust committed to them to give the necessary consent. A condition *sine qua non* if such consent is to be morally licit is precisely the requirement that the proposed experiment pose no "significant risk" (as this has been defined) to the persons committed to their care.

3. Research on the Unborn (in Particular, Embryonic Stem-Cell Research), Including Updated Scientific Evidence Regarding Effectiveness of Therapeutic Use of Adult Stem Cells, Continued Failure of Use of Embryonic Stem Cells to Effect Cures and Evidence of Harms They Can and Have Caused, Developments of Induced Pluripotent Stem Cells (IPPS)

The New Atlantis: A Journal of Technology and Society (Number 34, Winter 2012) provides us with a primer on stem-cell research. This Number is entirely devoted "to a major report on the stem cell debates, a comprehensive and up-to-date account of the scientific facts and the moral, political, and legal stakes. This is the inaugural report of an important new body, The Witherspoon Council on Ethics and the Integrity of Science." Among its board members are Robert George, J.D., D. Phil, Princeton University, cochairman with Donald Landry, M.D., Ph.D. of Columbia University Medical Center, Michael Birrer, M.D, Ph.D., Harvard Medical School, Eric Cohen, editor of *The New Atlantis*, William Hurlburt, M.D., Stanford Medical Center, Gilbert Meilaender, Ph.D., Valparaiso University, and Christopher Tollefsen, University of South Carolina.

The report, entitled "The Stem Cell Debates: Lessons for Science and Politics," is divided into seven major parts and two appendices. Of particular value are the following: (1) "Ten Common Misrepresentations," among them "Embryonic stem cells are superior to adult stem cells, or adult stem cells are superior to embryonic stem cells"; "A clear majority of Americans support embryonic stem cell research"; "Opposing embryonic stem cell research means opposing cures for suffering people"; "Opposing embryonic stem cell research is a matter of religious ideology." (2) "Lessons of the Stem Cell Debates," among them "Science Informs Ethics" and "Ethics Guides Science." (3) Appendix A: "The Science of Stem Cell Research," with in-depth and up-to-date material on the sources, potential, and serious problems with embryonic stem cells and the development of alternate sources or pluripotent stem cells not derived by the killing of human embryos; Appendix B: "The Promise of Stem Cell Therapies," in particular the ongoing successes in therapeutic use of adult stem cells. As can be seen this is a most important and current account of stem-cell research. [38]

The basic norm, clearly developed by *Donum vitae*, as we saw in the previous section and also in Chapter One, and obliquely reaffirmed by *Dignitas personae*, in nos. 24, 31, and clearly reaffirmed in 32,[39] rightly condemns as utterly immoral any non-therapeutic experimentation or research on human embryos. Any form of experimentation or research on a human embryo performed on it not for its own benefit but for that of others is unethical and gravely immoral, particularly if the experimentation is such as gravely to harm the unborn child. Any procedure whereby new human life is generated *in vitro* in order either to use it for implantation and gestation later on or to freeze it or to use it for experimental purposes is radically immoral and unjust, however good the motivation for doing so.

A. What Are Human Embryonic Stem Cells, and Why Are They Sought for Research?

Today embryonic stem-cell research is a matter of great interest. As noted, Appendices A and B of Number 34, Winter 2012 of *The New Atlantis* provide comprehensive summaries of this research and the promise and successes and problems found in using adult stem cells for therapeutic purposes, and the development of different kinds of induced pluripotent stem cells not derived by the intentional killing of unborn human life.

Embryonic stem cells develop very early in the human embryo after fertilization. They form the "inner cell mass" of the early embryo during the blastocyst stage, when the embryo is about to implant in the womb (the "outer mass" of the blastocyst is called the trophoblast and forms the placenta and other supporting and vital organs needed for the development of the unborn child within the mother). These cells go on to form the body of the developing human person. Although they are not "totipotential," as are the cells organized into a unitary whole in the preimplantation embryo, they are "pluripotential," since they have the capacity to develop into any of the more than two hundred kinds of cells that make up the adult human body. In theory, if these cells are extracted early enough during embryonic life, they can be cultured and manipulated to become the cells needed for specific therapeutic purposes. The cells thus produced can be transferred into an organ (e.g., the brain), where they can proliferate and replace or repair cells that are injured or dying because of some disease. With modern technology, there is reason to think that they can be designed to repair or replace muscle or brain cells, transplanted into human hearts or brains in order to treat such maladies as Parkinson's disease, Alzheimer's disease, and various heart diseases and in this way restore health to many people.[40]

Advocates of human embryonic stem-cell research point to the following *technical advantages* of such research: (1) embryonic stem cells are very flexible and may have potential to make any cell; (2) there is a never-ending supply — one embryonic stem-cell line can potentially provide an endless supply of cells with defined characteristics; and (3) they are readily available from embryos cryopreserved in *in vitro* fertilization clinics. Advocates also admit that there are some *technical disadvantages*: (1) they are very difficult to differentiate uniformly into a target-type cell or tissue; (2) they are immunogenic — such cells are likely to be rejected after transplantation; and (3) they are tumorigenic — capable of forming tumors.[41] As Richard Doerflinger — whom I consider one of the most well-informed and intelligent lay (nonscientific) authorities on stem-cell research — has said, human embryonic stem-cell lines "may develop genetic abnormalities preventing their use in humans for the foreseeable future."[42]

B. Why Research on Embryonic Stem Cells Is Gravely Immoral

Three principal methods, all of them intrinsically immoral, are currently being proposed for retrieving embryonic stem cells. The first is to induce the abortion of early embryos and retrieve their stem cells. The second is to produce embryos *in vitro* solely for the purpose of research, including stem-cell research. The third is to use the so-called spare embryos that have been produced *in vitro* for infertility treatment and cryopreserved. All three of these methods require the *intentional* killing of unborn human children and are hence intrinsically evil. The persons eager to obtain these cells want them *precisely because they are the cells of living human beings*. Were they the stem cells of canines, bovines, felines, simians, or dolphins, one would not want them (and members of People for the Ethical Treatment of Animals [PETA] and others would think it barbaric to kill embryonic dolphins or chimps or gorillas in order to get their stem cells). They thus frankly acknowledge that the beings they must kill are *human beings, members of the human species*.[43] But they claim that embryonic human beings are not *persons*, and that only persons have "rights." This claim, however, drives a wedge between *being a human being* and *being a person* and requires those who distinguish sharply between the two to offer a nonarbitrary criterion to distinguish which members of the human species are persons and which are not. But this, as we have seen in the chapter on abortion, is impossible.

C. Propaganda vs. Facts

Although some people — in particular, elites in our society, editorial writers for major news media, prominent academics, and politicians — claim that embryonic stem-cell research has led to therapies for a host of dread diseases (diabetes, Parkinson's disease, various cancers, etc.), this is not the case. As a matter of fact, at present there are *no* therapeutic treatments making use of embryonic stem cells, and *no* potential therapies are even in clinical trials. *Not a single human person has as yet benefited from such research!*

Adult stem cells have been used for years in treating patients. Some such treatments, such as the use of bone-marrow transplantation for leukemia and other blood diseases, antedated the knowledge that it was specifically stem cells that made the treatment work. Even now, many of the most exciting medical advances using stem cells rely on adult stem cells, including the recent creation of an artificial trachea and the successful treatment of HIV using bone marrow transplantation.[44]

In 2007, Doerflinger was able to cite seventy-five *new* reasons to reconsider the alleged need for stem-cell research that destroys human embryos, and he noted recent advances in adult stem-cell research and other alternatives to embryonic stem-cell research made between June 2006 and February 2007.[45]

On November 14, 2011, the Geron Corporation, which had for fifteen years spent hundreds of millions of dollars in embryonic stem-cell research and had FDA approval to test such cells on human persons to see whether they were therapeutically of value, stated that it would terminate its research on embryonic stem cells. This was a bombshell in the embryonic stem-cell industry, although some companies, notably Advanced Cell Technology, are pursuing such research with FDA approval. For some, Geron's action was a tragedy. Daniel Heumann, a board member of the Christopher and Dana Reeve Foundation, said: "I'm disgusted. It makes me sick. To get people's hopes up and then do this for financial reasons is despicable. They are treating us like lab rats." Quadriplegic Christopher Reeve became an icon for the campaign to use human embryonic stem cells. In the light of his courage and strength of personality, ethical reservations became petty quibbles and the sour scowls of naysayers. He was convinced that he and others would one day walk again thanks to the mysterious powers of human embryonic stem cells. This hope created the $3 billion California Institute for Regenerative Medicine (CIRM) and persuaded legislators in other states and countries to authorize embryo research. But, as Jared Lee reported in the November 19, 2011, edition of *BioEdge*, "these hopes have crashed and burned."

> In interviews scientists put on a brave face, but the news is a huge blow to supporters of the therapeutic potential of human embryonic stem cells. As critics of the ethically contentious treatment have argued for years, it now seems clear that embryonic stem cells will not lead to miracle cures. "Advances in the stem cell field are disruptive innovations that have the potential to supersede earlier innovations, hES [human embryonic stem] cells being one of those. I don't know if Geron looks at it that way, but I do," Roger Pedersen, a leading stem cell scientist at Cambridge, told *ScienceInsider*. Embryonic stem cells may have been the most hyped scientific innovation of a generation.[46]

D. Legitimate Sources of Stem Cells for Research

As the previous section clearly indicates, adult stem cells — and these are found in newborns — can be, have been, and are being used already for therapeutic treatments. Obtaining such cells does not require the destruction of human embryos. As Edmund D. Pellegrino, M.D., among others, has pointed out, "Creditable laboratories have identified a wide variety of sources for pluripotential cells with the capability of embryonic stem cells. For example, stem cells from the bone marrow, placenta, or umbilical cord of live births are already in use in treating leukemia. Work currently in progress indicates that such cells can be altered to develop into cartilage and bone tissue and used in replacing diseased bone tissue.... [N]eural stem cells [have been] successfully isolated from living nerve tissue ... and show promise for possible use in treating Parkinson's disease or brain injuries."[47] Since Pellegrino penned those lines, enormous advances have been made, as noted already, in therapies developed with the use of adult stem cells.

Those advocating continued research on adult stem cells note the following *technical advantages*: (1) special adult stem cells from bone marrow and umbilical cords that appear to be as flexible as embryonic types have been recently isolated; (2) they are easier than embryonic stem cells to differentiate into specific kinds of cells or tissues; (3) they are not immunogenic

— recipients who receive stem cells from their own cells and tissues will not reject transplants; (4) they are relatively easy to obtain; (5) they are non-tumoregenic.[48]

E. Proposed New Sources for Embryonic Stem Cells Obtained in Ways That Do Not Require the Killing of Human Beings During the Embryonic Stage of Their Existence

(1) Pluripotent Stem Cells From Adult Skin Cells

Undoubtedly, one of the most promising sources for pluripotent stem cells is adult skin cells. On November 20, 2007, both the *New York Times* and the *Washington Post* announced on their front pages that two teams of scientists had succeeded in turning human skin cells into what appear to be embryonic stem cells without making or destroying human embryos. The teams were headed by James A. Thompson at the University of Wisconsin and by Shinya Yamanaka in Japan.

(2) The President's Council on Bioethics 2005 "White Paper"

In May 2005, the President's Council on Bioethics published a white paper entitled *Alternative Sources of Human Pluripotent Stem Cells*.[49] The Council was seeking ways of obtaining pluripotent stem cells by methods "that would meet the moral standard of not destroying or endangering human embryos in the process."[50] The Council identified four broad approaches. "The stem cells could be derived: (1) by extracting cells from embryos already dead; or (2) by non-harmful biopsy of living embryos; or (3) by extracting cells from artificially created non-embryonic but embryo-like cellular systems (engineered to lack the essential elements of embryogenesis but still capable of some cell division and growth); or (4) by dedifferentiation of somatic cells back to pluripotency."[51]

Other sources for pluripotent stem cells *not* derived by the intentional killing of human embryonic persons are (5) Hurlbut's Altered Nuclear Transfer Proposal, (6) Altered Nuclear Transfer — Oocyte Assisted Reprogramming, (7) pluripotent stem cells in amniotic fluid, and (8) pluripotent stem cells from mice.

I will not go into the details and debates concerning these proposed sources for pluripotent stem cells not derived immorally by intentionally killing unborn human life. Pages 232-236 of the 2nd (2008) edition of this work were devoted to a comprehensive account. Today I advise readers to consult the Winter 2012 issue (Number 34) of *The New Atlantis*, to which reference has already been made. See pp. 69-74 of Appendix A for a good summary of such alternative sources of pluripotent stem cells.

4. Genetic Therapy

A. Church Teaching

In nos. 25-28 of Part Three *Dignitas personae* affirms:

> *Gene therapy* commonly refers to techniques of genetic engineering applied to human beings for therapeutic purposes, that is to say, with the aim of curing genetically based diseases, although recently gene therapy has been attempted for diseases which are not inherited, for cancer in particular. In theory, it is possible to use gene therapy on two levels: somatic cell gene therapy and germ line cell therapy. *Somatic cell gene therapy* seeks to eliminate or reduce genetic defects on the level of somatic cells, that is, cells other than the reproductive cells, but which make up the tissue and organs of the body. It involves procedures aimed at certain individual cells with effects that are limited to a single person. *Germ line cell therapy* aims instead at correcting genetic defects present in germ line cells with the purpose of transmitting the therapeutic effects to the offspring of the individual. Such methods of gene therapy, whether somatic or germ-line cell therapy, can be undertaken on a fetus *before his or her birth* as gene therapy in the uterus or *after birth* on a child or adult.

Continuing, the document declares:

> For a moral evaluation the following distinctions need to be kept in mind. Procedures used on somatic cells for strictly therapeutic purposes are in principle morally licit. Such actions seek to restore the normal genetic configuration of the patient or to counter damage caused by genetic anomalies or those related to other pathologies. Given that gene therapy can involve significant risks for the patient, the ethical principle must be observed according to which, in order to proceed to a therapeutic intervention, it is necessary to establish beforehand that the person being treated will not be exposed to risks to his health or physical integrity which are excessive or disproportionate to the gravity of the pathology for which a cure is sought. The informed consent of the patient or his legitimate representative is also required. The moral evaluation of germ line cell therapy is different. Whatever genetic modifications are effected on the germ cells of a person will be transmitted to any potential offspring. Because the risks

connected to any genetic manipulation are considerable and as yet not fully controllable, in the present state of research, it is not morally permissible to act in a way that may cause possible harm to the resulting progeny. In the hypothesis of gene therapy on the embryo, it needs to be added that this only takes place in the context of in vitro fertilization and thus runs up against all the ethical objections to such procedures. For these reasons, therefore, it must be stated that, *in its current state* [my emphasis], germ line cell therapy in all its forms is morally illicit.

It then concludes:

The question of using genetic engineering for purposes other than medical treatment also calls for consideration. Some have imagined the possibility of using techniques of genetic engineering to introduce alterations with the presumed aim of improving and strengthening the gene pool. Some of these proposals exhibit a certain dissatisfaction or even rejection of the value of the human being as a finite creature and person. Apart from technical difficulties and the real and potential risks involved, such manipulation would promote a eugenic mentality and would lead to indirect social stigma with regard to people who lack certain qualities, while privileging qualities that happen to be appreciated by a certain culture or society; such qualities do not constitute what is specifically human. This would be in contrast with the fundamental truth of the equality of all human beings which is expressed in the principle of justice, the violation of which, in the long run, would harm peaceful coexistence among individuals. Furthermore, one wonders who would be able to establish which modifications were to be held as positive and which not, or what limits should be placed on individual requests for improvement since it would be materially impossible to fulfil the wishes of every single person. Any conceivable response to these questions would, however, derive from arbitrary and questionable criteria. All of this leads to the conclusion that the prospect of such an intervention would end sooner or later by harming the common good, by favouring the will of some over the freedom of others. Finally it must also be noted that in the attempt to create *a new type of human being* one can recognize *an ideological element* in which man tries to take the place of his Creator. In stating the ethical negativity of these kinds of interventions which imply *an unjust domination of man over man,* the Church also recalls the need to return to an attitude of care for people and of education in accepting human life in its concrete historical finite nature.

The official U.S. Government website providing a detailed account of the current scientific status of research into genetic therapy is http://www.ornl .gov/sci/techresources/Human_Genome/medicine/genetherapy.shtml. It gives detailed information about the following topics: (1) What is gene therapy? (2) What is the current status of gene therapy research? (3) What are some current developments in gene therapy research? (4) What are some of the ethical considerations for using gene therapy? The ones listed are: What is normal and what is a disability or disorder, and who decides? Are disabilities diseases? Do they need to be cured or prevented? Does searching for a cure demean the lives of individuals presently affected by disabilities? Is somatic gene therapy more or less ethical than germ-line therapy? Preliminary attempts at gene therapy are exorbitantly expensive: Who will have access to them? Who will pay for their use?

B. Gene Therapy: Its Definition and Types

"Gene therapy," as the Working Party of the United Kingdom's Catholic Bishops' Joint Committee on Bioethical Issues has said, "is the intentional alteration of genes in cells or tissues in such a way as to treat or prevent an inherited disorder, or to make another pathological condition more amenable to treatment." Continuing, the Working Party describes two of the basic types of such therapy: "Such intervention is termed *somatic* gene therapy if the alteration affects only the individual on whom it is carried out. If the intervention takes place on the germ-line cells — that is, sperm, ova or their precursors — it is termed *germ-line* gene therapy, and will affect not only a particular individual but also his or her descendants."[52]

The goal of gene therapy is to treat human diseases by correcting the genetic defects underlying genetic maladies or by adding new genes to the patient in order to provide or enhance a given therapeutic operation.

In addition to these forms of gene *therapy* there exists also the possibility of genetic *enhancement*, i.e., efforts to improve or enhance, by genetic engineering, characteristics such as size, skin color, intelligence, etc. Speaking of this possibility W. French Anderson, one of the leading world authorities on gene therapy, had this to say: "To the extent that defects in these traits constitute truly damaging errors or disease, they ought to, and will, be treated with all the tools at our command [and efforts to treat these defects would then come under gene *therapy*]. But to the extent that they are not errors but rather normal human variations, the pursuit of forms of enhancement modification is fraught with risks for society." Anderson then goes on to enumerate some of these serious risks.[53] I will not here consider enhancement genetic engineering. At present, there are no good ethical reasons for attempting such engineering and many good moral reasons for not doing so; the medical hazards are as yet not even known: who decides and on what criteria, which genes to select for "enhancement," how one could avoid unjust discrimination in selecting those who would presumably benefit from such enhancement, etc. Thus, in what follows, attention focuses on gene *therapy*, and, in particular — for reasons to be given later — on *somatic gene therapy*.

C. How Gene Therapy "Works"

Today it is possible to treat or prevent a genetically based malady because of the breakthroughs that occurred with ever-increasing frequency in molecular biology and DNA research over the past half century. Each human cell, except for the mature red blood cell, has a nucleus containing *chromosomes*. Each chromosome is made up of DNA (deoxyribonucleic acid), which takes the form of a double-stranded helix, and attached to each strand of the helix is a series of alternating nucleotides called *bases*. DNA is the "genetic alphabet" and its bases are the "letters" of this alphabet. There are four, and only four, such bases or letters, namely, adenine (A), cytosine (C), guanine (G), and thymine (T), and the "words" of the genetic language or DNA are constructed of these "letters" or bases. The sequence of bases on either strand of the DNA constitutes a gene, the basic unit of heredity whereby traits are passed on from one generation to another.

Scientists now know a good deal about this genetic language. They realize that the substitution of even one "letter" for another can cause a cell to produce or not produce a given enzyme or protein essential for the normal functioning of the organism. If the organism is not functioning properly because of an error in the language of its DNA, it is possible, in light of new breakthroughs in molecular biology and recombinant DNA, to put the "right" letter into the pertinent genetic "word," to replace one that is "incorrect," etc., and in this way to correct a given genetically induced defect. In theory, such genetic therapeutic intervention can be done either to the body or to the somatic cells of the person afflicted with the malady — *somatic-cell* therapy as described above — or to the germ cells of the persons transmitting the genetic traits to their offspring through generation of human life — *germ-line* therapy as described above.[54]

The major problem, once the "correct gene" has been designed or produced, is to get it into appropriate body cells of the person receiving the therapy.

D. Strategies for Gene Therapy

According to Anderson, there are three basic approaches to the genetic correction of diseases, namely (1) *ex vivo*, (2) *in situ*, and (3) *in vivo*. The first requires removing cells from the patient, "correcting" them outside his body by inserting the normal gene, and then returning the corrected cells to the patient. The second introduces the new, correct gene, directly into the site of the disease within the body of the patient, either in the form of a "virus vector" (on this, see below) or naked DNA. The third approach, not yet developed sufficiently for practical use, requires developing "vectors" that can be injected directly into the bloodstream and carry the therapeutic gene to the proper cell tissue safely and efficiently.[55]

In addition, Anderson notes that all current (c. 1995-2000) clinical protocols for gene therapy are based on the idea of adding a normal gene rather that replacing or correcting the malfunctioning gene present in the patient's body. This approach assumes that the newly added gene will be introduced into a site in the genome different from that of the defective gene and that the new gene's expression will override the effects of the defective gene.[56]

E. Delivering Therapeutic Genes

The English Bishops' Working Group pointed out that effective gene therapy requires not only the recognition and isolation of the appropriate gene for effecting therapy but also an efficient delivery system. The latter — the delivery system — is called a *vector*.[57] Although the desired genes to be delivered into the cells of the patient needing therapy can be delivered by physical techniques (e.g., ingestion of an organic salt called calcium phosphate containing the appropriate DNA or the placing of DNA into fatty bubbles or liquid vesicles that can be fused with human body cells), such techniques have not as yet proved very effective. At present the most effective way to deliver therapeutic genes is through the use of *viruses* and *viral vectors*.

Viruses have a natural tendency to enter human cells and insert their genetic information into the genome of the cells that they enter. Thus therapeutic gene cells, developed through recombinant DNA, can be inserted into various kinds of viruses capable of introducing their genetic information into target cells and allow those genes to become a permanent and functional part of the host-cell genome. The newly introduced gene is a new cellular gene of the patient. However, the viruses themselves can often have bad effects on the cells of the person into whom they are introduced. But, again as a result of the advances made in molecular cellular biology, it is now possible to inactivate or remove deleterious viral genes, replacing them with the desired therapeutic genetic material.[58]

This type of genetic *somatic-cell* therapy has proved beneficial and successful in the treatment of several genetically based diseases, e.g., cystic fibrosis, adenosine deaminase deficiency (ADA) — a genetic disorder caused by the lack of the gene product adenosine deaminase and leading to abnormality of bone marrow cells, thus giving rise to serious infections — and there is hope that as time goes on more and more genetically based diseases can be treated by somatic-cell therapy.

F. *The Morality of Somatic-Cell Gene Therapy*

Somatic gene therapy raises problems similar to those posed by other forms of treatment. Such therapy is morally warranted so long as the risks posed by this new type of therapy are not significant when compared with the reasonable expectation that employment of such therapy will indeed bring great benefit *to the patient*. Somatic-cell gene therapy is today, of course, *experimental* in nature and does not constitute "standard" treatment. As with other experimental procedures (e.g., as kidney transplants were when they were first initiated), there is reason for reserving such therapy for serious diseases for which there is no satisfactory alternative treatment.[59] There is urgent need that, wherever possible, attempts at somatic therapy on human persons be preceded by studies on animals.

There is the possibility that somatic gene therapy may have side effects, possibly deleterious, affecting the germ-line or gametic cells. Such risk is not limited to gene therapy, as other medical treatments can risk harming the children conceived while their mothers, in particular, are undergoing treatment. To reduce the risk of unintentionally harming progeny, some have recommended, as Helen Watt has observed, that female patients participating in trials of somatic-cell therapy be required to use contraceptives.[60] As Watt goes on to note, correctly, "Those who recognize the use of contraception as incompatible with sexual integrity will wish to recommend, instead, the use of natural family planning — always assuming there really is no appreciable risk of transmitting an effect to the germ line."[61]

G. *Germ-Line "Therapy"*

At present such "therapy" seems unrealizable, and the risks entailed, particularly if human subjects (and their progeny — for such "therapy" affects not only particular individuals but all their descendants) are involved, are far too great, and even unknown, to warrant its use. Much more research needs to be done on animals before one can even begin to think of morally licit applications of such "therapy." The problems and risks raised by germ-line therapy are such as to provide serious grounds for thinking that it should never be carried out. Watt describes these serious risks — to the immediate subject, to future generations, to the human embryos that would no doubt be used for purely research purposes, etc. — in great detail in her excellent article, and I refer readers interested in pursuing the matter to it.[62] Such therapy is *not* to be regarded in any way as intrinsically evil. It is simply that at present, with other pressing health needs and in view of the serious and unresolved problems and unknown risks raised by this line of therapy, it would be better to leave it alone. But it might perhaps be morally licit in the future, once sufficient studies had been done on animals and there was reasonable hope that the terrible risks such therapy raises both for the individuals immediately affected and for their descendants could be avoided or minimized.

5. Prenatal and Preimplantation Screening

A. Church Teaching

Relevant magisterial teaching is given by Pope John Paul II and *Dignitas personae.* Pope John Paul II declared:

> Special attention must be given to evaluating the morality of *prenatal diagnostic techniques* which enable the early detection of possible anomalies in the unborn child. In view of the complexity of these techniques, an accurate and systematic moral judgment is necessary. When they do not involve disproportionate risks for the child and the mother, and are meant to make possible early therapy or even to favor a serene and informed acceptance of the child not yet born, these techniques are morally licit. But since the possibilities of prenatal therapy are today still limited, it not infrequently happens that these techniques are used with a eugenic intention which accepts selective abortion in order to prevent the birth of children affected by various types of anomalies. Such an attitude is shameful and utterly reprehensible, since it presumes to measure the value of a human life only within the parameters of "normality" and physical well-being, thus opening the way to legitimizing infanticide and euthanasia as well. (*Evangelium vitae,* no. 63)

Dignitas personae affirmed:

> Preimplantation diagnosis is a form of prenatal diagnosis connected with techniques of artificial fertilization in which embryos formed *in vitro* undergo genetic diagnosis before being transferred into a woman's womb. Such diagnosis is done *in order to ensure that only embryos free from defects or having the desired sex or other particular qualities are transferred* [emphasis in original]. Unlike other forms of prenatal diagnosis, in which the diagnostic phase is clearly separated from any possible later elimination and which provide therefore a period in which a couple would be free to accept a child with defects, in this case, the diagnosis before implantation is immediately followed by the elimination of an embryo suspected of having genetic or chromosomal defects, or not having the sex desired, or having other qualities that are not wanted. Preimplantation diagnosis — connected as it is with artificial fertilization, which is itself always intrinsically illicit— is directed toward the *qualitative selection and consequent destruction of embryos,* which constitutes an act of abortion. Preimplantation diagnosis is therefore the expression of a *eugenic mentality* that "accepts selective abortion in order to prevent the birth of children affected by various types of anomalies. Such an attitude is shameful and utterly reprehensible, since it presumes to measure the value of a human life only within the parameters of 'normality' and physical well-being, thus opening the way to legitimizing infanticide and euthanasia as well." (no. 22; reference to *Evangelium vitae,* no. 63)

The document went on to hold:

> By treating the human embryo as mere "laboratory material," *the concept itself of human dignity is also subjected to alteration and discrimination.* Dignity belongs equally to every single human being, irrespective of his parents' desires, his social condition, educational formation or level of physical development. If at other times in history, while the concept and requirements of human dignity were accepted in general, discrimination was practiced on the basis of race, religion or social condition, today there is a no less serious and unjust form of discrimination which leads to the non-recognition of the ethical and legal status of human beings suffering from serious diseases or disabilities. It is forgotten that sick and disabled people are not some separate category of humanity; in fact, sickness and disability are part of the human condition and affect every individual, even if some do not have direct experience of it. Such

discrimination is immoral and must therefore be considered legally unacceptable, just as there is a duty to eliminate cultural, economic and social barriers which undermine the full recognition and protection of disabled or ill people. (no. 22)

B. Current Methods of Screening the Unborn

The original purpose of prenatal screening was to help protect the health and life of both the unborn child and its mother. It had as its major emphasis the diagnosis or assessment of conditions to assist the physician in helping the unborn child to a more normal and healthy life. The development of sonography allowed one to see into the uterus and to observe the development of the embryo/fetus. In the past few decades since the proliferation of "fertility clinics" offering "new reproductive techniques" for making babies in the laboratory, there has been an explosion of technological tools used to examine the "product" (human embryo/fetus) and to identify (at times falsely) different chromosome anomalies (e.g., Down syndrome), different biochemical or molecular conditions with a genetic base, and other conditions such as spina bifida, cystic fibrosis, fragile X syndrome, and others.

Fragile X syndrome is a genetic syndrome that is the most common known single-gene cause of autism and the most common inherited cause of intellectual disability, ranging from mild to severe. It can also result in physical characteristics such as an elongated face, large or protruding ears, and larger testes; behavioral characteristics such as stereotypical movements (e.g., hand flapping); and social anxiety. It affects the fragile X mental retardation (*FMR1*) gene on the X chromosome, which is required for normal neural development. There is currently no drug treatment that has shown benefit specifically for fragile X syndrome, but medications are used to treat symptoms of attention deficit and hyperactivity, anxiety, and aggression. Supportive management is important for individuals with fragile X syndrome and may involve speech therapy, occupational therapy, and individualized educational and behavioral programs.[63]

Among these tools are, of course, such long used ones as sonography, amniocentesis, and chorionic villus sampling. There are many new ones, however, and more are being constantly developed by scientists and doctors in fertility clinics and IV centers to help them identify (at times falsely) human unborn babies either conceived naturally in the wombs of their mothers but of the wrong (= unwanted) sex — most frequently female — or manufactured by new reproductive techniques and found not to measure up to standards or, because of hyperfertilization and implantation, must be "reduced" (= killed in utero) because too many would threaten the survival of some. Among these new tools are ultrasonography (including *nuchal translucency ultrasound*), preimplantation genetic diagnosis (PGD), and blastocyst transfer.

Nuchal translucency sonography is a sonographic scan to help identify higher risks of chromosomal defects such as Down syndrome in a fetus, particularly for older women who have higher risks of such pregnancies. The scan is carried out at 11 to 13.6 weeks' gestation.[64]

Preimplantation genetic diagnosis (PGD) is described as follows by the Houston Fertility Institute:

> PGD ... is a breakthrough technology that improves the likelihood of having a healthy baby. PGD is most commonly performed when one or both partners carry a genetic disease, as it allows the couple to reduce the chance of transmitting the disorder to their children. The physicians and embryologists at Houston Fertility Institute are experts in this new area of reproductive health and have recently published articles on a new embryo biopsy technique that we [technicians at the Houston Fertility Institute] have pioneered in our embryology laboratories. The importance of having PGD performed at an experienced facility, such as Houston Fertility Institute, cannot be overemphasized.
>
> PGD is performed as a part of an *in-vitro fertilization* (IVF) cycle, during which multiple eggs are produced, retrieved from the ovaries, and fertilized with sperm in our embryology laboratory. IVF is necessary for the PGD procedure, because it allows us access to the embryos. On day five of embryo culture, the embryos are blastocysts, and typically over one hundred cells in size. One or two cells are removed from each embryo during a process called embryo biopsy, and a genetic evaluation is performed on all the embryos. *Only the healthy embryos* [my emphasis] are then transferred back into the uterus....
>
> The blastocyst culture and day-five embryo transfer procedure for in-vitro fertilization (IVF) facilitates selection of the best quality embryos for transfer. The concept of embryo quality is very important for couples who are experiencing infertility. With blastocyst embryo transfer, we [technicians at the Houston Fertility Institute] can transfer fewer embryos, thereby reducing risks for multiple pregnancies while still keeping our overall pregnancy rates at our Houston, Texas–area infertility treatment center very high.[65]

C. Moral Misuse of Prenatal Screening

When the U.S. Supreme Court in its 1973 ruling in *Roe v. Wade* struck down as unconstitutional state laws proscribing abortion on the grounds that such laws violated the "right to privacy" granted to pregnant women and their doctors by the Fourteenth Amendment, the pressure for diagnosing unborn children grew, and the legal penalty imposed on obstetricians for failing to warn or diagnose fetal anomalies became a driving force in obstetric care.

This barbaric consequence of legalizing abortion was illustrated for me a few years ago while I was visiting my daughter, Kathleen, in London. Her husband, James Boardman, a pro-life pediatric neurologist then finishing his residency, came home sickened one night because a newborn who was brought to him was blind in one eye. The needle used for an amniocentesis to determine whether he had Down syndrome had pierced that part of the brain where the eye develops. James told us that invasive procedures that jeopardize the unborn child (e.g., amniocentesis) are medically unnecessary in medical practice in which neither the doctor nor the patient is willing to abort, a judgment made also by the well-known champion of life Thomas W. Hilgers.[66]

D. Morally Good Uses of Prenatal Screening

Preimplantation diagnosis can, however, have truly *therapeutic ends* in view. For instance, it is possible to use gene therapy on a preimplantation embryo to correct a possible serious malady. Thus on February 3, 2000, the *London Times* (I happened to be in London at the time) reported that doctors had helped a married couple who had already had one child who suffered from cystic fibrosis to have a child free of this disease, despite the fact that they stood at risk of having another child so afflicted. What they had done was to have the couple provide the ovum and sperm, fertilize these gametic cells *in vitro*, and then subject the developing preimplantation embryo to a test to see whether it carried the genes responsible for cystic fibrosis. It did. But then the physicians introduced a viral vector carrying a gene to "correct" this problem, and they succeeded in doing so. The child was then implanted in the mother's womb, and approximately nine months later (early February 2000) a baby girl was born, totally free of cystic fibrosis.

Here the moral problem is that this child was not conceived in the mother's womb after a marital act but was rather "produced" in the laboratory in a petri dish and, had the gene therapy not been successful, the preimplantation embryo would have been "discarded" and not implanted in the mother's womb.

But would it be immoral to remove an early, preimplantation embryo from the womb by uterine lavage if there is serious reason to think that it suffers from a serious genetic malady that could be cured by the introduction of the "right" gene through gene somatic-cell therapy?

The Magisterium has not addressed this issue. Although *Donum vitae* condemns *in vitro* fertilization and the freezing of embryos (cryopreservation), "even when carried out in order to preserve the life of an embryo," as an offense contrary to human dignity because it exposes the embryo to grave risks of harm (cf. DV, I, 6), it had previously acknowledged that if such diagnosis respects the embryo's life and is directed toward its safeguarding, it can be morally licit (cf. DV, I, 2). Thus might it not be in conformity with magisterial teaching to remove an early embryo from the womb by uterine lavage, if there is serious reason for believing it to be subject to a devastating genetic disease, and, if there are good reasons for thinking that gene somatic-cell therapy would be successful, deliver the "correct" genes to the embryo, and then reintroduce it into the mother's womb for implantation? It seems to me that this may be a valid moral option.

By detecting neural tube anomalies such as spina bifida, it is frequently possible to engage in therapeutic actions on the developing embryo in the womb. For example, a shunt can be inserted into the child's brain and fluid causing pressure on the brain can be drained from it, thus providing great benefit to a child suffering from spina bifida. In fact, some years ago at a hearing at the U.S. Senate, sponsored by pro-life Senator Gordon Humphrey, I witnessed testimony from a couple with their physician and their child — now born and resting on her mother's lap — in which they described the wonderful surgery that had been done on the child while still in the womb, a therapeutic intervention indicated after prenatal diagnosis had shown that she suffered from a neural tube defect and that fluids were building up in her cranium, exerting pressure on her brain. This timely intervention was successful in minimizing the harm this child suffered.

E. Conclusion

Magisterial teaching provides solid guidance regarding prenatal diagnosis. In *Donum vitae* (I, 2), the Congregation for the Doctrine of the Faith declared such diagnosis "permissible if the methods used, with the consent of the parents who have been adequately instructed, safeguard the life and integrity of the embryo and its mother and do not subject them to disproportionate risks. But this diagnosis is gravely opposed to the moral law when it is done with the thought of possibly inducing an abortion depending upon the results: a diagnosis which shows the existence of a malformation or a hereditary illness must not be the equivalent of a death-sentence." Similar teaching is found in other relevant magisterial documents, such as John Paul II's *Evangelium vitae*, the Pontifical Council for Pastoral Assistance to Health Care Workers' *Charter for Health Care Workers*, and the U.S. bishops' *Ethical and Religious Directives for Catholic Health Care Services*.[67]

6. Genetic Counseling

In their *Ethical and Religious Directives for Catholic Health Care Services*, the U.S. bishops state: "Genetic counseling may be provided in order to promote responsible parenthood and to prepare for the proper treatment and care of children with genetic defects, in accordance with Catholic moral teaching and the intrinsic rights and obligations of married couples regarding the transmission of life" (no. 54). Genetic counseling, therefore, is morally legitimate in itself.

The need for such counseling is growing, as today we know that many, many diseases and anomalies affecting human persons are genetically based. In fact, a genetic component has been identified for over four thousand diseases, disorders, and traits, and as the Human Genome Project (see below) advances, and after virtual completion, more and more such diseases may be identified. As a result, today many persons, particularly married couples, are legitimately concerned to know whether there is likelihood that any children they may generate may be afflicted by some serious genetically induced malady. The moral issue concerns the *kind* of counseling to be given.

Today, in our secular society, many think that if genetic testing shows that a couple is at high risk of conceiving a child afflicted by a serious genetically based malady, that couple ought to take effective steps to prevent either the conception or birth of such a child. By effective steps for preventing conception, moreover, they mean various contraceptive procedures, in particular tubal ligation, and by effective steps for preventing birth, should tests *in utero* show that a child is, or may well be, afflicted by such a malady, they mean abortion. They may also recommend artificial insemination by a donor, *in vitro* fertilization (followed by preimplantation diagnosis, with "termination" of embryos identified as afflicted by a genetic malady), and other immoral methods of coping with the dangers that genetic testing may indicate. Obviously, a morally upright person cannot offer such "counseling."

Germain Grisez has provided very practical guidance for morally upright counselors, in particular, physicians who might be asked by their patients for advice on these matters. Obviously, a Catholic physician/counselor, or any morally upright counselor, should tell potential patients that he or she is committed to the good of human life and will never advise anyone even to consider contraception, sterilization, abortion, *in vitro* fertilization, etc. Because of the current climate in our society, physicians and others who refuse to provide such counseling may be vulnerable to legal malpractice suits. They ought therefore to seek competent legal advice. Grisez makes the following practical suggestion:

> You may be able to minimize your vulnerability arising from your nonconformity [to secular standards] by not only telling those who come to you where you stand but having them read, and perhaps even sign, a carefully drafted summary of your position on matters where your standards of good practice will diverge from those the courts would be likely to use. Without anticipating the legal advice you will receive, I think such a summary probably should include a clear statement that, as a matter of principle, you will not prescribe contraceptives, do sterilizations, or perform abortions; you will give no medical advice regarding these matters and no information about their availability; and in respect to these matters you will not refer patients to others from whom they might obtain any service, advice, or information that, as matter of principle, you would not provide personally.[68]

This seems eminently good, practical advice for counselors.

If a couple seeking counsel is not married, the results of a genetic test would either remove reasons for concern or disclose a reason, not necessarily conclusive but surely worth considering, for either abstaining from marriage or continuing one's search for a spouse. If the couple is married, negative results of genetic testing would of course allay any fears they might have. But if the tests disclosed that there were indeed risks of conceiving a child who would be afflicted by a genetic malady, the couple would then need helpful counseling. Above, a morally wrong kind of counseling was excluded.

The choice whether to accept the risk and seek to generate life through the conjugal act or to avoid doing so by the practice of periodic continence is, of course, the responsibility of the couple. The Magisterium of the Church clearly recognizes that the likelihood of generating a child who might suffer from a serious genetic illness provides a *serious* reason for deciding not to have a child for either a certain or indefinite period of time.[69] The couple might legitimately reach the conclusion (and their counselor might well concur and indeed recommend) that running the risk would be unfair to others or that they either could not fulfill or would be seriously tempted to omit fulfilling the responsibilities they would incur in caring for a child afflicted by the malady. Such a conclusion and/or recommendation would not be immoral.

The couple might conclude (and their counselor might well agree and recommend), however, that they courageously agree to accept the risk and by doing so firmly commit themselves to carry out the responsibilities they would incur should their child indeed be afflicted by the malady in question. Although some people, particularly in our secular culture, might argue that if a couple deliberately risks having a child who might suffer from a serious malady such as cystic fibrosis, they are being unjust, either to the child exposed to such a risk or to the larger society (which will have to help in providing suitable health care), or to both. I believe that those who argue this way are mistaken. If the child is generated, a new and precious human person has come into existence, and his or her life is of surpassing value and contributes to the common good. Frequently, the burdens such a child might himself suffer and present for others are highly exaggerated, while the possible benefits of the child's life, to himself or herself, to his or her parents, and to society as a whole, are ignored or minimized. Thus, as Grisez correctly says, "one cannot rule out the possibility that a couple could rightly decide that they need not abstain from possibly fertile intercourse, despite the probability that a child will be afflicted with a severe disease, genetic or other. Moreover, in the case of genetic diseases, a couple accept not only more or less risk; avoiding parenthood on this basis means also forgoing children who would themselves be healthy, though perhaps carriers of the genetic defect."[70]

7. The Human Genome Project

The genome is the sum of the genetic material that defines a biological species. The Human Genome Project (HGP) is an international research program whose goal is to map in detail the positions of genes on their respective chromosomes, to determine the complete nucleotide sequence of human DNA, and to localize the estimated 50,000 to 100,000 genes on each of the 46 human chromosomes within the human genome.[71] By late June 2000, this vast project was completed.

Human genome studies of genetically related disorders and diseases are of tremendous importance not only to scientists and physicians but to everyone. The major *moral* question is how this knowledge will be used. It can obviously be used to develop new kinds of genetic therapy, and it may perhaps become feasible to attempt some kinds of germ-line therapy that would not raise grave moral objections.

The greatest (and legitimate) fear people have is that, if genetic testing made possible by the HGP showed them susceptible to or carriers of serious genetic maladies, they would experience prejudicial and indeed unjust treatment from those who learn of their genetic defects or dispositions. Such unjust treatment could be extended by parents to children whose genetic propensities become known to them, by employers and potential employers, by health-care providers and insurance companies, and by the government. The possibility exists that some individuals would not be allowed to marry or to have children, that efforts to make sterilization and abortion compulsory would be made, etc.

But these potential problems are not *per se* the result of the Human Genome Project, which in itself is essentially a research project intended to enrich the human community by expanding its knowledge. The problems lie in the human heart and will, not in the HGP.

——————————— Endnotes for Chapter Six ———————————

1. In the introduction and first two parts of this chapter, I have adapted, with substantive additions and developments, some material from my earlier book *Human Existence, Medicine, and Ethics: Reflections on Human Life* (Chicago: Franciscan Herald Press, 1977), Chapter One, "Experimenting on Human Subjects." The matter presented here, however, is in essence a complete reworking of the issue.

2. Roger Wertheimer, "Philosophy on Humanity," in *Abortion: Pro and Con*, ed. Robert L. Perkins (Cambridge, MA: Schenkmann, 1975), pp. 107-108.

3. Today, of course, many influential authors explicitly claim that membership in the human species has absolutely *no* moral significance and that those who claim that it does are guilty of "speciesism." Among the more prominent and better-known advocates of this view are Michael Tooley (see his *Abortion and Infanticide* [Oxford and New York: Oxford, at the Clarendon Press, 1983], esp. pp. 61-76), Peter Singer (see his *Rethinking Life and Death: The Collapse of Our Traditional Ethics* [New York: St. Martin's Press, 1994], esp. pp. 202-206), and Joseph Fletcher ("Indicators of Humanhood," *Hastings Center Report* 2 [November 1972], 1-4). This denigration of the moral worth of human beings, a cornerstone of the culture of death, was criticized in Chapter Five. One of the finest philosophical rebuttals of this position is given by Patrick Lee, *Abortion*

and Unborn Human Life (Washington, DC: The Catholic University of America Press, 1997), Chapter One.

4. Karol Wojtyla, *Love and Responsibility*, trans. H. Willetts (New York: Farrar, Straus, Giroux, 1981), p. 41.

5. Paul Ramsey, *The Patient as Person: Explorations in Medical Ethics* (New Haven and London: Yale University Press, 1970), Chapter One, "Consent as a Canon of Loyalty with Special Reference to Children in Medical Investigation," pp. 1-58. This chapter is *must* reading on this subject.

6. See, for example, Benedict Ashley, O.P., and Kevin O'Rourke, O.P., *Health Care Ethics: A Theological Analysis* (4th ed., Washington, DC: Georgetown University Press, 1997), pp. 345-346.

7. Articles of the Nuremberg Tribunal, article 1; cited by Ramsey, *The Patient as Person*, p. 1.

8. The text of the *Declaration of Helsinki* can be found in Henry K. Beecher, *Research and the Individual* (Boston: Little, Brown, and Co., 1970), p. 227.

9. Gonzalo Herranz, "Christian Contributions to the Ethics of Biomedical Investigation: An Historical Perspective," in *Ethics of Biomedical Research in a Christian Vision: Proceedings of the Ninth Assembly of the Pontifical Academy for Life* (Vatican City, February 24-26, 2003), eds. Juan de Dios Vial Correa and Elio Sgreccia (Vatican City: Libreria Editrice Vaticana, 2003), pp. 126-145.

10. Here the *Charter* refers to Pius XII, "To the Doctors of the G. Mendel Institute," Nov. 24, 1957, in *AAS* 49 (1957), 1031. Pius XII spoke about this topic many times. A useful collection of his addresses on this subject can be found in *The Pope Speaks* 1.3 and 1.4 (1954). Among his principal addresses are those to the First International Congress on the Histopathology of the Nervous System (September 14, 1952), the Sixteenth International Congress of Military Medicine (October 19, 1953), and the Eighth Congress of the World Medical Association (September 30, 1954).

11. In a footnote at this point, the *Charter* quotes from the following passage from the Pontifical Council *Cor Unum*'s "Some Ethical Questions Relating to the Gravely Ill and the Dying" (June 27, 1981): "The patient cannot be the object of decisions which he will not make, or, if he is not able to do so, which he could not approve. The 'person,' primarily responsible for his own life, should be the center of any assisting intervention: others are there to help him, not to replace him." The full text of this document is found in *Enchiridion Vaticanum 7, Documenti ufficiali della Santa Sede 1980-1981* (Bologna: EDB, 1985), 1137, no. 2.1, 2.

12. The *Charter* cites this text from Pope John Paul II's Address to the World Congress of Catholic Doctors, October 3, 1982, published in *Insegnamenti di Giovanni Paolo II* 5.3 (Vatican City: Libreria Editrice Vaticana, 1983), p. 673, no. 4.

13. Here the *Charter* refers to Pope John Paul II's Address to the Participants at Two Congresses on Medicine and Surgery, October 27, 1980, published in *Insegnamenti di Giovanni Paolo II* 3.2 (Vatican City: Libreria Editrice Vaticana, 1981), pp. 1008-1009, no. 5.

14. The text of no. 72 of the *Charter* can be found in Pontifical Council for Pastoral Assistance to Health Care Workers, *Charter for Health Care Workers* (Boston: Pauline Books and Media, 1995), pp. 70-71.

15. For instance, Henry K. Beecher, *Research and the Individual,* pp. 18-19, 121ff.

16. Ramsey, *The Patient as Person*, p. 3.

17. National Conference of Catholic Bishops, *Ethical and Religious Directives for Catholic Health Care Services* (Washington, DC: United States Catholic Conference, 1995), no. 27.

18. In *The Patient as Person*, p. 8, footnote 6, Ramsey notes that "Sir Harold Himsworth said (1953) that the Hippocratic Oath can be given in a single sentence: *Act always so as to increase trust* (quoted by Ross G. Mitchell, 'The Child and Experimental Medicine,' *British Medical Journal* 4, no. 1 [March 21, 1964]: 726). This might better read: *Act always so as not to abuse trust; act always so as to exhibit faithfulness,* to deserve and inspire trust."

19. On this, I have already referred to the "personalistic norm" articulated by Karol Wojtyla in *Love and Responsibility*. Other excellent and eloquent defenses of the inviolable dignity of all human beings, all human persons, are set forth by Jacques Maritain, *The Person and the Common Good* (New York: Charles Scribner's Sons, 1947), Chapter 3; Mortimer Adler, *The Difference of Man and the Difference It Makes* (New York: Meridian, 1968).

20. Ramsey, *The Patient as Person*, p. 7.

21. Pontifical Council for Pastoral Assistance to Health Care Workers, *Charter for Health Care Workers*, p. 72, no. 73.

22. Ramsey, *The Patient as Person,* pp. 7-8.

23. Hans Jonas, "Philosophical Reflections on Experimenting with Human Subjects," in *Philosophical Essays: From Current Creed to Technological Man* (Chicago: University of Chicago Press, 1980), pp. 105-131.

24. The text of these Articles is given in Tom Beauchamp and James Childress, *Principles of Bioethics* (5th ed., Oxford-New York: Oxford University Press, 2001), p. 511.

25. Pontifical Council for Pastoral Assistance to Health Care Workers, *Charter for Health Care Workers*, p. 72, no. 73.

26. Ibid., p. 77, no. 81.

27. Ibid. Here the internal citation is from the same address of Pope John Paul II, ibid.

28. Richard McCormick, S.J., *How Brave a New World? Dilemmas in Bioethics* (Garden City, NY: Doubleday, 1981), chapter four, "Proxy Consent in the Experimental Situation," pp. 61-62; and chapter six, "Sharing in Sociality: Children and Experimentation," pp. 87-98. Chapter four had originally been published in *Perspectives in Biology and Medicine* 18 (1974), 2-20; chapter six had originally been published in *Hastings Center Report* 5:3 (May 1975), 26-31.

29. Here I want to note that I believe, with others, that as children grow they become capable of exercising their intellect and power of free choice. According to the *Code of Canon Law*, "minors," i.e., individuals under eighteen years of

age, "on completion of the seventh year ... [are] presumed to have the use of reason" (*"Minor ... expleto autem septennio, usum rationis habere praesumitur"*) (canon 97.2). Those who have reached the use of reason, I believe, can give personal free and informed consent to be subjects of non-therapeutic as well as therapeutic research/experiments. However, I believe that the parents of minor children can veto such authorization.

30. On this, see my essay "Experimenting on Human Subjects," *Linacre Quarterly* 41.3 (November 1974), 238-252, and also my *Human Existence, Medicine, and Ethics: Reflections on Human Life* (Chicago: Franciscan Herald Press, 1977), pp. 21-28; Ramsey, *A Reply to Richard McCormick: The Enforcement of Morals: Nontherapeutic Research on Children.*

31. Ramsey, *The Patient as Person*, pp. 12-14.

32. Grisez, *The Way of the Lord Jesus*, Vol. 2, *Living a Christian Life* (Quincy, IL: Franciscan Press, 1993); emphasis added.

33. Congregation for the Doctrine of the Faith, *Donum vitae* (1987), 1.4, *AAS* 80 (1988), 81-83. Italics in original. At this point a footnote, no. 29, is given. It reads: "Cf. Pope John Paul II, Address to a Meeting of the Pontifical Academy of Sciences, October 23, 1982: *AAS* 75 (1983), 37: 'I condemn, in the most explicit and formal way, experimental manipulations of the human embryo, since the human being, from conception to death, cannot be exploited for any purpose whatsoever.'"

34. See National Conference of Catholic Bishops, *Ethical and Religious Directives for Catholic Health Care Services*, no. 51: "Non-therapeutic experiments on a living embryo or fetus are not permitted, even with the consent of the parents." See also *Charter for Health Care Workers*, no. 82.

35. Ibid., no. 31, which reads in part: "In instances of nontherapeutic experimentation, the surrogate can give this consent *only if the experiment entails no significant risk to the person's well being*" (emphasis added).

36. I made this accusation in the first edition of this book.

37. See the Australian bishops' *Code of Ethical Standards for Catholic Health and Aged Services in Australia.* In no. 6.6 of this document, we read: "Research involving vulnerable people must only be undertaken when the knowledge to be obtained is sufficiently important to warrant involving such vulnerable people and this knowledge cannot be obtained by other means.... *Non-therapeutic experimentation must involve no significant risk at all*" (emphasis added).

38. Accessible at http://www.thenewatlantis.com/docLib/20120125_TNA34TOC .pdf. It is possible to pay for a copy online if one is not a subscriber.

39. See E. Christian Brugger, "Stem Cells for Dummies," *Zenit*, March 24, 2009, http://www.zenit.org/article-25472?l=english. Accessed May 12, 2012.

40. A good presentation of this matter is given by Edmund D. Pellegrino, M.D., "Human Embryos and the Stem Cell Controversy," *The NaProEthics Forum* 4.6 (November 1999), 2-3. See also Edward J. Furton and Micheline M. Mathews-Roth, M.D., "Stem Cell Research and the Human Embryo, Part One," *Ethics & Medics* 24.8 (August 1999), 1-2.

41. On this, see testimony of Rev. Tadeusz Pacholczyk given July 30, 2005, to the Pennsylvania Conference of Catholic Bishops; see http://www.Catholicculture .org/culture/library/view.cfm?recnum=6570.
42. Doerflinger, in a letter to the U.S. House of Representative made public April 29, 2004. See http://www.catholicnews.com/data/stories/cns/0403293.htm. Among Doerflinger's important essays on stem-cell research published between 1999 and 2006 are the following: "Human Cloning and Embryonic Stem Cell Research after Seoul," in *The National Catholic Bioethics Quarterly* 6.2 (Summer 2006), 339-350 (reprinting congressional testimony of March 7, 2006); "The Many Casualties of Cloning," *The New Atlantis* (Spring 2006), 60-70; "Cloning Chaos," *National Review Online* (December 13, 2005), at www.nationalreview .com/comment/doerflinger200512130824.asp; "Confronting Technology at the Beginning of Life: A Morally Grounded Policy Agenda for the United States," in Charles Colson and Nigel Cameron (eds.), *Human Dignity in the Biotech Century: A Christian Vision for Public Policy* (Downers Grove, IL: Inter-Varsity Press 2004), pp. 221-239; "Experimentation on Human Subjects and Stem Cell Research," in Kevin T. McMahon, S.T.D., ed., *Moral Issues in Catholic Health Care* (Philadelphia, PA: Saint Charles Borromeo Seminary, 2004), pp. 93-107; "Retrospective and Prospective: The Public Policy Debate on Embryo Research," in Nicholas C. Lund-Molfese and Michael L. Kelly, eds., *Human Dignity and Reproductive Technology* (Lanham, MD: University Press of America 2003), pp. 97-109; "Testimony on Embryo Research and Related Issues," in *The National Catholic Bioethics Quarterly* 3.4 (Winter 2003), 767-786; "The Ethics and Policy of Embryonic Stem Cell Research: A Catholic Perspective," in Nancy E. Snow, ed., *Stem Cell Research: New Frontiers in Science and Ethics* (Notre Dame, IN: University of Notre Dame Press, 2003), pp. 143-166; "The Science and Politics of Stem Cell Research," in L. Gormally, ed., *Culture of Life — Culture of Death* (London: The Linacre Centre, 2002), pp. 299-307; "The Policy and Politics of Embryonic Stem Cell Research," *The National Catholic Bioethics Quarterly* 1.2 (Summer 2001), 135-143; "The Ethics of Funding Embryonic Stem Cell Research: A Catholic Viewpoint," in *Kennedy Institute of Ethics Journal* 9.2 (June 1999), 137-150.
43. See, for example, Nicholas Wade, "Embryo Cell Research: A Clash of Values," *New York Times*, July 2, 1999, A21.
44. *The New Atlantis,* no. 34 (Winter 2012), p. 17, referring to the study of Gautam Naik, "Lab-Made Trachea Saves Man," *Wall Street Journal*, July 8, 2011, http:// on.wsj.com/pXMnUs; Gero Hutter et al., "Long-Term Control of HIV by CCR5Δ32/Δ32 Stem-Cell Transplantation," *New England Journal of Medicine* 360.7 (2009): 692-698; Kristina Allers et al., "Evidence for the Cure of HIV Infection by CCR5Δ32/Δ32 Stem Cell Transplantation," *Blood* 117.10 (2011): 2791-2799- H6956-7).
45. For this article see http://www.stemcellresearch.org/alternatives/75newreasons .pdf. Accessed May 12, 2012.
46. See *BioEdge*, November 19, 2011.

47. Pellegrino, "Human Embryos and the Stem Cell Controversy," 3. Pellegrino cites the following scientific sources to support his affirmations: P. Rubinstein et al., "Outcomes among 526 Recipients of Placental-Blood Transplants from Unrelated Donors," *New England Journal of Medicine* 399.22 (November 26, 1998), 1565-1577; R. Lewis, "Human Mesenchyma Stem Cells Differentiate in the Lab," *The Scientist* 13 (April 12, 1999), 1ff.; Claire Lowry, "Adult Human Brain Stem Cells Reproduce in Vitro," *UniSci Science and Research News*, April 28, 1999.

48. On this, see Rev. Tadeusz Pacholczyk, cf. endnote 41 above.

49. The President's Council on Bioethics, *Alternative Sources of Human Pluripotent Stem Cells: A White Paper* (Washington, DC: The President's Council on Bioethics, 2005).

50. Ibid., p. 2.

51. Ibid., p. 3.

52. *Genetic Intervention on Human Subjects: The Report of a Working Party of the Catholic Bishops' Joint Committee on Bioethical Issues* (London: The Catholic Bishops' Joint Committee on Bioethical Issues, 1996), p. 6. Members of the Working Party were Dr. A. P. Cole (Chairman), Rev. John Berry, John Duddington, Dr. Ian Jessiman, Dr. John McLean, Agneta Sutton, and Dr. Helen Watt.

53. W. French Anderson, "Gene Therapy. I. Strategies for Gene Therapy," *Encyclopedia of Bioethics*, 911.

54. On all this, see *Genetic Intervention on Human Subjects*, pp. 6-15; Anderson, "Genetic Therapy," in *The New Genetics and the Future of Man*, ed. Michael Hamilton (Grand Rapids, MI: Eerdmans, 1972), pp. 109-117.

55. Anderson, "Gene Therapy. I. Strategies for Gene Therapy," 908.

56. Ibid.

57. Ibid., 909f.; *Genetic Intervention on Human Subjects*, p. 12.

58. Anderson, "Gene Therapy I. Strategies for Gene Therapy," 909f.

59. See L. Archer, "Genetic Testing and Gene Therapy," in *Man-Made Man: Ethical and Legal Issues in Genetics*, eds. P. Doherty and A. Sutton (Dublin: Open Air, 1997), p. 38.

60. This is recommended, for instance, by the British Gene Therapy Advisory Committee in its *First Annual Report, November 1993-December 1994* (London: Health Departments of the United Kingdom, 1995), pp. 5-6. Helen Watt calls attention to this in her very helpful essay "Human Gene Therapy: Ethical Aspects," in *Human Genome, Human Person, and the Society of the Future: Proceedings of the Fourth Assembly of the Pontifical Academy for Life* (Vatican City, February 23-25, 1998), eds. Juan de Dios Vial Correa and Elio Sgreccia (Vatican City: Libreria Editrice Vaticana, 1999), p. 256, footnote 6.

61. Watt, "Human Gene Therapy: Ethical Aspects," p. 256.

62. Ibid., pp. 256-268.

63. For fragile X syndrome see http://en.wikipedia.org/wiki/ Fragile_X_syndrome. Accessed May 12, 2012.

64. For nuchal transparency scanning see http://en.wikipedia.org/wiki/Nuchal_ scan. Accessed May 12, 2012.

65. See http://www.hfi-ivf.com/in-vitro-fertilization/pdg. Accessed May 12, 2012.

66. See Thomas W. Hilgers' essay "Prenatal and Pre-Implantation Genetic Diagnosis: Duty or Eugenic Prelude?" in *Human Genome, Human Person, and the Society of the Future*, p. 186.

67. Charter for Health Care Workers; *Ethical and Religious Directives for Catholic Health Care Services* (Washington, D.C. United State's Conference of Catholic Bishops, 2009), directive 50.

68. Grisez, *The Way of the Lord Jesus*, Vol. 3, *Difficult Moral Questions* (Quincy, IL: Franciscan Press, 1997), p. 300. See material online at http://twotlj.org/.

69. See, for example, Pope Paul VI, encyclical Humanae vitae, no. 10.

70. Grisez, *Difficult Moral Questions*, p. 302. See http://twotlj.org/.

71. On this, see Albert Moraczewski, "Genes and Ethics," Ethics & Medics 16.5 (May 1991), 2; see also National Institutes of Health Web site: http://www .nhgri.nih.gov/HGP/, "The Human Genome Project," 2/16/2000.

CHAPTER SEVEN

Euthanasia, Assisted Suicide, and Care of the Dying

Introduction: The Contemporary Movement for Euthanasia and Assisted Suicide

In 1935, the first Voluntary Euthanasia Society was founded in London, and a Euthanasia Society was established in the United States in 1938, but by the early 1970s neither had had much success in gaining support. At the beginning of 1975, the U.S. Euthanasia Society was reactivated as the Society for the Right to Die, and by the beginning of the 1990s support for euthanasia and physician-assisted suicide in the English-speaking world had grown enormously. Public opinion polls in the United States and Britain during the last decade have shown increasing willingness to sanction euthanasia and assisted suicide both morally and legally, and those agitating for change are no longer, as Daniel Callahan, president of the Hastings Center (an influential think tank on bioethical issues), has noted, "a small minority, the usual reformist suspects, but a larger, more influential group of academics, physicians, legislators, judges, and well-placed and well-organized lay people."[1]

To account for this sea change in public opinion, Callahan points to

a growing fear of a long, lingering death, the consequence of changes in the way people die occasioned by more chronic illness and more death in old age; the publicity given to a number of cases where seemingly conservative resistance kept people alive longer than most people found tolerable; ... the AIDS epidemic, with its well publicized cases of young people dying miserable deaths from a particularly noxious and degrading disease ...; the potent Anglo-American movement toward greater self-determination and autonomy — fostered most explicitly on the political left but implicitly abetted ... by the libertarian strains so prominently espoused by conservatives for free market solutions to social problems, and perhaps a diminished willingness on the part of many to accept the pain and suffering of dying as an acceptable fact of life.[2]

The reasons Callahan cites have undoubtedly contributed to the growing success the movement is enjoying.[3] Note, in particular, that he singles out the emphasis on autonomy in contemporary society and an unwillingness to accept pain and suffering. In his encyclical *Evangelium vitae*, Pope John Paul II points to an exaggerated and false understanding of individual autonomy and to hedonism as critical factors contributing to the culture of death (cf. *Evangelium vitae*, nos. 20, 23). I believe that another major factor helping to win acceptance of euthanasia and assisted suicide is the idea that *personal* life, as distinct from "merely" biological life, requires exercisable cognitive abilities. This dualistic understanding leads many to conclude that once an individual no longer has such exercisable abilities or when there is danger that they will be lost because of disease or illness, then that individual's biological life is of no value to him or her and that he or she is better off dead than alive; one's life is no longer worth living. Another contributing factor, I believe, is the acceptance of abortion. It is frequently justified on the grounds that the life destroyed is merely "biologically human" and not "personal," and it is at times resorted to as a kind of "mercy killing" or euthanasia of unborn children diagnosed as suffering from maladies that will, so it is alleged, make their lives burdensome and miserable.

Pope John Paul II offers insights into the reasons accounting for the appeal euthanasia has for many today. Thus he writes in *Evangelium vitae*:

> In the sick person the sense of anguish, of severe discomfort, and even of desperation brought on by intense and prolonged suffering can be a decisive factor. Such a situation can threaten the already fragile equilibrium of an individual's personal and family life, with the result that, on the one hand, the sick person, despite the help of increasingly effective medical and social assistance, risks feeling overwhelmed by his or her own frailty; and on the other hand, those close to the sick person can be moved by an understandable even if misguided compassion. All this is aggravated by a cultural climate which fails to perceive any meaning or value in suffering, but rather considers suffering the epitome of evil, to be eliminated at all costs ... [and assumes] a certain Promethean attitude which leads people to think that they can control life and death by taking the decisions about them into their own hands.... As well as for reasons of a misguided pity at the sight of the patient's suffering, euthanasia is some-

times justified by the utilitarian motive of avoiding costs which bring no return and weigh heavily on society. Thus it is proposed to eliminate malformed babies, the severely handicapped, the disabled, the elderly, especially when they are not self-sufficient, and the terminally ill. (no. 15)

Although euthanasia and physician-assisted suicide are becoming more and more accepted as morally right and legally necessary, these forms of intentional killing of the innocent remain intrinsically immoral. The *Catechism of the Catholic Church*, referring to the Vatican *Declaration on Euthanasia*, ably summarizes what Catholic faith holds. It recognizes that "whatever its motives and means, direct euthanasia consists in putting an end to the lives of handicapped, sick, or dying persons," and is therefore "morally unacceptable" (no. 2277). Continuing, it declares: "Thus an act or omission which, of itself or by intention, causes death in order to eliminate suffering constitutes a murder gravely contrary to the dignity of the human person and to the respect due to the living God, his Creator. The error of judgment into which one can fall in good faith does not change the nature of this murderous act, which must always be forbidden and excluded" (ibid.).

In this chapter I will proceed as follows. (1) I will clarify the terminology used in debates over euthanasia. (2) I will set forth the major arguments given to support what I call the "ethics of euthanasia," including the argument to gain legal approval of voluntary active euthanasia. (3) I will offer a critique of the "ethics of euthanasia" and show why a willingness intentionally to kill a human person is absolutely incompatible with respect for his dignity as a person. (4) I will develop what I will call the "ethics of benemortasia" or of caring, and only caring, for the dying. In developing this alternative to the "ethics of euthanasia," I will identify criteria that help us to distinguish between "ordinary" or "proportionate" medical treatments and "extraordinary" or "disproportionate" treatments. The former are morally required, whereas the latter can, and at times ought to, rightly be refused. (5) I will then call attention to a very helpful book published in 2012 called *Debating Euthanasia*, co-authored by Emily Jackson, a UK lawyer and ardent champion of euthanasia and assisted suicide, and John Keown, a well-known defender of the absolute inviolability of innocent human life, whose contribution to this book completely devastated Jackson's spurious reasoning, and also to developments in the legalization of euthanasia and assisted dying. (6) I will next take up the care to be given persons who are judged to be permanently unconscious or in the so-called persistent vegetative state. (7) I will conclude with a discussion of living wills and advance directives. Naturally I will integrate more recent studies where doing so is helpful.

1. Clarifying the Terminology

The Vatican *Declaration on Euthanasia* (1980) defines euthanasia as "an action or an omission which of itself or by intention causes death, in order that all suffering may in this way be eliminated. Euthanasia's terms of reference, then, are to be found in the intention of the will and of the methods used" (Part II). This is a very clear and precise definition, explicitly and rightly noting that one can kill another "in order that all suffering may in this way be eliminated" by acts of *omission* as well as by acts of *commission*. This is most important to recognize, because advocates of euthanasia seek to win support by claiming that so-called passive euthanasia, which for them encompasses "allowing" a person to die of some underlying pathology by withholding or withdrawing medical treatments, is already regarded as morally and legally permissible and that, therefore, "active" euthanasia ought also to be recognized as morally and legally permissible.[4] This is completely false.

The term "euthanasia" is derived from the combination of two Greek words, *eu* (good or well) and *thanasia* (death), and originally meant a good or happy death. But today, as the Vatican *Declaration on Euthanasia* makes clear, it has acquired the meaning of "mercy killing." In fact the revised edition of *The Random House College Dictionary* gives the following as the first meaning of "euthanasia": "1. Also called **mercy killing**, the act of putting to death painlessly a person suffering from an incurable and painful disease or condition."[5]

Euthanasia takes the following forms: 1. *Active euthanasia* (at times called "direct" or "positive" euthanasia), in which someone intentionally chooses to kill a person by an act of commission, can be either (a) *voluntary active euthanasia*, when it is performed on persons who give free and informed consent to being killed mercifully; (b) *nonvoluntary active euthanasia*, when performed on individuals who are not capable of giving free and informed consent to being killed mercifully; or (c) *involuntary active euthanasia*, when done to individuals who refuse to give free and informed consent to being killed mercifully but who nonetheless are so killed. 2. In *passive euthanasia* (at times called "indirect" or "negative" euthanasia) someone brings about the death of a person for merciful reasons by an act of omission, i.e., by withholding or withdrawing medical treatments that could preserve that person's life, precisely in order to bring about death. Like active euthanasia, passive euthanasia can be (a) *voluntary,* when the person killed gives free and informed consent to the withholding or withdrawing of treatments precisely as a way of bringing about his or her own death; (b) *nonvoluntary*, when the person so killed is incompetent and incapable of giving consent; or (c) *involuntary*, when the person so killed refuses to consent to the withholding or withdrawing of life-preserving treatments.[6]

Today the euthanasia movement is principally concerned with establishing the moral rightness and legal permissibility of *active voluntary euthanasia*, claiming erroneously that *passive euthanasia*, both voluntary and nonvoluntary, has already been recognized as morally and legally permissible. Many euthanasia advocates are also agitating for acceptance of *active nonvoluntary euthanasia*, and, as will be seen, they clearly hold it to be the morally right way of "treating" many incompetent patients.

Physician-assisted suicide is accurately defined by one of its champions, Dr. Timothy E. Quill, as "the act of making a means of suicide (such as a prescription for barbiturates) available to a patient who is otherwise physically capable of suicide and who subsequently acts on his or her own. It is distinguished from voluntary euthanasia, where the physician not only makes the means available but is the actual agent of death upon the patient's request."[7] Thus the principal difference between euthanasia and assisted suicide is that in euthanasia a person other than the one killed is the principal cause of the killing whereas in assisted suicide the person killed is himself or herself the principal cause, while the physician or other person (spouse, etc.) formally cooperates in the killing act and is, as it were, an instrumental cause. Since it is usually a physician who "assists" in the suicide, the expression "physician-assisted suicide" is most common in the literature. The most prominent practitioner and advocate of physician-assisted suicide, of course, is the notorious Dr. Jack Kevorkian,[8] popularly known as "Dr. Death," who was convicted of murder and sentenced to prison in 1999.

Since the moral and juridical issues regarding physician-assisted suicide are basically the same as those regarding euthanasia, in what follows I will speak only of euthanasia and the ethics of euthanasia. The rationale justifying physician-assisted suicide is the same as that underlying euthanasia. Those in favor of euthanasia support physician-assisted suicide, while those rejecting euthanasia as intrinsically immoral similarly repudiate physician-assisted suicide.

Note, above all, that active euthanasia, brought about by an act of commission, and passive euthanasia, achieved through an act of omission, are morally the same. Each is the *intentional killing* of an innocent human person for reasons of mercy. Such *intentional killing* of an innocent person for reasons of mercy is completely different from the choice (intention) to withhold or withdraw medical treatments from a person because the *treatments* in question are either useless or burdensome, realizing that the person will die without such treatments. In euthanasia, one chooses to kill either by an act of commission or of omission because one judges that the *life* of the person to be killed is either useless or excessively burdensome and that the person is better off dead than alive. In what I shall call "benemortasia," one refuses to kill a person because one respects his or her life as something incomparably good; one rather chooses to withhold or withdraw *treatments* that are either futile (useless) or impose unnecessary burdens upon the dying person. This is a key distinction, frequently ignored today, that will be developed further in this chapter.

2. The "Ethics of Euthanasia"

The "ethics of euthanasia" has been developed by a great many persons. Although the euthanasia movement began in the 1930s,[9] it picked up momentum in the 1970s, particularly after the Supreme Court's *Roe v. Wade* abortion decision in 1973, and the 1970s witnessed a host of books and articles setting forth the rationale underlying euthanasia.[10] The arguments advanced in the 1990s (another decade of great agitation for the euthanasia movement) are rooted in the same ideology.[11] I will first consider the rationale underlying the drive for voluntary active euthanasia and then the rationale underlying the movement for nonvoluntary active euthanasia.

A. Voluntary Active Euthanasia

(1) The "Principle of Autonomy"

The argument justifying voluntary active euthanasia morally and also for sanctioning it by law is fundamentally the following: In voluntary active euthanasia, the patient, even if not terminally ill, gives free and informed consent to being killed mercifully. The patient wants to die. The patient's desire to die is, moreover, understandable because of the pain and/or suffering experienced. Pain relievers may not be wholly effective in eliminating pain and other discomforts, including embarrassment, humiliation arising from the illness, a desire to alleviate the burdens his or her care imposes on others, etc. The patient has reached a mature and settled judgment that he or she is better off dead than alive. Since the person to be killed mercifully gives free and informed consent to being killed, no injustice will be done. Respect for this person's integrity and autonomy require one to honor his or her request to die. In fact, not to do so is not only to fail to respect the person's autonomy and dignity; it is to compel him or her to live in a way he or she believes is a horrible mockery of all he or she holds dear and to force him or her to die a miserable, pain-ridden death. Thus the request of such persons to be killed ought to be honored; carrying it out is, in fact, an act of kindness or beneficence. Not only is voluntary active euthanasia morally right, but it ought also to be protected by law. To continue its prohibition is cruel to those who are made to suffer needlessly and infringes on the liberty of those who would choose to be killed or to kill in order to prevent needless suffering.[12] Indeed, as several champions of voluntary active euthanasia put matters, "death control, like birth control, is a matter of human dignity. Without it persons become puppets."[13]

From this we can see that the major argument given to justify voluntary active euthanasia is rooted in the premise that human persons are autonomous, i.e., that their freedom of self-determination includes the freedom to choose to be killed when doing so is judged reasonable on the grounds that they are better off dead than alive, that their lives are no longer of any value to them, and that others have the duty to respect their choice to be killed mercifully rather than bear the indignity of a life no longer worth living. Meaningful human dignity, in this understanding, consists in the ability to control one's own life and death and to determine the manner of one's demise.[14]

Voluntary active euthanasia, therefore, is justified on an alleged "principle of personal autonomy," or on the right of persons to be in control of their own life and death. As Peter Singer puts it, linking the right to die to the right to life, "the most important aspect of having a right to life is that one can choose whether or not to invoke it. We value the protection given by the right to life only when we want to go on living. No one can fear being killed at his or her own persistent, informed and autonomous request."[15]

(2) "Personal" Life vs. "Biological" Life

But voluntary active euthanasia also rests on the dualistic presupposition, implicit if not explicit, that physical, bodily life is radically distinct from "personal" life. The former is merely "biological" in nature; the latter, personal or meaningful life, consists in the exercisable ability to communicate, to make judgments, to reason. This dualistic presupposition is, as we will see, more central to the defense of nonvoluntary euthanasia, but it is likewise prominent in the defense of voluntary active euthanasia mounted by many of its more ardent advocates. Thus Joseph Fletcher, elaborating on the right of autonomous persons to exercise their dominion over physical nature, including bodily life and its processes, had this to say:

> Physical nature — the body and its members, our organs and their functions — all of these things are a part of "what is over against us," and if we live by the rules and conditions set in physiology or another *it* we are not *thou*.... Freedom, knowledge, choice, responsibility — all these things of personal or moral stature are in us, not *out there*. Physical nature is what is over against us, out there. It represents the world of *its*.[16]

Similarly, Marjorie Reiley Maguire rails against the "physicalistic ethic that left moral man at the mercy of his biology" and condemned him to "await the good pleasure of biochemical and organic factors and allow these to determine the time and manner of his demise." Technological man, Maguire continues, now realizes that he has the moral right to intervene "creatively" and "to terminate his life through either positive action [active voluntary euthanasia] or calculated benign neglect [passive voluntary euthanasia] rather than await in awe the dispositions of organic tissues."[17] Similarly, John Harris and Singer sharply distinguish mere biological life from personal life, claiming that persons have a right to choose death rather than become depersonalized through debilitating illnesses.[18]

B. Nonvoluntary Euthanasia

Although the contemporary legal battle is over voluntary active euthanasia, advocates of the "ethics of euthanasia" likewise maintain that nonvoluntary euthanasia is also the right moral choice to make on behalf of many incompetent patients and that this ought to be legally permissible. As noted earlier, nonvoluntary euthanasia is used to describe the mercy killing of patients who are *not capable* of giving or withholding consent to being killed mercifully, but whose lives are judged no longer of any value to them.

(1) "Quality of Life" Judgments Justifying Nonvoluntary Euthanasia

Two major arguments are given to justify nonvoluntary euthanasia, or the mercy killing of incompetent individuals. The first is based on the "quality of life" and the judgment that an incompetent person's life is no longer of any value to him or to her and that killing such a person is a benefit rather than a harm. Arguments based on "quality of life" judgments have been advanced by many euthanasia supporters. Among the more ardent advocates of nonvoluntary euthanasia, in particular the "beneficent" mercy killing of handicapped newborns, are Glanville Williams, Marvin Kohl, H. Tristram Englehardt, Jr., Robert F. Weir, Anthony Shaw, Raymond S. Duff, and A. G. M. Campbell.[19] Frequently nonvoluntary euthanasia, particularly in the case of newborns, is administered by withholding or withdrawing life-preserving measures (including feeding, even by mouth, e.g., some celebrated cases of Down syndrome babies killed by "benign" neglect). The life-preserving measures are withheld or withdrawn precisely as a means of bringing about death, and the killing is justified on the grounds that the individuals killed are, because of their low quality of life, better off dead than alive. Different advocates of nonvoluntary euthanasia based on a poor quality of life differ greatly, however, in identifying "criteria" to determine whether one's quality of life is so bad that death is a benefit and not a harm. Although quite frequently nonvoluntary euthanasia is accomplished by an act of omission (so-called passive euthanasia), its advocates hold that active euthanasia is also morally justifiable and preferable to passive euthanasia because the former is quicker than the lingering death frequently resulting from nontreatment.[20]

The basic argument is simply this: one can determine that an individual's quality of life is so poor that continued existence is for that person not a benefit but a burden. Thus, killing that person is an act of benevolence or kindness, for by killing that person, whose life has been judged to be no longer worth living, one is doing something good.

(2) Nonpersonhood and Nonvoluntary Euthanasia

The justification of nonvoluntary euthanasia based on "quality of life" judgments does not deny the personhood of those to be killed mercifully. Another argument to justify nonvoluntary euthanasia, whether by an act of commission (active) or by one of omission (passive), is that those killed are either not yet persons or are no longer persons. Thus their intentional killing can be likened to the killing of other animals for reasons of mercy.

Joseph Fletcher, Michael Tooley, and Peter Singer are among the most vociferous champions of this latter claim (these authors, and many others, likewise justify abortion, as we saw in a previous chapter, on the grounds that the unborn cannot be regarded as persons).[21] They argue that abortion is frequently justified because intrauterine examination has disclosed that the unborn entity suffers from some serious (or not too serious) malady (e.g., Down syndrome, Tay-Sachs disease, cystic fibrosis, etc.), and that one ought to prevent its birth and subsequent experience of a life not worth living, what one could call euthanasia of the unborn. But at times, prenatal examination does not take place or fails to detect some serious (or not too serious) malady. Since both the unborn and the newborn are not, in their judgment, persons because they lack exercisable cognitive abilities, their parents ought to have the right to kill them to spare such infants a burdensome life.

Here it is worth noting that John Harris, a leading advocate of euthanasia, justified the withholding of nutrition and hydration by means of tubes from Tony Bland, an Englishman said to be in the so-called persistent vegetative state, on the grounds that Bland could no longer be considered a "person" because he had no exercisable cognitive faculties and was hence "no longer capable of possessing any interests at all" — an ability which Harris deems necessary if an entity is to be regarded as a "person" — and that, consequently, "death was in his best interests." Harris held that the withdrawing of tubally provided food and hydration from Bland was done precisely in order to bring about his death — a clear case of nonvoluntary euthanasia.[22] In another section of this chapter I will discuss in more detail the care to be given persons in the so-called persistent vegetative state, and we will see that some hold that withholding or withdrawing the provision of food and hydration from such persons is justified as the withholding or withdrawing of *useless* and/or *burdensome* treatment, with the subsequent death not intended, and not as an act of euthanasia by an act of omission. But Harris clearly sees such withholding or withdrawing of nutrition and hydration as the *intentional* killing of a human being who is no longer to be regarded as a person, as an act of nonvoluntary but justified euthanasia.

C. The Legal or Jurisprudential Issue

Although the champions of euthanasia approve of both voluntary and nonvoluntary euthanasia, whether active or passive, as morally good choices that ought to be legally permissible, the major goal of euthanasia supporters today is to win legal approval of voluntary active euthanasia. At present, the law of homicide (at least in the United States) protects the lives of all innocent human persons who have survived birth by strictly prohibiting intentionally killing them. Thus the law now regards active euthanasia, even if voluntary, as criminal homicide. This accounts for the great contemporary

agitation clamoring for a change in the legal status. Here I will merely summarize the basic argument advanced by apologists for euthanasia to effect a
change in the law. It can be stated as follows:

> By definition, if euthanasia is voluntary, the person to be killed merci-
> fully gives free and informed consent to being killed; hence killing him
> or her does no injustice. The person's desire to be killed mercifully is
> reasonable in view of the suffering and/or pain and/or humiliation he or
> she experiences; at times others, too, are suffering terribly, psychologically,
> or economically, or both. Killing this person, who after all, freely consents
> to being killed and may even be begging to be killed, is thus a reasonable
> way to end all this suffering. Although some people in our society regard
> such killing as immoral for various reasons, it would be cruel and unjust
> to impose their values on those who freely choose to be killed and on
> those who seek to compassionately execute their choice. Thus voluntary
> active euthanasia ought to be legally permissible.

This argument would seem to find legal support in the understanding of
the Fourteenth Amendment undergirding the 1992 Supreme Court decision
in *Planned Parenthood v. Casey*. In that case, Justices David Souter, Anthony
Kennedy, and Sandra Day O'Connor gave as one of the major reasons for
reaffirming the "central holding" of *Roe v. Wade* the meaning of "liberty"
in the Fourteenth Amendment. According to them, matters "involving the
most intimate and personal choices a person may make in a lifetime, choices
central to personal dignity and autonomy, are central to the liberty protected
by the Fourteenth Amendment. At the heart of liberty is the right to define
one's own concept of existence, of meaning, of the universe, and of the mystery of human life."[23] The drive to legalize voluntary active euthanasia has
had great success in the Netherlands and other European countries and has
been legalized in several states in America. At present three states, Oregon,
Montana, and Washington, have specific laws that allow for legal assisted
suicide. Thirty-six states prohibit assisted suicide. Common law prohibits
assisted suicide in seven states, but four states have no laws regarding assisted
suicide. In most of the United States, and in many countries, passive forms of
euthanasia, such as refusing treatment in order to bring about death — and
not because the treatments are *either unduly burdensome or useless* (on this,
see below) — and withholding life-saving treatments, are legal if voluntarily
chosen by the person determined to be terminally ill. Unsuccessful efforts
have been made to legalize euthanasia in other states, e.g., California. It

should be noted that in Montana the voters did not vote to legalize euthanasia; rather a judge made the ruling. In addition popular referenda on the issue, when held in states, show that the people oppose such legalization.

D. Summary and Conclusion: The "Ethics of Euthanasia"

Arthur Dyck, a Protestant theologian teaching at Harvard University, is a champion of innocent human life, both prior to birth and throughout life until death. In my opinion, Professor Dyck gives us one of the most accurate and succinct summaries of the major claims upon which the "ethics of euthanasia" is based — claims he subsequently countered with the truths underlying what he called the "ethics of benemortasia." According to Dyck, the case for active voluntary euthanasia rests on the following presuppositions:

> (1) that the dignity that attaches to personhood by reason of the freedom to make moral choices demands also the freedom to take one's life or to have it taken when this freedom is absent or lost; (2) that there is such a thing as a life not worth living, a life that lacks dignity, whether by reason of distress, illness, physical or mental handicaps, or even sheer despair or whatever reason; (3) that what is sacred or supreme in value is the "human dignity" that resides in the rational capacity to choose to control life and death.[24]

The first and third of these presuppositions, taken together, constitute the so-called principle of autonomy invoked by so many today to provide a moral and jurisprudential justification of euthanasia. The second of these presuppositions is also at the heart of the alleged justification of nonvoluntary euthanasia, along with the claim that some of the non-competent individuals who are to be killed mercifully are not persons because they lack exercisable cognitive abilities. This second presupposition implies a dualism, one that regards physical, bodily life as an instrumental good: a good *for* the person, not a good *of* the person, and thus different in kind from the truly *personal* goods that perfect the person and are thus goods *of* the person, goods such as knowledge, free choice, meaningful interpersonal relationships, etc., i.e., goods whose very being depends on consciousness.

3. Critique of the "Ethics of Euthanasia"

Here I will focus on the following: (A) the claim that voluntary euthanasia is justified by human autonomy, (B) the contention that nonvoluntary euthanasia is justified on the basis of "quality of life" judgments, (C) the dualism underlying the entire euthanasia movement, and (D) the reasons why voluntary active euthanasia ought not to be legalized.

A. Autonomy and Voluntary Euthanasia vs. the Sanctity of Life

As we have seen, the basic argument for voluntary euthanasia is this: the person to be killed mercifully gives free and informed consent to being killed in this way. He or she chooses death, regarding it as a benefit. In doing so, the person is simply exercising his or her autonomy. Respect for this autonomy should therefore lead others, including doctors, to confer the benefit of a merciful death on the person.

But a doctor, even one not opposed in principle to euthanasia, would refuse to kill a patient, even if the patient begged to be killed, if he thought that the patient still had a worthwhile life to live. Thus, as the authors of a superb study prepared by a group of British Catholics rightly point out, "*it is precisely the judgement that a patient no longer has a worthwhile life which will seem to justify euthanasia*," and, continuing, they affirm: "***But precisely that contention is inconsistent with recognising the continuing worth and dignity of the patient's life.***"[25] In a magnificent passage, these authors then show why this is so:

> In any apparent conflict between, on the one hand, the requirement that we do not deny equal human dignity and respect for the sanctity of human life and, on the other, the putative claims of respect for autonomy, the principle of the sanctity of human life must always trump those claims. For recognition of equal human dignity is fundamental to recognition of all human beings as subjects of justice. There is no authentic conflict between rightly respecting the sanctity of human life and rightly respecting autonomy. The exercise of human autonomy in giving shape, direction, and character to a human life is not a source of value and dignity at *odds* with the fundamental source of human worth and dignity in human nature itself. For ... what makes it reasonable to recognise human nature as the source of our basic worth and dignity as human beings is the fact that our nature in its development is intrinsically directed to human fulfilment and human good. And what best makes sense of the ideal of respect for autonomy is the role played by free choice in the achievement of that fulfilment to which our nature is directed; for self-determining choice is integral to that achievement. But if the moral significance of autonomy is understood in that way, then the value of autonomy is derivative from, and reflective of, that which gives value to our humanity. So

it should be clear that the claims of autonomy cannot properly extend to choices, which are inconsistent with recognising the basic worth and dignity of every human being.[26]

In other words, human autonomy (self-determination) is not unlimited. Its *rightful* exercise enables us to achieve our fulfillment, our perfection, but it is subservient to our *good as persons*. I have cited this passage at length not only because it is, in my opinion, so powerful, but also because much that is said in it fits in beautifully with Pope John Paul II's correct understanding of legitimate human autonomy and the role that a false notion of autonomy has played in the development of the culture of death.

Legitimate human autonomy, or self-government, is rooted in our capacity to determine our lives in and through our self-determining acts of free choice. Pope John Paul II, as we saw in Chapter Two, emphasized the truth that "it is precisely through his acts that man attains perfection [= the "fulfillment" referred to in the above passage] as man, as one who is called to seek his Creator of his own accord and freely to arrive at full and blessed perfection by cleaving to him" (*Veritatis splendor*, no. 71). Our freely chosen deeds, as the Pope stresses, "do not produce a change merely in the state of affairs outside of man, but, to the extent that they are deliberate choices, they give moral definition to the very person who performs them, determining his *profound spiritual traits*" (no. 71). They are a "*decision about oneself* and a setting of one's own life for or against the Good, for or against the Truth, and ultimately, for or against God" (no. 65). In other words, as we saw in Chapter Two, we *give to ourselves our identity as moral beings in and through the actions we freely choose to do*.

Moreover, as John Paul II likewise rightly stressed, human freedom of choice, our legitimate autonomy, must be guided, if we are to exercise it rightly, by the *truth*. Human freedom and autonomy are not unlimited, creative of the moral order. Human freedom is exercised rightly and in a way conducive to human fulfillment or perfection only when guided by the *truth*. This truth is rooted ultimately in God's wise and loving plan for human existence, the eternal law, and God has so made us that we are capable of participating actively in this wise and loving plan through our knowledge of the practical truths necessary to guide our choices so that they can lead us to our perfection, and our knowledge of these truths is what we know as natural law (*Veritatis splendor*, nos. 38-45; cf. Chapter Two, pp. 68-72). When human autonomy is conceived as the creator and arbiter of good and evil, of right and wrong, we are no longer able to guide our choices by the truth but only by subjective and changing human opinions (cf. *Veritatis splendor*, nos. 35-37), and human autonomy, so conceived, gives birth to the culture of death (cf. *Evangelium vitae*, no. 19).

In short, human autonomy, human freedom of choice, is limited. It is valued precisely because we can exercise it with a view to our flourishing or fulfillment as persons living in communion with others. By exercising it in accord with the truth, we choose in such a way that we give to ourselves our identity as persons willing to respect the truth and to shape our lives in accord with it. If our choices seriously undermine in us our capacity to flourish as human persons, and if, *a fortiori*, they aim to damage aspects of this capacity in others, there is no reason to respect such choices. And the intentional killing of ourselves or others, no matter what the reason, is a choice that sets us against the inherent goodness of human life, of this great and incomparable good gift that God has given us. In choosing to *kill*, more-over, we give to ourselves the identity of *killers*. This is the reason, as Vatican II reminds us, why morally bad choices, such as the choice to *kill* innocent human life, not only poison society and dishonor the Creator, but "harm their perpetrators more than those who are harmed by them" (*Gaudium et spes*, no. 27).

B. "Quality of Life" Judgments and Justice

We have seen that two principal arguments are advanced to justify non-voluntary euthanasia. One claims that the individuals to be killed merci-fully, although certainly members of the human species, are no longer to be regarded as persons because they lack presently exercisable cognitive faculties, etc. Since this claim has been sufficiently refuted in the chapter on abortion, it is not necessary to discuss it here.

The second asserts that even if we grant that the individuals to be killed mercifully are indeed persons, their "quality of life" is so poor that life is no longer of any benefit to them and that death can be regarded as a kindly release from a burdensome and/or useless existence demeaning to human persons. This claim is utterly incompatible with the justice due to human persons. "Quality of life" judgments are inescapably arbitrary and unjust. Different authors assign different qualities that one needs to possess "mean-ingful" life, and the same authors at times list different qualities in differ-ent apologias for their position. More significantly, the qualities alleged to make life worthwhile (intelligence, ability to respond to stimuli, awareness of others, etc.) all admit of enormous differences in degree. But some cutoff point has to be assigned, above which the quality of life is "meaningful," and below which it is not, so that death can be mercifully administered. Such cutoff points are arbitrarily asserted, with different authors assigning different "weight" to different factors and different degrees of ability within the chosen criteria. It is evident that this way of determining who should live and who should die is utterly arbitrary and unjust.[27]

C. Dualism and Euthanasia

Advocates of euthanasia are in essence dualists. They regard human persons as consciously experiencing subjects, free to do as they choose, whose bodily life is merely an instrumental good, a good *for* persons, i.e., consciously experiencing subjects. When this life becomes burdensome, it is, for them, no longer of value; it is rather a burden that the experiencing subject is free to set aside. As the authors of *Euthanasia, Clinical Practice and the Law* so perceptively say, "propaganda puts into the mouth of the potential, theoretical suicide [or advocate of euthanasia]: 'I belong to myself, and I can set conditions on which I will consent to go on living.' Life is regarded as a good or bad hotel, which must not be too bad to be worth staying in."[28] But our bodily life is integral to our lives as persons; it is not something foreign to it. Human persons are bodily persons, and bodily life is not merely, as we saw in a previous chapter, a useful or instrumental good *for* the person, but it is rather integral to the human person, an aspect of his or her *being*. One cannot respect a human person without respecting his or her bodily life. In addition many arguments demonstrating that this claim is false were marshaled in Chapter Four, on abortion, and by Christopher Kaczor in his 2011 book, *The Ethics of Abortion: Women's Rights, Human Life, and Justice.*

The dualism underlying euthanasia is false. Human persons are bodily beings, whose bodies are integral to their being as persons. When God created human persons, "male and female he created them" (Gn 1:27), i.e., men and women of flesh and blood. He did not create conscious minds to which he then added a body as an afterthought. Moreover, when the Father's only-begotten Son, his uncreated Word, became man to show us how deeply God loves us, he did not become a conscious mind using a body as his instrument; rather, he became "living flesh" (*sarx egeneto*, as the Greek of Jn 1:14 reads). Although human persons are *more* than their bodies because their life-giving principle, the principle that makes their bodies to be *human* bodies, is a spiritual soul, they are nonetheless *bodies, living flesh*. If a person breaks his or her arm, he does not damage his property or break an "instrument"; he or she hurts *himself* or *herself.*

The bodily life of a human person, however heavily burdened it may be, is still that person's life, his very being. To attack one's life is to attack one's person. One cannot kill a person's body without killing the person. Although the latter's soul is immortal, the soul is not the "I," the self,[29] for the self is a unit of body and soul. Christians believe that Christ has conquered death, so that death has lost its sting. But death itself is not good; it is the deprivation of life, and life is a good, and an incalculable good *of* the person. To judge that a person's life no longer has any value, that it is worthless, is to judge that a *person* no longer has any value, that a *person* is worthless.

Here it is worth recalling what Dr. Leo Alexander, who took part in the Nuremberg trials after World War II, had to say about "medical science under dictatorship." After a careful study of the "culture of death" characteristic of the Third Reich, he showed that it has its origins in the acceptance of mercy killing. He concluded: "Whatever proportion these crimes [of the Nazis] finally assumed, it became evident to all who investigated them that they had started from small beginnings.... It started with the acceptance of the attitude, basic in the euthanasia movement, *that there is such a thing as a life not worthy to be lived.*"[30]

D. Voluntary Active Euthanasia and the Law

We have already seen the major argument advanced to secure the legalization of voluntary active euthanasia, namely, that it is not unjust because the person to be killed freely consents to being so killed and that its legal proscription violates that person's liberty and the liberty of those who want, compassionately, to honor the person's request to be killed mercifully.

The basic counterargument, advanced with great skill by Grisez and Boyle, can be summarized as follows. Legalizing euthanasia without stringent governmental regulation would inevitably be unjust because some persons who would not freely consent to being killed mercifully would surely be pressured or coerced into giving consent to such killing, and these persons would unjustly be deprived of the protection that the current law of homicide extends to them. But to avoid this kind of injustice, strict governmental regulation would be indispensable. But government involvement, including the use of tax monies, would for this purpose infringe on the liberty of all those citizens who find such killing abhorrent and who do not wish their government to be involved in such killing, undertaken, moreover, not for the *common* good, but to serve the *private* interests of individuals. Legalizing euthanasia without government regulation would unjustly endanger the lives of those who might then be pressured into giving consent to being killed mercifully; legalizing it with strict governmental supervision would infringe on the liberty of others; since voluntary active euthanasia cannot be legalized without causing injustice to those to be killed or unjustly infringing on the liberty of citizens who find government involvement in such killing for some individuals' private good repugnant, it cannot be legalized without doing injustice. Therefore, it ought not to be legalized.[31]

4. The "Ethics of Benemortasia"

"Benemortasia" is a term meaning a "good" or "happy" "death" (from the Latin, *bene* [good] and *mortasia* [death]), coined by Arthur Dyck of Harvard University, who, as we have seen already, vigorously opposes the "ethics of euthanasia." A similar term, "agathanasia" (from the Greek *agathos, agathe* [good] and *thanasia* [death]), was coined by the late Paul Ramsey, for many years professor of Christian ethics at Princeton University and a champion of the culture of life vs. the culture of death.[32]

I believe that the "ethics of benemortasia" can be adequately set forth by reflecting on and developing the following truths: (1) it is always wrong, and utterly incompatible with love for God and neighbor, intentionally to kill innocent human life; (2) in caring for the dying, a proper love for life requires one to make use of "ordinary" or "proportionate" means of preserving life, but one is free to withhold or withdraw "extraordinary" or "disproportionate" means of doing so.

A. The Intrinsic Good of Human Life and the Evil of Intentional Killing

We believe, and rightly so, that human persons are radically different in kind from other animals and that, because they are, they are beings of moral worth, whose lives are precious. The ultimate reason why human life is precious is that it is a good and great gift of God, a created participation in his life. He has given it to us to guard and protect, to be its stewards. But "why," the authors of *Euthanasia, Clinical Practice and the Law,* inquire, "cannot we stewards of our life return it to its rightful owner when the indications are that it has served its purpose and that God is recalling it to himself? Why cannot we then hasten death?" Their answer to this question is eloquent:

The Christian response is that one's stewardship of one's life does not include the choice to terminate the stewardship itself. We did not ourselves participate in initiating the gift and task of that stewardship; we could not accept it on conditions chosen by us. Why God should have brought us (or anyone) into existence as "persons created for their own sake" is deeply mysterious. So we should not be particularly surprised if we also find it mysterious that God sees meaning and value in every part — even the most miserable and reduced — of the lifespan he allots us. But that God can and does is central to the faith of Israel and to Christian faith. His ways are not our ways, and the particular workings of his purposes are inscrutable to us. The conditions of our stewardship, then, are provided by God's commandments or "mandates." Men and women can come (though not without the risk of uncertainty and confusion) to a knowledge of those commandments by a conscientious exercise of "natural" reason, i.e., even without the benefit of God's self-disclosure.... In that self-disclosure there is revealed a commandment which, as explained through Scripture and the tradition of the Church, forbids us to intend to terminate our life. It has always been Christian belief that that expression of God's will holds good in all the circumstances and conditions of life.... We are all in the hands of a loving God who has given us each a life to be lived out in loving worship of him and in loving service of our neighbour, in preparation for a further life of perfect fulfillment with the God of all love and consolation.... The ultimate source of the dignity and inviolability of the human being is God's creative love and loving purpose, which are at the depth of the mystery of every human person, and uniquely for everyone.[33]

The life God has given us includes our bodily life, which is integral to our *being* as human persons. So true is this that "to regard the body as a prison, or as an instrument or detachable launching rocket of the *real* person, is incompatible with the faith in which incarnation and redemption are central.... The good of human life, protected by God, is the good of bodily life. One cannot justify an attack on that life, even in one's own person, by arguing that one's bodily life is useless or an encumbrance to one's *real* vocation as a person. Reverence for that bodily life is thus integral to one's earthly existence."[34]

As John Paul II reminds us in *Veritatis splendor*, love for our neighbor requires us to respect our neighbor's *good*, and we can do this only by respecting his *goods*, the goods perfective of him at the various levels of his existence, goods such as *life* itself (cf. nos. 12, 13). One cannot love one's neighbor if one judges the neighbor to be better off dead than alive, if one *wills* that he or she be dead.

B. Criteria for Distinguishing Between "Ordinary" ("Proportionate") and "Extraordinary" ("Disproportionate") Treatments

(1) Relevant Church Teaching and Its Interpretation

Two major documents of the Church's Magisterium clearly distinguish between "ordinary" or "proportionate" treatments — i.e., treatments that one is morally obliged to use in order to respect the dignity of human life and rightly to exercise one's stewardship of it — and "extraordinary" or "disproportionate" treatments — i.e., treatments that one is at liberty to withhold or withdraw in exercising stewardship over one's own or another's life. We reviewed the teaching in one of these documents, the Vatican *Declaration on Euthanasia* (1980) in Chapter One, and here we will note its relevance. The other document is a 1957 address of Pope Pius XII to a congress of anesthesiologists. In the course of his remarks, Pius had this to say:

> ... normally one is held to use only ordinary means [to prolong life] — according to the circumstances of persons, places, times, and culture — that is to say, means that do not involve any grave burden for oneself or another. A stricter obligation would be too burdensome for most men and would render the attainment of the higher, more important good too difficult. Life, health, all temporal activities are in fact subordinated to spiritual ends. On the other hand, one is not forbidden to take more than the strictly necessary steps to preserve life and health, so long as he does not fail in some more important duty.[35]

This statement of Pius XII is obviously relevant to the distinction between "ordinary" and "extraordinary" means of treatment and to the criteria for determining whether it is morally appropriate to withhold or withdraw treatment. Here he indicates that "ordinary" medical treatment is that kind of treatment which offers reasonable hope of benefiting the subject without imposing unacceptable burdens on the subject or others, whereas "extraordinary" medical treatment is treatment that imposes unacceptable burdens on the subject and/or others. The Pope did not himself address the *specific* criteria for distinguishing between treatments that are ordinary and those that are extraordinary. Rather, he outlined a general approach that seems clear enough, but one which obviously requires more specification.

(2) Legitimate vs. Illegitimate "Quality of Life" Judgments

Note that the Vatican *Declaration* affirms that in assessing treatments it is proper to take "into account the state of the sick person and his or her physical and moral resources." Here the *Declaration* makes it clear that, although it is *always* gravely immoral to kill a person mercifully because one judges that the "quality" of his or her life is so wretched that he or she would be better off dead than alive, it is legitimate to consider the "quality" of his or her life *in relationship to specific kinds of treatments* for a person *in that condition*, i.e., with that "quality of life." What would not be too risky, painful, burdensome, etc., for an otherwise healthy teenager or adult might well be so for persons suffering from advanced stages of lethal diseases, etc. Thus, for instance, an amputation of a limb would not be "disproportionate" or "extraordinary" for an otherwise vigorous youth or mature adult but would be so for someone suffering from advanced pancreatic cancer or something similar. Such "quality of life" judgments, which bear on the uselessness or burdensomeness of specific kinds of *treatments* for persons in *specific kinds of conditions*, are not the same as "quality of life" judgments asserting that those persons' *lives* are no longer of any value.[36] The late John R. Connery, S.J., summed this matter up well when he said that while the Catholic tradition has repudiated a quality of life ethic that would deny persons needed medical care simply on the basis of the poor quality of their lives, it nonetheless "allowed quality of life considerations in decisions about prolonging life *if they were related to the means themselves.*"[37]

C. Criteria for Determining Whether Treatments Are "Ordinary" ("Proportionate") or "Extraordinary" ("Disproportionate")

We will be helped to discover the criteria for withholding or withdrawing treatments (= criteria for distinguishing between "ordinary/proportionate" and "extraordinary/disproportionate" treatments) by first considering non-suicidal reasons for refusing treatment. As Grisez and Boyle have noted,

> Individuals who are competent can refuse treatment upon themselves without the intent to end their own lives, which would be their motive if they appraised their future prospects and decided that they would be better off dead. Such refusal of treatment, including treatment without which life will be shortened, can be based upon *objectionable features of the treatment itself, its side effects, and its negative consequences.* An individual who has no desire to die can take such factors into account and decide that life without treatment, so long as life lasts, will be better than life with it. Such a decision is not a choice of death.[38]

A human person, in short, can refuse a treatment — choose that it be withheld or withdrawn — without adopting by choice a proposal to kill himself or herself. The treatment refusal is based on the judgment that the treatment itself, or its side effects or deleterious consequences, are so burdensome that undergoing the treatment is not morally obligatory. The treatment in question is truly "extraordinary/disproportionate" since the burdens it imposes far exceed the benefits likely to result from its use.

What are some major reasons for refusing treatment on these grounds? Here too Grisez and Boyle offer helpful criteria that flesh out the general guidelines given by Pius XII and the Vatican *Declaration.* They write:

> First, sometimes treatment is experimental or risky; ... second, some treatment is itself painful or brings about other experienced conditions which are undesirable; ... third, in many cases, the requirements for the application of medical care would interfere with the activities and experiences which one desires during the time [of life] remaining; ... fourth, many persons object to certain forms of care on the basis of some principle [for example, Jehovah's Witnesses refuse blood transfusions because they believe that this is immoral, the equivalent of taking life, and others refuse organ transplants from the newly dead because they fear that the organs were taken while the "donor" was still alive]; ... fifth, there is a variety of reasons why persons find medical care psychologically repugnant; ... sixth, in many cases medical care for one individual makes very severe demands upon others.[39]

To the reasons for making a given treatment unduly burdensome assigned by Grisez and Boyle in the above paragraph, we can add the cost of some medical treatments; one is not obligated to bankrupt his or her family in order to undergo a treatment. All these factors are *objectively discernible features in the treatment itself, its side effects, and its negative consequences that impose undue burdens on the patient and/or others.* One can rightly reject such treatments and withhold them or withdraw them. The choice to do so is not suicidal, rooted not in the "ethics of euthanasia" but rather in the "ethics of benemortasia." We could say that *excessive burdensomeness* is the major criterion for determining whether a proposed treatment is "extraordinary/disproportionate." Excessive burdensomeness is, as it were, the genus, and species of such burdensomeness include the treatment's riskiness, its bad side effects and bad consequences on the life of the person, the excessive pain of the treatment, treatments judged morally or psychologically repugnant, and excessive expense that would imperil the economic security of the patient, the patient's family, and/or the community. Withholding or withdrawing such treatments is not a choice to kill oneself or another for merciful reasons. It is *not* euthanasia. One does not judge a *life* excessively burdensome; one judges a *treatment* excessively burdensome. And, as we have seen already, in making this judgment, the "physical and moral resources of the patient" — his or her "quality of life" in *that* sense — can rightly be taken into account.

In addition to the criterion of *burdensomeness*, another criterion that enables us to judge whether a given treatment, for a given patient, is "extraordinary/disproportionate" and hence not morally required is the criterion of *usefulness*. In the Catholic tradition, a means has been judged useless in the strict sense if the benefits it promises are nil or useless in a wider sense if the benefits conferred are insignificant in comparison with the burdens it imposes.

The authors of *Euthanasia, Clinical Practice and the Law* provide a very detailed analysis of the reasons why a competent patient may rightly refuse treatment. In addition to excessive risk or financial cost, they identify four potentially acceptable reasons for rejecting treatment because it is "extraordinary/disproportionate." These are: "a) the burdens attendant on treatment impress one as more than one can cope with; b) the burdens attendant on treatment seem hardly warranted by the promised benefits; c) treatment is not worthwhile because a dying patient has reason to think that he no longer has an obligation to seek to prolong his life; d) treatment is straightforwardly futile, i.e., inappropriate to the biological nature of one's condition, as, for example, when putatively curative treatment is offered to someone in an irreversible state of dying."[40]

In summary, we can say that the two principal criteria for determining whether to withhold or withdraw a treatment because it is "extraordinary/disproportionate" are *burdensomeness* and *uselessness*. The former is the major criterion, insofar as the relative uselessness of many treatments is contingent upon the burdens they impose when compared with the benefits they bring. But what is most important is that these criteria draw attention to the *burdensomeness* and/or *uselessness* of the means used to preserve life. They do not lead one to conclude that treatments are to be withheld or withdrawn because of a judgment that the patient's *life* is either burdensome or useless — and this, as we have seen, is the judgment reached in the "ethics of euthanasia." Judgments of the burdensomeness and/or uselessness of treatments are compatible with a respect and love for the dignity of human life, which is *always* a precious good, a gift from God, no matter how heavily burdened it may be.

D. Summary: The Presuppositions of the "Ethics of Benemortasia"

A fitting conclusion for this section is provided, I believe, by Arthur Dyck, who, as we have seen, coined the term "benemortasia." Just as he ably set forth the presuppositions underlying the "ethics of euthanasia," so he also neatly expressed the presuppositions underlying the "ethics of benemortasia." These are:

1. A human being's life is not solely at the disposal of that person; every human life is part of a human community that is held together in part by respect for life and love for the lives of its members.
2. The dignity of the person, by reason of his freedom of choice, includes the freedom of dying persons to refuse non-curative, death-preventing interventions, but it does not include the freedom to choose death and to set one's will against life.
3. Every life has some worth. Life itself is a precious good; it is an intrinsic good, a good *of* the person, not merely a useful or instrumental good, a good *for* the person.
4. The supreme good is God himself, to whom the dying and those who care for the dying are responsible.[41]

5. *Debating Euthanasia*, by Emily Jackson and John Keown

Jackson's thesis: We owe those experiencing permanent and irreversible suffering and others worried that this may happen to them to do all we can to alleviate their distress, and in a small number of cases we must "allow" people to have their lives ended quickly and painlessly if they cannot be helped in any other way and believe that death offers the only possible relief from their suffering.

Definitions: Euthanasia is commonly done by a doctor using a lethal injection; if a relative or friend administers something lethal this is "mercy killing." V*oluntary active euthanasia* (VAS) differs from *involuntary* or *passive* euthanasia, when a person's life is ended without his or her request. Causing someone's death by withdrawing life-preserving treatment is sometimes called *passive euthanasia*, but Jackson prefers to speak of "treatment withdrawal" as the proper way to designate ending the life of a person unable to give consent. Assisted suicide (AS) differs from euthanasia and mercy killing because the agent bringing about the person's death is the person himself or herself (1-2).

Here — and later in her essay — Jackson falsely equates treatment withdrawal as a form of euthanasia or assisted dying.

Keown's argument: It has always been against the law and medical ethics for doctors or other health-care personnel intentionally to kill their patients. Keown's paper is a reasoned argument to keep it that way. The purpose of his essay is to add support to an international consensus opposing "assisted dying" by showing (1) that VAE/AS would breach the basic human right not to be intentionally killed; (2) that the case for euthanasia on request logically leads to euthanasia without request; and (3) that it pressures the competent but vulnerable to ask for an earlier death and would lead to death without request for the non-competent.

He considers ten arguments alleged to support euthanasia and physician assisted suicide. These are the following: A. Autonomy; B. Compassion; C. Legal Hypocrisy; D. A Right to Suicide; E. Public Opinion; F. Legal Failure; G. The Netherlands; H. Oregon; I. Religion, and J. Economics. I will not consider Keown's rebuttal of all ten arguments; rather I will illustrate how he refutes Jackson's presentation of these arguments with his rebuttals of A. Autonomy and B. Compassion.

He offers five arguments against autonomy: (i). autonomy vs. the principle of the inviolability of human life; (ii) the autonomous few vs. the vulnerable many; (iii) how autonomous; (iv) some patients better off dead?; (v) autonomy's "slippery slope." I will summarize the first two. The first shows clearly why the claim that autonomy justifies decriminalizing euthanasia is false. A person's self-determining choice (exercise of autonomy) does not make what is chosen morally good or bad. "Autonomy is valued precisely because its exercise makes for the well-being and flourishing of those who possess it. But it is clear that many self-determining choices damage the well-being of the life of the chooser and the lives of those affected by those choices. Autonomy has limits; one of the most important is the cardinal ethical principle of the inviolability of life (of persons not involved in unjust aggression [and the patients cared for by doctors and healthcare personnel are not so involved]); this principle is sometimes called the 'sanctity of life' (which has religious connotations), but it can stand on purely philosophical grounds." The second shows that decriminalization would prejudice the vulnerable, both those who are autonomous and those who are not, making some elderly persons feel guilty for being a burden or pressuring them to choose "assisted dying" or being pressured by family members to do so.

The "compassion" apologia for "assisted dying" notes that "we shoot horses, don't we?" and claims that VAE/AS must be made available to terminally ill patients as a way of ending suffering they can no longer endure. Four reasons show how fallacious all this is. The first is that compassion is not a moral principle but a laudable emotion. Some of the most compassionate members of the health-care community — doctors, nurses, and others — are leading opponents of VAE/PAS. True "com-passion" means "suffering with" their patients, caring for them, not killing them, affirming the patient's worth and acting in solidarity with them. We kill suffering animals out of mercy, but we should not treat human persons as animals. The second is compassion's "slippery slope." If compassion justifies giving a terminal or dying patient a lethal injection, it would also justify giving one a lethal injection if he were physically unable to commit suicide; it would also justify doing so to a terminally ill, dying person incapable of making a request for such an injection, or to non-terminally ill patients suffering from chronic rheumatic arthritis and similar painful maladies. The third is that the kind of palliative care pioneered by Cecily Hastings, founder of the hospice movement, meets the needs of suffering patients much better than do VAE and PAS — 95 percent of UK physicians engaged in palliative medicine agreed with this statement: *With improvement in palliative care, good clinical care can be provided within existing legislation ... and patients can die with dignity.* The fourth is that legalizing VAE and PAS violates the physician's (and other health-care workers') vocation to heal and erodes the trust in their doctors to which patients have a right.

6. Caring for the Permanently Unconscious and Persons in the " 'Persistent' Vegetative State"

Introduction

I will (a) comment on the so-called *persistent* vegetative state; (b) present John Paul II's address and its significance; (c) consider the negative responses given to it by a large number of American theologians; and (c) present the definitive defense of his position by the Congregation for the Doctrine of the Faith in August 2007.

A. Comments on the " 'Persistent' Vegetative State"

At the end of International Congress "Life-Sustaining Treatments and Vegetative State: Scientific Advances and Ethical Dilemmas" (Rome, March

17-20, 2004), cosponsored by the Pontifical Academy for Life and the World Federation of Catholic Medical Associations (FIAMC), the FIAMC issued a statement in which the scientists who participated in the congress offered several considerations regarding the nature of this alleged "state," among them the following:

1) Vegetative State (VS) is a state of unresponsiveness, currently defined as a condition marked by: a state of vigilance, some alternation of sleep/wake cycles, absence of signs of awareness of self and of surroundings, lack of behavioural responses to stimuli from the environment, maintenance of autonomic and other brain functions.

2) VS must be clearly distinguished from: encephalic death, coma, "locked-in" syndrome, minimally conscious state. VS cannot be simply equalled to cortical death either, considering that in VS patients islands of cortical tissue which may even be quite large can keep functioning.

3) In general, VS patients do not require any technological support in order to maintain their vital functions.

4) VS patients cannot in any way be considered terminal patients, since their condition can be stable and enduring.

5) VS diagnosis is still clinical in nature and requires careful and prolonged observation, carried out by specialized and experienced personnel, using specific assessment standardized for VS patients in an optimum controlled environment. Medical literature, in fact, shows diagnostic errors in a substantially high proportion of cases. For this reason, when needed, all available modern technologies should be used to substantiate the diagnosis.

6) Modern neuroimaging techniques demonstrated the persistence of cortical activity and response to certain kinds of stimuli, including painful stimuli, in VS patients. Although it is not possible to determine the subjective quality of such perceptions, some elementary discriminatory processes between meaningful and neutral stimuli seem to be nevertheless possible.

7) No single investigation method available today allows us to predict, in individual cases, who will recover and who will not among VS patients.

8) Until today, statistical prognostic indexes regarding VS have been obtained from studies quite limited as to number of cases considered and duration of observation. Therefore, the use of adjectives like "permanent" referred to VS should be discouraged, by indicating only the cause and duration of VS.[42]

Note that in no. 8, the scientists who participated in this important congress explicitly declare that the adjective "permanent" *not* be used to describe the condition because such use is not warranted by the facts. Note also that in no. 6, the scientists indicate that persons in the "vegetative" state may be able to experience pain.

The October 15, 2007, issue of the *New Yorker* magazine carried an article by Jerome Groopman that confirmed the findings of the medical scientists given above.[43]

B. Pope John Paul II's Address of March 20, 2004

(1) Context and Key Themes

This address, given at the conclusion of the International Congress "Life-Sustaining Treatments and Vegetative State: Scientific Advances and Ethical Dilemmas," was based on the latest medical and scientific findings relevant to the "vegetative" state.[44]

Among the principal ideas Pope John Paul articulated are the following:

1. *"A man, even if seriously ill or disabled in the exercise of his highest functions, is and always will be a man,* and he will never become a 'vegetable' or an 'animal' " (no. 3; emphasis in original).

2. *The right of the sick person, even one in the vegetative state, to basic health care.* Such care includes "nutrition, hydration, cleanliness, warmth, etc." and "appropriate rehabilitative care" and monitoring "for clinical signs of eventual recovery" (no. 4).

3. *The moral obligation,* in principle, *to provide food and water to persons in the "vegetative" state by tubal means:* "I should like to underline how the administration of food and water, even when provided by artificial means, always represents a *natural means* of preserving life, not a medical act. Its use, furthermore, should be considered, in principle, *ordinary and proportionate,* and as such morally obligatory, insofar as and until it is seen to have attained its proper finality, which in the present case consists in providing nourishment to the patient and alleviation of his suffering" (no. 4; emphasis in original).

4. *The need to resist making a person's life contingent on its quality:* "[I]t is not enough to reaffirm the general principle according to which the value of a man's life cannot be made subordinate to any judgment of its quality ... ; it is necessary to promote the *taking of positive actions*

as a stand against pressures to withdraw hydration and nutrition as a way to put an end to the lives of these patients" (no. 6; emphasis in original).

5. *The principle of solidarity:* "It is necessary, above all, *to support those families* who have had one of their loved ones struck down by this terrible clinical condition" (no. 6; emphasis added).

(2) Comments

John Paul II emphasized that the providing of food and water even by artificial means is to be regarded "*in principle*" (emphasis added) " '*ordinary and proportionate,*' and as such morally obligatory." Thus, although such provision is obligatory in principle, the Pope allowed for those cases in which the provision of nutrition and hydration would not be appropriate, either because they would not be metabolized adequately or because their mode of delivery would be gravely burdensome.

As the Australian bishops have noted, "the Pope's statement does not explore the question whether artificial feeding involves a medical act or treatment with respect to insertion and monitoring of the feeding tube. While the act of feeding a person is not itself a medical act, the insertion of a tube, monitoring of the tube and patient, and prescription of the substances to be provided do involve a degree of medical and/or nursing expertise. To insert a feeding tube is a medical decision subject to the normal criteria for medical intervention."[45] I bring this up because some may claim that, since providing food/water by tubal means requires a medical act to insert the tube, such feeding is itself a medical treatment and not an act of caring. This is not true. But the insertion of a feeding tube, particularly through enteral and not perienteral means, is neither futile nor burdensome in almost all cases.

C. Definitive Defense of His Address by the Congregation for the Doctrine of the Faith's August 1, 2007, "Responses to Certain Questions of the United States Conference of Catholic Bishops Concerning Artificial Nutrition and Hydration"

This brief document and the Commentary attached to it are luminously clear. I will thus reproduce the texts here in full. It is very unusual for the CDF to issue explanatory commentaries on its brief responses to questions raised by bishops. The texts are as follows:

RESPONSES TO CERTAIN QUESTIONS
OF THE UNITED STATES CONFERENCE OF CATHOLIC BISHOPS
CONCERNING ARTIFICIAL NUTRITION AND HYDRATION

First question: Is the administration of food and water (whether by natural or artificial means) to a patient in a "vegetative state" morally obligatory except when they cannot be assimilated by the patient's body or cannot be administered to the patient without causing significant physical discomfort?

Response: Yes. The administration of food and water even by artificial means is, in principle, an ordinary and proportionate means of preserving life. It is therefore obligatory to the extent to which, and for as long as, it is shown to accomplish its proper finality, which is the hydration and nourishment of the patient. In this way suffering and death by starvation and dehydration are prevented.

Second question: When nutrition and hydration are being supplied by artificial means to a patient in a "permanent vegetative state," may they be discontinued when competent physicians judge with moral certainty that the patient will never recover consciousness?

Response: No. A patient in a "permanent vegetative state" is a person with fundamental human dignity and must, therefore, receive ordinary and proportionate care which includes, in principle, the administration of water and food even by artificial means.

The Supreme Pontiff Benedict XVI, at the Audience granted to the undersigned Cardinal Prefect of the Congregation for the Doctrine of the Faith, approved these Responses, adopted in the Ordinary Session of the Congregation, and ordered their publication.

Rome, from the Offices of the Congregation for the Doctrine of the Faith, August 1, 2007.

William Cardinal Levada
Prefect

Angelo Amato, S.D.B.
Titular Archbishop of Sila
Secretary

COMMENTARY

The Congregation for the Doctrine of the Faith has formulated responses to questions presented by His Excellency the Most Reverend William S. Skylstad, President of the United States Conference of Catho-

lic Bishops, in a letter of July 11, 2005, regarding the nutrition and hydration of patients in the condition commonly called a "vegetative state."
The object of the questions was whether the nutrition and hydration of
such patients, especially if provided by artificial means, would constitute
an excessively heavy burden for the patients, for their relatives, or for the
health care system, to the point where it could be considered, also in the
light of the moral teaching of the Church, a means that is extraordinary
or disproportionate and therefore not morally obligatory.

The Address of Pope Pius XII to a Congress on Anesthesiology, given
on November 24, 1957, is often invoked in favor of the possibility of
abandoning the nutrition and hydration of such patients. In this address,
the Pope restated two general ethical principles. On the one hand, natural reason and Christian morality teach that, in the case of a grave illness,
the patient and those caring for him or her have the right and the duty
to provide the care necessary to preserve health and life. On the other
hand, this duty in general includes only the use of those means which,
considering all the circumstances, are ordinary, that is to say, which
do not impose an extraordinary burden on the patient or on others. A
more severe obligation would be too burdensome for the majority of
persons and would make it too difficult to attain more important goods.
Life, health and all temporal activities are subordinate to spiritual ends.
Naturally, one is not forbidden to do more than is strictly obligatory to
preserve life and health, on condition that one does not neglect more
important duties.

One should note, first of all, that the answers given by Pius XII
referred to the use and interruption of techniques of resuscitation. However, the case in question has nothing to do with such techniques. Patients
in a "vegetative state" breathe spontaneously, digest food naturally, carry
on other metabolic functions, and are in a stable situation. But they are
not able to feed themselves. If they are not provided artificially with food
and liquids, they will die, and the cause of their death will be neither an
illness nor the "vegetative state" itself, but solely starvation and dehydration. At the same time, the artificial administration of water and food
generally does not impose a heavy burden either on the patient or on his or
her relatives. It does not involve excessive expense; it is within the capacity
of an average health care system, does not of itself require hospitalization,
and is proportionate to accomplishing its purpose, which is to keep the
patient from dying of starvation and dehydration. It is not, nor is it meant

to be, a treatment that cures the patient, but is rather ordinary care aimed at the preservation of life.

What may become a notable burden is when the "vegetative state" of a family member is prolonged over time. It is a burden like that of caring for a quadriplegic, someone with serious mental illness, with advanced Alzheimer's disease, and so on. Such persons need continuous assistance for months or even for years. But the principle formulated by Pius XII cannot, for obvious reasons, be interpreted as meaning that in such cases those patients, whose ordinary care imposes a real burden on their families, may licitly be left to take care of themselves and thus abandoned to die. This is not the sense in which Pius XII spoke of extraordinary means.

Everything leads to the conclusion that the first part of the principle enunciated by Pius XII should be applied to patients in a "vegetative state": in the case of a serious illness, there is the right and the duty to provide the care necessary for preserving health and life. The development of the teaching of the Church's Magisterium, which has closely followed the progress of medicine and the questions which this has raised, fully confirms this conclusion.

The *Declaration on Euthanasia*, published by the Congregation for the Doctrine of the Faith on May 5, 1980, explained the distinction between proportionate and disproportionate means, and between therapeutic treatments and the normal care due to the sick person: "When inevitable death is imminent in spite of the means used, it is permitted in conscience to take the decision to refuse forms of treatment that would only secure a precarious and burdensome prolongation of life, so long as the normal care due to the sick person in similar cases is not interrupted" (Part IV). Still less can one interrupt the ordinary means of care for patients who are not facing an imminent death, as is generally the case of those in a "vegetative state"; for these people, it would be precisely the interruption of the ordinary means of care which would be the cause of their death.

On June 27, 1981, the Pontifical Council *Cor Unum* published a document entitled *Some Ethical Questions Relating to the Gravely Ill and the Dying*, in which, among other things, it is stated that "There remains the strict obligation to administer at all costs those means which are called 'minimal': that is, those that normally and in usual conditions are aimed at maintaining life (nourishment, blood transfusions, injections, etc.). The discontinuation of these minimal measures would mean in effect willing the end of the patient's life" (no. 2.4.4.).

In an address to participants in an international course on forms of human preleukemia on November 15, 1985, Pope John Paul II, recalling the *Declaration on Euthanasia*, stated clearly that, in virtue of the principle of proportionate care, one may not relinquish "the commitment to valid treatment for sustaining life nor assistance with the normal means of preserving life," which certainly includes the administration of food and liquids. The Pope also noted that those omissions are not licit which are aimed "at shortening life in order to spare the patient or his family from suffering."

In 1995 the Pontifical Council for Pastoral Assistance to Health Care Workers published the *Charter for Health Care Workers*, paragraph 120 of which explicitly affirms: "The administration of food and liquids, even artificially, is part of the normal treatment always due to the patient when this is not burdensome for him or her; their undue interruption can have the meaning of real and true euthanasia."

The address of John Paul II to a group of bishops from the United States of America on an *ad limina* visit, on October 2, 1998, is quite explicit: nutrition and hydration are to be considered as normal care and ordinary means for the preservation of life. It is not acceptable to interrupt them or to withhold them, if from that decision the death of the patient will follow. This would be euthanasia by omission (cf. no. 4).

In his address of March 20, 2004, to the participants of an International Congress on "Life-sustaining Treatments and Vegetative State: Scientific Progress and Ethical Dilemmas," John Paul II confirmed in very clear terms what had been said in the documents cited above, clarifying also their correct interpretation. The Pope stressed the following points:

1) "The term *permanent vegetative state* has been coined to indicate the condition of those patients whose 'vegetative state' continues for over a year. Actually, there is no different diagnosis that corresponds to such a definition, but only a conventional prognostic judgment, relative to the fact that the recovery of patients, statistically speaking, is ever more difficult as the condition of vegetative state is prolonged in time" (no. 2). (Terminology concerning the different phases and forms of the "vegetative state" continues to be discussed, but this is not important for the moral judgment involved).

2) In response to those who doubt the "human quality" of patients in a "permanent vegetative state," it is necessary to reaffirm that "the intrinsic

value and personal dignity of every human being do not change, no matter what the concrete circumstances of his or her life. *A man, even if seriously ill or disabled in the exercise of his highest functions, is and always will be a man,* and he will never become a 'vegetable' or an 'animal'" (no. 3).

3) "The sick person in a vegetative state, awaiting recovery or a natural end, still has the right to basic health care (nutrition, hydration, cleanliness, warmth, etc.), and to the prevention of complications related to his confinement to bed. He also has the right to appropriate rehabilitative care and to be monitored for clinical signs of possible recovery. I should like particularly to underline how the administration of water and food, even when provided by artificial means, always represents a *natural means* of preserving life, not a *medical act*. Its use, furthermore, should be considered, in principle, *ordinary* and *proportionate*, and as such morally obligatory, to the extent to which, and for as long as, it is shown to accomplish its proper finality, which in the present case consists in providing nourishment to the patient and alleviation of his suffering" (no. 4).

4) The preceding documents were taken up and interpreted in this way: "The obligation to provide the 'normal care due to the sick in such cases' (Congregation for the Doctrine of the Faith, *Declaration on Euthanasia*, p. IV) includes, in fact, the use of nutrition and hydration (cf. Pontifical Council *Cor Unum, Some Ethical Questions Relating to the Gravely Ill and the Dying*, no. 2, 4, 4; Pontifical Council for Pastoral Assistance to Health Care Workers, *Charter for Health Care Workers*, no. 120). The evaluation of probabilities, founded on waning hopes for recovery when the vegetative state is prolonged beyond a year, cannot ethically justify the cessation or interruption of *minimal care* for the patient, including nutrition and hydration. Death by starvation or dehydration is, in fact, the only possible outcome as a result of their withdrawal. In this sense it ends up becoming, if done knowingly and willingly, true and proper euthanasia by omission" (n. 4).

Therefore, the Responses now given by the Congregation for the Doctrine of the Faith continue the direction of the documents of the Holy See cited above, and in particular the Address of John Paul II of March 20, 2004. The basic points are two. It is stated, first of all, that the provision of water and food, even by artificial means, is in principle an ordinary and proportionate means of preserving life for patients in a "vegetative state": "It is therefore obligatory, to the extent to which, and for as long as, it is shown to accomplish its proper finality, which is the hydration and nourishment of the patient." It is made clear, secondly, that this ordinary means of sustaining life is to be provided also to those in a "permanent vegetative state," since these are persons with their fundamental human dignity.

When stating that the administration of food and water is morally obligatory *in principle*, the Congregation for the Doctrine of the Faith does not exclude the possibility that, in very remote places or in situations of extreme poverty, the artificial provision of food and water may be physically impossible, and then *ad impossibilia nemo tenetur*. However, the obligation to offer the minimal treatments that are available remains in place, as well as that of obtaining, if possible, the means necessary for an adequate support of life. Nor is the possibility excluded that, due to emerging complications, a patient may be unable to assimilate food and liquids, so that their provision becomes altogether useless. Finally, the possibility is not absolutely excluded that, in some rare cases, artificial nourishment and hydration may be excessively burdensome for the patient or may cause significant physical discomfort, for example resulting from complications in the use of the means employed.

These exceptional cases, however, take nothing away from the general ethical criterion, according to which the provision of water and food, even by artificial means, always represents a *natural means* for preserving life, and is not a *therapeutic treatment*. Its use should therefore be considered *ordinary and proportionate*, even when the "vegetative state" is prolonged.

7. Advance Directives

An advance directive is a document by which a person makes provision for health-care decisions in the event that, in the future, he or she is no longer competent to make such decisions for himself or herself. Advance directives are of two main types: (1) the "living will" and (2) the "durable power of attorney for health care." A third type of advance directive (3) is a hybrid of these two.

A. The Living Will

This is a signed, witnessed or notarized document that allows a patient to direct that specified life-sustaining treatments be withheld or withdrawn if the patient is in a terminal condition and unable to make health-care decisions. Since an attending physician who may be unfamiliar with the signer's wishes and values has the authority to carry out the directives of the will, its terms may be interpreted in a way not envisioned by its signer. Moreover, the language used in such documents is often vague and general and fails to distinguish clearly the difference between a suicidal intention (to forgo treatment precisely as a way of ending one's life) and the non-suicidal intention to forgo treatment because of the treatment's uselessness or burdensomeness. Frequently, models of a living will are promoted by supporters of euthanasia, using language that is easy to interpret in a way favorable to euthanasia. Because of these features of the so-called living will — a document prepared in advance of the time when one will be in a situation calling for careful judgment about the appropriateness or non-appropriateness of specific treatments — it seems to me (and to others who have examined this issue far more deeply than I) that it is not advisable to make use of a "living will" as an advance directive regarding one's health care.

B. The Durable Power of Attorney

This is a signed, witnessed or notarized document in which the signer designates an agent to make health-care decisions for him or her in the event that he or she becomes incompetent. The agent must, of course, be chosen with great care since the agent will have great power and authority to make decisions about whether health care is to be provided, withheld, or withdrawn. The signer of such a document has the obligation to discuss his or her values, wishes, and instructions with the agent before and at the time the document is signed, and the agent must be willing to respect and carry out the signer's wishes.

The major advantage of appointing a health-care decisions agent is that it leaves decision making in the hands of a person of one's own choosing. Obviously, a Catholic will choose only someone who respects and lives up to the Church's teaching on the dignity of human life. The Catholic Conference for the District of Columbia issued a pastoral letter containing a set of criteria for selecting a health-care agent with the power of attorney. These are most useful, in my opinion. Thus I here reproduce them:

- Appoint someone who has the strength of character to make good judgments in painful circumstances.
- Appoint someone who you know you can trust to make decisions on the basis of the Church's teaching. The prudent person will select an agent who will act as he or she would have acted in whatever circumstances evolve.

- No one should agree to act as an agent for another person if that person would expect or require the agent to make decisions which disregard the teaching of the Church. It is not morally acceptable to carry out immoral decisions on behalf of someone else. No agent and no physician should ever feel obliged to act contrary to their well-informed consciences, even on behalf of another person.

- Appoint someone who is likely to be available to care for you in the distant future.... [I]t may be advisable to name alternate agents, in the event that your first choice proves unable or unwilling to act for you when the need arises.

- Discuss the specifics of your directive with the person whom you wish to choose as your agent....

- Generally avoid: 1. Stating that you wish to reject certain treatments under all circumstances except in case of imminent death or when one's present medical condition makes it clear in advance that such treatments would be futile; 2. Stating without qualification that you want medical remedies restricted in the event that you become permanently unconscious or terminally ill. Such stipulation can amount to providing a premature self-diagnosis. You should allow your health care agent and physician latitude to offer you appropriate care based on your actual condition.

- Include a provision regarding treatment at the time of imminent death. Recall that the Church allows a person on the verge of death to refuse a treatment which would result in only a burdensome prolongation of life. Your advance directive should authorize your agent to observe this norm.

- Periodically review the provisions of your directive.... Make copies of your directive and distribute them to your agent and each of your health care providers and anyone else you deem appropriate.[46]

The Patients Rights Council (accessible at http://www.patientsrightscouncil .org/site/about-the-prc/, formerly known as the International Task Force on Euthanasia and Assisted Suicide) has developed a very worthwhile document called the "Protective Medical Decisions Document." This is a durable power of attorney for health-care documents specifically prohibiting suicide, assisted suicide, and euthanasia. It is a document fully compatible with Catholic teaching and can be ordered from the council.

I advise persons not to sign living wills, which are vigorously promoted by euthanasia advocates. Rather, appoint a person whom you trust to be your agent by giving him or her durable power of attorney. Consider making use of the Protective Medical Decisions Document available from the International Task Force on Euthanasia and Assisted Suicide.[47]

————————————— Endnotes for Chapter Seven —————————————

1. Daniel Callahan, "Foreword" to *Euthanasia Examined: Ethical, Clinical and Legal Perspectives*, ed. John Keown (Cambridge: Cambridge University Press, 1995), pp. xiii-xiv.
2. Ibid., p. xiv.
3. On factors contributing to acceptance of the euthanasia movement, see also Patrick Nowell-Smith, "In Favour of Voluntary Euthanasia," in *Principles of Health Care Ethics*, ed. Raanan Gillon (New York: John Wiley & Sons, 1994), pp. 754-755.
4. See, for example, the following: Nowell-Smith, "In Favour of Voluntary Euthanasia," pp. 751-761; Joseph Fletcher, "Ethics and Euthanasia," *American Journal of Nursing* 73 (April 1973), reprinted in *To Live and to Die*, ed. Robert H. Williams (New York: Springer Verlag, 1973).
5. The *Random House College Dictionary* (rev. ed., New York: Random House, 1996), p. 456.
6. On this, see Germain Grisez and Joseph Boyle, *Life and Death with Liberty and Justice: A Contribution to the Euthanasia Debate* (Notre Dame, IN: University of Notre Dame Press, 1979), pp. 86-87. This excellent work, now three decades old, remains one of the finest studies available to show that respect for the intrinsic goodness of human bodily life absolutely proscribes euthanasia of any kind. I am in great debt to the authors, whose work, unfortunately, has never received the attention it merits for both its moral and jurisprudential arguments against euthanasia.
7. Timothy E. Quill, "Death and Dignity," in *Last Rights: Assisted Suicide and Euthanasia Debated*, ed. Michael M. Uhlmann (Washington, DC/Grand Rapids, MI: Ethics and Public Policy Center/William B. Eerdmans Publishing Co., 1998), pp. 327-328. Quill's essay originally appeared in his book *Death and Dignity: Making Choices and Taking Charge* (New York: Norton, 1993).
8. See Jack Kevorkian, "A Fail-Safe Model for Justifiable Medically Assisted Suicide," in *Last Rights*, pp. 263-296; originally published in *American Journal of Forensic Psychiatry* 13.1 (1992).
9. Among the early advocates of euthanasia were Glanville Williams, an English lawyer, and Joseph Fletcher, at that time an Anglican clergyman. Glanville's most important work advocating euthanasia was his *Sanctity of Life and the Criminal Law* (New York: Alfred A. Knopf, 1957). Fletcher devoted a chapter defending euthanasia in his *Morals and Medicine* (Boston: Beacon Press, 1960), a work reprinted in the 1970s and 1980s. During the 1970s, Fletcher wrote frequently in defense of euthanasia (see endnote 10).

10. Three authors in particular wrote extensively (and influentially) on the subject, namely, Joseph Fletcher (a professor at the Episcopal Theological School in Cambridge, MA, and later at the University of Virginia), Daniel Maguire (a Catholic theologian teaching at Marquette University), and Marvin Kohl (a philosopher at the State University of New York in Buffalo). Among Fletcher's writings on the subject at this time were: "Ethics and Euthanasia" (see endnote 4); "The Patient's Right to Die," in *Euthanasia and the Right to Death*, ed. A. B. Downing (London: Peter Owen, 1969), pp. 66-69; and "The 'Right' to Life and the 'Right' to Die," in *Beneficent Euthanasia*, ed. Marvin Kohl (Buffalo: Prometheus Books, 1975). Maguire authored a book and several essays, among them *Death by Choice* (New York: Doubleday, 1974); "The Freedom to Die," in *New Theology No. 10,* ed. Martin Marty and Dean Peerman (New York: Macmillan, 1974); and "A Catholic View of Mercy Killing," in *Beneficent Euthanasia*. Among Kohl's contributions to the literature was his essay "Voluntary Beneficent Euthanasia" in the volume he edited, *Beneficent Euthanasia*. That volume ended with "A Plea for Beneficent Euthanasia," pp. 233-236, written by Kohl and Paul Kurtz (editor of the *Humanist*) and signed by Fletcher, Maguire, several Nobel laureates, physicians, religious leaders, and academics.

11. More contemporary articulations of the "ethics of euthanasia" include the following: Nowell-Smith, "In Favour of Voluntary Euthanasia," pp. 751-762; John Harris, "Euthanasia and the Value of Life," in *Euthanasia Examined* (see endnote 1 for details), pp. 6-22; Jean Davis, "The Case for Legalising Voluntary Euthanasia," in ibid., pp. 83-95; Ronald Dworkin, *Life's Dominion: An Argument about Abortion, Euthanasia, and Individual Freedom* (New York: Harper, 1993); Dworkin, "Do We Have a Right to Die?" in *Last Rights* (see endnote 7 for details), pp. 75-94; Peter Singer, *Rethinking Life and Death: The Collapse of Our Traditional Ethics* (New York: St. Martin's Press, 1995); Derek Humphrey and Ann Wickett, *The Right to Die: Understanding Euthanasia* (New York: Harper & Row, 1988).

12. This, in essence, is the argument advanced by a host of writers. See, for instance, Kohl, "Voluntary Beneficent Euthanasia," esp. pp. 131-133, where he emphasizes that voluntary euthanasia is rooted in a respect for the dignity of the person to control his or her own life; Fletcher, "Ethics and Euthanasia," "The 'Right' to Life and the 'Right' to Die"; Maguire, "The Freedom to Die." Dworkin believes it is tyrannical to oppose a person's well-considered decision to ask to be killed mercifully: "making someone die in a way ... that he believes [is] a horrifying contradiction of his life, is a devastating, odious form of tyranny" (*Life's Dominion . . .* , p. 217). See also Harris, "Euthanasia and the Value of Life," pp. 14-16.

13. Fletcher, "The Patient's Right to Die," p. 69. See also Maguire, "The Freedom to Die," pp. 188-189.

14. Thus Kohl, one of the leading proponents of "beneficent euthanasia," distinguishes sharply between the dignity human beings have by reason of their nature as members of the human species — he refers to this as dignity — and the dignity human persons have insofar as they are capable of controlling their

own lives — dignity — and his contention is that it is dignity that is at stake in the issue of euthanasia and that this dignity justifies the "right to die" and to choose to be killed mercifully, a choice that others are obliged to respect. See his "Voluntary Beneficent Euthanasia," pp. 132-133.

15. Singer, *Rethinking Life and Death*, pp. 218-219.

16. Fletcher, *Morals and Medicine*, p. 211.

17. Maguire, "The Freedom to Die," pp. 188-189. It is instructive to note that both Fletcher and Maguire explicitly link the freedom to choose death (in euthanasia) to the freedom to control conception by contraceptive methods. This helps one see the link between acceptance of contraception and the culture of death. See Chapter Four.

18. Harris, "Euthanasia and the Value of Life," pp. 8-9; Singer, *Rethinking Life and Death*, pp. 180-183, 202-206.

19. Marvin Kohl, *The Morality of Killing: Sanctity of Life, Abortion and Euthanasia* (Atlantic Highlands, NJ: Humanities Press, 1974), pp. 81-96; Glanville Williams, *Sanctity of Life*, p. 316; Williams, "Euthanasia," *Medico-Legal Journal* 41 (1973), 22; H. Tristram Englehardt, Jr., "Ethical Issues in Aiding the Death of Young Children," in *Beneficent Euthanasia*, pp. 180-192; Robert F. Weir, *Selected Nontreatment of Handicapped Newborns* (New York: Oxford University Press, 1984), esp. pp. 188-223; Anthony Shaw, "Dilemmas of 'Informed Consent' in Children," in *Death, Dying, and Euthanasia*, ed. Dennis J. Horan and David Mall (Frederick, MD: University Publications of America, 1984), pp. 75-90; Raymond S. Duff and A. G. M. Campbell, "Moral and Ethical Dilemmas in the Special-Care Nursery," in *Death, Dying, and Euthanasia*, pp. 91-104.

20. See, for example, Weir, *Selective Nontreatment of Handicapped Newborns*, pp. 215-221.

21. Fletcher, "Indicators of Humanhood: A Tentative Profile of Man," *Hastings Center Report* 2 (November 1972), 1; "Four Indicators of Humanhood — The Enquiry Matures," *Hastings Center Report* 4 (December 1974), 5-7; Tooley, "Abortion and Infanticide," *Philosophy and Public Affairs* 2 (1972), 37-65, esp. 44-48; Singer, *Rethinking Life and Death*, pp. 202-206.

22. Harris, "Euthanasia and the Value of Life," pp. 7-8, 17-18.

23. Supreme Court of the United States, *Planned Parenthood of Southeastern Pennsylvania et al. v. Robert P. Casey*, June 29, 1992, p. 9. An excellent analysis and critique of this decision is Russell Hittinger, "Et Tu, Justice Kennedy?" *Crisis* 10.8 (September 1992), 16-22.

24. Arthur Dyck, "Beneficent Euthanasia and Benemortasia: Alternative Views of Mercy," in *Beneficent Euthanasia*, p. 127.

25. *Euthanasia, Clinical Practice and the Law*, ed. Luke Gormally (London: The Linacre Centre for Health Care Ethics, 1994), pp. 131, 132; emphasis, including boldface, in the original. The first part of this truly excellent volume upholding the sanctity of life and providing devastating criticism of the rationale to justify euthanasia contains a reprint of the important Linacre Centre Working Party Report, whereas the second part contains the submission made on behalf

of The Linacre Centre to the House of Lords' Select Committee on Medical Ethics. Among the members of the Working Party were Luke Gormally, John Mahoney, S.J., G. E. M. Anscombe, and John Finnis.

26. Ibid., p. 132.
27. The best treatment of the injustice of "quality of life" criteria for determining who should live and who should die is given by Grisez and Boyle in *Life and Death with Liberty and Justice*, chapter 6.
28. *Euthanasia, Clinical Practice and the Law*, p. 42.
29. As St. Thomas says, commenting on St. Paul's teaching on the resurrection of the body, *"anima mea non est ego"* ("my soul is not me") (*In 1 Cor. 15*).
30. Leo Alexander, "Medical Science Under Dictatorship," in *Death, Dying, and Euthanasia*, p. 584. Alexander's essay, which should be read by everyone who wants to understand the evil of euthanasia, originally appeared in the *New England Journal of Medicine* 241 (1949), 39-47.
31. See Grisez and Boyle, *Life and Death with Liberty and Justice*, pp. 154-168.
32. Ramsey proposed the term "agathanasia" in his long essay, "On (Only) Caring for the Dying" in his *Patient as Person* (New Haven: Yale University Press, 1970), pp. 113-164. Dyck developed his analogous notion of "benemortasia" in two essays: "An Alternative to an Ethics of Euthanasia," in *To Live and to Die*, pp. 98-112, and in "Beneficent Euthanasia and Benemortasia: Alternative Views of Mercy," in *Beneficent Euthanasia*, pp. 117-129.
33. *Euthanasia, Clinical Practice and the Law*, pp. 53-54.
34. Ibid., p. 55.
35. Pope Pius XII, "The Prolongation of Life: An Address to an International Congress of Anesthesiologists," as reprinted in *Death, Dying, and Euthanasia*, p. 284.
36. This matter is clearly discussed in *Euthanasia, Clinical Practice and the Law*, pp. 43-45.
37. John R. Connery, S.J., "Prolonging Life: Its Duty and Its Limits," in *Moral Responsibility in Prolonging Life Decisions*, ed. Donald McCarthy and Albert Moraczewski, O.P. (St. Louis: Pope John XXIII Medical-Moral Research and Education Center, 1981), p. 133.
38. Grisez and Boyle, *Life and Death with Liberty and Justice*, p. 260.
39. Ibid., pp. 268-269.
40. *Euthanasia, Clinical Practice and the Law*, p. 66.
41. Dyck, "An Alternative to an Ethics of Euthanasia," in *To Live and to Die*, pp. 111-112; Dyck provides a similar list, omitting the fourth, in "Beneficent Euthanasia and Benemortasia: Alternative View of Mercy;" in *Beneficent Euthanasia*, pp. 128-129. I have modified somewhat his way of articulating these presuppositions.
42. FIAMC and Pontifical Academy for Life, "Joint Statement on the Vegetative State," available at http://www.vatican.va/roman_curia/pontifical_academies/acdlife/documents/rc_pont-acd_life_doc_20040320_joint-statement-veget-state_en.html.

43. Jerome Groopman, "Silent Minds: Scan Technology and Vegetative Patients," *New Yorker*, October 15, 2007.

44. See the review of the International Congress's work by Richard Doerflinger, "John Paul II and the 'Vegetative' State," *Ethics & Medics* 29.6 (2004).

45. Australian bishops, Briefing Note on the Obligation to Provide Nutrition and Hydration, "09-05-04," available at http://www.bioethicsperth.org.au/Upload%5CBriefing%20%20note%20broch.pdf.

46. Roman Catholic Bishops of the District of Columbia, *Care of the Sick and Dying: A Pastoral Letter* (Washington DC: The District of Columbia Catholic Conference, 1994), p. 28.

47. Note that the Anti-Euthanasia Task Force, presided over by Rita Marker, is now known as the Patients Rights Council. The same document is available from them.

CHAPTER EIGHT

Defining Death and Organ Transplantation

1. Part One: Defining Death

Introduction[1]

A current issue of crucial importance focuses on the definition of death and on criteria for determining that a person has died. This issue is critical because it is possible to save the lives of persons who are threatened by death because one or more of their vital organs — the heart, lungs, liver, etc. — no longer function. Although paired vital organs such as kidneys can be provided for them by living donors, such donors cannot be used as the source of unpaired vital organs such as the heart, but a possible source for such organs (and of paired vital organs as well) is the "body" of a person who has just died. But organ transplants from a cadaver *must* take place almost immediately after death. Were the transplantation delayed, the organs in question would quickly deteriorate and would no longer be of any help in preserving the lives of those in need of them.

In the legitimate desire to obtain a life-saving organ for a fellow human being whose life can be saved by transplant surgery, it is necessary firmly to resist any temptation to diminish care of a dying person because he or she happens to be a prospective donor. This is the reason why the World Medical Assembly, at a 1968 meeting in Sydney, Australia, accepted the principle that there be complete separation of authority and responsibility between the physician or group of physicians charged with caring for the dying person and the physician or group of physicians whose task is to care for the person in need of an organ. It is for this reason that one of the provisions of the Uniform Anatomical Gift Act is the following: "The time of death shall be determined by a physician who attends the donor at his death, or, if none, the physician who certifies the death. This physician shall *not* participate in the procedures for removing or transplanting a part."[2]

Our legitimate concern in the practical order to protect the dignity of the dying person is paralleled, or *ought* to be paralleled, in the intellectual order with a concern to separate the question of defining death and the use of organs for transplants. The late Paul Ramsey forcefully made this point when he said:

> If in the practical order we need to separate between the physician who is responsible for the care of a prospective donor, and the physician who is responsible for a prospective recipient, do we not need in the intellectual order to keep the question of the definition of death equally discrete from the use of organs in transplantations? If only the physician responsible for a dying man should make the determination that he has died, with no "help" from the medical team that has in its care a man who needs a borrowed organ, should not also the definition of death and the tests for it that he uses be ones that he thinks are sound or were agreed to by the profession without having transplantation in view? There would be too little protection of life attained in the practical order by entirely separating the authority and responsibility of the teams of physicians if the definition of death and the tests used for it have already been significantly invaded by the requirements of transplant therapy. If no person's death should *for this purpose* be hastened, then the definition of death should not *for this purpose* be updated, or the procedures for stating that a man has died be revised as a means of affording easier access to organs.[3]

Since the end of the 1960s a widely accepted criterion — in addition to the pulmonary-coronary criterion — has been the "neurological criterion" (popularly but mistakenly known as "brain death"). This has been accepted in some form of law throughout the world and in the United States. Thus in 1981 this consensus was well articulated by the members of the U.S. President's Commission for the Study of Ethical Problems in Medicine and Biomedical and Behavioral Research. The 1981 report of the Commission advocated statutory enactment of a Uniform Definition of Death Act.[4] This act provides that an individual who has sustained either (1) irreversible cessation of circulatory and respiratory functions or (2) irreversible cessation of *all* functions of the *entire* brain, *including the brain stem* (my emphasis), is dead.[5] Thus the Presidential Commission for the Study of Ethical Problems in Medicine and Biomedical and Behavioral Research's Report *Defining Death: A Report on the Medical, Legal and Ethical Issues in the Determination of Death* declared: "if the functioning of the brain is the factor which principally integrates any organism which has a brain, then if that function is lost, what is left is no longer as a whole an organic unity."[6] According to this rationale, neurological criteria for death did not represent a new *definition* of death, but just gave more precise criteria for determining that bodily death had occurred.

The donation of organs for transplantation was welcomed by the Catholic Church. In 1956, Pope Pius XII taught that donation of organs after death was not "a violation of the reverence due to the dead"; rather, it was an expression of "merciful charity shown to some suffering brothers and sisters."[7] Pius's teaching —reaffirmed by Pope John Paul II (on this, see below) has been incorporated into number 2296 of the *Catechism of the Catholic Church*, which reads as follows: "Organ donation after death is a noble and meritorious act and is to be encouraged as an expression of generous solidarity."

Pius XII also recognized that determining the time of death was a matter of *medical* rather than *theological* or *magisterial* competence. "It remains for the doctor, and especially the anaesthesiologist, to give a clear and precise definition of 'death' and the 'moment of death' of a patient who passes away in a state of unconsciousness."[8]

A. Purpose and Scope

Catholic scholars who accept magisterial teaching are debating this controversial issue. Some affirm, others deny, the validity of the "neurological criterion" for determining that a person has died. The purpose of the first part of this chapter is to answer the question "Are those who reject as invalid the 'neurological criterion' for determining that a human person has died disloyal Catholics?" This question must be asked because the most authoritative magisterial statement is that made by the late Pope John Paul II in his address of August 29, 2000, to the 16th Annual Conference of the Transplant Society. In this address, no. 5, he declared:

> It is a well-known fact that for some time certain scientific approaches to ascertaining death have shifted the emphasis from the traditional cardio-respiratory signs to the so-called *"neurological" criterion*. Specifically, this consists in establishing, according to clearly determined parameters commonly held by the international scientific community, the complete and irreversible cessation of all brain activity (in the cerebrum, cerebellum and brain stem). This is then considered the sign that the individual organism has lost its integrative capacity.... [I]t can be said that the criterion adopted in more recent times for ascertaining the fact of death, namely the *complete* and *irreversible* cessation of all brain activity [emphasis in original], if rigorously applied, does not *seem* [my emphasis] to conflict with

the essential elements of a sound anthropology. Therefore a health-worker professionally responsible for ascertaining death can use these criteria in each individual case as the basis for arriving at that degree of assurance in ethical judgement which moral teaching describes as "moral certainty." This moral certainty is considered the necessary and sufficient basis for an ethically correct course of action. Only where such certainty exists, and where informed consent has already been given by the donor or the donor's legitimate representatives, is it morally right to initiate the technical procedures required for the removal of organs for transplant.[9]

In other writings on this issue, John Paul II, like his predecessor Pius XII, made it clear that the competence to set forth the criteria for determining that a human person has died is **not** within the competence of the Magisterium. Thus, for example, in his "Discourse to the Participants of the Working Group of the Pontifical Academy of Sciences at a meeting held in Rome December 10-14, 1989,"[10] he said that two tasks must be addressed. The first concerns *scientists, analysts, and scholars* (my emphasis), who "must pursue their research and studies in order to determine as precisely as possible the exact moment and the indisputable sign of death. For, once such a determination has been arrived at, then the apparent conflict, between the duty to respect the life of one person and the duty to effect a cure or even save the life of another, disappears. One would be able to know at what moment it would be perfectly permissible to do what had been definitely forbidden previously, namely, the removal of an organ for transplanting, with the best chances of a successful outcome." A second task concerns moralists, philosophers, and theologians who must exercise the virtue of prudence in finding appropriate solutions to new problems and new aspects of age-old problems in light of new data.[11]

Note that John Paul said that the neurological criterion did not *seem* to conflict with the demands of a sound anthropology.

On September 8, 2008, *L'Osservatore Romano* (Italian version) published "*I Segni della morte: A quarant'anni dal rapporto di Harvard*" ("The Signs of Death: 40 Years after the Harvard Report") by Lucetta Scaraffia, a professor of contemporary history at the Rome university "La Sapienza." Scaraffia's article was summarized in the Italian journal *Chiesa*. Here I shorten and paraphrase this summary:

> Forty years ago, on August 5, 1968, the *Journal of the American Medical Association* published the "Harvard report" that established the total

cessation of brain activity as determining that a person has died. All of the countries of the world rapidly adopted this standard. The Catholic Church did also, particularly in reports in 1985 and 1989 from Working Groups of the Pontifical Academy of Sciences. John Paul II accepted these reports and reaffirmed this acceptance in his Allocution to the 16th International Congress of the Transplantation Society, on August 29, 2000. This position was defended by [many highly regarded Italian moral theologians and Vatican officials].... Beneath the surface, however, doubts were growing in the Church, as illustrated by an entire chapter of a book published recently in Italy: Paolo Becchi's *I Segni della morte e la questione dei trapianti* ["The Signs of Death and the Question of Transplants"]. Becchi is professor of the philosophy of law at the universities of Genoa and Luzern, and a pupil of a Jewish thinker who dedicated concerned reflections to the question of the end of life, Hans Jonas. According to Jonas, the new definition of death established by the Harvard report was not motivated by any real scientific advancement, but rather by the need for organs for transplants. It is especially in the Church that critical voices are gaining strength. On January 3-4, 2005, the Pontifical Academy of Sciences again met to discuss the question of the "signs of death," and the experts present — philosophers, jurists, neurologists from various countries — found themselves in agreement in maintaining that brain death is not the death of a human being, and that the criterion of brain death, not being scientifically credible, should be abandoned.

This conference shocked Vatican officials who accepted the Harvard report [and prevented] publication of the proceedings. A substantial number of the speakers then gave their texts to the publisher, Rubbettino. The result was a book with the Latin title *Finis Vitae,* edited by Professor Roberto de Mattei, deputy director of the National Research Council.... The book was published in two editions, in Italian (in 2007) and English [not published until several years later]. It presented eighteen essays, half of them by scholars who had not participated in the conference of the Pontifical Academy of Sciences, but shared its views. These include Professor Becchi. Among those who did speak at the conference, special mention should be made of Josef Seifert and of the German philosopher Robert Spaemann, who is highly respected by Pope Joseph Ratzinger, who, as Pope Benedict XVI, has never spoken directly on this question.... But it is known how much he respects the arguments of his friend Spaemann. Another contributor to *Finis Vitae* was the respected German Catholic philosopher Wolfgang Waldstein.[12]

It is significant that Scaraffia's article was published in *L'Osservatore Romano*. Although this paper "acts as an official outlet of the Holy See only in the section 'Our Information,' which presents the appointments, audiences, and activities of the pope. Almost all of its articles are printed without advance review by the Vatican authorities, and fall under the responsibility of the authors and the director of the paper, Professor Giovanni Maria Vian. This does not change the fact that the article has broken the silence on views questioning the 'Harvard Report' in a newspaper that in any case is known as 'the pope's newspaper.'"

B. Reasons For Questioning the "Neurological Criterion"

Since the mid-1990s, an increasing number of philosophers, bioethicists, and physicians, Catholic and non-Catholic alike, have provided further evidence and arguments to reinforce doubts that some had had for many years regarding the validity of the "neurological criterion" for determining that a human person was dead. The most significant critic has been D. Alan Shewmon, M.D. The current state of doubts and confusion over the validity of this criterion (popularly known as "brain death") was well expressed by the United States President's Council on Bioethics Report of 2008, *Controversies in the Determination of Death*:

> There remains considerable public confusion, both about the meaning of the term "brain dead" and about its relation to the death of a human being. There is persistent dissent by some clinicians, philosophers, and other critical observers who have never been convinced that "brain death" is, indeed, the death of the human being. There are, as well, pressures against insisting that declaring death, or at least "organ donation eligibility," requires the irreversible loss of function in the whole brain. And, perhaps most important, there are critics who have published evidence of ongoing integrated bodily activities in some persons meeting the criteria of "whole brain death" and who have claimed that this evidence invalidates the rationale for today's consensus position.

C. Procedure

Since my concern focuses on the obligation of Catholic scholars to render "loyal submission of the will and intellect ... , in a special way, to the authentic teaching authority of the Roman Pontiff, even when he does not speak *ex cathedra*" (*Lumen gentium*, no. 25), I will now proceed as follows:

1. Summarize a valuable review of *Finis Vitae* to illustrate the problem;
2. Summarize Paolo Becchi's "*I Segni della morte e la questione dei trapianti*";
3. Summarize the view of D. Alan Shewmon, M.D., R. D. Truog, M.D., and J. Flacker on transplanting vital organs;
4. Summarize the view of Edmund D. Pellegrino, M.D.;
5. Summarize the position of Nicanor Austriaco, O.P., on the criterion to determine that a person has died;
6. Summarize the position of Germain Grisez, Peter Ryan, S.J., Patrick Lee, and myself on this issue.

I will then offer a conclusion.

(1) Finis Vitae: *Is Brain Death Still Life?*

Randy Engel's extensive review of this book is very helpful.[13] I present my own paraphrase and summary of major points developed in this review. In his introduction, Paul A. Byrne reports that in 2004, Pope John Paul II asked a group of faithful lay Catholics to collaborate with the Pontifical Academy of Sciences (PAS) to reexamine in depth the issues of "brain death" and unpaired vital organ transplantation. Previous official meetings held by the PAS on these critical matters in 1985, and again in 1989, were with few exceptions dominated by scientists and physicians who accepted the "brain death" criterion and did little to show the true nature and implications of the controversies surrounding the definition of "brain death" as a valid criterion for true death and the institutionalized practice of excising unpaired vital organs from living persons for transplantation purposes. One of the key provisos imposed on organizers of the meeting by the Vatican was that both sides of the issues, pro and con, be equally represented at the conference.

On February 3-4, 2005, "The Signs of Death" Conference was convened in Vatican City by the PAS. At the conclusion of the conference, the usual preparations were made to print and distribute the proceedings of the conference, but at the eleventh hour, the printing was called off without any explanation.

This was more than a bureaucratic error, and this became evident when the PAS organized another conference on September 11-12, 2006, under the same title, "The Signs of Death." But this time the Vatican did not require that all points of view, pro and con, be represented. Participation was limited to those in favor of "brain death," and the proceedings were printed and distributed without any delay.

Byrne and his colleagues who opposed "brain death" decided to publish their papers from the original 2005 "Signs of Death" conference under the auspices of the National Research Council of Italy. The Italian version of *Finis Vitae,* edited by Professor Roberto de Mattei, was published in 2006. And in 2009, the English version was edited and updated by Dr. Byrne and published in 2011 by the Life Guardian Foundation. The eighteen papers published in *Finis Vitae* in opposition to the "brain death" criterion were written by world-class neurologists, philosophers, neonatologists, jurists, and bioethicists. Four of the authors, in addition to Byrne and Bishop Fabian Bruskewitz of Lincoln, Nebraska, are respected as good and loyal Catholics and are members of the Pontifical Academy of Life, namely, Robert Spaemann, Josef Seifert, Wolfgang Waldstein, and D. Alan Shewmon; and the first three are personal friends of Pope Benedict XVI.

Here, summarized, are some of the arguments advanced by contributors to *Finis Vitae* to discredit "brain death." Spaemann declared:

> The new definition of death as "brain death" makes it possible to declare people dead while they are still breathing and to bypass the dying process in order to quarry spare parts for the living from the dying. Death no longer comes at the end of the dying process, but ... at its beginning. The [Harvard] commission intended to provide a new definition [of death], clearly expressing their main interest. It was no longer the interest of the dying to avoid being declared dead prematurely, but other people's interest in declaring a dying person dead as soon as possible.[14]

Spaemann reminded card-carrying donors and their families to be aware that "[a] transplantation physician professionally sides with the recipient, **not** the donor of organs."[15] The practical application of this obvious conflict of interest is that the donor card may become the donor's death warrant.

Another contributor, Cicero Galli Coimbra, M.D., Ph.D., a clinical neurologist at the Federal University of Sao Paulo, Brazil, pointed out, "nowadays many brain injured patients conceivably evolve to deep coma and are submitted to diagnostic procedures for BD/BSD [brain death/brain-stem death] *without having even received the current standard of basic care to prevent further brain injury from secondary insults* [emphasis added]. Among these tests is the apnea test for determination of 'brain death,' which is administered for the ultimate benefit of the organ recipient, not the injured patient."[16]

The need to end the practice of carrying out the deadly apnea test on potential organ donors to determine "brain death" is another major theme found in *Finis Vitae*. While this test is often categorized as "cardinal," "essential," "central," or "mandatory," in reality, it has no therapeutic purpose whatsoever for the potential donor. Its primary purpose is to determine whether the patient can or cannot breath on his own in order to declare him "brain dead," and thus eligible to be an organ donor. True informed consent concerning the nature of and dangers posed by the test are usually withheld from family members lest they withhold support for the test, without which the transplantation protocol cannot proceed.[17] In another of Coimbra's essays, "The Apnea Test — A Bedside Lethal 'Disaster' to Avoid a Legal 'Disaster' in the Operating Room," the neurologist states that the apnea test administered to the seriously brain injured patient may cause "irreversible damage to brain tissue," and even death.[18]

Coimbra maintains that the apnea test is not only "undoubtedly unethical" but it is also "technically useless for its own intended or declared purpose of characterizing the irreversible loss of respiratory reflex." Coimbra notes that "too many lives have been lost during the last decades of blindness, when the diagnosis of 'death' has been applied to the silent brain receiving critical levels of blood supply.... A patient who would have hopelessly died years ago may now recover by novel and effective therapies developed from improved knowledge on the pathophysiology of coma."[19]

Josef Seifert, Wolfgang Waldstein — also members of the Pontifical Academy of Life — and Bishop Fabian Bruskewitz agreed with Spaemann and Coimbra and contributed essays to *Finis Vitae*. Seifert and Waldstein, like their German-language colleague Spaemann, have long argued against the validity of "brain death" as a criterion for determining that a human person has died. In addition to their essays in *Finis Vitae*, they have written frequently to criticize this criterion.

In addition to his essay in *Finis Vitae*, Spaemann's clear presentation during an international bioethical conference that took place in Rome in October 2002 is most valuable. It is published in Italian as "La morte della persona e la morte dell'essere umano," in *Lepanto* 162.21 (December 2002).

(2) Paolo Becchi's "I Segni della morte e la questione dei trapianti"

Becchi begins by noting that the "brain death" criterion reflected scientific knowledge at the time it was so widely accepted because it seemed to prove the theory that patients in an irreversible coma were destined to die of cardiac arrest in a short time; moreover, it greatly helped the development of transplant surgery; finally, it would not constitute mercy killing because a patient whose brain had completely stopped working was dead, and therefore removing his vital organs would not kill him.

But in the United States this definition was soon challenged and reconsidered. Strong philosophical doubts about the new definition of death were raised immediately by the great philosopher Hans Jonas, who voiced strong objections to it a month after the Harvard report. According to Jonas we do not know exactly the borderline between life and death, and a definition introduced with the clear intention to encourage the removal of organs cannot replace that cognitive deficit.

Next Becchi stressed two crucial points on this subject. The first one concerns the possibility of checking total brain death on the basis of the norms and tests now in use. What they show is that brain death is a telltale symptom of the *near* brain death of the whole human body, *not* the death of the whole human body.

The first point was considered by two U.S. medical doctors, Robert Truog and James Flacker, in a 1992 essay.[20] According to these authors, proved scientific research shows that patients who respond to current clinical criteria and neurological tests for brain death do not necessarily lose all brain functions. This proves that the complete cessation of these would not be diagnosable on the basis of the standard tests in use. To support their theory, they showed: (1) the endocrine-hypothalamic function of these patients does not fail, even after they were declared in brain death according to the tests then in use; (2) a weak electrical activity is demonstrated in many of these patients; this activity is concentrated in some areas of the cerebral cortex, and it is destined to stop after twenty-four to forty-eight hours; (3) some patients unexpectedly go on responding to external stimuli, as the rise in heart rate and in blood pressure after the surgical cut to excise organs shows (these observations refer to patients declared brain dead on the basis of only clinical British criteria, which refer to the brainstem condition); (4) many patients declared brain dead still have spinal reflexes. Therefore one cannot rule out lower brainstem involvement in spinal marrow activity.

On the basis of a careful analysis of these elements the two authors came to the conclusion that current clinical means do not and cannot prove the cessation of *all* functions of the entire brain, but only of some, and at most they can diagnose only cortical death. The second point has been illustrated above all by D. Alan Shewmon, an authoritative American neurologist, who changed his mind during his career; at first strongly supporting brain death and then becoming one of the most prominent opponents of the theory. His critique is based on empirical examinations of many patients declared brain dead but who nonetheless grew, spontaneously healed minor infections from within, etc.[21]

(3) The Views of D. Alan Shewmon, M.D, R. D. Truog, and J. Flacker on Transplanting Vital Organs

These authors reject the "neurological criterion," as we have seen, and Shewmon's empirical studies are regarded by many as perhaps the strongest scientific evidence demonstrating the demise of the claim that a human person is dead if there is irreversible cessation of the functioning of the entire brain, including the brain stem.

But they both hold that it would be a mistake to conclude that rejection of the "brain death" criterion automatically entails the end of vital organ transplantation from the (still-living) bodies (= persons) of those deemed brain dead. Shewmon, for example, asks, "What if ... in a very particular circumstance it were possible to remove unpaired organs, including even the heart, from a live donor *without causing or even hastening death?*" He then goes on to suggest that this *is* possible and to outline the procedures to be followed.

Here it seems best to cite in full Shewmon's proposal. He writes as follows:

> Consider a patient on morally extraordinary (disproportionate) life support (typically a ventilator), who is about to have that support licitly withdrawn and who, independent of that decision, also wants to donate organs. Suppose also a high probability that the patient will die very quickly upon termination of that support. Instead of the withdrawal taking place in the intensive care unit, however, it is done in the operating room with surgical teams poised. Perhaps, with the patient's consent, arterial catheters have been placed in readiness to perfuse at an appropriate time the organs of interest with a cold ischemia-protective solution. The life support is then discontinued and asystole awaited. After a brief interval (short enough not to damage the transplantable organs but long enough for moral certainty that spontaneous recovery will not occur) the organs of interest are perfused and the surgical teams begin their work.
>
> In such a scenario, the patient would probably not yet be dead at the moment of organ removal. Cardiopulmonary resuscitation could be

successful, but it would constitute an extraordinary means that has been decided ahead of time to be legitimately forgone. In the absence of circulating blood, however, "vital" organs are no longer vital, including even the nonbeating heart; their mere presence in the body contributes nothing to the body's physiological integrity or remaining brief span of life (perhaps on the order of tens of minutes); therefore, their removal would neither cause nor even accelerate death. It is generally accepted that healthy individuals may licitly donate a single kidney or a piece of liver on the dual basis that (1) the functional integrity of their body is not compromised and (2) the gift of life for the recipient sufficiently justifies the risks of surgery and the structural mutilation. The retrieval of unpaired vital organs in the manner described above would seem to be morally equivalent, at least in principle, to these classic examples of licit live donation.[22]

Shewmon believes that this approach to transplant surgery merits further research, and he encourages such study and research "in order to reassure the transplant community that the conceptual demise of 'brain death' would not necessarily entail the demise of organ transplantation, although it would surely require a radical change in the *modus operandi* for obtaining donor organs." Truog holds the same position. But Shewmon, in his "Dead Donor" essay, adds the following caveat:

> The foregoing discussion *does not* [emphasis added] constitute advocacy of any particular transplantation protocol. It addresses the very precise and limited question of whether it is possible in principle to remove vital organs without causing or hastening death or violating the time-honored injunction *primum non nocere*. My conclusion is yes, it is possible in principle. *But before deciding whether it would be prudent to put this principle into practice in today's society, many other factors, which are outside the scope of this paper, must be considered, such as whether donor consent can be guaranteed to be truly informed and free; whether, in the case at hand, apnea off life support can be predicted with medical and moral certainty; whether such eviscerating procedures respect human dignity even if they might not cause or hasten death; whether the risk of public misperception that this is utilitarian killing can be minimized; and so on. If the answer to one or more of these "whethers" is a "no,"* ... *then it behooves us to hold off implementing the otherwise intrinsically ethical procedure until all the circumstantial details are worked out* [emphasis added].[23]

(4) The Position of Edmund D. Pellegrino, M.D.

Edmund Pellegrino, an internationally recognized and respected bioethicist, was chairman of the President's Council on Bioethics when it prepared and released its famous white paper, *Controversies in the Determination of Death* (December 2008). In his own personal statement Pellegrino summarizes the Council's white paper in this way:

> Loss of somatic integration of the organism as a whole as a result of brain death was proposed nearly thirty years ago by the then-President's Commission. In recent years, this criterion has been cast into doubt by a long series of clinical observations. A list, from the work of neurologist Alan Shewmon, is presented in Chapter Four of the white paper. Strenuously debated in the past, the criterion of somatic integration enjoys waning support today.... The Council's white paper [Leon Kass, former chairman of the Council, was key in its new formulation of a definition of death] offers a more attractive philosophical argument, i.e., loss of the capacity by the apneic patient for *active spontaneous engagement with the environment* [my emphasis] through the function of breathing. The patient lacking this capacity is said to be "dead," even if respiratory function and cell metabolism are sustained by mechanical ventilation because they are not, then, the result of "spontaneous" respiration. However, other patients kept alive "artificially" — by pacemakers, defibrillators, vasopressors, ventricular assist devices, artificial nutrition and hydration, etc. — are not, by that fact alone, considered to be "dead." Patients with respiratory paralysis due to poliomyelitis or cervical spine trans-section have lived with the assistance of respirators for many years.[24]

The possibilities of organ transplantation require us to shorten the time for observation/deliberation in the interests of preserving the vitality of organs to be transplanted. We must declare a donor to be dead as soon as possible, by one or the other of two standards, both subject to increasing uncertainty about their validity. Pellegrino thus considers the comparative reliability of the neurological and the cardiopulmonary standards.

He says that the "Dead Donor Rule" "has been the anchor for the moral and social acceptability of organ transplantation protocols from their earliest days." Its first demand in any ethically legitimate transplantation protocol for retrieving organs from nonliving, healthy donors is to have certainty that the donor is dead, nor can his death be hastened or end-of-life care compromised in any way. Pellegrino then notes serious failures to observe the DDR, several involving infants.

He asks, "Which standard should be preferred — the neurological or the cardiopulmonary?" Pellegrino considers the objections leveled against both. He concludes: "Taking everything into account, I believe that ... with the cardiopulmonary standard there is a higher degree of certainty of death than there is with a heart-beating donor, because heart, lung, and brain have all ceased functioning."

Having said all this, he then asks whether transplantation of vital organs from nonliving donors can be ethically acceptable and, if so, under what conditions? This, he says, is a matter of prudential or practical reasoning. "How can we act ethically in the face of relative clinical doubt?" Although we may not, at present, have absolute certainty that the "donor is dead," a sufficient degree of moral certainty to warrant such an action may be attainable if the requirements for prudent decision-making are satisfied. But what does this entail? Pellegrino's answer to this very difficult matter, it seems to me, is the following:

> Relative moral certitude does not substitute for scientific certitude. But, properly weighed, it can give a legitimate warrant for necessary action in the face of unavoidable uncertainty. This is the situation within which ordinary decisions in daily life are made. Clinical prudence seeks to avoid both the error of inaction, which would deprive the recipient of a needed transplant, and the error of premature action, which would deprive the donor of life. Fidelity to beneficence and the prudential approach to decisions aim to avoid both the paralysis of inaction and the harmful use of ineffective medical treatments. Prudence must not be confused with self-protective cowardice. It is the decision to act for a good end in the morally optimal way despite persistent uncertainty about the outcome.

Much as I respect Pellegrino, I find this account unacceptable. For instance, how is "relative moral certainty" to be "weighed"? It is not something quantifiable like a pound of butter or a liter of gasoline, nor is there some common denominator to which it and something else can be reduced, nor can it be some kind of feeling. There must be some *reasons* why moral certainty that a person is dead is possible. Pellegrino is himself, I believe, aware of this, and he addresses the matter in a section of his essay called "Futility in the Decision Process." There he writes as follows: "Clinical futility is present when any medical intervention is: (1) *ineffective*, i.e., unable to change the natural history of a disease or its trajectory towards death; (2) *non-beneficial*, i.e., unable to satisfy any good or value perceived by the patient or his or her surrogate; and (3) *disproportionately burdensome* to the patient, physically, psychologically, or financially. Balancing the relationship among those three criteria is at the heart of prudent, precautionary, and proportionate action. This formulation accommodates the physician's expertise with respect to effectiveness and the patient's values with respect to benefits, and it results in shared decision-making regarding the proportionality of benefits and burdens." I am still not satisfied, but it is possible that I have not properly understood Pellegrino's position and am not being fair to him. If so, I apologize.

Pellegrino's personal reflections continue with reflections on the need always to *care* for the patient, the value of palliative care, and on remaining ambiguities and problems, but the essence of his reflections on the inadequacy of the neurological criteria and preference for the cardiopulmonary criteria have been set forth.

(5) The Position of Nicanor Giorgio Pier Austriaco, O.P., Ph.D., S.T.L

Nicanor Austriaco, Ph.D. (in biology from Massachusetts Institute of Technology), S.T.L. (from the Dominican House of studies, Washington, DC), teaches biology at Providence College, Providence, Rhode Island. He endorses the devastating criticism of the "neurological criterion" mounted by Shewmon and others. Austriaco holds that the only real sign of the death of a human person is the loss of the *human organism*. "An organism," he writes, "can be defined scientifically as a discrete unit of living matter that follows a self-driven, robust developmental pathway that manifests its species-specific self-organization.... An organism's organization gives it its ability to live and to grow in a species-specific manner. Thus, the signature sign for the presence or the absence of the organism, and thus the presence or absence of its life, is the presence or the absence of its organization, its bodily integrity."[25]

This is Austriaco's basic argument. Much of his essay, however, is devoted to a critique of what he refers to as the "radical capacity for sentience" argument. This argument, he claims, is opposed to a realistic, scientific, Thomistic anthropology or understanding of the human person as a bodily organism of a specific kind. He maintains that "anyone who accepts the logic of the radical capacity for sentience argument he embraces must also endorse the brain stem and the neocortical definitions for death, putting the lives of the most disabled of neurologically disabled patients at risk."

I maintain that Austriaco misunderstands the so-called "radical capacity for sentience" argument. A brief presentation of that argument and its purpose is given in the last section of this paper.

(6) The position of Germain Grisez, Peter Ryan, S.J., Patrick Lee, and William E. May

Their position was originally advanced at a "Scholars' Forum on Brain Death" in Washington, DC, April 1-11, 2008, devoted to Shewmon's work. Shewmon was present and actively participated in the discussions. Although a few rejected his critique of the neurological criterion, a majority of those in attendance accepted it. But some of us, led by Grisez and Ryan and Lee, argued that the entities Shewmon claimed were human persons who survived brain death, e.g., T. K., a Japanese boy declared brain dead when he was several months old yet lived until he was nineteen, were in fact *not* human beings.

Why? Our argument can be summed up as follows: A human being is a rational animal. An animal is a sentient organism. In human beings and other mammals, sentience includes such functions as seeing, hearing, feeling pain and pressure, perceiving, imagining, remembering, desiring, fearing, being angry, etc. Embryonic mammals do not actually perform such actions, but they have within themselves the resources to develop themselves, so they do have this capacity. Since embryonic mammals have the resources — the genetic and epigenetic composition and structure —actively to develop sentient capacities for themselves, they too are sentient organisms. The rationality that differentiates human beings from other animals includes such functions as conceptual thought, reasoning, and making deliberate choices. An organism that has the capacity for these types of actions is a human individual. Human embryos and fetuses are human organisms because they too have the internal resources to develop themselves to the stage where they will be able to perform the actions characteristic of the human kind. But the organisms that Shewmon identified as living human persons who have survived brain death, e.g., T. K., is therefore not a mammalian, let alone a human organism.

But Austriaco objects that our argument is falsified by sound biology. Biologically, not only the brain, but other parts of the nervous system are necessary for a mammal's sentient functioning, and the death of the organism involves the loss of the nervous system as a whole, not only of the brain. Our objection is that total brain death is not a sound criterion for the death of a mammalian organism. The premises are true, but the conclusion does not follow. An organism loses the capacity for a function if it irreversibly loses any part of what is necessary for that function. Therefore, if some parts of a mammal's brain are necessary for its sentient functioning, then its irreversible loss of its whole brain entails the loss of its radical capacity for sentient functioning, and its death necessarily follows from the loss of its whole brain or of whatever part of its brain is necessary for the capacity for sentient functioning.

He further claims that our argument proves too much if it proves anything. One step in that argument is the proposition that the complete loss of specifically human capacities is a substantial change, namely, the person's passing away. It is obvious, however, that before some people die, many completely and irreversibly lose their specifically human capacities — their capacities for reasoning and making free choices. Yet such people plainly are not dead. Although their neocortex is not functioning, they are nonetheless living human persons alleged to be in the "vegetative state." Thus, unless it is shown beyond reasonable doubt that someone has lost the capacity for any sort of consciousness, one cannot be sure beyond reasonable doubt that the individual has lost the capacity for specifically human functioning. Therefore, our claim that the total loss of specifically human capacities is a human being's passing away does not warrant treating such individuals as nonpersons.

Our position does not lead to the conclusion that everyone who is unconscious and will never regain consciousness is already dead. It means that the loss of the *capacity* for consciousness is death. When a patient still warm and pink and breathing is in question, we admit that death has occurred when, and *only* when, it is shown beyond reasonable doubt that there no longer is any *capacity* for consciousness.

Patients confidently judged to be unconscious after careful and repeated examinations have sometimes later told about undergoing those examinations. The immediately exercisable capacity to respond to stimuli is one thing; consciousness is another. Thus, to establish beyond reasonable doubt even the fact that a patient is unconscious is far more difficult than is generally supposed. Pathological unconsciousness is one thing; the loss of the capacity for consciousness is another.

Thus our argument does not lead, as Austriaco charges, to an endorsement of neocortical death nor does it put the most vulnerable in our society, e.g., people in the so-called "permanent" vegetative state at risk of life. It does not because our position is grounded in the *Thomistic* principle that "nothing is in the mind [an immaterial faculty, not a material one to be identified with the brain] that has not been some way *in the senses.*" The human intellect, unlike the divine and angelic, is a faculty of a being who is a composite of soul and body — and the body is integral to the being of the human person. For us to form concepts, make judgments, and reason (intellectual acts), we must first "separate" or "abstract" forms present in our sensory powers, the external senses of sight, hearing, touch, smell, taste, and the "internal" senses of imagination and memory, or what Aquinas called the *vis cogitative,* the "cogitative power." But as long as we have a composite being made of spiritual soul and body (made alive by the soul or animating principle) we have what Austriaco calls a living human organism. His critique is misplaced.[26]

Nonetheless, as Grisez and Lee say explicitly at the conclusion of their essay, "the present paper has been concerned exclusively with the adequacy of total brain death as criterion for the death of a human individual. The judgment that this criterion — or any other criterion — of death is met is an entirely different matter. Nothing that we have said should be mistaken as supporting the adequacy of the procedures that have been used in pronouncing patients brain dead."[27]

Conclusion

The summary presented here of contemporary debates and discussions shows, I am convinced, that the best scientific and scholarly studies demonstrate as false the claim that a human person is dead if the functioning of the entire brain, including the brain stem, has been irretrievably lost — the "neurological criterion/criteria." The brain is *not,* as those defending this claim insist, the primary integrator of the entire human body. A more holistic criterion has been developed to demonstrate that the human organism is dead, and it is only when there is moral certainty that a person has really died that his or her corpse can be buried or cremated or that vital organs can, with proper consent, be excised from his or her body and transplanted into the bodies of persons in need of them.

Must Catholic scholars who, in light of new scientific evidence, dissent from the teaching of Pope John Paul II be regarded as disloyal Catholics? As I have argued elsewhere,[28] after carefully examining relevant passages in Vatican II's Dogmatic Constitution on the Church, *Lumen gentium,* in particular no. 25, on the obligation to give religious submission of will and intellect to teachings proposed by the Roman pontiff authoritatively but not irrevocably and definitively (i.e., *ex cathedra*), and also to John Paul's insistence that competence for determining criteria to show that a person has died is one within the competence of scientists and doctors, *not* popes or bishops, I conclude that today Catholic scholars and doctors who reject the neurological criterion for a more holistic one are not acting in a disloyal way.

2. Part Two: Transplanting Organs From the Living

Today the transplanting of vital organs, such as a kidney, a portion of the liver, etc., from one living person to another in desperate need of a vital organ is commonplace. We intuitively and instinctively judge that the giving of a part of one's own body to help a gravely or even mortally ill fellow human person is not only morally justifiable but an act of heroic charity.

The Magisterium of the Church praises the self-giving of vital organs by living persons. Pope John Paul II has frequently remarked on the moral liceity of the self-giving of vital organs, and he has likewise clearly indicated the limits of such self-giving. Thus, in his Address to the First International Congress of the Society for Organ Sharing, he said, first, that "a transplant, and even a simple blood transfusion, is not like other operations. It must not be separated from the donor's act of self-giving, from the love that gives life. The physician should always be conscious of the particular nobility of his work; he becomes the mediator of something especially significant, the *gift of self* which one person has made ... so that another might live." He then articulated the norm: "A person can only donate that of which he can deprive himself without serious danger or harm to his own life or personal identity, and for a just and proportionate reason."[29]

The *Catechism of the Catholic Church*, in taking up organ transplants *inter vivos*, says: "*Organ transplants* are in conformity with the moral law if the physical and psychological dangers and risks to the donor are proportionate to the good that is sought for the recipient."[30] And finally, the bishops of the United States declare: "The transplantation of organs from living donors is morally permissible when such a donation will not sacrifice or seriously impair any essential bodily function and the anticipated benefit to the recipient is proportionate to the harm done to the donor.... [T]he freedom of the prospective donor must be respected."[31]

Nonetheless, the proper way to justify organ donations from living persons is a matter of debate among Catholic theologians. In fact, when this kind of surgery became possible around the middle of the twentieth century, it stirred controversy among them.[32] Some leading theologians of the time, among them Marcellino Zalba, S.J., wondered how one could justify a procedure in which a healthy human person (the donor) willingly suffers mutilating surgery and the risk of health problems, perhaps serious ones, in the future when his own life and health are not imperiled. The mutilating surgery could hardly be regarded as therapeutic for the donor and hence could not, in their judgment, be justified by the principle of totality, according to which one could justify the mutilation of one's own person (e.g., the amputation of a gangrenous limb or the excision of cancerous testicles) in order to protect one's own life.[33]

Gerald Kelly, S.J., provides the reasons why he and theologians of his day concluded that the principle of totality could not be used to justify such procedures: "This principle [that of totality] can be applied only when there is the subordination of part to whole that exists in the natural body. No such subordination exists between human persons or between the individual and society. Each person is a distinct entity, with a distinct finality. No matter how lowly his condition, he is not subordinated to others in the order of being."[34] Some theologians, nonetheless, sought to justify organ transplants *inter vivos* by "extending" the principle of totality. A radical presentation of this line of thinking, extending the principle to embrace the total good of the person, including the "spiritual" good of the donor, who allegedly benefits spiritually by the self-giving of his vital organs, was presented by Martin Nolan, O.S.A.[35] His attempted justification, rooted in a dualistic understanding of the human person, was soundly criticized by others, in particular by the great Protestant ethicist, Paul Ramsey, who characterized it as the "sticky benefits" theory.[36] In addition, Pope Pius XII, who had himself invoked the principle of totality to justify mutilating surgery on one's own person when necessary to protect the person's health and life as a whole, explicitly declared that this principle could not be used to justify organ transplants among the living.[37]

Realizing that organ transplants among the living cannot be justified by the totality principle, other theologians, preeminently Gerald Kelly, S.J., followed the lead first suggested by Bert Cunningham, C.M., in his doctoral dissertation, *The Morality of Organic Transplantation* (Washington, DC: The Catholic University of America Press, 1944), that the self-giving of one's own vital organs could be justified by the principle of fraternal charity or love when doing so is of great benefit to the recipient, with the proviso that the harm suffered by the donor is limited and morally acceptable. This view, endorsed and developed by Kelly, was soon accepted by many moral theologians. They distinguished between *anatomical* and *functional* integrity, arguing that only the latter was necessary for bodily and personal integrity.

Some theologians, preeminently Germain Grisez, argue that organ transplants from the living can be justified by the principle of double effect.
According to this principle, an action having two effects — one good, the
other bad — is morally good provided that the action is not morally wrong
for other reasons, that the evil is not intended, that the evil is not the means
to the good, and that there is a "proportionate reason" for tolerating or
accepting the bad effect. Grisez argues, correctly in my opinion, that the
"principle of totality" is itself, if analyzed properly, an instance of double
effect. However, the *physical* "directness" of the causing of harm and the
physical "indirectness" of the causing of the benefit led many theologians to
think that a special principle was needed to justify the "mutilation" involved
in necessary surgical interventions on one's own body (the malfunctioning
or diseased organ, e.g., the gall bladder, was first removed physically, causing
a "mutilation" before the healing would take place).

But if we analyze the matter from a moral perspective, we can see that
the "object" morally specifying the chosen act (on this see *Veritatis splendor*,
no. 78) is not the harm done to the person but rather the removal of the
organ or part of the body, with, as its resulting effects, the "mutilation" (the
evil effect) and the "protection" or "restoration" of health (the good effect).
Thus, in analyzing morally the reason why one is justified in submitting to
"mutilating" surgery to protect one's own life and health, Grisez writes:

> It can be morally good and even obligatory to remove a part of the
> body essential to some physiological or psychic function, when doing so
> of itself also protects or promotes health: the detriment to function may
> not be intended as a means to the other end, but may only be accepted
> as a side effect. For example, a person sometimes should consent to the
> cutting off of an infected or cancerous limb or nonvital organ when that
> is necessary to prevent the infection or cancer from doing great harm to
> the body as a whole. Indeed, this is so even when the part removed is itself
> healthy, if removing it has natural consequences which are necessary for
> the health of the body as a whole and which cannot be brought about
> in another way. For example, a man suffering from breast cancer may
> consent to the surgical removal of his normal testicles in order to stop the
> hormones which are aggravating the cancer.[38]

Similarly, Grisez argues, the same norms can be applied to the self-giving
of vital organs. The morality of giving them depends on how the freely chosen act relates one to the relevant goods: healthy functioning and life itself.

If the harm (including the mutilation) suffered by the donor — but in no way *intended* either by him or those involved in the transplant — does not impair his functional integrity, the evil suffered is an unintended side effect of an act of self-giving. However, were the donor's own functional integrity and hence his own health and life to be impaired, the choice would be to impede or damage his own health as a means to some good end, but one can never intend or choose evil for the sake of good to come.[39]

Although theologians differ among themselves on the proper way to justify the self-giving of vital organs by living donors, today all agree that it is morally permissible, under given conditions, for live donors to donate paired organs to those who are in need of them. Moreover, the Church's Magisterium praises those who generously give such organs, while at the same time clearly noting the limitations of such self-giving.

--------------------- Endnotes for Chapter Eight ---------------------

1. I want to thank my colleagues E. Christian Brugger and Mark Latkovic for reading, correcting, and improving an earlier draft of this paper.
2. "Uniform Anatomical Gift Act, Section 7 (b)," as printed in Alfred M. Sadler, Jr., M.D.; Blair L. Sadler, LL.B.; and E. Blythe Stason, J.D., "The Uniform Anatomical Gift Act: A Model for Reform," *Journal of the American Medical Association* 206 (December 9, 1968), 2506.
3. Paul Ramsey, *The Patient as Person* (New Haven: Yale University Press, 1970), p.103.
4. http://bioethics.georgetown.edu/pcbe/reports/past_commissions/defining_death.pdf.
5. U.S. President's Commission for the Study of Ethical Problems in Medicine and Biomedical and Behavioral Research, *Defining Death: A Report on the Medical, Legal and Ethical Issues in the Determination of Death* (Washington, DC: U.S. Government Printing Office, 1981), p. 41.
6. Ibid., p. 36, n. 4 quoting Germain Grisez and Joseph A. Boyle, Jr., *Life and Death with Liberty and Justice* (Notre Dame, IN: University of Notre Dame Press, 1979), p. 77.
7. Pope Pius XII, "Allocution to Eye Specialists," May 14, 1956.
8. Pope Pius XII, "Address to an International Congress of Anesthesiologists," November 24, 1957.
9. http://www.vatican.va/holy_father/john_paul_ii/speeches/2000/jul-sep/documents/hf_jp-ii_spe_20000829_transplants_en.html.
10. "Discourse of John Paul II to the Participants of the Working Group," *The Determination of Brain Death* ... , no. 6, in *Working Group on the Determination of Brain Death and Its Relationship to Human Death* (December 10-14, 1989) (Pontificiae Academiae Scientiarum Scripta Varia, 83), eds. R. J. White, H. Angstwurm, and I. Carrasco de Paula (Vatican City: Pontifical Academy of Sciences, 1992), p. xxvi.

11. Ibid.
12. See *L'Osservatore Romano*, Italian version, September 9, 2008. It can be paraphrased as follows: "According to the journalist Lucetta Scarrafia, Paolo Becchi was the author of a chapter entitled '*I Segni della morte e la questione dei trapianti*' ('The Signs of Death and the Question of Transplants') in a book published in Italian. Becchi was a follower of Hans Jonas, a philosopher who for more than 20 years had opposed so-called brain death and the Harvard Report, which he claimed was not rooted in scientific knowledge but was motivated by a desire to get vital organs for transplant purposes. As a result of Becchi's work, a book was published in Italian in 2007 called *Finis Vitae*, and published in English in the following year and revised in 2011, containing the studies of 18 scientists, theologians, and philosophers, all of whom strongly criticized and rejected the Harvard Report and the criteria used to determine brain death."
13. Randy Engle, "*Finis Vitae* — Is 'Brain Death' True Death?", review of *Finis Vitae*, in *Renew America*, January 12, 2012, accessible at http://www.renewamerica.com/columns/engel/120117.
14. Spaemann, "Is Brain Death the Death of the Human Being?", *Finis Vitae*, p. 260.
15. Ibid., p. 262.
16. Cicero Galli Coimbra, "Are 'Brain Dead' (or 'Brain-Stem Dead') Patients Neurologically Recoverable?", *Finis Vitae*, p. 335.
17. Cicero Galli Coimbra, "The Apnea Test — A Bedside Lethal 'Disaster' to Avoid a Legal 'Disaster' in the Operating Room," *Finis Vitae*, p. 135.
18. Ibid., pp. 136, 137.
19. Ibid., p. 161.
20. R. D. Truog and J. C. Fackler, "Rethinking Brain Death," *Critical Care Medicine* 20.12 (1992), 1705-1713; "Organ Transplantation without Brain Death," *Annals of the New York Academy of Science* 913 (2000), 229-239.
21. See http://www.brainharmony.org/neuroethics.html, where Shewmon lists publications and public presentations of his writings on "brain death."
22. "Recovery from 'Brain Death' ... ," 82. In "Brainstem Death, Brain Death and Death," 128-129 Shewmon elaborates on this proposal.
23. "Brainstem Death, Brain Death and Death," 129. See also his " 'Brainstem Death,' 'Brain Death,' and Death: A Critical Re-Evaluation of the Purported Evidence," *Issues in Law and Medicine* 14.2 (1998), 125-145.
24. See http://bioethics.georgetown.edu/pcbe/reports/death/index.html.
25. For a more comprehensive account of Austriaco's views see his essay, "Is the Brain-Dead Patient *Really* Dead?" *Studia Moralia* 41 (2003), 277-308. See also his article "In Defense of Bodily Integrity as a Criterion for Death: A Response to the Radical Capacity Argument," *The Thomist* 73 (2009), 647-659, and his book *Biomedicine and Beatitude: An Introduction to Catholic Bioethics* (Washington, DC: The Catholic University of America Press, 2011).
26. Germain Grisez and Patrick Lee, "Total Brain Death: A Reply to Alan Shewmon," *Bioethics* 26.5 (2012), 275-284. In my judgment Mortimer Adler's 1968 book, *The Difference of Man and the Difference It Makes* is a very good presen-

tation of the difference between what he calls "perceptual thinking" (e.g., our imagining a dog and, in doing so, imagining a dog of a certain color, size, etc.), and a concept (a mental construct that is universal and capable of existing only in a nonmaterial faculty of the human animal, and not in the brain of a subhuman, nonpersonal animal). It requires, within the entitative makeup of *human animals,* a nonmaterial faculty, the mind, which includes its cognitive dimension, intellect, and its choosing dimension, freedom of will.

27. Ibid., 284.

28. See my article "Responding to Teachings Proposed for Determining That a Person Has Died," *Fellowship of Catholic Scholars Quarterly* 34.1 (Fall 2011), 17-20. See note to that article and citation from Ref. Gonzalo Miranda, Dean of the School of Bioethics at the Ateneo Romano della Regina Apostolorum.

29. Pope John Paul II, Address to the First International Congress of the Society for Organ Sharing, *L'Osservatore Romano*, English ed. (June 24, 1991), 2.

30. *Catechism of the Catholic Church*, no. 2296. **NB:** Here I give the text as required by the "Modifications from the *Editio Typica*" (based on the definitive Latin text promulgated on September 8, 1997). The text found in editions of the *Catechism* prior to that date is somewhat different.

31. National Conference of Catholic Bishops, *Ethical and Religious Directives for Catholic Health Care Services* (Washington, DC: United States Catholic Conference, 1995), no. 30.

32. For a discussion of the debates that took place, see a series of articles by Gerald Kelly, S.J., in *Theological Studies* 16 (1955), 391-396; 17 (1956), 341-344, 557-561; 18 (1957), 228-230, 570-572.

33. On the "principle of totality" see John Gallagher, C.S.B., "The Principle of Totality: Man's Stewardship of His Body," in *Moral Theology Today: Certitudes and Doubts*, ed. Donald G. McCarthy (St. Louis: Pope John XXIII Medical-Moral Research and Education Center, 1984), pp. 217-242.

34. Gerald Kelly, S.J., *Medico-Moral Problems* (St. Louis: The Catholic Hospital Association, 1957), p. 247.

35. Martin Nolan, O.S.A., "The Principle of Totality in Moral Theology," in *Absolutes in Moral Theology?*, ed. Charles E. Curran (Washington, DC: Corpus Books, 1968), pp. 232-248.

36. Paul Ramsey, *The Patient as Person: Explorations in Medical Ethics* (New Haven, CT: Yale University Press, 1970), chapter 4, "The Self-Giving of Vital Organs," pp. 165-197, esp. pp. 178-181.

37. See, for example, Pope Pius XII, "Allocution to a Group of Eye Specialists" (May 14, 1956), as found in *The Human Body: Papal Teaching*, selected and arranged by the Monks of Solesmes (Boston: St. Paul Editions, 1960), nos. 645ff.

38. Germain Grisez, *The Way of the Lord Jesus*, Vol. 2, *Living a Christian Life* (Quincy, IL: Franciscan Press, 1993), p. 542.

39. Here I paraphrase and in some ways modify ibid., p. 543.

Bibliography and Resources

NOTE

The endnotes for each chapter provide extensive bibliographical references for the issues specific to each chapter. Here I provide information on (1) a Select Bibliography of Texts, Encyclopedias, and Anthologies, (2) a list of important Journals and Periodicals, and (3) Centers and Web sites of Particular Value for Catholic Perspectives on Bioethics.

Select Bibliography of Texts, Encyclopedias, and Anthologies

Ashcroft, Richard Edmund, Angus Dawson, Heather Draper, and John McMillan, eds. *Principles of Health Care Ethics*. 2nd ed. Philadelphia: J. P. Lippincott, 2007. The first edition of this massive work of over 800 pages was edited by Raanon Gillan. The best item in it is a brilliant essay by John Finnis and Anthony Fisher, O.P., "Theology and the Four Principles of Ethics," a devastating and accurate critique of the highly influential work of Beauchamp and Childress referred to below.

Ashley, Benedict, O.P., and Kevin O'Rourke, O.P. *Health Care Ethics: A Theological Analysis*. 5th ed. Washington, DC: Georgetown University Press, 2007. In my opinion the fourth edition is superior to the fifth. For a review of the fifth edition see my "Review Essay" in *The National Catholic Bioethics Quarterly* 7.2 (Summer 2007), 409-417.

———. *Ethics of Health Care: An Introductory Textbook*. 2nd ed. Washington, DC: Georgetown University Press, 1994.

Austriaco, Nicanor Pier Giorgio. *Biomedicine and Beatitude: An Introduction to Catholic Bioethics*. Washington, DC: The Catholic University of America Press, 2012. The bibliography is very extensive.

Beauchamp, Thomas, and James Childress. *Principles of Biomedical Ethics*. 3rd ed. New York: Oxford University Press, 1994. This is a widely used and highly influential work; in it, personal autonomy trumps everything.

Cataldo, Peter, and Albert S. Moraczewski, O.P., eds. *Catholic Health Care Ethics: A Manual for Ethics Committees.* Braintree, MA: National Catholic Bioethics Center, 2002. This is very useful and was published in a binder divided into sections so that new material can be easily inserted. The Center has since moved to Philadelphia.

Fisher, Anthony, O.P., *Catholic Bioethics for a New Millennium*, Cambridge, England, and New York, Cambridge University Press, 2011.

Griese, Orville. *Catholic Identity in Health Care: Principles and Practice.* Braintree, MA: Pope John XXIII Medical-Moral Research and Education Center, 1987.

Grisez, Germain. *The Way of the Lord Jesus.* Vol. 2, *Living a Christian Life.* Quincy, IL: Franciscan Press, 1993. Chapter Eight of this volume, entitled "Life, Health, and Bodily Inviolability," is a short and excellent treatise on bioethics, pp. 459-552.

———. *The Way of the Lord Jesus.* Vol. 3, *Difficult Moral Questions.* Quincy, IL: Franciscan Press, 1997. Many of the questions analyzed in detail by Grisez in this volume concern bioethical issues.

Jackson, Emily, and John Keown. *Debating Euthanasia.* Volume 3 in the Debating Law Series. London: Hart Publishing, 2012.

Kaczor, Christopher. *The Ethics of Abortion: Women's Rights, Human Life, and the Question of Justice.* New York: Routledge, 2011.

McCormick, Richard A., S.J. *How Brave a New World? Dilemmas in Bioethics.* Garden City, NY: Doubleday, 1978. Although dated, this work embodies a proportionalist method of making moral judgments incompatible with Catholic teaching. It is, however, very influential.

———. *The Critical Calling: Reflections on Moral Dilemmas Since Vatican II.* Washington, DC: Georgetown University Press, 1989. The same comments as given previously apply here.

Post, Stephen Garrad, ed. *Encyclopedia of Bioethics.* 3rd rev. ed. New York: McGraw-Hill, 2005. Five volumes paginated consecutively. The first edition was published in 1978. This is basically oriented in a secularist direction. In the first edition, there was an entry on "Marriage." This is now called "Marriage and Other Significant Relationships."

Ramsey, Paul. *The Patient as Person.* New Haven: Yale University Press, 1970. Although an old work, it is still one of the best, despite a few problematic positions.

————. *Ethics at the Edges of Life: Medical and Legal Intersections*. New Haven: Yale University Press, 1978. Another superlative work.

Shannon, Thomas A., ed. *Basic Writings of the Key Ethical Questions That Surround the Major Biological Possibilities and Problems*. 4th ed. New York: Paulist Press, 1993. Biased toward proportionalism.

Smith, Janet, and Christopher Kaczor. *Life Issues, Medical Choices: Questions and Answers for Catholics*. Cincinnati: Servant Book from St. Anthony Messenger, 2007. This brief work is written clearly and is fully in accord with Catholic teaching.

Tonti-Filippini, Nicholas. *About Bioethics*. Melbourne: Connor Court, 2011.

Walters, Leroy, ed. *Bibliography of Bioethics*. Detroit: Gale Research Co., 1975-present. An annual bibliography, the most complete of its kind, classified systematically.

Important Journals and Periodicals

BioEdge. This is a very helpful weekly newsletter summarizing current developments in bioethics from a deeply Catholic perspective. It is published by Australasian Bioethics Information, whose Web site is http://www.australasianbioethics.org. It is headquartered in Australia.

Catholic Medical Quarterly: Journal of the Guild of Catholic Doctors. A quarterly journal published by the Guild of Catholic Doctors in England.

Ethics & Medics: The Bulletin of the National Catholic Bioethics Center on Moral Issues in the Health Care Sciences. Inaugurated in 1975, this is a very useful monthly periodical, ordinarily four pages in length and containing two brief but significant essays on an issue in bioethics. It is published by the National Catholic Bioethics Center (formerly called the Pope John XXIII Medical-Moral Research and Education Center).

Hastings Center Report. This is published bimonthly by the Hastings Center, a nonpartisan organization that carries out educational and research programs on ethical issues in medicine. In addition to the bimonthly *Report*, the Center issues occasional studies on selected topics.

Health Progress. This journal, formerly called *Hospital Progress*, is published ten times a year by the Catholic Health Association of the United States.

Issues in Law and Medicine. This is a quarterly publication of the National Legal Center for the Medically Dependent and Disabled, Inc., the Horatio P. Storer Foundation, Inc., and the American Academy of Medical Ethics, Inc. Essays in this journal are uniformly of high scholarly quality and pro-life in orientation.

Journal of the American Medical Association (JAMA). A weekly, professional journal for physicians; many articles are quite technical; others deal with ethical issues from various perspectives, unfortunately too often utilitarian in nature.

Linacre Quarterly. This is the official publication of the Catholic Medical Association, formerly called the National Federation of Catholic Physicians' Guilds.

The NaProEthics Forum. Bimonthly publication of the Pope Paul VI Institute, Omaha, Nebraska, this was published regularly for several years but is no longer being published. That is unfortunate, as it carried good material.

The National Catholic Bioethics Quarterly. Published by the National Catholic Bioethics Center (see below) and edited by Edward Furton, this is without a doubt the premier scholarly quarterly on bioethical issues published under Catholic auspices. It is must reading for anyone seriously interested in the issues taken up in this book.

New England Journal of Medicine. This is a very prestigious and scholarly weekly journal. Articles are frequently very technical; most ethical issues are addressed from a secularist point of view but at times some very excellent pieces appear.

Centers and Web Sites of Particular Value for Catholic Perspectives on Bioethics

The most important center for Catholic perspectives on bioethics in the United States is the **National Catholic Bioethics Center**, formerly called the Pope John XXIII Medical-Moral Research and Education Center. It publishes its bulletin, *Ethics & Medics,* and numerous monographs on bioethical issues. For many years, it has sponsored, with the help of the Knights of Columbus, workshops on specific topics in bioethics for the bishops of the United States, Canada, and Latin America, publishing papers given at these workshops in volumes of proceedings. John Haas is current president of the Center. Its Web site is http://www.ncbcenter.org.

Another very important center for Catholic perspectives on bioethics is the **Anscombe Bioethics Centre**, Oxford. This takes the place of **The Linacre Centre** in London, which for more than thirty years sponsored excellent research in bioethics. Among the Linacre Centre's publications is its Working Party Report on Euthanasia, *Euthanasia, Clinical Practice and the Law*, edited by Luke Gormally, and cited frequently in the endnotes for Chapter Seven.

The **Center for Health Care Ethics**, while representing the Catholic tradition, seeks dialogue with the many other ethical traditions represented in the United States. Its Web site is http://chce.slu.edu.

The **Joseph P. and Rose F. Kennedy Institute of Ethics**, although located on the campus of a major Catholic university (Georgetown), does not, on the whole, support magisterial teaching and presents a wide variety of views on bioethical matters. Currently a very strong Catholic voice is found in Professor John Keown, an Englishman who is widely known and respected as an authority on euthanasia and assisted suicide. Its Web site is http://kennedyinstitute.georgetown.edu/index.htm.

Additional Web Sites

In addition to the Web sites noted above, the following organizations, with their Web sites, are valuable resources for those interested in Catholic perspectives on bioethics.

Culture of Life Foundation: http://www.culture-of-life.org. This is an excellent source for relevant essays and other information on contraception, abortion, the generation of human life, euthanasia, etc.

International Federation of Catholic Medical Associations: http://frblin.club.fr/fiamc/welcome.html. Another good source.

Patients Rights Council: http://www.patientsrightscouncil.org. This was formerly the **International Task Force on Euthanasia and Assisted Suicide.** An excellent source for material on euthanasia and allied subjects.

Pontifical Academy for Life: http://www.academiavita.org/portal.jsp?lang=english. A very important source. Publications of the Academy are most significant and helpful.

Pontifical Academy of Sciences: http://www.vatican.va/roman_curia/pontifical_academies/acdscien. Another very important source.

Pontifical Council for Health Pastoral Care: http://www.healthpastoral.org. Also important.

United States Conference of Catholic Bishops Pro-Life Office: http://www.nccbuscc.org/prolife. This is the source for many very important articles, etc.

Center for Bioethics and Culture Network: http://www.cbc-network .org. Under the leadership of Jennifer Lahl, this non-Catholic center is a valuable source of information supporting pro-life activities.

Coalition of Americans for Research Ethics: Do No Harm: http://www.stemcellresearch.org. This is the best source for information on stem cell research, adamantly opposed to killing human beings in their embryonic stage in order to obtain pluripotent stem cells.

Center for Bioethics and Human Dignity: http://www.cbhd.org. This Center, located at Trinity International University in Deerfield, Illinois, is a pro-life Protestant bioethics organization completely opposed to abortion, euthanasia, etc. It publishes an important journal and issues newsletters regularly that are of help.

Index

for generating new human life as "begotten, not made," 84-87

May, Elaine Tyler, book on 50th anniversary of "the pill," 147; firm advocate of contraception, 147f; forced in honesty to recognize that many young women today and gynecologists/obstetricians advocate the Fertility Awareness Method and this in time has led some to conclude that NFP is morally and scientifically better than artificial contraception, 147f

McCormick, Richard, S.J., advocates tubal ligation as most effective way to prevent conception when pregnancy might endanger a woman's life, 142, 156 (endnote 44), criticized by Klaus 142, 156 (endnote 45); justifies spousal use of homologous *in vitro* fertilization and embryo transfer as legitimate way to generate new human life, 98, 117 (endnotes 39 and 40), criticized by Ashley, 98, 116, rationale for proxy consent for noncompetent "voiceless" persons as subjects of both therapeutic and non-therapeutic experimentation, 216f, 246 (endnote 38)

N

New Atlantis: A Journal of Technology and Society (Number 34, Winter, 2012) provides a primer on stem-cell research, 223-225

new reproductive technologies: kinds of described, 89-94 (artificial

fertilization, artificial insemination, *in vitro* fertilization and embryo transfer, alternative technologies using male and female gametic cells such as sperm intrafallopian tube transfer [SIFT] and gametic intrafallopian tube transfer [GIFT], and cloning or agametic reproduction); ethical argument to show immorality of all forms of non-marital generation of new human life, 95-100; basic theological reason why human life ought to be generated only through a marital act: the life of human beings, made in the image of God whose Son (Word) became and is a human being, ought, like God the Father's only Son, "to be begotten, not made," 101-102

new reproductive technologies, Church teaching on: Vatican *Instruction on Respect for Human Life in Its Origin and on the Dignity of Procreation*, 34, 37, 88; Pius XII, 87f; Pontifical Academy for Life "Reflections on Cloning," 88f

Nuremberg Code, cardinal principle governing experimentation on human subjects, 210

P

Papal Commission on Population, the Family, and Natality, dualistic understanding of human person, severing the "person" (= consciously aware subject) and his body at core of argument of